Communications
in Computer and Information Science 53

T0216753

Djamshid Tavangarian   Thomas Kirste
Dirk Timmermann   Ulrike Lucke
Daniel Versick (Eds.)

Intelligent Interactive Assistance and Mobile Multimedia Computing

International Conference, IMC 2009
Rostock-Warnemünde, Germany, November 9-11, 2009
Proceedings

 Springer

Volume Editors

Djamshid Tavangarian
Thomas Kirste
Dirk Timmermann
Ulrike Lucke
Daniel Versick

Faculty of Computer Science and Electrical Engineering
University of Rostock
Rostock, Germany

{djamshid.tavangarian, thomas.kirste, dirk.timmermann,
ulrike.lucke, daniel.versick}@uni-rostock.de

Library of Congress Control Number: 2009938060

CR Subject Classification (1998): H.5, H.2.4, I.2.9, I.2.11, C.5.3, K.8

ISSN   1865-0929
ISBN-10   3-642-10262-X Springer Berlin Heidelberg New York
ISBN-13   978-3-642-10262-2 Springer Berlin Heidelberg New York

springer.com

© Springer-Verlag Berlin Heidelberg 2009
Printed in Germany

Typesetting: Camera-ready by author, data conversion by Scientific Publishing Services, Chennai, India
Printed on acid-free paper   SPIN: 12783953   06/3180   5 4 3 2 1 0

Message from the Chairs

The starting day of the IMC 2009 conference coincided with the 20th anniversary of the Berlin Wall coming down, reuniting Germany after more than 40 years of separation. We took this as a good sign as we also hoped for the joining of worlds that previously were poles apart, to talk about innovative assistive technologies for the next few decades.

Ubiquitous computing will point out new kinds of applications in the twenty-first century: to access and process information anywhere, anyplace, and anytime; to support users in their every-day life. Alone inside computer science, this is associated with a number of sub-disciplines, each addressing individual aspects of ubiquitous computing, each characterized by individual contributions and research challenges, and each having its individual platforms in the world-wide community. With IMC 2009 we sought to bridge this gap.

From a bottom-up perspective, infrastructures for ubiquitous computing are being enabled by rapidly emerging communications systems, based on different wireless technologies as well as utilizing such technologies for cellular architectures, for personal communications, and for wireless local area networks. From a top-down perspective, applications like intelligent assistance with a high degree of autonomy require sensing, aggregation, and interpretation of contextual data for understanding and supporting the personal needs of the users in time. A number of cross-cutting issues emerge in putting together these perspectives, finally bringing up the main subjects of the IMC 2009 conference:

- Enabling the electronic assistant to understand the user's goals and preferences as well as the individual strategies employed by the user for achieving these goals
- Sensing and understanding the user's personal environment and the ways the environment influences his activities and strategies
- Providing intuitive interaction by supporting novel input technologies as well as tailored information visualization techniques
- Making this support available in the user's environment, e.g., smart home, smart office, etc.
- Modeling, simulating, and rapidly deploying new scenarios, architectures, and tools for interactive mobile applications
- Managing security, privacy, and trust in sensor-rich dynamic environments

The conference aims to provide an international forum for researchers, students, and professionals in order to present current research results on these subjects, and to bring together experts from both academia and industry for the exchange of ideas and discussion of future challenges. In this way, researchers from various fields all over the world are working together hand in hand in order to bridge the gap between theoretical possibilities and technical necessities. The vision of intelligent assistive systems is now within reach.

The IMC 2009 program consisted of three invited talks from international experts, four tutorials on fundamental techniques related to the conference topics, nine regular paper sessions, and a short paper / poster session. We received close to 50 submissions from 15 countries world-wide. Based on the anonymous reviews provided by members of the international Program Committee, the Steering Committee recommended accepting 50% of the contributions as regular papers and another 15% as short papers with poster presentation. To our regret there were a few interesting papers that we had to reject. However, the reviewing results showed a high quality as well as an interesting variety of submissions.

We would like to thank all authors for carefully preparing the results of their work submitted to IMC 2009, thus enabling an interesting and high-quality conference program. Moreover, we are deeply grateful to all members of the Program and Steering Committees for their efforts in quickly and thoroughly evaluating the papers. Finally, our special thanks go to the organizers Ulrike Lucke and Daniel Versick for their great work. They handled all the organizational tasks as well as the communications, the electronic submission, reviewing, and publication procedure in an efficient and timely manner.

As another reference to recent German history, we were pleased to welcome our conference guests in the formerly "hidden" part of Germany. Our conference venue was a newly established resort in Rostock-Warnemünde, directly at the shore of the Baltic Sea in the north-eastern part of Germany. Despite Rostock being an old hanseatic city, open to the world, with a long tradition in shipping and trading, 20 years ago nobody would have bet on gathering international researchers at the beach of Warnemünde today!

November 2009   Djamshid Tavangarian
                                                                      Thomas Kirste
                                                                   Dirk Timmermann

Organization

The International Conference on Intelligent Interactive Assistance and Mobile Multimedia Computing 2009 – IMC2009 – was organized by the Faculty of Electrical Engineering and Computer Science of Rostock University.

Executive Committee

General Chair   Djamshid Tavangarian (Rostock, Germany)
Steering Committee   Michael Beigl (Braunschweig, Germany)
                                    Andreas Heuer (Rostock, Germany)
                                    Ali Hurson (Missouri, USA)
                                    Christopher Lueg (Hobarth, Australia)
                                    Fabio Paterno (Pisa, Italy)
                                    Claudia Roda (Paris, France)
Program Co-chairs   Thomas Kirste (Rostock, Germany)
                                    Dirk Timmermann (Rostock, Germany)

Program Committee

Uwe Baumgarten	Björn Gottfried	Christian Müller-Schloer
Regina Bernhaupt	Jan Gulliksen	Jörg Nolte
Marcus Bick	Niels Henrik Helms	Adam Pawlak
Arndt Bode	Bernd Klauer	Kari-Jouko Räihä
Hendrik Bohn	Stefan Knauth	Frank Reichenbach
Clemens Cap	Birgitta König-Ries	Alessandro Saffiotti
Giuseppe Ciaccio	Antonio Krüger	Klaus Schmid
Giovanni Chiola	Rolf Kruse	Daniel Sinnig
Stefan Fischer	Rainer Malaka	Bodo Urban
Peter Forbrig	Mahmoud Mofaddel	Janet Wesson
Hans-Werner Gellersen	Behzad Moshiri	Bernd E. Wolfinger

Organization Team

Ulrike Lucke
Daniel Versick

Institutions

Universität Rostock

Gesellschaft für Informatik

IEEE

German Chapter of the ACM

ITG

VDE

Table of Contents

Mobile Communication

Context Awareness

Semantics

System Development

Intelligence

Security and Privacy

Short Papers

Assistive Systems:
A Paradigm Shift in Technology and Medical Care

Michael Meyer, Arthur F. Pease, and Michael Lang

Siemens AG Germany, Healthcare Sector
Karlheinz-Kaske-Str. 2, 91052 Erlangen, Germany
michael-meyer@siemens.com

Abstract. Medical diagnostic procedures are overwhelming physicians with data. In response, doctors are turning to computer programs that help them assess and interpret results. Newly-developed software is now providing fast, accurate decision support. An army of algorithms is being developed. Built on expert knowledge and capable of learning from experience, these systems are pointing out anomalies in radiology exams, providing decision support in a range of fields, and optimizing split-second decision making in high-speed industrial processes. As such systems harvest knowledge, there will be no limit to what we will learn from them.

1 Introduction

For most industrialized countries, the demographic, structural and social changes are resulting in a higher proportion of elderly people within the population. The social and financial impact of this change cannot be met by today's medical system and the public institutional care systems. Hence the transition of elderly people into medical care centers and institutional care has to be reduced or delayed, and work intensive tasks within these facilities have to be facilitated. Assistive systems are therefore demanded at the elderly people's home as well as in institutional medical care.

An Ambient Assisted Living (AAL) environment is an integration of stand-alone assistive technologies, with elements of smart homes, and telehealth services. AAL refers to technical systems that support people in need of assistance in their everyday lives, to promote personal independence and to improve the availability and quality of health and social care services in the home. New market potentials are created at the interface between traditional sectors such as health services, care, medical technology, housing and the IT industry on the other. The use of ICT and the establishment of networks between everyday objects, social players and the welfare system mean high requirements have to be met regarding the reliability, user acceptance and serviceability of the IT based solutions.

One important application is a continuous monitoring of activities and behavior of the elderly user based on diverse sensor modalities. This enables the system to recognize and assess the current situation, to provide assistance and to call external support if needed. In this context robots can be of use in order to provide additional sensing capabilities. In addition, it is expected that future intelligent robots will provide

D. Tavangarian et al. (Eds.): IMC 2009, CCIS 53, pp. 1–11, 2009.

physical assistance tasks in home and care facilities. They will also feature a close integration into intelligent environments.

2 Harvest without End[1]

Patterns previously invisible to machines and humans are today providing insights that make medical treatments increasingly personalized and effective, production more customized and efficient, and intelligence — whether in a security camera or a picture archiving system — more distributed and flexible. Across the board — from health care to energy management, and from finance to security and sales — information is being mined from machines, processes and experts, and crystallized into machine knowledge used by algorithms. These algorithms, which range from systems that can interrogate cardiac data for anomalies to the analysis of sales information to predict a customer's probability of consummating an order, are becoming our invisible assistants.

2.1 Experts Inside

Regardless of the class of problems they are engineered to solve, assistants provide support in an area humans are ill equipped to deal with: discovering trends in huge databases. In the medical area, for instance, this process begins with data mining. "We are taking various patient data sources, mining them to build predictive models, and embedding the results in applications that allow physicians to dynamically interact with the information in a computer aided detection (CAD) environment," says Alok Gupta, PhD, vice president of the CAD and Knowledge Solutions Group at Siemens Medical Solutions (SMS) in Malvern, Pennsylvania.

For SMS, the spot where this avalanche of data converges is a comprehensive knowledge platform for medical decision support called the Remind (Reliable Extraction and Meaningful Inference from Nonstructured Data) platform. The ultimate invisible assistant, "Remind will make it possible to dynamically integrate medical images, in-vitro diagnostic information, and genetic information into a patient's profile, providing personalized decision support based on analysis of data from large numbers of patients with similar conditions," explains Bharat Rao, PhD, senior director of Knowledge Solutions for Healthcare Providers at Siemens Medical Solutions in Malvern and inventor of the Remind platform. Remind adds up to a diagnostic crossroads for Siemens' imaging-related businesses and its more recently acquired in-vitro businesses, now known as Siemens Diagnostics (for more, see Pictures of the Future, Spring 2007, p. 54). "The vision is to integrate the information from imaging and laboratory tests into a single database, and eventually a single patient record," says Gupta.

On the long road to realizing the Remind vision, Siemens is developing an army of invisible assistants designed to support physicians as "second readers."

The idea is that once a specialist has examined a scan, he or she can run the appropriate assistant to increase the probability that nothing has been missed. Known as

---

[1] This article by Arthur F. Pease was originally published in the Siemens brochure "Pictures of the Future", pages 89-91, Spring 2008.

knowledgedriven products, these assistants (which plug into Siemens' syngouser interface) offer computer aided detection of lung nodules, colon polyps, breast lesions, and much more.

Other assistants support physicians in accelerating the process of accurately quantifying functions such as cardiac ejection fraction and vessel flow abnormalities, and in providingcomparative analysis of images produced at different times and from different imaging modalities.

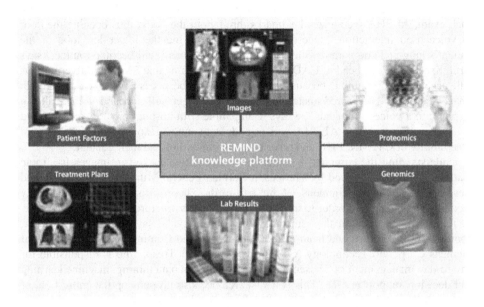

Fig. 1. By combining different sources of medical information in a single database, the Remind platform will support the creation of new, specialized decision-support assistants

Among the many assistants heading for commercialization is one that extracts a 4D model (3D over time) of the aortic valve from ultrasound data "that will allow physicians to interrogate it regarding a variety of real-time, quantitative functions," says Helene Houle, a senior sonographer with Siemens Ultrasound in Mountain View, California, who worked closely with Siemens Corporate Research in Princeton on its development. Another assistant now under joint development will create a 3D interactive model of the heart from computer tomography (CT) data. The model, now in prototype, will display the outlines of the beating heart and provide information regarding anomalies in the volume of blood pumped by the atria.

But such assistants are just the beginning. "We are looking at what it would mean to add genetic information to the imaging data in these products," says Gupta. With this in mind, Siemens is working with an expanding group of medical centers in the context of the EUfunded Health-e-Child program (see Pictures of the Future, Spring 2007, p. 72). The program, which is coordinated by SCR and the CAD group, is developing an integrated health-care platform for pediatric information designed to provide seamless integration of traditional sources of biomedical information, as well as emerging sources, such as genetic and proteomic data.

2.2 Voice Command

As medical assistants multiply and their underlying databases expand, new systems of addressing this cornucopia of information will be needed. One solution that is approaching market introduction in 2008 is Automatic Localization and Parsing of Human Anatomy (ALPHA). Trained on a huge anatomical database and capable of learning with each exam, ALPHA recognizes landmarks throughout the body, thus opening the door to voicebased interaction. "Questions such as 'show me the lower left lobe of the patient's lung and compare it with the previous two exams,' will become routine," says Arun Krishnan, PhD, head of CAD research and development at SMS in Malvern. "This will accelerate throughput, because it will no longer be necessary to search through image sets to find a desired anatomical slice. The target will appear automatically in response to a voice command," he says. Compatible with hospital picture archiving and communication systems, ALPHA will provide a quantum leap in terms of the rapid accessibility of CT, MR, PET, and other imaging modalities and their content.

Understanding the complex meanings and information locked in images is a topic that is also being examined by Theseus, a German Federal Ministry of Education and Research project led by Siemens. "A big part of the Theseus vision is to automatically recognize image data in order to transform it from an unstructured to a structured state, so that it can be used in the semantic Web for retrieval," say Dr. Hartmut Raffler, coordinator of Theseus and head of the Information and Communications Division of Siemens Corporate Technology (CT). Adds Dr. Volker Tresp, who is responsible for day-to-day management of Theseus and is a specialist in data mining, machine learning and decision support at CT, "This is a vast area because it opens up the entire field of picture, video, multimedia and content archives for deep exploration as they relate to security, robotics, entertainment, environmental sciences, and much more."

Specifically, a research area within Theseus known as "Medico" is building an intelligent, scalable picture archiving and search system (that could be supported by ALPHA) capable of retrieving images by content. Suppose, for in stance, that a cardiologist is examining MR images of a patient with a pulmonary valve deficiency. "To help determine whether the deficiency warrants surgery, he might ask Theseus to show him images of pulmonary valves that look similar to the one he is looking at in terms of morphology and function before and after surgery," says Dr. Dorin Comaniciu, head of the Integrated Data Systems department at Siemens Corporate Research and one of the initiators of Theseus Medico.

2.3 Communicative Cameras

But the areas of application for this kind of search engine extend well beyond medical uses. Says Ramesh Visvanathan, PhD, head of the Real-time Vision and Modeling Department at SCR, "In the context of the Theseus project, our Vision Center of Competence in Munich is defining metadata languages for the automatic identification of video content. In terms of security applications, for instance, this will mean that cameras will be able to track a target of interest by describing it in a standardized language and passing the information from one camera to another." The technology would thus make it possible to follow an intruder as he or she leaves one camera's field of view and enters the area monitored by another camera.

And what about the quality of the images that intelligent systems select? Regardless of whether an image originates in a surveillance camera or a medical database, the highest quality must be guaranteed if the evaluation of its content is to be reliable. Image retrieval systems therefore need a way of ensuring selection of the best available images. Work now in the pipeline at Beijing's Tsinghua University that is sponsored in part by Siemens may provide an answer. "The idea is to develop an assistant that will select the best and most relevant images for doctors from large data sets," says Comaniciu. Trained by using the criteria doctors themselves use for selecting images, the assistant may even be able to enhance images that are less than perfect.

2.4 Algorithms and Automation

Just as intelligent assistants are rapidly reproducing in the health-care universe, they are also beginning to populate other areas — particularly in industry. In steel production, for instance, the trend toward total automation is leading to increasing use of decentralized intelligence.

"Depending on the grade of steel, the manufacturing components involved may have individual strategies for monitoring and managing each step while taking a collective view ofthe process," says Dr. Michael Metzger, a specialist in steel industry solutions at Corporate Technology in Munich. He explains that this boils down to the use of "algorithms stationed near associated actuators working together to solve a control problem within a community of machines." Such systems must, furthermore, be able to learn at lightning speed. "In order to accomplish this," says Metzger, "these systems are based on control and optimization process models that are themselves based on relationships derived from physics and expert knowledge. But they must also be able to learn from the huge amount of data produced by an automation system, thus enabling the control system to respond optimally in real time to variables such as rolling force and temperature," he explains.

As in health care, a process of customization is in full swing here. This begins with expert knowledge and data mining, which discover key parameters, such as deformation historyand cooling rate for a given grade of steel. Then, to optimize results for a particular order, the entire production process is simulated — including neural networks and learning algorithms. Once optimized in the virtual world, the information is transferred to the rolling mill and put to the test. Values for each process step are taken and compared against the simulated (and thus optimized) values. "As a result," says Metzger, "the models learn how to improve themselves based on this comparison. Ultimately," he adds, "such systems will provide decision support and finally decision automation."

2.5 Digital Repairmen

Not only do learning systems keep track of what works best under a complex variety of circumstances. They also keep an eye on the long-term factors that cause machine wear and tear, and predict when service should be performed with a view to minimizing downtime. With this in mind, in 2007 Siemens established a strategic program called the Machine Monitoring Initiative. "The project will tap basic research throughout the organization in data mining, learning systems and decision support," says Claus Neubauer, a data integration specialist at SCR. The results will be used to automate the prediction and scheduling of maintenance on everything from power, rail and communication networks to MR scanners and windmill gearboxes.

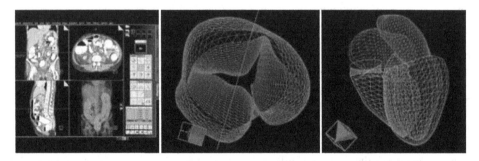

Fig. 2. Medical assistants recognize anomalies in the intestine (left), in the function of the aortic valve (center), and in the amount of blood pumped by the atria of the heart over time

Predicting when machines will need maintenance and which parts will need to be replaced may sound like a tall order, but what about predicting whether a customer will actually purchase a wind park or an MR scanner? Surprisingly, agents are already zeroing in on this kind of information as well. Research conducted at SCR has come up with an agent technology that is "70 to 80 percent accurate," says Amit Chakraborty, who leads the Modeling and Optimization program at SCR. "In providing this decision support, the agent takes many factors into account, including customer reliability, competitors, and sales force information," he adds.

2.6 Intelligence Everywhere

Naturally, given the fact that they are weightless, not particularly expensive to produce, and capable of incrementally increasing the productivity of hardware, invisible agents will eventually pop up just about everywhere. The trend toward decentralized intelligence in highly automated production facilities will have its counterparts in traffic and rail management, building and home automation, safety and security technology, power generation and distribution, and of course health care. The implications of these invisible entities for entertainment, information accessibility, security, environmental protection, and the way humans communicate, organize, work and live could be profound.

"We should keep in mind that this is all about solutions that support human activities," says CT's Raffler. "Based on this, agents will understand what we are looking for, present results more intelligently than is now possible, answer questions, deal with large bodies of unstructured data, compose services, and propose new processes for solving problems."

Information, something we produce more of with every passing second, will become increasingly valuable as we learn to mine it, combine its streams, and refine its messages. What lies ahead, in short, is a harvest without end.

3 Digital Decision Support[2]

The Maastro Clinic is a leading cancer treatment facility located in the vicinity of Maastricht University in the Netherlands. The clinic's Radio Therapy section has a friendly reception area where patients referred from numerous other Dutch hospitals await cancer screenings, follow-up treatments, and treatment simulations. To provide the best possible treatment for these patients, and improve cancer research, the facility houses an interdisciplinary team of radiation therapy specialists, biologists, physicists, and computer scientists, as well as experts from Siemens Healthcare, all of whom have access to high-tech medical equipment and state-of-the-art software.

A key member of the team is Professor Philippe Lambin, a radiation oncologist who is medical director of the Maastro Clinic. "We're conducting research on a computer-aided decision-support system for personalized treatment of patients with lung cancer," Lambin explains.

"We're doing this because a study carried out by Maastricht University revealed that most doctors are unable to reliably assess how well their treatments are working, and therefore have difficulty in choosing the right treatment. We plan to improve predictions of the effectiveness of radiation therapies with the help of sophisticated software." The software Lambin is referring to is based on Remind, a data mining comtool from Siemens (Pictures of the Future, Spring 2006, p. 9).

Remind (Reliable Extraction and Meaningful Inference from Nonstructured Data) statistically analyzes all types of medical information, including everything from physicians' letters to medical images and laboratory diagnoses, and then identifies specific patterns. A research prototype system tested at the Maastro clinic is able to predict the two year survival rate of lung cancer patients with high accuracy. The twoyear survival rate is used by doctors to assess the success of individual radiation treatments. At the moment, 47 percent of all lung cancer patients survive for the first two years after diagnosis, if their cancer is detected at an early stage.

The first commercial application of Remind is Soarian Quality Measures software, which can measure quality of care from patient records based on established standards. At the Maastro Clinic, however, Remind is being optimized for cancer research in a research project that calls for Siemens experts to work with clinic specialists on site.

The system requires as much medically relevant patient data as possible to issue statistically meaningful prognoses. Such data includes sociological information on the individual in question, measurements taken with imaging methods, and biological data such as cell division biomarker analyses. Remind analyzes and links more than 100 of these parameters. In this research project, Remind then computes the likelihood of two year survival, and the risk of side effects, for various treatment options

---

[2] This article by Michael Lang was originally published in the Siemens brochure "Pictures of the Future", pages 92-94, Spring 2008.

for a patient. The intention is to help physicians select the optimal treatment for each individual patient. capability and radiation sensitivity, which can be determined through gene and blood biomarker analyses. Remind analyzes and links more than 100 of these parameters.

In this research project, Remind then computes the likelihood of two year survival, and the risk of side effects, for various treatment options for a patient. The intention is to help physicians select the optimal treatment for each individual patient.

3.1 Combining Diagnostics and Treatment

Maastro physicians can use state-of-the-art Siemens technology for their diagnoses and treatments. For instance, a combined positron emission tomography (PET) and computer tomography (CT) scanner makes it possible to obtain 3D images of the lungs in spite of breathing- related movement — a must in the case of lung cancer patients. The PET unit uses a lowradiation marker substance to provide crosssectional images that depict biochemical and physiological processes, while the CT details the anatomy and location of the tissue being studied.

The combination of both technologies provides doctors with information on the type of tumor they're dealing with, as well as its precise shape and position. When it comes to treatment, one of Lambin's preferences is adaptive radiotherapy. This Siemens solution provides oncologists with a 3D data set of the patient, which allows them to optimally adapt a radiation procedure to the position and size of the tumor in question.

Here too, Remind supports physicians with prognoses and treatment planning assistance by assessing the results from a database of post-treatment examinations. Lambin describes this combination of diagnostics and treatment therapy as "computer-aided theragnostics."

Another aspect of this research project is to configure Remind to predict the relative probability of typical radiation therapy side effects, such as esophagitis (perforation of the esophagus). This is achieved on the basis of parameters such as radiation dose, treatment time, concomitant chemotherapy, and the concentration of white blood cells. The intention is that such a tool helps doctors to recognize early signs of esophagitis, thus avoiding premature discontinuation of therapeutic treatment.

The next step in the research project will be to include the costs of potential complications associated with the therapy in question. Lambin's primary goal for 2008 is to broaden the system's database. "To make a fairly accurate prediction of the survival rate after a specific therapy, we need to have at least 500 to 1,000 patients in our database," he says. "We also need an external dataset to validate the predictions — that's the bottleneck."

The Maastro research database now contains data on approximately 1,000 patients, 500 of whom were diagnosed with lung cancer. In order to expand this database, the Maastro Clinic has plans to establish a digital network link with hospitals in Leuven and Liège in Belgium, and in Groningen in the Netherlands. Due to data security considerations, however, Maastro's Remind system will only be given anonymous parameters via the link; the data itself will remain in other clinics. The resulting broader research database will make a completely new type of clinical research possible. This is because specialists in Maastricht plan to use the data to simulate clinical studies, much in the same way the pharmaceutical industry uses machine-learning-based software to simulate experiments.

3.2 Digital Radiology

Dr. Marco Das works in the Department of Diagnostic Radiology at Aachen University Hospital, which is located around 40 kilometers from the Maastro Clinic. The focus of his work is the detection of growths in the lungs, such as cancers, metastases, and benign tumors. The clinical routine here involves using CT to create 3D data sets of the lung, after which Das searches for suspicious-looking structures in digital images. Das examines 30 to 40 patients this way every day, meaning that he only has a couple of minutes for each diagnosis.

To raise the probability that no tumor is overlooked, a second radiologist double-checks all of his findings. Das also utilizes CAD (computer- aided detection) software that may eliminate the need for a second radiologist, as is already the case at many hospitals. CAD is a technology based on pattern recognition and not on artificial intelligence. CAD systems for lungs analyze differences in thickness in lung tissues and compare these with stored images of typical lung tumor patterns. They are therefore able to recognize such patterns in other CT images as well.

3.3 Tumor Marker

"All of this functions very well in practice," says Das, who uses syngo Lung- CAD software from Siemens. The system examines lungs for tumors even before a radiologist has finished making his or her assessment. It takes the software only around four minutes to check up to 700 image slices, each of which is one millimeter thick — and it works even faster with thicker layers and a correspondingly lower number of images.

After Das completes his diagnosis, he analyzes the results produced by the software, which means there's no waiting time in between. The software automatically marks suspicious areas with red circles. "All studies to date show that CAD software has had a positive effect on the accuracy of radiologist diagnoses," says Das. The system does make errors, however. These take the form of false-positive diagnoses, which, according to Das, don't cause any major problems, since they can quickly be spotted by an experienced radiologist.

"CAD programs are very good as second readers, but they'll never replace radiologist diagnoses because a doctor's experience is the key to evaluating results," says Das. An additional advantage offered by the new syngo CT Oncology software — which includes syngo LungCAD functionality — is that it helps to accelerate diagnostic decision making, according to Das. For instance, doctors need to measure changes in tumor size in order to determine whether a treatment is working. Until recently this was done by manually calculating a tumor's diameter onscreen. Such measurements are extremely imprecise, however, and can vary from doctor to doctor. Syngo CT Oncology, on the other hand, improves measurement accuracy by automatically calculating the volume of all different types of tumors. It also enables

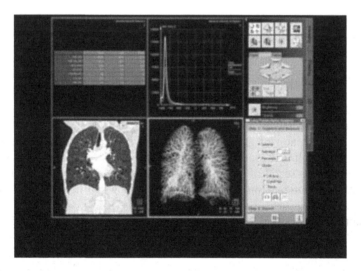

Fig. 3. Siemens software supports accurate diagnostic decision making regarding lung tumor characteristics

doctors to determine tissue density — a measurement that cannot be performed manually. Tissue density, in turn, provides an initial indication of whether or not a tumor is malignant.

Such measurements are also often used on patients with emphysema, a disease usually caused by smoking that destroys the alveoli in the lungs. Here, syngo InSpace4D Lung Parenchyma Analysis software from Siemens measures density distribution throughout the entire lung, whereby a diseased lung will, due to its burst alveoli, have more free air in its tissue (and will therefore be less dense) than a healthy lung. "This software solution makes it possible for the first time ever to quantify the early stages of emphysema and thus to effectively monitor treatment," says Das. "This used to be an extremely difficult process requiring several indirect tests."

3.4 Virtual Colonoscopy

Colon cancer screenings are another application where computeraided detection is very helpful. Dr. Anno Graser from the Institute for Clinical Radiology at Munich University Hospital uses syngo Colonography with PEV (Polyp Enhanced Viewing) software to review the results of virtual colonoscopies. Unlike physicians in Aachen, Graser does not have a second radiologist and therefore relies on PEV software for a second opinion.

"The program, which can be used by any doctor, delivers very good results, as long as the colon has been properly cleansed beforehand," says Graser, who also tested the software in several studies. He's not only satisfied with the program's accuracy, but also happy that "the software simplifies and accelerates the entire process." In Graser's institute, it only takes four minutes, in fact, for the program to calculate the PEV results — about as long as it takes a gastroenterologist.

Graser has been screening one or two patients per day with the system since he concluded his clinical studies of the software. But there is still some resistance to the new technology. "Health insurance companies in Germany only pay for conventional colonoscopies, unless you have a situation where an intestinal infection or obstruction would not allow for such a procedure," he explains.

Nevertheless, patients prefer the virtual procedure because it's much shorter than the conventional one. Another major benefit is that its polyp detection software is extremely sensitive, thus improving the chances of early detection. "These benefits are going to help the system achieve a major breakthrough in terms of acceptance," says Graser.

Qualitative Locomotion Patterns in Convex Spaces

Björn Gottfried

Centre for Computing Technologies
University of Bremen, Germany
bg@tzi.de

Abstract. This paper presents a qualitative spatial representation in order to describe locomotion patterns. This is useful for smart environments in order to let the system monitor the behaviours of inhabitants. Then, the monitored behaviours can be evaluated using the proposed representation in order to provide assistance according to the behaviours the inhabitants show.

The new representation abstracts from specific sensor technologies. Instead, it determines what the sensory system to be used has to afford. Therefore, this work is regarded as a framework about spatiotemporal patterns found between the sensory level and the application level. Since there exists a constrained class of locomotion patterns for convex indoor environments, according constraints are applied to both the sensory system and the representation.

Core result is that this approach enables a new design concept for spatiotemporal assistance systems. While previous work has shown the limitations of methods that relate interpretations of behaviours to specific locations, it shows that specific locations are sometimes difficult to define. Instead we propose to relate interpretations of behaviours to locomotion patterns which are not necessarily bound to specific locations.

1 Introduction

Providing an employee or inhabitant in a smart environment assistance requires to determine his behaviour. The most fundamental behaviours people obey are locomotion behaviours in order to get from one place to another one. This is the reason why smart environments need to support locomotion behaviours. That is to say, a smart environment should take into account where someone is and which paths he takes. Then, the environment gets smarter by making use of this information, which amounts to monitor and interpret the user's locations and changes of locations. An example is given in [6] where meetings are supported by a smart conference room in which in particular locomotion behaviours let the system know about what is going on. Hence, the application problem at hand consists in distinguishing typical locomotion patterns. Further approaches investigating locomotion patterns for specific purposes include [5,8,11,16].

The paper is structured as follows. In Section 2 a problem is identified that motivates our approach which is presented in Section 3. This approach allows the

D. Tavangarian et al. (Eds.): IMC 2009, CCIS 53, pp. 13–24, 2009.

definition of locomotion patterns, as introduced in Section 4. While a number of examples demonstrate the application of the discussed representation, Section 5 shows how the approach deals with imperfect data, and hence, how it manages realistic scenarios. A final discussion closes the paper in Section 6.

2   Interpretations Based on Locomotion Patterns

In [6] domain knowledge on a given environment is employed in order to identify relevant locations and possible motion paths for the given assistance system. The role of people is directly related to those locations: when standing or moving at some presentation area they are assumed to held a presentation, while being at other locations they are assumed to sit at a table in the audience. Similarly, specific paths are distinguished: those covered when people entering the conference room, looking for a seat, and those covered when going to the presentation area or back to the seat. Relating motion behaviours to regions is in fact a common technique [12,9]. The strategy [6] applies could be referred to as the *location-interpretation strategy*: behaviours are interpreted with reference to the locations where those behaviours have been observed. But then, the authors identify the problem that the system might come to wrong conclusions when a person accidently leaves an area that is designated to a specific purpose, and hence, role the system attaches to that person: the interpretation fails.

A more flexible approach would rather attach specific roles of people to locomotion behaviours instead of to specific locations or regions. This has the advantage that people are not confined to specific regions they must not leave. We will therefore propose a calculus that enables the robust analysis of how a person behaves in a room independent from specific locations but depending on how the given locomotion patterns look like. As opposed to the *location-interpretation strategy* we call this the *locomotion-interpretation strategy*. Clearly, situations are conceivable in which both strategies cooperate.

3   A Locomotion Calculus for Convex Spaces

In order to investigate locomotion patterns a smart environment is assumed that is equipped with sensors determining positions of people or mobile robots moving around. For a sensor independent solution, we expect that the given sensory system is able to register mobile objects crossing the view of a specific sensor. Then, there are basically two factors influencing how objects are located. First, depending on the number of sensors deployed the location of a mobile object can be determined more or less precise. Second, the specific configuration of sensors determines which places can be distinguished in the given environment. We shall analyse the distinguishable locations for a particular sensor setup, and consequently, the locomotion patterns that can be discriminated. We generalise from this example and come up with a calculus for the class of locomotion patterns of closed convex spaces. Such spaces are found in most indoor environments.

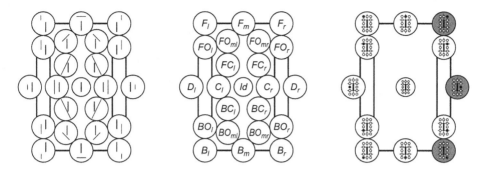

Fig. 1. The 23 $\mathcal{BA}_{23}$ relations that can be distinguished between two line segments in the two-dimensional plane. Left: Example arrangements. Centre: Mnemonic labels. Right: Twelve relations exist when describing the positions of points. The three highlighted relations remain in convex spaces when assigning FO_r and BO_r to D_r.

3.1 $\mathcal{BA}_{23}$

In [3] a relation algebra has been introduced with 23 relations among intervals in two dimensions. These relations are shown in Fig. 1. They form a qualitative representation in that they abstract from precise quantitative locations. Having two intervals which are determined by their endpoints we are faced with a four-dimensional configuration space that consists of precise values. The abstraction from precise quantities means to define equivalence classes of locations that are considered to be identical in the chosen representation. For instance, when an object is left of another object, level with it, it is said to be *during left*, D_l for short (see the relation on the left hand side of the neighbourhood graph in Fig. 1). In this way, each conceivable relation among two linear disconnected objects in two dimensions can be represented. The considerations of sequences of such relations describe relative locomotion patterns among pairs of objects.

3.2 $\mathcal{BA}_3$

Here we shall consider a class of locomotion patterns that are frequently found in indoor environments. Analysing the constraints satisfied for such patterns, a new calculus with only 3 base relations is identified. It will be shown below how locomotion patterns are described using this approach.

We start by the observation that indoor spaces are in most cases distinguished by having a convex, e.g. rectangular, ground plan; or, to be more precise, such a ground plan will usually be concave since gaps exist for doors and windows, but then the boundary is lying on its convex hull. Therefore, attaching a number of sensors at the walls, they are arranged on a convex shape. Enumerating them clockwise and conceiving two adjacent sensors as the start- and endpoint of an interval, we would have only those 10 relations shown on the right hand side of the neighbourhood graph in Fig. 1, that is those relations with the index

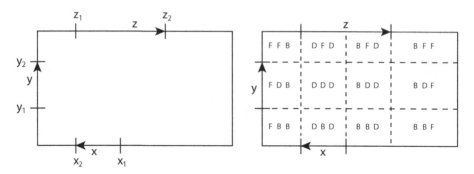

Fig. 2. Left: A rectangular room equipped with six sensors x_1, x_2, y_1, y_2, z_1, and z_2. Right: The line of sights of the sensors tessellate the ground plan into twelve regions.

r; henceforth, by the term sensor we refer to such a sensor pair comprising two adjacent collinear sensors. Having more than two sensors on the same wall, there are two additional relations, F_m and B_m, if we would relate the sensors themselves. A final constraint is that we assign FO_r and BO_r to D_r since we will not be in need of such overlap relations. Then, mobile objects that are represented by points (i.e. degenerated intervals) lie in one of the three highlighted relations to each sensor pair (right hand side of Fig. 1). The resulting system of relations is $\mathcal{BA}_3 = \{F_r, D_r, B_r\}$.

3.3   An Example

On the left hand side of Fig. 2 a rectangular ground plan of a room is given together with six sensors called x_1, x_2, y_1, y_2, z_1, and z_2. They are arranged in pairs clockwise oriented and stored in the list $S = \langle x, y, z \rangle$. Considering their line of sights orthogonal to their arrangements along the walls a tessellation of the ground plan is obtained for which each place can be uniquely indexed (right hand side of Fig. 2). $_xF_r$ denotes the region called *front right* induced by sensor x, while $_yF_r$ denotes *front right* induced by sensor y. Furthermore, P_x denotes the set of x-distinguishable places, i.e. $P_x = \{_xF_r, \,_xD_r, \,_xB_r\}$. While P_x just refers to the x-tessellation of the ground plan, $P_s = P_x \cap P_y \cap P_z$ denotes the whole tessellation shown in Fig. 2 induced by the sensors contained in S. A specific place is accordingly given by, for instance, $p = \,_xD_r \cap \,_yD_r \cap \,_zD_r$ denoting that region which is left of the centre of the room.

Since in $\mathcal{BA}_3$ every relation has the index r, for *right of*, we simplify the description by omitting this index. Additionally, in the following the first letter refers to what x senses, the second what y senses and the last one what z senses. For example, $_xD_r \,_yB_r \,_zD_r$ simplifies to DBD, which denotes the region nearby sensor x.

4   Qualitative Locomotion Patterns

Fig. 3 shows the trajectory of a mobile object travelling through the room. The table in Fig. 3 shows the qualitative labels of the places occupied by the mobile

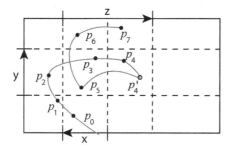

Position	Qualitative Label
p_0	DBD
p_1	FBB
p_2	FDB
p_3	DDD
p_4	BDD
p_5	DDD
p_6	DFD
p_7	BFD

Fig. 3. A motion trajectory measured at eight positions

on its path. There are no two equal places following directly each other, like p_4 and p_4', since no sensor recognises such changes as from p_4 to p_4'. Labels are printed in black whenever they change. Usually only one label changes at a time. But two cases exist in which more changes occur simultaneously, namely when sensors share their line of sights (as for x_2 and z_1) or when places are crossed diagonally (as when changing from p_0 directly to p_2). Maximally two sensors share their line of sights, namely whenever two of their components, as x_2 and z_1, are precisely opposite to each other.

In the following, a number of locomotion patterns will be analysed given such sequences of qualitative places as in the table in Fig. 3. For this purpose, it is shown that these qualitative places define a metric on which locomotion patterns can be defined. Then, a sequence t is defined by the qualitative positions the travelling object subsequently occupies:

(D1) $t \equiv \langle p_0, p_1, \ldots, p_{n-1} \rangle, \ p_i \in P_s, \ i = 0, 1, \ldots, n-1, \ n \geq 1$

4.1   A Metric on Qualitative Places

Pairs of places can be related by the distance of the according relations that describe those places. Since the relations in $\mathcal{BA}_3$ are in a total order, the distance between a pair of relations, r_i and r_j, is defined as follows:

(D2) $\forall_{r_i, r_j \in \mathcal{BA}_3} : |r_i - r_j| \equiv \begin{cases} 0 & \text{if } r_i = r_j \\ 1 & \text{if } r_i = D \wedge (r_j = F \vee r_j = B) \\ 2 & \text{else} \end{cases}$

The distance between qualitative places, p_i and p_j, is then defined by the sum of the distances of relations for all sensors:

(D3) $\forall_{p_i, p_j \in P_s} : d(p_i, p_j) \equiv |_x r_i - {}_x r_j| + |_y r_i - {}_y r_j| + |_z r_i - {}_z r_j|, {}_s r_k \in \mathcal{BA}_3$

In this way, the Manhatten distance is realised as opposed to the Euclidean distance [10]. But then, the problem occurs that distances are counted twice whenever two sensors share a line of sight. For example, when getting from DBD to FBB two neighbouring places are subsequently visited although two labels change, namely for sensor x and for sensor z (see Fig. 2).

In order to solve this problem we register such cases, i.e. the sets $\mathcal{S}_{Double}^1$ and $\mathcal{S}_{Double}^2$ include those sensor components which have a line of sight in common with another sensor, either at the transition of BD or DF. That is, we have to register only one of those sensors because such a transition is to be counted exactly once. In our example it holds $\mathcal{S}_{Double}^1 = \{z_1\}$ since the line of sight of z_1 equals that one of x_2 which is z's transition at BD; additionally, it holds $\mathcal{S}_{Double}^2 = \{\}$ since there is no doublet at a transition between D and F. Then, the distance for a pair of relations depends on the according sensor s:

$$(D4) \quad \forall_{s \in S} \forall_{{}_s r_i, {}_s r_j \in \mathcal{B}\mathcal{A}_3} : |{}_s r_i - {}_s r_j| \equiv \begin{cases} 0 & \text{if } {}_s r_i = {}_s r_j \ \vee \\ & (s \in \mathcal{S}_{Double}^1 \wedge {}_s r_i = B \wedge {}_s r_i \neq {}_s r_j) \ \vee \\ & (s \in \mathcal{S}_{Double}^2 \wedge {}_s r_i = F \wedge {}_s r_i \neq {}_s r_j) \\ 1 & \text{if } {}_s r_i = D \wedge ({}_s r_j = F \vee {}_s r_j = B) \\ 2 & \text{else} \end{cases}$$

Equation D4 is to be used in equation D3 and for the transition between DBD to FBB we obtain 1. With these definitions a metric space on P_s is obtained:

Proposition 1 (Metric).

(P_s, d) defines a metric space, with the metric $d : P_s \times P_s \to \mathbb{N}_0$.

Proof. P_s satisfies the following four axioms of a metric:

1. $\forall_{p_i, p_j \in P_s} : d(p_i, p_j) \geq 0$

   (1) $\forall_{p_i, p_j \in P_s} \forall_{s \in S} \forall_{{}_s r_i, {}_s r_j \in \mathcal{B}\mathcal{A}_3} : \qquad d(p_i, p_j) = \sum_{s \in S} |{}_s r_i - {}_s r_j| \qquad \text{(D3)}$

   (2) $\forall_{s \in S} \forall_{{}_s r_i, {}_s r_j \in \mathcal{B}\mathcal{A}_3} : \qquad\qquad 0 \leq |{}_s r_i - {}_s r_j| \leq 2 \qquad\qquad \text{(D2)}$

   (3) $\forall_{s \in S} \forall_{{}_s r_i, {}_s r_j \in \mathcal{B}\mathcal{A}_3} : \qquad\qquad 0 \leq \sum_{s \in S} |{}_s r_i - {}_s r_j| \leq 2 \cdot |S| \qquad (1), (2)$

   (4) $\forall_{p_i, p_j \in P_s} : \qquad\qquad\qquad\qquad 0 \leq d(p_i, p_j) \qquad\qquad\qquad (D3), (3)$

2. $\forall_{p_i, p_j \in P_s} : d(p_i, p_j) = 0 \leftrightarrow p_i = p_j$

   (1) $\forall_{p_i, p_j \in P_s} : \qquad\qquad\qquad\qquad d(p_i, p_j) = 0 \qquad\qquad\qquad \text{hypothesis}$

   (2) $\forall_{{}_s r_i, {}_s r_j \in \mathcal{B}\mathcal{A}_3} : \qquad\qquad \sum_{s \in S} |{}_s r_i - {}_s r_j| = 0 \qquad\qquad (1), (D3)$

   (3) $\forall_{{}_s r_i, {}_s r_j \in \mathcal{B}\mathcal{A}_3} \forall_{s \in S} : \qquad\qquad |{}_s r_i - {}_s r_j| = 0 \qquad\qquad\qquad (2)$

   (4) $\forall_{{}_s r_i, {}_s r_j \in \mathcal{B}\mathcal{A}_3} \forall_{s \in S} : \qquad\qquad {}_s r_i = {}_s r_j \qquad\qquad\qquad (3), (D2)$

   (5) $\forall_{p_i, p_j \in P_s} : \qquad\qquad\qquad\qquad p_i = p_j \qquad\qquad\qquad\qquad (4)$

3. $\forall_{p_i,p_j \in P_s} : d(p_i, p_j) = d(p_j, p_i)$

(1) $\forall_{p_i,p_j \in P_s} \forall_{s r_i, s r_j \in \mathcal{BA}_3} :$ $\qquad d(p_i, p_j) = \sum_{s \in S} |_s r_i - {}_s r_j|$ (D3)

(2) $\forall_{s r_i, s r_j \in \mathcal{BA}_3} :$ $\qquad \sum_{s \in S} |_s r_i - {}_s r_j| = \sum_{s \in S} |_s r_j - {}_s r_i|$ (1), commutat.

(3) $\forall_{s r_i, s r_j \in \mathcal{BA}_3} \forall_{p_i,p_j \in P_s} :$ $\qquad \sum_{s \in S} |_s r_j - {}_s r_i| = d(p_j, p_i)$ (2), (D3)

4. $\forall_{p_i,p_j,p_k \in P_s} : d(p_i, p_k) \leq d(p_i, p_j) + d(p_j, p_k)$

(1) $\forall_{s \in S} \forall_{p_i,p_k \in P_s} \forall_{s r_i, s r_k \in \mathcal{BA}_3} :$ (D3)

$$d(p_i, p_k) = \sum_{s \in S} |_s r_i - {}_s r_k|$$

(2) $\forall_{s \in S} \forall_{s r_i, s r_k, s r_m \in \mathcal{BA}_3},$ (D2)

$_s r_m = {}_s r_i \lor {}_s r_m = {}_s r_k \lor$

$(_s r_m = D \land {}_s r_i \neq {}_s r_k) :$

$$|_s r_i - {}_s r_k| = |_s r_i - {}_s r_m| + |_s r_m - {}_s r_k|$$

(3) $\exists_{s \in S} \forall_{s r_i, s r_k, s r_m \in \mathcal{BA}_3},$ (D2)

$_s r_m \neq {}_s r_i \land {}_s r_m \neq {}_s r_k \land$

$(_s r_m = D \rightarrow {}_s r_i = {}_s r_k) :$

$$|_s r_i - {}_s r_k| < |_s r_i - {}_s r_m| + |_s r_m - {}_s r_k|$$

(4) $\forall_{s \in S} \forall_{s r_i, s r_k, s r_m \in \mathcal{BA}_3} :$ (2), (3)

$$|_s r_i - {}_s r_k| \leq |_s r_i - {}_s r_m| + |_s r_m - {}_s r_k|$$

(5) $\forall_{p_i,p_m,p_k \in P_s} :$

$$d(p_i, p_k) \leq d(p_i, p_m) + d(p_m, p_k)$$ (4), (D3)

(6) $\forall_{p_i,p_j,p_k \in P_s} :$

$$d(p_i, p_k) \leq d(p_i, p_j) + d(p_j, p_k)$$ (6), $j \triangleq m$

Note how (D3) defines the connection between the places in P_s and the relations in $\mathcal{BA}_3$ via the sensors in S; this is how some steps can be explained in the proof, for instance, from line (4) to line (5) in the proof of the second axiom. Eventually, the proof assumes that there are no sensors in S sharing a line of sight. Its generalisation is straightforward.

4.2   Shortest and Indirect Paths

A trajectory t describes the shortest path between p_0 and p_{n-1} when, with each step on this path, the distance to the target place gets shorter:

Proposition 2 (Shortest Path).

$$shortest\text{-}path(t) \leftrightarrow \forall_{p_i \in t \text{ with } i \in \{1,2,...,n-1\}} : d(p_i, p_{n-1}) < d(p_{i-1}, p_{n-1})$$

Conversely, an indirect path is taken when there is at least one pair of subsequent places for which the distance to the target gets longer:

Proposition 3 (Indirect Path).

$$indirect\text{-}path(t) \leftrightarrow \exists_{p_i \in t \ with \ i \in \{1,2,...,n-1\}} : \ d(p_i, p_{n-1}) > d(p_{i-1}, p_{n-1})$$

Counting the number of roundabout routes a measure of complexity of the trajectory can be computed. In the example, already p_1 is identified as a roundabout route since its distance to p_7 (which is 4) is larger than the distance between p_0 and p_7 (which is 3). Fig. 4 shows from the left to the right three trajectories with an increasing degree of complexity.

Note that normally there exist more shortest paths depending on the number of sensors involved (see Fig. 5). Similarly, a number of different roundabout routes exist with the same degree of complexity. In order to tell them apart, a further extension would not only count the number of backward steps. Additionally, the sensors along which backward steps are performed can be differentiated.

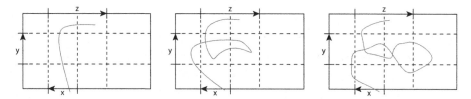

Fig. 4. Three paths of different complexity

Another remark concerns straight paths. A straight path is a shortest path. However, if there are obstacles on the shortest path the smart environment needs to take this into account. For this purpose, intermediate places are defined whenever there is an obstacle. Then, shortest paths are defined among intermediate places as well as among the last intermediate place and the destination place.

4.3   Running on a Spot

A running on a spot occurs when a person is running to and fro, for example while giving a lecture. The occupied area can be arbitrarily large depending on the character of the presenter. Therefore, we propose not to confine artificially the presentation area. Instead the approach tracks the presenter and determines the type of his spatial activity. Thereby, typical patterns can be looked for. They involve the repetitive coming back to the front or a characteristic stop and go while he is talking. As an example we describe the detection of a running to and fro pattern in the following.

At first, the *circulation direction* is to be distinguished for each sensor. For instance, BBB might change to FBB via DBB; in this case we say that the circulation direction of the first sensor runs left of the reference sensor. This

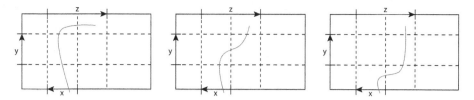

Fig. 5. Three different shortest paths

notion has been used in previous work in order to denote that other objects follow an anticlockwise path around the reference object (sensor) in the non-convex case [4].

Here we are interested in recognising that the circulation direction changes, since this is the case when someone is running to and fro. A change in circulation direction is what we shall call a *reversal*. The circulation direction ρ can take two different ways, or alternatively, there is no circulation at all:

(D8)

$$\forall_{r,r' \in \mathcal{BA}_3 \ \wedge \ succ(r)=r'} : \rho(r,r') \equiv \begin{cases} l & \text{if } (r = \mathsf{B} \wedge r' = \mathsf{D}) \vee (r = \mathsf{D} \wedge r' = \mathsf{F}) \\ r & \text{if } (r = \mathsf{F} \wedge r' = \mathsf{D}) \vee (r = \mathsf{D} \wedge r' = \mathsf{B}) \\ \epsilon & \text{else} \end{cases}$$

A trajectory t comprises a reversal, denoted by ϱ, if there is a change in the circulation direction:

(D9) $\varrho(t) \leftrightarrow \exists_{i,j,k \in \{0,1,\ldots,n-1\} \wedge i < j < k \wedge p_i, p_j, p_k \in t} : \rho(r_i, r_j) \neq \rho(r_j, r_k)$

Counting the number of reversals which occur within a region or within a temporal interval different degrees of this type of running to and fro behaviour can be computed. Fig. 6 gives three examples with no reversal, one reversal and two reversals.

5   Imperfection

How does this approach deal with imperfect data? For an analysis we shall distinguish between inaccuracy, imprecision, and incompleteness as three modes of imperfection [20].

Incompleteness arises as soon as at least one of the sensors fails, i.e. we obtain a description which is only based on the remaining sensors. For instance, if z fails we can distinguish only nine places, if y fails we can even distinguish only four different places. This shows how crucial the sensor arrangement is in order to distinguish as many places as possible. Important to note is that whenever a sensor fails, a valid description can still be derived, though this description is less precise than a description based on all sensors.

Inaccurate data are mainly due to imperfect sensor technologies or noisy environments. From the given sensor arrangement we know that specific combinations are impossible, such as FFF. If such a description is generated, the system

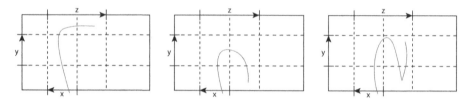

Fig. 6. Left: Path has no reversal. Centre: Path has one reversal along y (a change from B to D and from D to B). Right: Path has two reversals along y (BD, DB, BD).

can derive that something went wrong. From the previous description, however, it can be inferred which sensor works imperfect. If the previous description is DFD, then z seems to have made a mistake. This is because this previous description was still valid and a neighbouring place of FFB, the only configuration where x and z respond with F. Another valid configuration would have been BFF which we would take if the previous valid configuration would have been BFD or FDF; in this case the system would derive that something went wrong with sensor x.

Imprecision is the third mode of imperfection we shall look at. It concerns the precision with which locations are determined. Since we decided to use a qualitative representation we abstract from precise locations, i.e. we have a coarse description. We are therefore not able to determine precise locations or precise trajectories unless we are willing to deploy further sensors in order to obtain a finer tessellation of the ground plan. On the other hand, we do not have to rely on measurement tools which work particularly precise, that is the description is quite robust. The only question that remains is whether we are able to derive anything meaningfully from such a coarse description. This is what we have shown in the previous sections.

6   Discussion

The presented work has not made specific assumptions on the sensors to be used. Motion sensors could be used as well as other sensors which would capture lines of sight. Distinguishing discrete places as in the proposed approach the use of smart floors would also work [17]. This shows the generality of the proposed representation. In [15,14] further positioning techniques, in particular for indoor environments, are surveyed and [7] provides an overview of location systems for ubiquitous computing.

We are currently investigating how it helps to determine relative sensor positions in order to let the system decide itself which failures occur. So far, each sensor that fails would simply leave an incomplete description. Such relative interval-interval descriptions are discussed in [3], and other related approaches that are mainly different in that they make other distinctions, are found in [2].

In smart environments a frequently applied method consists in learning typical behaviours by collecting large quantities of sensory data [1]. The introduced

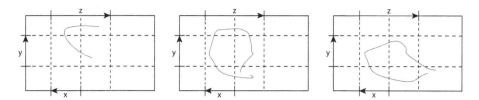

Fig. 7. Left: a reversal along x. Centre: reversals along x and y. Right: reversals along x, y, and z.

representation, and similar other subsets of $\mathcal{BA}$ relations, could also be employed in the context of learning. Here, however, we follow another approach and define behaviour patterns without the need for learning.

Groups of moving objects pose yet other challenges. RFID readers might be a good choice to tell apart individuals of a group of people within such sensor systems [18]. New patterns involving more people would arise; they would give the smart environment further hints about what is going in the environment. An overview of current approaches to movement analysis can be found in [13], and in particular concerning groups, [19] provides a classification scheme for behaviours of collectives.

Eventually, the investigated confines of convex spaces enable a clearly laid out analysis of locomotion patterns that relies on only three relations. But the used concepts do generalise to concave spaces. For the latter, more relations have to be taken into account that describe the possible positions of mobile objects in relation to their more complex, i.e. concave, environment. Such relations can be derived from Fig. 1. In all these cases, qualitative locomotion patterns can be derived that enable to follow the *locomotion-interpretation strategy*.

References

1. Aztiria, A., Izaguirre, A., Basagoiti, R., Augusto, J.C.: Learning about preferences and common behaviours of the user in an intelligent environment. In: Gottfried, B., Aghajan, H. (eds.) Behaviour Monitoring and Interpretation – Smart Environments. IOS Press, Amsterdam (2009)
2. Dylla, F.: Qualitative Spatial Reasoning for Navigating Agents. In: Gottfried, B., Aghajan, H. (eds.) Behaviour Monitoring and Interpretation – Smart Environments. IOS Press, Amsterdam (2009)
3. Gottfried, B.: Reasoning about Intervals in Two Dimensions. In: Thissen, W., Wieringa, P., Pantic, M., Ludema, M. (eds.) Proceedings of the IEEE International Conference on Systems, Man & Cybernetics, The Hague, The Netherlands, October 10–13, pp. 5324–5332. IEEE Press, Los Alamitos (2004)
4. Gottfried, B.: Characterising Meanders Qualitatively. In: Raubal, M., Miller, H.J., Frank, A.U., Goodchild, M.F. (eds.) GIScience 2006. LNCS, vol. 4197, pp. 112–127. Springer, Heidelberg (2006)
5. Gottfried, B.: Spatial health systems. In: Bardram, J.E., Chachques, J.C., Varshney, U. (eds.) 1st International Conference on Pervasive Computing Technologies for Healthcare (PCTH 2006), Innsbruck, Austria, November 29 – December 1, p. 7. IEEE Press, Los Alamitos (2006)

6. Hein, M., Burghardt, C., Giersich, M., Kirste, T.: Model-based Inference Techniques for detecting High-Level Team Intentions. In: Gottfried, B., Aghajan, H. (eds.) Behaviour Monitoring and Interpretation – Smart Environments. IOS Press, Amsterdam (to appear, 2009)

7. Hightower, J., Borriello, G.: A Survey and Taxonomy of Location Systems for Ubiquitous Computing. Technical Report UW-CSE 01-08-03, University of Washington, Computer Science and Engineering, Box 352350, Seattle, WA 98195 (2001)

8. Kiefer, P., Schlieder, C.: Exploring context-sensitivity in spatial intention recognition. In: Gottfried, B. (ed.) BMI 2007, vol. 296, pp. 102–116. CEURS (2007)

9. Kiefer, Y., Stein, K., Schlieder, C.: Rule-based intention recognition from spatio-temporal motion track data in ambient assisted living. In: Gottfried, B., Aghajan, H. (eds.) Behaviour Monitoring and Interpretation – Smart Environments. IOS Press, Amsterdam (2009)

10. Krause, E.F.: Taxicab Geometry: An Adventure in Non-Euclidean Geometry. Dover Publications, Inc., Mineola (1987)

11. Kritzler, M., Lewejohann, L., Krüger, A.: Analysing Movement and Behavioural Patterns of Laboratory Mice in a Semi Natural Environment Based on Data collected via RFID. In: Gottfried, B. (ed.) BMI 2007, vol. 296, pp. 17–28. CEURS (2007)

12. Kurata, Y., Egenhofer, M.: Interpretation of Behaviours from a Viewpoint of Topology. In: Gottfried, B., Aghajan, H. (eds.) Behaviour Monitoring and Interpretation – Smart Environments. IOS Press, Amsterdam (2009)

13. Laube, P.: Progress in Movement Pattern Analysis. In: Gottfried, B., Aghajan, H. (eds.) Behaviour Monitoring and Interpretation – Smart Environments. IOS Press, Amsterdam (2009)

14. Liu, H., Darabi, H., Banerjee, P., Liu, J.: Survey of wireless indoor positioning techniques and systems. IEEE Transactions on Systems, Man, and Cybernetics, Part C: Applications and Reviews 37(6), 1067–1080 (2007)

15. Millonig, A., Brändle, N., Ray, M., Bauer, D., Van Der Spek, S.: Pedestrian Behaviour Monitoring: Methods and Experiences. In: Gottfried, B., et al. (eds.) Behaviour Monitoring and Interpretation – Smart Environments. IOS Press, Amsterdam (2009)

16. Millonig, A., Gartner, G.: Monitoring pedestrian spatio-temporal behaviour. In: Gottfried, B. (ed.) BMI 2007, vol. 296, pp. 29–42. CEURS (2007)

17. Steinhage, A., Lauterbach, C.: Monitoring Mov. Behav. by means of a Large Area Proximity Sensor Array. In: Gottfried, B., Aghajan, H. (eds.) BMI 2008, vol. 396, pp. 15–27. CEURS (2008)

18. Weinstein, R.: RFID: a technical overview and its application to the enterprise. IT Professional 7(3), 27–33 (2005)

19. Wood, Z., Galton, A.: Collectives and their Movement Patterns. In: Gottfried, B., Aghajan, H. (eds.) Behaviour Monitoring and Interpretation – Smart Environments. IOS Press, Amsterdam (2009)

20. Worboys, M.F., Clementini, E.: Integration of imperfect spatial information. Journal of Visual Languages and Computing 12, 61–80 (2001)

Mobile Interaction with Geo-Notes: A Gesture-Driven User Interface for Browsing User-Generated Content in Mobile Web Applications

Hidir Aras and Denis Huber

TZI, University of Bremen
Research Group Digital Media
28359 Bremen, Germany
aras@tzi.de, denis.huber@googlemail.com

Abstract. Mobile web studies undertaken in 2008 confirm the dominance of social networking in the mobile web – where we have huge amounts of (mostly tagged) user-generated content (UGC) that call for appropriate methods for retrieval and highly interactive user interfaces. Unfortunately, existing mobile (social) web applications are less interactive and do rarely exploit user-provided tags or the user's context for improving mobile interaction with such data. In this paper we present an approach and a map-based mobile social web application that allows for exploring the folksonomy space and related geo-referenced resources utilizing a gesture-driven orientation-based menu. Our prototype that runs on pen-based mobile devices was evaluated in a user study and yields promising results.

Keywords: mouse gestures, context-aware tag clouds, mobile ajax, user generated content, orientation menus, mobile map applications.

1 Introduction

Recent studies report that the mobile web grows several times faster than the "wired" web and at the same time confirm the dominance of social networking in the "mobile" web[1] yielding high user participation. In contrast to this, a field exploration described by Cui et al. [5] depicts clearly that users were less satisfied with mobile user experience on most existing mobile sites. But, emerging new technical trends [9] in "Mobile Web 2.0" such as mobile UGC, mobile Ajax and new forms of input facilities using 3G/4G mobile devices, e.g. touch, motion sensor etc. aim to create more interactive and intuitive to use web applications, thus, enriching mobile user experience. Furthermore, mobile systems increasingly exploit contextual information [1, 16] in order to adapt their services to the user's context, such as location, time or user preferences. Hence, a more intuitive and "intelligent" mobile access to the web is a key challenge of today's mobile social web applications – where we have amounts of

---

[1] Khan, M. A. Mobile Web grows eight times faster than wired Web: British study (from Nielson Online). Mobilemarketer: www.mobilemarketer.com, 5th January, 2009.

D. Tavangarian et al. (Eds.): IMC 2009, CCIS 53, pp. 25–36, 2009.

UGC that call for appropriate treatment. Unfortunately, existing mobile web applications do rarely exploit user-provided tags or the user's context affording highly interactive user interfaces. One main reason in the past used to be the static nature of content provided and technical restrictions of client-side interaction using early mobile web browsers that may have been resolved in more recent browser generations. Looking closer into existing mobile social web applications, we see that mostly simple tag-based search and ranked lists are used to find web resources, e.g. bookmarks, photos etc. utilizing folksonomies. While social web applications for desktop systems often feature various kinds of a tag cloud combined with keyword search to access the data of a social network, for map-based mobile applications only a few applications offer more.

In this paper we present our approach and a mobile prototype for browsing geo-referenced UGC. We integrate the interaction of the user with the spatial context, i.e. the user's location/region directly into our gesture-based interaction paradigm. We utilize the user's current position and orientation to explore tag clouds in the current or a neighboring area using simple and intuitive mouse gestures. The interaction can be controlled dynamically by using different types of gestures allowing for revising, canceling or expanding gesture execution. Starting point for our mobile web application are geo-notes, i.e. geo-referenced notes having temporal, spatial and topical attributes (tags) created by mobile users.

In order to avoid additional recognition hardware we used mouse gestures and the Ajax technology for realizing the dynamic web interface that runs on appropriate mobile browsers. The remainder of this paper is structured as follows. After surveying the state of the art, we describe our concept, the user interface, implementation issues and show first results of our user evaluation.

2   Related Work

Tag clouds as visual information retrieval interfaces represent weighted lists that are visualized using different font sizes. More frequent items or words are represented with a bigger size and more bold than less frequent items [13]. Further improvements to tag cloud layout where distance between tags has meaning have been discussed by Hassan-Montero and Herrero-Solana [8]. Interactive tag maps and tag clouds were used also for exploring large spatio-temporal data sets for information visualization and geo-visualization techniques [15]. The VisGets approach described by Doerk et al. [6] investigates how coordinated visualizations using filters (spatial, temporal and topical) can improve search and exploration of information in the World Wide Web. In our work, we employ the tag cloud approach as an information retrieval interface to browse UGC in a certain geographic region while extending the classic tag cloud using spatial, temporal and topical filters. Ahern et al. [2] present in their work World-Explorer, a visualization tool for location-aware devices that uses "representative tags" for arbitrary areas in the world to expose geo-referenced photos in Flickr as the main web content. Representative tags result by analyzing tags associated with geo-referenced photos by using knowledge aggregation based on multi-level clustering and TF-IDF-based[2] scoring of tags. The authors perform a qualitative evaluation

---

[2] Term Frequency (TF) – Inverse Document Frequency (IDF).

to analyze the visualization benefits in browsing this type of content. The visual interface in this work allows for interaction with the aggregated representative tags as "primary tags" and "drops down" related photos and "secondary tags" as an extension in order to browse the map area around a primary tag. In contrast to this work, we distinguish between current and neighbored local regions for mobile users in order to browse to tag clouds in other neighbored regions executing simple atomic or complex gestures.

Mobile information access considering contextual information emerged as an important research area with the increasing availability of mobile devices and higher bandwidths in 3G wireless networks. In the SmartKom project [16] a mobile prototype was developed that allowed for gesture interaction to interact with a city map. The system was able to process deictic gestures ("show this object") as well as multi-level gestures for zooming to a particular level or restricting the search area ("encircling") by using 2-point gestures. Though using the mouse to allow interaction via free hand mouse gestures has attracted much interest recently these kinds of gestures reveal an interaction problem [11] that results from limited user feedback, e.g. users easily cause navigation errors when unknowingly executing a gesture.

Bau et al. [3] present a dynamic guide for learning gesture-based command sets. The OctoPocus system can be applied to a wide range of single-stroke gestures and recognition algorithms. The described approach can be adapted to mark-based gestures significantly improving input time. Furthermore, it has been shown that users can better learn, execute and remember gesture sets if the current state of recognition is revealed to the user and gestures represented in a graphical form that shows the optimal path for remaining alternatives. For that reason, we utilize icons that represent the menu items for visual feedback in our menu structure that is assembled dynamically during gesture execution. An early study by Kurtenbach et al. [10] investigated learning and performance with marking menus in real world situations showing the potential of marking menus. Finally, Zhao et al. in [17] indicate that this approach has the potential to significantly increase the number of items in a marking menu that can be selected efficiently and accurately, while requiring less physical input space to perform the selections, making it particularly suitable for pen-based mobile devices.

3 Gesture-Driven Interaction

UGC in social network applications usually is marked with keywords that describe the data. In our application we let users create data in form of geo-notes that have temporal, spatial (e.g. GPS coordinates) and thematic attributes, i.e. a list of tags. Users are allowed to feed an initial profile, i.e. name or interests that we utilize to filter out non-relevant geo-notes or restrict the data presented. A geographic region with a pre-defined radius, e.g. 50 meters around the user position is set as the current spatial context of the user. In order to explore geo-notes within range a tag cloud is created from all relevant geo-notes considering tag frequencies and other contextual parameters for the current or a hypothetic user context. Relevant geo-notes that are interlinked with the created tag cloud terms are selected by analyzing tag similarities. The interaction on a map is realized via a multi-layer, i.e. hierarchical menu structure that opens up as a "compass-shaped" menu to allow for execution of simple or complex mouse gestures. Our experiments revealed that different forms of simple gestures (deictic, mimetic and emblematic) are necessary for realizing intuitive and flexible interactions. Using specific gestures a user is able to generate tag clouds for the current or neighboring regions following specified menu paths that utilize the eight directions, i.e. north, north-east, east etc.

3.1 Context-Aware Tag Clouds

We use an extended form of a tag cloud that considers beside tag frequencies as the main parameter also contextual information such as current user position, time and user interests. The tag cloud is created dynamically performing the following general procedure:

1. Retrieve all time-valid geo-notes in a region around the current user position.
2. Compare all geo-notes in that region with the profile of the current user.
3. Select relevant items according to some similarity measure, e.g. tag similarity.
4. Generate tag cloud using several contextual parameters as constraints.

In the generated tag cloud (see example in Figure 1) the terms are ordered alphabetically. Geo-notes that are related with each tag cloud term can be reached by clicking on the term or category the user is interested in. The user can then thumb through each individual geo-note by clicking the appropriate control buttons, while the geo-notes are visualized on the map via a pin icon on their geographic coordinates. In order to browse to tag clouds of neighborhood regions north, north-east, east etc. a compound gesture must be executed using the gesture-driven menu (Figure 2). The implemented gesture types are described in more detail below.

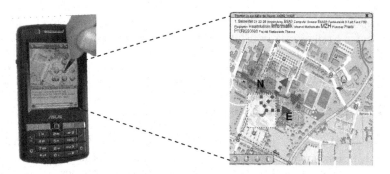

Fig. 1. Mobile prototype, tag cloud and neighborhood exploration

3.2 Interaction Metaphor

We encode the gestures in a menu structure that is realized as a compass-shaped menu. It opens up when the user selects a location on the map by using the input device (Figure 1). Menu items are arranged spatially around the center using appropriate icons. The distance from the center of the menu to each individual item is equal.

Menu items encode specific system functions such as zooming etc. or represent entry points to underlying layers for realizing hierarchical menus.

A gesture is executed by moving the input device, e.g. stylus or mouse from the center of the menu in one of the eight directions to select the respective destination item. In the case of nested menus selecting an item can open another similar menu, where items are organized around the current position of the input device. In order to execute an item from a hierarchical menu a compound gesture is required, e.g. center/north-west/south-east. We designed our menu structure by encoding three types of mouse gestures that are applied for different types of actions. We employed deictic gestures (Figure 3, r.) to select a user region for showing or interacting with relevant geo-notes.

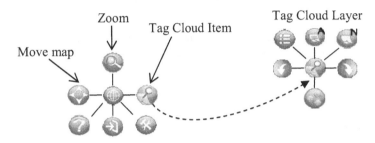

Fig. 2. Gesture-driven menu structure. Start layer (l.) and underlying tag cloud layer (r.).

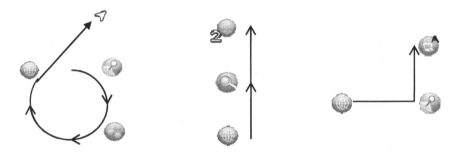

Fig. 3. Mimetic (l.), emblematic (m.) and deictic (r.) gestures

Using mimetic gestures we are able to slide the map or change to a different tag cloud that is generated for regions nearby. An example for changing to the tag cloud located north-east is shown in Figure 3 (l.). The mouse gesture interaction starts by selecting the current user position then following to the "tag cloud icon" (east) where the second menu layer (Figure 2, r.) opens up. The stylus follows to the "change cloud icon" (south) where arrows that reflect the eight geographic orientations appear as the third layer around the center, i.e. the stylus. In our example, we move to the north-east arrow. The described complex gesture is initiated by following the mouse without removing the stylus from the touch screen until the destination item is reached. Consequently, releasing the input device at the destination executes a certain gesture. Gestures can be canceled or revised partly by returning back to a previous layer or releasing the input device. We realized "zooming" on the map using emblematic gestures where the input device is moved from a start position to an end position (see Figure 3, m.). Apart from showing only a part of the original user region zooming also affects the generation of the tag cloud where geo-notes in a restricted or enlarged area are considered. Other interactions have been realized accordingly using one of the three available gesture types in combination.

3.3 System Architecture

Our prototype was realized using the Model View Controller (MVC) architecture. System data such as icons, text or tags are stored in the model. JavaScript is used to realize client-side interaction with the user interface. In our work we used the open source browser Minimo[3] from Mozilla because of its most complete support of Ajax functionality at that time. The Controller component is responsible for asynchronous data loading, modification or storage and sends required data from the relational database to the presentation layer where they are integrated using DOM tree manipulation of the HTML document. Gestures are realized using mouse events such as MouseOver, MouseDown etc.

4 Evaluation

In order to assess the described interaction paradigm we conducted a user study using our prototype. Users had to perform tasks in a browsing or search scenario using the available basic gestures of the system. The goal of our evaluation was to test general system and interaction parameters while focusing on the gesture-driven interaction regarding ease of use, general usability and satisfaction. Because of the absence of a baseline system that had the characteristics of the described approach, i.e. gesture-interaction utilizing directly the users (spatial) context for browsing UGC, we conducted the user study balancing qualitative and quantitative metrics to prove the general applicability of our application on mobile devices.

Users were given a one-page handbook describing their task and a description to learn the icon symbols of our menu structure. A supervisor was advised to answer questions in case of problems and record the time a user completed a single task in order to be able to assign the gestures to the performed tasks respectively. The test runs were held in a lab using the same set-up as planned for a field test using wireless LAN and the technical set-up described in section 4.1. The users performed the tests in a stable position[4] while holding the mobile device in their hands, i.e. not walking around. User movement in field was simulated through map scrolling. The users had to imagine their current position on the map. Our evaluation process covered as basic steps the generation of user data, the task-based user evaluation and recording of user activity, a standardized questionnaire and the evaluation analysis. We tested subjective user impressions using appropriate standardized SUS [4] and QUIS [14] questionnaires that

---

[3] http://www-archive.mozilla.org/projects/minimo/

[4] The field study described in [5] showed that most mobile users stand or sit in a stable position to use their mobile device.

contained general questions and questions related to the HCI experience. Properties such as simplicity, consistency, reliability, understandability and other aspects such as screen size, fonts, icons, familiarity were used to find out about sources of dissatisfaction and satisfaction with the interaction. The recording of user activities served to verify the answers given by the users. Subject of the analysis were properties such as success of gestures, task completion, gesture duration, learning effect. Possible indicators for user satisfaction might be, if the users state that, they used shorter menu paths, i.e. number of used menu items, the gestures failed rarely, they seldom returned back to previous menu nodes during gesture execution for completing a task. We also compared the duration for completing a task using different gestures at the beginning and at the end of the test, in order to prove a certain learning effect. The less time a gesture interaction took for completing a task the more effective the interaction was regarded. Further indicators, such as the number of needed gestures per task and certain interaction patterns, e.g. user cancels a gesture after a specific time or looks at a certain number of geo-notes, observed from the user activity have been subject to our analysis as well. Starting point of the user evaluation was the creation of user data. For this a set of 6 test persons used the prototype to create geo-notes from the categories study, computer science, lecturer, food, leisure and public transport. We gave each user a topic he mainly focused on – but users could also create geo-notes in any of the other areas. In order to avoid side-effects concerning familiarization with the system we excluded the data-creating users from the user evaluation in the second step. User registration and session management allowed us to protocol each user activity during the interaction with the system.

4.1 Technical Set-Up

Our prototype evaluation was performed using a client-server system that consisted of a PC (AMD Athlon 64 X2, Dual Core, 5000+, 3 GB RAM, 100 Mbit/s Ethernet network connection) and a mobile handheld device of the type HTC tyTN II (256 MB ROM, 128 MB RAM, 240x320 pixel screen size) with Windows Mobile 6. The server was running the Windows Vista Business Edition. For the wireless connection with the mobile device we used a 54 Mbit/s wireless router.

4.2 Experimental Tasks

User scenarios and task-based evaluation can be used to simulate realistic interactions [7]. The test persons get tasks that cover all or most important parts of the systems interaction capabilities. For the task-based evaluation we selected 10 users (7 male, 3 female) ranging in age from 21 to 28. We used a typical user scenario for students, i.e. a student new to the campus needs to explore the university, he needs to know where his faculty is, where he has lectures, where he can eat something, etc. From this basic user scenario we tailored seven tasks for the test persons that we describe in Table 1 as a chain of basic gesture actions. Tasks have been formulated explicitly, such as: "1.Use the deictic gesture for showing all available topics in your current location and select your computer science department.", "3. Explore your nearby regions using the *change-to nearby-tag cloud* gesture (see Figure 3, 1.), in order to find your library." etc. In some tasks we explicitly instructed the users to use a gesture to ensure the usage of all gesture types we want to test and restrict the systems degree of freedoms given that some task could be performed using alternative interactions. We also advised the users that we want to test the system, not themselves. This advice was proposed by Schweibenz et al. [12] in order to exclude usage errors that results from being nervous. The user tests were conducted on four separate days. Each test took between 7 and 15 minutes. The completion of the forms took approximately 10 minutes for each user.

Table 1. Used interactions and corresponding gesture types

Task	Interactions	Gesture types
1	Show all topics	deictic
2	Read geo-notes	-no gestures used
3	Zoom	emblematic
4	Show/change tag cloud, nearby area	deictic, mimetic
5	Move map	mimetic
6	Show all topics	deictic
7	Move map, create geo-note	mimetic, deictic

4.3 Questionnaires

A standardized questionnaire was used to test and analyze the subjective impressions of the users and the interaction. Users had to answer questions related to the system, general- and gesture interaction, graphical user interface etc. respectively (Table 2). We used the SUS form for general system questions and for the others the QUIS.

Table 2. Structure of the questionnaire form

Questionnaire (SUS + QUIS)	
Personal information	User test name, age, gender, date, time etc.
General part (Experiences ...)	Mobile devices, social tagging, maps, gestures
System part	
-General system (SUS)	General impression about system and its usage

-Interaction (QUIS)
    -      general
    -      gesture
	Subjective satisfaction with the HCI,
	Learning/remembering gestures, task completion

-Screen & GUI (QUIS)	Labeling, icons, pos. of screen elements, fonts
-System properties (QUIS)	Reliability, performance, error correction, feedback

5 Results

5.1 Questionnaires

After the task-based user study we applied the SUS evaluation scale to assess general impressions about the system prototype and its usage. The SUS scale yields a single score representing an overall measure for the usability of the system being studied. The scores have a range of 0 to 100. An average score of 81.5 represents a high acceptance in our case. For our QUIS evaluation of general HCI issues and the gesture-based interaction we gained similar results. We applied a scale of 1 to 5 to a set of questions from the areas we described in Table 2.

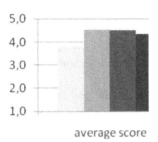 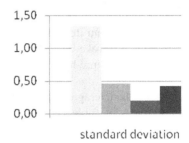

average score   standard deviation

Fig. 4. Mean (μ) and std. deviation (σ) for the four tested categories (from left to right): system, screen & GUI, general interaction and gesture interaction.

The overall average scores of the usability tests for the regarded areas are visualized in Figure 4. For the entire user study we reach an overall average score of 4.3 and standard deviation of 0.66. Apparently, the interaction parts of the prototype have been scored higher than the system parameters such as performance, error correction etc. In order to get a more detailed insight into the gesture-based interaction we left out non-gesture related interaction parameters and investigated general parameters related to gestures e.g. remembering, canceling gestures as well as individual gesture interactions such as map moving, zooming, changing tag clouds etc. Here, the users quoted that they used 2.5 menu items per gesture in the average – which can be regarded as an indicator of the cognitive load the user needs to deal with during each single interaction step. Concerning the gesture interaction, general parameters ($\mu=4.1$, $\sigma=0.51$) seem to be scored lower than the individual gesture interactions ($\mu=4.5$, $\sigma=0.33$). One reasonable explanation could be that external factors like not being familiar with stylus usage may have been the reason why single gesture interactions were scored higher.

5.2 User Activity Analysis

We logged each gesture interaction that starts when a user executes a special mouse event (stylus on screen) and ends when the user lifts up the stylus from the touch screen. We also logged clicks on menu buttons and map actions like moving etc. Each action was stored along with date and time, in order to be able to assign it to a specific task and a user test. The entire interaction protocol was stored in the database when the user logged out. Important indicators that we looked at more closer were duration of one or more gestures that have been used to complete a task, number of menu nodes that have been used, menu nodes where the user returned back to a previous menu node, failed gestures and the number of totally used gestures to complete a single task. Gesture duration was calculated by recording the time in seconds from the

Table 3. Averages for all tested interactions

Duration in sec	Path length	Revised steps	Failed gestures	Number of gestures
25.9	4.07	0.33	0.95	1.75

beginning (stylus down) until the end of the gesture execution by releasing the input device at the destination. The path length was recorded by counting the transitions from one to another menu item that the stylus had passed for a specific gesture. For simplicity reasons we broke this rule for two exceptional cases: We regarded a circular motion in a used gesture having a path length of 1. Deictic gestures also had been given a path length of 1.

Table 3 shows the average scores from all user tests for the gesture-based tasks we described previously in Table 1. Task 2 was not included because it does not use gestures but was inserted as a transition step for the remaining tasks. Having an average path length of 4.07 and 1.75 gestures per task in the average we get an average path length per gesture of approximately ~2.3 that a user needed to remember. We could not compare each single task directly because of the used different gesture types in each task that could affect the task duration significantly. But we could compare tasks 1, 3, 6 (Table 4) regarding effectiveness of the task. Here, the user had to perform a gesture that had a path length of 2. We see that the duration of the used gesture(s) per task reduced to 10.9 seconds - which is half the time needed executing task 1 - though the used gesture was not used before. This learning effect, i.e. increased familiarity with the interaction paradigm can also be observed looking at the reduced number of failed gestures or canceled steps at the end. The duration time and the reduced error rate show an improvement by trend, while other values do not get worse.

Table 4. Comparison of gesture tasks 1, 3 and 6

Task	Duration (s)	Path length	Revised steps	Failed gestures	Number of gestures
1	**22.7**	**2.6**	**0.1**	1	**1.3**
2	-	-	-	-	-
3	**12.1**	**3.2**	**0.9**	1.1	**1.5**
4	61.9	7.6	0.7	0.5	2.4
5	18	3	0	0.5	1.5
6	**10.9**	**2**	**0**	**0.4**	**1**
7	29.8	6	0.3	2.2	2.8

In Table 5 we calculated the interaction values per task per gesture, i.e. we divide the interaction values by the number of gestures in order to obtain, e.g. the gesture duration per gesture etc.

Though we cannot observe clear trends regarding all aspects we see that the average path length stays at about 2 and the number of canceled/returned steps remains lower than 0.4, while the number of failed gestures is not higher than 1. As we stated before, since we cannot compare each single gesture types and the individual tasks directly, we can affirm a certain positive learning effect.

Table 5. Interaction results per task per gesture

Task	Duration (s)	Path length	Revised steps	Failed gestures	Number of gestures
1	17.46	2	0.08	0.77	1
3	8.07	2.13	0.6	0.73	1
4	25.8	3.17	0.29	0.21	1
5	12	2	0	0.33	1
6	10.9	2	0	0.4	1
7	10.64	2.14	0.11	0.79	1
Ø				**0.538**	

5.3 Verification of the User Evaluation

In order to gain a more objective view on the evaluation we compared the protocols and the user evaluation results. From the user protocols we calculated approximately 2.3 menu items per gesture which more or less complies with the result of 2.5 of the user study. A paired t-Test (t=0.802, P=0.443) showed the differences not to be significant. Analyzing the number of menu items when performing a gesture, the users stated, that they rarely returned back to a previous menu node, i.e. revised a gesture. Analyzing the recorded protocols we got a value of 0.33 menu items per gesture which corresponds to 14% if we consider an average path length of 2.3, i.e. the results are here again comparable. The analysis concerning the number of failed gestures shows us a different picture. The users stated that the gestures did not fail often though from the protocols we calculated a mean value of 0.95 failed gestures per interaction or 0.54 per gesture (Table 5). A possible explanation for this maybe that wrong stylus usage like canceling gestures by removing the stylus from the screen was not regarded as a system failure or disadvantage but their own. Another possible explanation for the high rate of canceled gestures in the protocols may have been performance issues of the client-side prototype. The used mobile browser was stated as reacting too slow – particularly the used rendering engine to draw the menu structure. Less familiarity with pocket PC usage or stylus may be regarded as further reasons for the increased number of failed gestures. Despite these facts, we can conclude, that in a short time we could approve a learning success, i.e. the mean gesture failure rate reduced from 0.75 to 0.31 from task 3 to 6. User judged the gesture execution as positive (a score of about 4 points from 5), i.e. a low error rate of 0.2. Task completion was assessed 4.3 points from 5.

6 Summary and Future Work

Mobile access to the "Social Web" has to consider several contextual factors as well as to offer an intuitive interaction paradigm to deal with amounts of user-generated data in social networking applications. In this paper we presented an approach and a map-centric social web application for browsing UGC exploiting tag semantics, orientation and mouse gestures. A first user study using SUS and QUIS evaluation implies that our application provides an efficient and easy to use interaction paradigm – though there is room for more comprehensive field tests and a deployment over time in real contexts in the future. Moreover, it would also be important to investigate variant user interfaces utilizing different gesture types. For touch or finger-based input that we aim to support in future prototypes we would need dedicated designs and appropriate modifications to the menu structure and the gesture execution. Finally, exploring the folksonomy space using a visual interaction paradigm could be improved using additional modalities in combination.

References

1. Abowd, G.D., et al.: Cyberguide: A mobile context-aware tour guide. ACM wireless networks 3, 421–433 (1997)
2. Ahern, S., Naaman, M., Nair, R., Yang, J.: WorldExplorer: Visualizing Aggregate Data from Unstructured text in Geo-Referenced Collections. In: JCDL 2007, Vancouver, British Columbia, Canada (2007)
3. Bau, O., Mackay, W.E.: OctoPocus: A Dynamic Guide for Learning Gesture-based Command Sets. In: UIST 2008, Monterey, California, USA (2008)
4. Brooke, J.: SUS - A quick and dirty usability scale. Redhatch Consulting Ltd., United Kingdom (1986)
5. Cui, Y., Roto, V.: How people Use the Web on Mobile Devices. In: International World Wide Web Conference in 2008, Beijing, China (2008)
6. Doerk, M., et al.: VisGets – Coordinated Visualizations for Web-based Information Exploration and Discovery. IEEE Transactions on Visualization and Computer Graphics 14(6) (2008)
7. Fraser, N.M., Gilbert, G.N.: Simulating speech systems. Computer Speech and Language 5, 81–99 (1991)
8. Hassan-Montero, Y., Herrero-Solana, V.: Improving Tag-Clouds as Visual Information Retrieval Interfaces. In: International Conference on Multidisciplinary Information Sciences and Technologies, InSciT 2006, Mérida, Spain, October 25-28 (2006)
9. Jeon, J., Lee, S.: Technical Trends of Mobile Web 2.0: What Next? In: International World Wide Web Conference in 2008, Beijing, China (2008)
10. Kurtenbach, G., Braxton, W.: User Learning and Performance with Marking Menus. In: Proceedings of the SIGCHI conference on Human factors in computing systems, Massachusetts, United States, pp. 258–264 (1994)
11. Midgley, L., Vickers, P.: Socially-enhanced mouse gestures in the Firefox browser. In: Proceedings of the 12th International Conference on Auditory Display, London, UK (2006)
12. Schweibenz, W., Thissen, F.: Qualitaet im Web Benutzerfreundliche Webseiten durch Usability Evaluation. In: Benutzerorientierte Methoden der Usability Evaluation, ch. 7, pp. 116–195. Springer, Berlin (2002)
13. Sinclair, J., Cardew-Hall, M.: The folksonomy tag cloud: when is it useful? Journal of Information Science 34, 15 (2007)
14. Slaughter, L., Norman, K.L.: Assessing users' subjective satisfaction with the Information System for Youth Services (ISYS). In: VA Tech Proc. of Third Annual Mid-Atlantic Human Factors Conference, Blacksburg, March 1995, pp. 164–170 (1995)
15. Slingsby, A., Dykes, J., Wood, J., Clarke, K.: Interactive Tag Maps and Tag Clouds for the Multiscale Exploration of Large Spatio-temporal Datasets. In: Proceedings of the 11th international Conference information Visualization, July 04 - 06 (2007)
16. Wahlster, W. (ed.): SmartKom: Foundations of Multimodal Dialogue Systems. Springer, Heidelberg (2006)
17. Zhao, S., Balakrishnan, R.: Simple vs. Compound Mark Hierarchical Marking Menus. In: UIST 2004, Santa Fe, New Mexico, USA (2004)

Realization of Tangible Mobile Human Machine Interfaces Using Wireless Personal Area Networks

Jens Ziegler and Leon Urbas

Dresden University of Technology,
Chair of Distributed Control Systems Engineering,
01062 Dresden, Germany
jens.ziegler@tu-dresden.de
leon.urbas@tu-dresden.de
http://www.et.tu-dresden.de/ifa/

Abstract. Using mobile computers like laptops or personal digital assistants (PDA) in a process industries environment places high demands on robustness and security of the equipment and requires the optimization of the complete system for the respective task. This paper firstly addresses these requirements. Subsequently a novel approach is introduced concerning the creation of highly specialized interaction schemes using wireless personal area networks. A conceptual model to formalize interactions within wireless networks and a reference implementation are presented. It is demonstrated that this approach helps to facilitate the development of highly specialized interaction schemes for field applications.

Keywords: Wireless, Personal Area Network (PAN), Human Machine Interaction (HMI).

1 Introduction

Mobile computers are omnipresent in daily life. Mobile phones, PDAs and so called sub-notebooks provide numerous services for communication, information acquisition, self-organization and many more. Established interaction devices are miniaturized keyboards or increasingly touch-sensitive displays as input method and small displays in conjunction with sounds or vibration as feedback for actions as output method. Hence the provided services are adapted to handling and displaying on these interaction schemes. This has two consequences. Firstly only services that are displayable and operable with these techniques are provided. Secondly, the usability of services using the offered interaction scheme is extensively disregarded because there are no feasible alternatives available. Novel input devices like 3D-mice or speech input are available but only rarely supported by common mobile applications. For the application domain of industrial field equipment this is not acceptable. Industrial plants are mostly specialized, unique solutions with numerous complex, interconnected tasks. Every

D. Tavangarian et al. (Eds.): IMC 2009, CCIS 53, pp. 37–48, 2009.

task contributes to the efficiency of the plant and thereby to its profitability. Accordingly optimal adaptation of every field device on the respective task is indispensable. This is also valid for mobile computers in this application domain. Typical applications for mobile computers are the supply of information at any place and time, self-localization, orientation and navigation inside plants, the configuration and parameterization of field devices and plant units, as well as the storage and forwarding of user input. For each of these tasks highly adapted interaction schemes could significantly increase efficiency and usability. However in field applications this is not only a question of the intrinsic demands. There are numerous restrictions caused by the workspace (lighting conditions, noise level, missing desktop), as well as limitations caused by user demands (protective clothing, necessity of one-handed or free-handed operation, variable working posture) or safety regulation. These restrictions have a significant effect on the configuration of interaction schemes and have already been comprehensively investigated [1]. It has been shown, that the established interaction schemes are not suitable for field operation. Therefore many specialized concepts and devices for interaction have been developed [2]. At present mobile computers opened up a wide field of application. They are used e.g. by fire departments, police and armed forces. In the process industry however there are no mobile computers in the field. Hence it is essential to analyze the reasons for that and to draw conclusions for future developments.

In our opinion it is not sufficient just to develop new input or output devices. The separate consideration of hardware and software leads to the one-sided consideration of ergonomics. The development of an integrated concept that seamlessly combines the implementation of special interaction techniques with the design of adaptive software applications can therefore considerably improve the usability of mobile applications in a process industries environment.

2   Related Work

A lot of work has been done to develop novel input and output techniques. A comprehensive morphological analysis of the input/output design space is presented in [3]. It is shown that most input devices can be considered as compositions of a number of input primitives. This analysis is the foundation of our investigations. It is necessary to investigate text input devices, because they are the common input schemes common for mobile applications. In [4] a survey of mobile text entry techniques is given. Both key-based and stylus-based text entry are considered. A practical investigation of the efficiency and usability of keypads from different devices is given in [5]. To develop integrative solutions for tangible mobile Human Machine Interface (HMI) systems we also have to consider the specifics of mobile devices. A detailed examination of the factors size and portability of mobile computers in regard to their range of application as well as the resulting formal principles for application design is presented in [6]. It is shown that the use of mobile computers raises a range of new challenges, so classical design criteria and common control concepts have limited suitability for mobile applications. An introduction of the characteristics of visualization on small displays is given in [7]. Design principles for multimodal applications and services for mobile computers are discussed in detail in [8]. There are several approaches to realize integrative, context-aware solutions for mobile HMI-systems. An important step towards freely configurable interactive systems is made in [9], where the necessity for the adaptability of interaction devices and applications is described in detail. It is recognized that the composition of input devices to more complex input systems can lead to a key improvement in the operability of an application. However the model-driven approach mentioned there is not suitable for tangible HMI-systems because device configuration has to be done offline. In [10] an interactive mobile maintenance support system is presented. This project focuses on a multimodal information presentation. Model-based development of multimodal and multi-device user interfaces in context aware environments is comprehensively investigated in [11]. An innovative framework for context-aware, user-centered, mobile interactions is presented in [12]. This framework allows an adaptation of the application to changing user and environmental properties at runtime. We recognized that there are feasible solutions for specialized input devices as well as for interactive mobile applications, but there is still a gap in between. In this paper we present a middleware that fills this gap.

The next section of this paper defines requirements for tangible mobile HMI-systems in a process industries environment. This is followed by a presentation of our experimental design. We then present a conceptual model and a reference implementation. We close this paper with a short application example.

3   Requirements for Tangible Mobile HMI-Systems in a Process Industries Environment

The use of mobile devices in a process industries environment places a number of specific requirements to the system as well as to the underlying interaction techniques. In addition to higher reliability and quality demands there are a number of domain specific user requirements. The work is characterized by constantly recurring workflows. Interactive mobile applications can be highly optimized on these workflows. On the other hand the user is confronted with various restrictions. He or she may have to wear protective clothing including gloves, needs to use tools and must handle equipment. Since the work space covers the whole plant area the user must stay mobile. Narrow gangways, stairs and other obstacles must be considered. Normally there is no desktop available so that devices must be held in a hand or fastened on the user's body. Particles, liquids and lubricants continuously stain all device surfaces. These factors make high demands on the used devices [13,14].

Robustness: Devices and input techniques must be insensitive to contamination, humidity, mechanical shock, high temperatures and electro-magnetic contamination.

Usability: Devices must be usable single-handed, or even hands-free, while wearing protective clothing. The user must be able to clearly distinguish different interactions without seeing his or her hands. Interactions must give a perceptible feedback.

Ergonomics: Devices must be lightweight and manageable single-handedly. It should be possible to fasten the devices at the user's body or clothing. Because wires are a serious source of danger, connections must be wireless.

Replaceability: Due to frequently changing work procedures it is beneficial for the user to be able to modify the input scheme by replacing one input device with another at run-time of the system. This replacement must be transparent for the application.

The user requirements are manifold, so interaction schemes must be highly variable. They must be adaptable to the existing restrictions as well as to the users preferences. A promising approach to meet these demands is to separate the interaction devices from the mobile computer. In this case the user can select the best-suitable device for the requested task without the need to change the mobile computer or the application running on it. For this reason we present a reconfigurable communication system for interaction devices. This system is able to establish wireless, configuration-free ad-hoc networks between interaction devices and the mobile computer on which the application is running. All devices, all data and all methods are represented in a consistent manner. Thus devices with the same functionality can easily be interchanged. Devices with different functionality can be used in parallel. Applications and services can recognize changes and adapt themselves dynamically, so that they remain operable at any time.

4   Experimental Design

As initial point for development we set up an experimental design of a reconfigurable system consisting of several interaction devices and a mobile computer as demonstrated in Figure 1. The system consists of four devices, a keyboard, a hands-free device with gesture recognition and force-feedback, a single-handed device with a number of pushbuttons and a turning wheel, and a mobile computer with a display. These devices are fastened ergonomically to the user's lower arm, hand and waist. This device composition builds the interaction scheme. Each device is again a composition of interaction primitives. The single-handed device is a layout composition of three pushbuttons and a one-dimensional direction encoder. The hands-free device is a merge composition of two one-dimensional acceleration encoders for the X- and Y-axis and a force-feedback. The layout composition of 12 pushbuttons forms the keyboard. These buttons are connected with a decoder that maps the input onto a character or a direction command. The device composition is redundant since the single-handed-device can replace the hands-free-device and vice versa because the output domain is equivalent. The mobile computer controls the personal area network, runs the application and offers a graphical user interface as general output method. The network

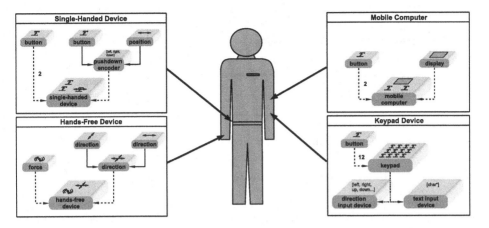

Fig. 1. Experimental Design of a mobile HMI-system

is structured as a star with the mobile device acting as the single master. All devices use a common network interface. Inputs, outputs, states, parameters and events are represented in a common conceptual model.

5   Conceptual Model

5.1   Input/Output Design Space

Card et. al. give an extensive morphological analysis of the design space of input devices [3]. We employ this analysis to define the design space for mobile interaction devices as well. As mentioned there, Human Machine Interaction can be considered as communication in an artificial language between a human and an application. The transmission medium is a set of input and output devices. The language is defined by a vocabulary of interaction primitives and a set of composition operators. According to [3] this vocabulary may be represented by a six-tuple consisting of a manipulation operator as a physical interface, an input domain and an output domain, a resolution function that maps the input domain set onto the output domain set, and finally a set of meta information and device properties. There are three composition operators defined in [3]. The combination of at least two devices with differing vocabulary creates a device with extended vocabulary. This is known as a merge composition. The spatial collocation of two devices is called layout composition. A connect composition is defined as a mapping from of the output domain of one device onto the input domain of another device. Figure 2 demonstrates the composition at the example of a computer mouse.

The design space can be realized by an integrative interaction system consisting of specific interaction devices and highly adapted software applications. We present a conceptual model that formalizes the definition and processing of interaction vocabularies for different devices.

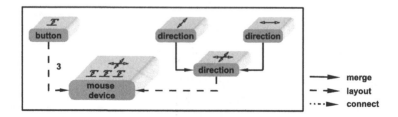

Fig. 2. Composition of a computer mouse device

5.2 Design Space Conceptual Model

Information Model. Manipulation operators in multimodal interaction devices are considerably more multifaceted than in [3] because in principle any physical value can be used as an input or output. Therefore it is essential to define suitable transformation operation to translate the arbitrary, device-specific input domain into a common and well-defined output domain. Using a suitable formalization of the above-mentioned composition operations and a well-defined output domain it is possible to seamlessly exchange devices in a network. The output domain consists of the common elementary data types like integer, float or string. In addition we defined artificial data types like positions, directions, events or gestures. Each data type is represented by a data object that holds the data value and provides methods for data access. The data objects also provide semantic information that the application can use to interpret the data value. Type and amount of this meta information are data type dependent. A device itself is represented by a uniform device object. Therefore the information model defines a device data type. Each device in the network must define a device object.

Communication Model. If a device application wants to publish information to the network, it has to create a respective data object. For the application this data object acts as a data structure that defines a *read()* and a *write()* operation. The device is therefore represented as a set of data objects. To distinguish the objects, they are identified with a user-definable identifier. For the underlying communication system the data object acts as one endpoint of a communication channel. If two or more devices in the network create data objects with the same identifier, the communication system synchronizes their data values continuously. It recognizes any changes and publishes them to the desired recipients. If a new device joins the network the network master discovers the data objects of the device starting with the mandatory device object. All discovered data objects will be automatically assigned for synchronization. This mechanism needs no user action. The synchronization mechanism is transparent for the application since no timing restrictions or transmission requirements have to be considered. Hence an asynchronous data access is mapped onto a synchronous message transport. An easy event-notification mechanism also allows the implementation of event-driven applications. The composition of two or more data objects can be considered as a merge composition. A layout composition can be realized using meta data. A connect operation is in principle an enhancement of the transformation operation and needs no further consideration. Thus the communication model realizes all composition operations defined in the input/output design space.

Applying the Conceptual Model. We want to demonstrate our model using the example of the computer mouse. The input domain consists of three binary inputs with clearly defined functionality and a two-dimensional motion vector. We use a rather simple resolution function to map these inputs onto an output domain, that consists of two data objects. An *event data object* handles the binary inputs meanwhile a *navigation data object* handles the motion input and defines the intended motion direction(e.g. x-axis and y-axis). An example application implements three data objects, an *event data object*, a *navigation data object* and a *string data object*. Providing that the appropriate data objects have the same identifiers, the communication system synchronizes the data objects permanently. If the user moves the mouse in a certain direction this information will be written to the local *navigation data object* and automatically published to the remote *navigation data object* of the application. The event-notification mechanism notifies this data change to the application. Figure 3 illustrates this sequence.

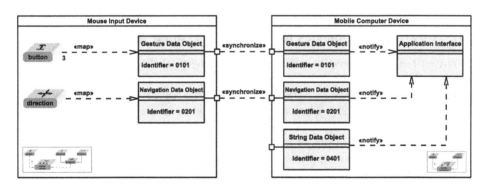

Fig. 3. A simple PAN using the Conceptual Model (simplified)

If we now add a joystick device that also offers a navigation data object the communication system adds its data objects at runtime so that both input devices interact with the example application. This change of the input scheme is transparent for the application. We can also add a text input device that offers a *string data object*. Since the application implements an appropriate data object the device can directly be used without any configuration. The resulting network is shown in Figure 4.

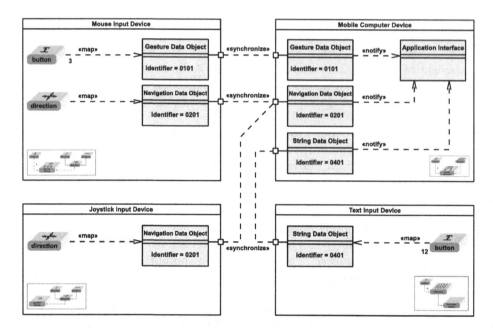

Fig. 4. A more complex PAN using the Conceptual Model (simplified)

6   Implementation

6.1   Network Technologies for Wireless Personal Area Networks

As stated before we need to realize a wireless network to avoid harms caused by wires. There are several transmission technologies available for wireless data connections. *Bluetooth 2.1+EDR* and *IEEE 802.15.4* are both very common technologies [16,20,21,22]. They are well-established in industrial applications. However *Wireless USB* and *Bluetooth 3.0+HS* are promising technologies for next generation applications [17,25]. *IEEE 811.2* is a standard for local area networks, but it is also applicable for our purposes. For example, *Bluetooth 3.0+HS* core specification integrates the *IEEE 802.11g* lower layers [17].

Several network technologies are based on these transmission technologies. The *Human Interface Device (HID)* protocol is part of the *USB* specification [15,24] and covers devices that are used by a human to control a machine, for example keyboards or pointing devices. *Bluetooth* defines a *HID Profile* for wireless connectivity [15,18]. *Universal Plug and Play (uPnP)* is used to establish IP-based networks between intelligent devices for the entertainment industry, home automation and multimedia computer systems [19]. *ZigBee* is a protocol stack based on *IEEE 802.15.4* [21,22]. *ZigBee* is intended to realize low-latency, low-power personal area networks [23].

These state-of-the-art network technologies are fully developed and powerful. They provide a large and extensible functionality. They are tested and well-established. Certainly they are consequently adapted, new transmission technologies like *Wireless USB* are capable to replace actual technologies. Specifications are changing fluently. To cope with this versatile technological foundation, we define a Network Technology Mapping Layer that provides simple, deterministic and configuration-free network access and a consistent device representation. We can also state that none of the aforementioned technologies provides a consistent and formalized information and communication model. To realize tangible, configuration-free interaction schemes we however need self-describing devices with well-defined interfaces. For this reason we use the Design Space Conceptual Model presented before to define a common, technology-independent interface for any application data.

6.2   Network Technology Mapping

To realize a technology-independent network behavior we define a Network Technology Mapping Layer that maps the real network layer onto a logical network interface with consistent behavior (in many cases the real behavior is equivalent). The logical network is a master-slave-network with a star topology. The network master manages all devices in the network, negotiates communication parameters with each slave and controls network access with a time-division multiple access procedure. The assignment of the available time slices depends on the requirements of the slaves. Flow control is realized with a simple message-response procedure. Thereby multiple messages to a single slave can be embedded into a single envelope-message. The underlying transmission technology is responsible for transport security and reliability. Figure 5 illustrates the basic structure of the communication system.

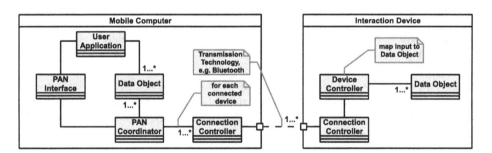

Fig. 5. Structure of the communication system

6.3   Realization

We realized the network master on an *Acer n300 PDA* running a *Windows Mobile 5.0*. The slave system is realized on an *ATMEL AVR* 8-bit microcontroller using a stand-alone *Bluetooth* module. We used the *Bluetooth* transmission technology because it is available in most mobile devices. Figure 6 illustrates a prototypical realization of our experimental design.

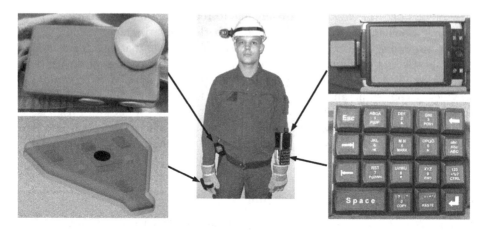

Fig. 6. A plant worker equipped with a tangible mobile HMI-system

7 Application

We use the presented system in a comparative evaluation of different input schemes. In collaboration with industrial partners we created a maintenance workflow based on typical work steps in the process industries domain. We perform this workflow on an experimental plant at an industrial scale. During the evaluation, our subjects have to wear protective clothing. They are aided by an interactive mobile maintenance assistance system which provides all necessary information like task lists error lists, equipment information or parameters. The subjects have to perform visual and acoustic inspections, install equipment, read sensor values, and do some experiments. The results of each work step as well as the information obtained have to be transferred to the maintenance assistance system using various interaction schemes. Afterwards the subjects are asked to sum up their experience in a comprehensive questionnaire. The results of the evaluation are not in the scope of this paper. Nevertheless a preliminary review indicates that our approach provides significant advantages over standard input schemes provided by mobile computers. We could notice a good acceptance of our system.

8 Conclusion

We stated problems and requirements for tangible mobile HMI-systems in a process industries environment. We could motivate the use of wireless personal area networks for specialized interaction devices. We showed that the composition of simple input devices to complex interaction systems can lead to highly optimized, user-centered and problem-adapted interaction techniques for mobile applications. We presented a communication system that allows a technology-independent realization of wireless personal area networks for tangible mobile HMI-systems.

In future work we will evaluate various interaction schemes to find optimal network configurations for different tasks in the process industry. We will also improve the mechanisms that adapt application control and information presentation to the available interaction devices.

References

1. Pascoe, J., Ryan, N., Morse, D.: Using While Moving: HCI Issues in Fieldwork Environments. ACM Transactions on Computer-Human Interaction 7(3), 417–437 (2000)
2. Ruegge, I.: Einsatzpotenziale, Nutzungsprobleme und Loesungsansaetze mobil tragbarer Informations- und Kommunikationstechnologien, Dissertation, Bremen (2006)
3. Card, S.K., Mackinlay, J.D., Robertson, G.G.: A Morphological Analysis of the Design Space of Input Devices. ACM Transactions on Information Systems 9(2), 99–122 (1991)
4. MacKenzie, I.S., Soukoreff, R.W.: Text entry for mobile computing: Models and methods, theory and practice. Human-Computer Interaction 17, 147–198 (2002)
5. Curran, K., Woods, D., Riordan, B.O.: Investigating text input methods for mobile phones. Telematics and Informatics 23(1), 1–21 (2006)
6. Gorlenko, L., Merrick, R.: No wires attached: Usability challenges in the connected mobile world. IBM Systems Journal 42(4) (2003)
7. Chittaro, L.: Visualizing Information on Mobile Devices. Computer 39(3), 40–45 (2006)
8. Blum, R., Khakzar, K.: Design Guidelines for PDA User Interfaces in the Context of Retail Sales Support. In: Jacko, J.A. (ed.) HCI 2007. LNCS, vol. 4551, pp. 226–235. Springer, Heidelberg (2007)
9. Dragicevic, P., Fekete, J.-D.: Support for Input Adaptability in the ICON Toolkit. In: International Conference on Multimodal Interfaces, pp. 212–219. ACM, New York (2004)
10. Burmeister, R., Pohl, C., Bublitz, S.: SNOW - A multimodal approach for mobile maintenance applications. In: Proceedings of WETICE 2006, pp. 131–136. IEEE Press, New York (2006)
11. Schaefer, R.: Model-Based Development of Multimodal and Multi-Device User Interfaces in Context-Aware Environments. Shaker Verlag, Aachen (2007)
12. Lopez-Jaquero, V., Montero, F., Gonzalez, P.: AB-HCI: an interface multi-agent system to support human-centred computing. IET Software 3(1), 14–25 (2009)
13. Yorka, J., Pendharkar, P.C.: Human-computer interaction issues for mobile computing in a variable work context. Int. J. Human-Computer Studies 60, 771–797 (2004)
14. Buergy, C.: An Interaction Constraints Model for Mobile and Wearable Computer-Aided Engineering Systems in Industrial Applications, Dissertation, Darmstadt (1999)
15. USB - Device Class Definition for Human Interface Devices (HID), V. 1.11, http://www.usb.org
16. Bluetooth Specification, V. 2.1 + EDR, www.bluetooth.org
17. Bluetooth Specification, V. 3.0 + HS, www.bluetooth.org
18. Bluetooth - Human Interface Device (HID) Profile, V. 1.0, www.bluetooth.org
19. UPnP - Device Architecture, V. 1.0, www.upnp.org

20. IEEE Std 802.15.3a-2008. IEEE, New York (2008)
21. IEEE Std 802.15.4-2006. IEEE, New York (2006)
22. IEEE Std 802.15.4a-2007. IEEE, New York (2007)
23. ZigBee Pro/2007 Specification, Rel.17, www.zigbee.org
24. Universal Serial Bus Specification, V. 2.0 incl. Errata (2002), http://www.usb.org
25. Wireless Universal Serial Bus Specification, V.1.0 incl. Errata 2005 and (2007), http://www.usb.org

On-the-Fly Device Adaptation Using Progressive Contents

Conrad Thiede, Heidrun Schumann, and René Rosenbaum*

University of Rostock, Germany
University of Rostock, Germany
University of California Davis, U.S.A.

Abstract. In this publication we propose a device adaptation approach based on progressive contents. Such representations are inherently scalable, created once, and multiply used for different kinds of device. Computationally inexpensive on-the-fly adaptation is achieved by a preview-wise progressive data refinement with fully client-based resource assessment and estimation continuously predicting whether provided system resources will be exceeded. Our approach considers resource consumption in screen space, computing power, and during transmission of the required data. Due to its flexible and uncomplex manner, it is a much more general solution to content and device adaptation problem compared to related approaches. This is underlined by empirical results we got from first experiments and a typical use case.

Keywords: device adaptation, progressive refinement, resource assessment, smart environments.

1 Introduction

The constantly increasing volume of contents to be processed and displayed are one of the main challenges in modern computing. The sheer amount of data results in long response times, heavily overloaded displays, and thus, unacceptable content presentation. While this already affects most stationary hardware, the problem is much worse in smart environments [17] characterized by a heterogeneous device scenery. These problems are not new and different approaches to overcome them have been proposed [1]. However, usually only single aspects of the associated issues are addressed, a limited range of output devices is considered, or the solutions lack of flexibility [8]. Thus, new and more general ideas and approaches are required.

Progressive transmission and refinement is a strategy to overcome resource limitations and has a long tradition in image and multimedia communication [15]. By providing the viewer with continuous previews and thus intermediate feedback, a highly responsive viewing and browsing experience can be achieved. It

* Thanks to Deutsche Forschungsgemeinschaft (DFG) for funding parts of this research.

D. Tavangarian et al. (Eds.): IMC 2009, CCIS 53, pp. 49–60, 2009.

has been shown, that this feature can also be used to prioritize and highlight important contents [12] and may be applied to various kinds of data [7].

In this publication we propose a novel approach for device adaptation of graphical contents based on the beneficial properties of *progression*. Progressive contents are inherently scalable and thus allow for flexible adaptation to heterogeneous devices using a single "*multi-purpose*" data-stream only. The main idea of the introduced approach is to refine the contents as long as the respective device is able to provide the resources required for its appropriate transmission, decoding, and display. Resource estimation based on the assessment of past consumption is applied to predict if the data belonging to the next progression stage can still be transmitted and handled without violating predefined user demands. If the required resources can no longer be provided, the refinement is stopped and the best content representation for the respective output device is considered to be found. This process is computed on-the-fly at client side and requires no prior knowledge to data or device. We assessed the approach for raster imagery and geometry resulting from the hierarchical treemap display and achieved a highly adapted content representation.

To show the novelty of our proposal, Section 2 reviews the State of Art in related research. Section 3 is concerned with the fundamental concepts of progressive content presentation serving in Section 4 as the foundation to introduce our device adaptation approach. Section 5 discusses the achieved results followed by a typical use case (Section 6). Conclusions and directions for future work follow in Section 7.

2   Related Work

Smart environments are not limited by presenting visual contents at certain orders or at specific output devices. Thus, the diverse range and strongly varying properties of possible configurations as well as the potential change of a particular output device require means for flexible adaptation.

Most of the adaptation approaches proposed in literature take only into account the properties of the data and the visualization goal [5]. Although of exceptional importance, device characteristics are usually neglected due to the sheer complexity of the problem if multiple of the influencing factors are considered. Related solutions are usually concerned with single aspects only [1]. The proposal by Mao [9] focuses on the communication channel between two devices. Thereby, it is distinguished in bandwidth, minimal bandwidth, and latency. The paper concludes that it is of exceptional importance to consider the amount of data during adaptation. In [6] the authors state that the viewing properties of the output device as screen size and resolution are important factors to also take into account.

As it is common sense that regarding the usability of interactive viewing devices, fast response rates are of higher importance than quality. Thus, processing speed must be considered as a crucial factor for device adaptation. It can be exactly assessed at client-side and only approximated at server-side. However, most of recently published adaptation strategies considering processing speed are server-based. A related approach focusing on the adaptation of tree-dimensional content has been introduced by KIM ET AL. [8]. Here, content customization is based on a generic schema of the MPEG-21 framework. The approach relies on a-priori knowledge to the output device, but does not require any modification at client side. Although this is a useful strategy for smart environments, the approach can not handle interactive changes and an individual content representation for each viewing device is required.

To summarize, several approaches are concerned with the adaptation of visual contents to heterogeneous output devices. Most of them, consider semantical aspects to adapt the visual representation only and neglect other main characteristics of the output device. Due to the complexity of the problem, a meaningful solution is still an open research question.

3   Progressive Content Presentation

Progressive processing became popular in the early days of the World Wide Web, when limited bandwidth was a big issue. To shorten the long latency times during the loading of imagery, the proposal of refining contents was a real relief. The basic idea of progressive imagery is to organize the encoded data in such a way that the decoding of a truncated stream leads to a restored image with less detail [15]. Thus, content previews can be given during a still running transmission, and with little data received, first conclusions can already be drawn. Due to its success, the approach has later also been applied to other kind of data [7,11] or to overcome other resource limitations [10].

Although technical benefits have always been in focus of research, progression may also be applied to support semantical aspects of content display. One of the applied concepts are Regions of Interest (RoIs) [12] that allow for demand-driven previews by placing most important data at the beginning of the stream. As

Fig. 1. Example and application of a *progressive treemap* providing a tour-through-the-data and uncomplex adaptation to a variety of viewing devices

the resulting presentation sequence allows for an incremental buildup of knowledge, it can be a valid means to enhance the conveyance of data characteristics (cf.Figure 1) [11,12]. Such a static or even interactive *tour-through-the-data* supports well-accepted visualization principles as the Information seeking mantra [13] – Overview first, zoom and filter, then details-on-demand – and is able to provide uncluttered views even for small devices and large amounts of data.

All progressive contents are based on an inherent hierarchical structure that allows for the data abstractions required to provide previews. This structure is key for the scalability feature and its flexible "multi-purpose" application. By implementing the paradigm - *Compress Once: Decompress Many Ways* [14, p.410], progressive contents are assumed to be created once, but to used multiple times. This is possible by transmitting, processing, and displaying the respective data in different traversal orders of the hierarchy and requires no further processing if the stored data is appropriately compressed and allows for random access [12].

While examples for a successful application of progressive imagery can widely be found in literature and practice, progressive geometry is not very common. An example demonstrating the mentioned technical and semantical benefits is the *progressive treemap* [11] illustrated in Figure 1. Treemap is a widely accepted technique to visualize hierarchical data [16]. Each node of the hierarchy is represented by a single rectangle. These rectangles are shown as nested sets in a way that a certain node spans all the nodes of its subtrees. The progressive treemap refines the hierarchy top-down, whereby the resulting presentation sequence can be interactively influenced by user-defined RoIs.

4   On-the-Fly Device Adaptation

Viewer of large visual contents have often no clues if the data to be displayed exceeds the resources available at the output device. If so, the user is usually confronted with heavily delayed interaction feedback or overloaded displays. To overcome this, we introduce a strategy that takes advantage of progression to adapt the contents to the respectively available resources.

4.1   The Adaptation Procedure

In current communication systems supporting progressive content refinement (see Figure 2 and [11]), the data is assessed as *original content*. *Encoding* (hierarchisation, compression) and permanent *Storage* of the resulting *Progressive content* occur on *Server*-side. *Traversal* accesses the transformed content whenever it is requested and transmits the different previews to client side. The *Client* consists of a single *Decoding and Adaptation* unit. This tier manages the progressive content display and is the only processing stage that has to be extended to allow for device adaptation. *Progressive selection* successively extracts the still encoded individual previews from the received data. The belonging data is then passed to a *Decompression* and *Postprocessing* component and displayed.

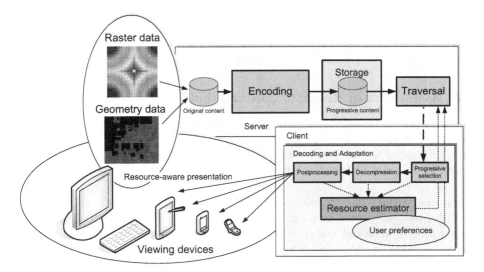

Fig. 2. A common processing pipeline for progressive data handling extended by components that allow for on-the-fly adaptation to heterogenous viewing devices

The main idea of our adaptation approach is to make use of the scalable coding and incremental presentation of progressive contents. During presentation the contents are preview-wise refined as long as the display device provides the resources required to transmit, process, and show the belonging data appropriately. The inherent overview-then-detail principle thereby nicely corresponds to the increasing resource consumption during presentation – first previews require little, detailed previews much resources. A *Resource estimator* decides whether the next preview can be displayed. This leads to either the next data request or signalization of the end of the adaptation procedure. The *Resource estimator* consists of the following 3 procedures:

1. Assessment of resource consumption of current preview in order to gain knowledge about the capabilities of the system (Section 4.2)

2. Estimation of future resource consumption in order to be able to predict system behavior for next preview (Section 4.3)

3. Completion of adaptation if estimated resource consumption exceeds pre-defined system criteria determined by *User preferences*.

User preferences describe the desired system behavior and might be different for every viewer. To allow for flexible adaptation, we consider the following common properties: (1) maximal *response time* as an important usability aspect, (2) maximal *data volume* to include limits in transmission time or costs, and (3) maximal *visual distortion* to consider quality reduction imposed by scaling large contents to small screen property. These attributes may be interactively specified or predefined based on prior empirically findings. *User preferences* may also be used to influence the generation of previews [11].

If the refinement process is completed, the most appropriate content presentation for the respective device is considered to be found.

4.2   Assessment of Resource Consumption

In our approach resource consumption is continuously assessed in order not to violate the specified user preferences. The following list indicates the resources that are related to the desired system behavior and shows how they can be assessed for scalably-coded imagery and treemap geometry.

Response time. This demand strongly corresponds to the processing power provided by the system. To assess processing power for image or geometry data we propose to measure the time required for a full decoding and display of a certain preview at client side. The capabilities of the device are considered to be used up if the measured processing time exceeds the desired response time.

Data volume. This demand corresponds to the use of the communication channel of the system. It can simply be assessed by measuring and summing the volume of the incremental image data bins or geometrical primitives that are received at client side. In contrast to others, this system resource can be very accurately measured. The calculated data volume must be smaller than the desired maximal data volume.

Visual distortion. Visual distortion is caused by limited display property and can be assessed by measuring visual clutter. This involves many semantic factors, varies dependent on the kind of data and its representation, and thus is difficult to quantify in a rigorous manner.

Visual distortion can be seen as a measure how well the content representation matches the available display space. Due to the continuous detail enhancement during progressive refinement, the match steadily increases towards a certain threshold and decreases if it is exceeded. This threshold is considered to be the best match between representation and display space.

As for raster imagery all pixels are arranged on a uniform grid, there is no traditional cluttering. However, displaying an image on screen resolutions that are smaller than the image resolution leads to multiple image pixels for each screen pixel. Although often not negatively influencing data representation, it results in increased response times and data volumes and should therefore be avoided. Thus, it is meaningful to chose the screen resolution of the device as the matching threshold.

Assessing clutter for geometry is difficult and varies strongly dependent on the respective context [3,4]. Due to the fact that primitives of the considered treemap display do not overlap, it is not subject to traditional clutter. However, some primitives may become very small and indistinguishable and it is meaningful to avoid their further refinement. As a generally valid clutter threshold is difficult to state, we apply a value that has been empirically determined for the used treemap implementation.

4.3   Estimation of Future Resource Consumption

Prediction of the future resource consumption is introduced to avoid the needless transfer of data that leads to a violation of the desired system behavior. Here, we take advantage of the fact that progressive contents usually imply a specific characteristic in data distribution. However, we are aware of the fact that exact resource estimation is difficult if not even impossible.

Our prediction strategy is based on the assessment and evaluation of the resource consumption that was required for previous previews. Dependent on the ability to apply static or dynamically calculated values to estimated future consumption, the proposed strategies are labeled *static* and *dynamic estimation.*

Static estimation. Due to the hierarchical structure of the underlying image or geometry data the data volume and processing time required to show two subsequent previews are often not arbitrary. Especially for scalable imagery usually encoded with defined decomposition schemes the hierarchy is a-priori known and thus can be used for prediction. A prime example is the Discrete Wavelet Transform (DWT) [14], where the number of reconstructed pixels increases by factor 4 with every successive level. For such schemes resource consumption of the next preview can be estimated by multiplying the respective factor to the requirements that were assessed for the current preview.

Dynamic estimation. The structure of arbitrary hierarchical geometry is not required to provide a linearly increasing number of primitives with every successive level. Thus, static prediction is only of use if hierarchies are balanced and there is a-priori knowledge to the respective increase. To be able to cope with arbitrary geometries, we propose dynamic estimation. The foundation of this strategy is the ability to detect changes in data structure and system properties by calculating differences in previously estimated and exactly assessed resource consumption. In order to flexibly adjust the estimation to recent changes, the increase factor may vary for each successive preview and thus is calculated right before the preview is to be requested. To be able to consider a range of former preview, we take advantage of average and median filters of different length. These filters have the beneficial advantage to aggregate and smooth the gained prediction values and thus allow for adaptation to tendencies and temporal changes. The respective length thereby determines how many previous refinement stages are considered for current prediction. As the respectively chosen filter length strongly influences the quality of the estimation (cf. to results section 5), we also propose to adjust the length dependent on the quality of previous predictions. Filters of long length increase the performance of predictions for preview sequences that can be well estimated, filters of short length for refinements with strongly varying prediction quality. We propose to start with a short length filter and to increase its length if estimation is sufficiently accurate. If estimation quality decreases, the filter length should be reduced.

4.4   Adaptation in Interactive Systems

Modern communication systems usually allow for an interactive steering of data transmission and processing. This leads to individually designed previews and in turn to an unpredictable resource consumption that might cause the proposed estimation strategies to fail.

There are two different options to adjust the adaptation procedure to the properties of interactive systems: (1) extending the fully client-based approach to a client-server based strategy or (2) performing adaptation without resource estimation. The basic idea of the first proposal is to force the traversal component at server-side to deliver "predictable" previews. As the prediction approach is known at server side, this can be easily implemented and might even lead to better adaptation results. However, the original fully client-based approach can be much easier migrated into existing systems. The second option omits the resource estimation stage and thus might require the transfer and processing of data that exceeds resource limitations. Although a still ongoing data transfer or processing can always be stopped whenever this is detected, the used resources are spent without contributing to better adaptation.

5   Results

In this section, we provide results we got from first experiments using the introduced adaptation strategy applied to raster imagery and hierarchical geometry. The strategy is based on resource assessment and prediction. As the used assessment methods are not novel, we focus in the following on prediction. To demonstrate the wide applicability, we tested our proposals with different hardware and achieved similar results. The results stated below are gained on a modern workstation. The ordinary raster image used in the experiments is of size 3452×2300 and was scalably encoded using a 7-level DWT. For creating treemap geometry we used a data set that was provided for the 2003 *InfoVis contest* on the display of hierarchical data (*logs_A_03-01-01.xml*, 11 levels, 76551 nodes, strongly unbalanced). Thus, the following results cover the performance we got from simple and rather challenging test data.

5.1   Estimating Response Time and Amount of Data

To show the applicability of our approach and to gain new insight for its appropriate parameterization, we assessed estimation accuracy for the introduced strategies. To achieve this, the time required to process the data up to a certain progression level was measured. We empirically determined a linear dependency between response time and amount of data (average difference: 6.7%). As the resulting statements are similar, they are shown for response time only. Figure 3 illustrate the achieved results for raster (left) and geometry data (right).

For image data it can be stated that prediction based on the Median(all) filter taking into account all currently available data performs best. It achieves the

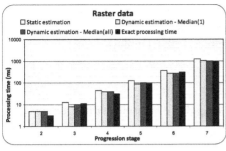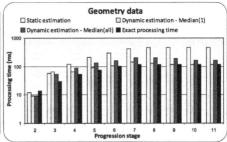

Fig. 3. Comparison of performance of the introduced estimation approaches and their parameters for image (left) and geometry data (right)

smallest average (avg: 18%) and smallest maximal prediction error (max: 54%). This is mainly due to the steadily increasing data amount and the dynamic nature of the prediction. Although, static prediction using a meaningful increase rate of factor 4 is able to produce the smallest minimal error (min: 1%), it estimates worse in other progression stages (avg: 27%). The Median(1) filter covers only the last progression stage and performs on average better (avg: 23%) than static prediction. We also tested the performance of average filters. Due to sensitivity to outliers, the estimation was in most cases worse then using Median filters. Outliers appear especially in time assessments at early progression stages. This is mainly due to the fact that the applied software-based time measurement fails if increments are very small. This, however, does not limit the applicability of our approach.

Contrary to well-structured image data, estimating response time for the given geometry was difficult. Strong variances from one preview to another and the property that the increment in data volume even decreases in later progression levels (cf. Figure 3/right) caused the static prediction to fail. Here, the Median(1) filter performed best (avg: 25%, min: 2%, max: 117%) as its short filter length adapts quickly to the changing structure of the data. The Median(all) filter has a longer coverage and thus provides slower adaptation (avg: 63%, min: 40%, max: 81%).

To consider real-world applications characterized by varying system resources we also assessed the performance for strong changes in CPU load (5-95%). However, this seams not to influence the estimation as strong as expected. Best filter for imagery is again Median(all) (avg: 20%, min: 2%, max: 38%). For geometry, both median filters show similar performance (Median(1) - avg: 160%, min: 30%, max: 220% / Median(all) - avg: 120%, min: 6%, max: 310%). Worst performs static prediction (avg: 210%, min: 14%, max: 570%).

The achieved results demonstrate that exact estimation of the consumed computing power without prior knowledge to the data is difficult. The prediction often varies by 20-30% and thus gives just a rough estimation of actual resource consumption. However, if applied to our adaptation approach the performance is often sufficient. Only if the user places its thresholds within the error range, the refinement will terminate too early or late. The average prediction error is a good indicator for the probability for such unintended behavior. In applications where high adaptation accuracy is crucial, we suggest to apply one of the adjustments proposed for interactive systems (cf. Section 4.4).

5.2   Estimating Visual Distortion

The performance of the introduced approaches for distortion estimation are different for images and geometry. Due to the options for an accurate assessment of screen and image resolution, distortion prediction for image data is exact. However, if one of the inherent image resolutions does not match with the screen resolution the adapted resolution will be smaller than required for the device. In this case, we propose to check if the current or next progression level matches the screen resolution closer and to use the better solution. As already stated is it currently unsolved how to assess and estimate distortion for geometry in a rigorous manner. However, the assessment we used in our experiments is computationally inexpensive and a valid means for adaptation of treemap geometry.

6   A Typical Use Case for Our Approach

The proposed strategies are valid solutions for multiple problems in smart environments. The discussed use case is a smart meeting room [2] consisting of many different display devices. Meetings are typical events where images and data visualizations are shown and discussed. As the treemap is a typical information display with a broad applicability and acceptance [16], it may also be applied in this scenario.

The traditional procedure for displaying contents is its static representation on the viewing device that provides the most resources, e.g. a high-performance workstation connected to a high-resolution projector. This allows for fast system response and little visual distortion, but has the significant drawback that just a single view to the content is shown on a single display. If the same presentation is displayed on a strongly limited device, content representation and interaction are poor.

By applying the introduced adaptation approach, the available resources may be used much more efficiently. In group work it is often useful to provide the respective contents on many viewing devices. We refer to this case as "*parallel refinement*". Presentation adapted by the proposed strategy are highly responsive, non distorted, and interactive for all shown refinement stages and viewing devices. The semantic benefits of progressive refinement further allow for an improved conveyance of the presented information by different views to the data. Whenever the final presentation on a certain device is reached, the user is able to switch to another device in order to see the remaining presentation stages. The fact that different devices stop at different stages further allows for later comparison of the different previews and for extraction of further information from those contents not part of a particular representation or hidden by clutter.

Information has often to be viewed privately, e.g. on a Smartphone, PDA, or netbook, before to be shown to the public. The proposed approach refines and presents the contents, maybe under interactive modification, until the resource limits of the device are reached. By moving the content to other viewing devices providing more resources, the viewer is able to share his insights whenever desired. We refer to this case as *"sequential refinement"*.

Compared to the traditional content presentation using a single view and display, the introduced approach allows for much more flexibility. Single centrally stored content is shown in many incremental views and is adapted to all desired viewing devices. To achieve this, the approach requires no a-priori knowledge to the data, is low complex and completely accomplished at client side.

7   Conclusions

The diverse range of heterogeneous viewing devices requires strategies for flexible content adaptation. Existing solutions usually focus on semantical aspects and provide poor system performance. We proposed an approach that can be applied to most kinds of devices and considers response rate, data volume, and visual distortion. Our adaptation strategy is based on progressive contents and on-the-fly resource assessment and prediction. Device adaptation is achieved by completing refinement whenever it is predicted that handling the next progression stage violates desired system behavior. We achieved the best results by dynamic estimation using a median filter (average estimation error: 18-25%) that covers all (images) or just the last progression stage (geometry). A rather beneficial property of our approach is that progressive contents are encoded just once and can be multiply used for different devices. This solution is computationally inexpensive, overcomes many of the problems stated in literature for device specific content adaptation, and has a wide variety of applications.

In future work we will implement this approach for other kinds of data and application fields. Furthermore, we plan to compare its performance to a profile-based approach founded on prior knowledge to the different influencing factors. However, our next step will be concerned with the development of more accurate predictions schemes specifically regarding visual distortion.

References

1. Bandelloni, R., Berti, S., Paternó, F.: Mixed-Initiative. In: Trans-Modal Interface Migration Proceedings Mobile HCI, pp. 216–227. Springer, Heidelberg (2004)
2. Burghardt, C., Reisse, C., Heider, T., Giersich, M., Kirste, T.: Implementing scenarios in a Smart Learning Environment. In: Proceedings of 4th IEEE International Workshop on Pervasive Learning (2008)
3. Ellis, G., Dix, A.: The plot, the clutter, the sampling and its lens: occlusion measures for automatic clutter reduction. In: AVI 2006: Proceedings of the working conference on Advanced visual interfaces, pp. 266–269. ACM, New York (2006)

4. Ellis, G., Dix, A.: A Taxonomy of Clutter Reduction for Information Visualisation. IEEE Transactions on Visualization and Computer Graphics, IEEE Educational Activities Department 13, 1216–1223 (2007)
5. Fujishiro, I., Furuhata, R., Ichikawa, Y., Takeshima, Y.: GADGET/IV: A Taxonomic Approach to Semi-Automatic Design of Information Visualization Applications Using Modular Visualization Environment. InfoVis 00, 77 (2000)
6. Skorin-Kapov, L., Komericki, H., Matijasevic, M., Pandzic, I., Mosmondor, M.: MUVA: a Flexible Visualization Architecture for Multiple Client Platforms. Journal of Mobile Multimedia 1, 3–17 (2005)
7. Lee, H., Desbrun, M., Schröder, P.: Progressive encoding of complex isosurfaces. In: SIGGRAPH 2003, pp. 471–476. ACM Press, New York (2003)
8. Kim, H., Joslin, C., Di Giacomo, T., Garchery, S., Magnenat-Thalmann, N.: Device-based decision-making for adaptation of three-dimensional content. In: The Visual Computer, vol. 22, pp. 332–345. Springer, Heidelberg (2006)
9. Mao, S., Bushmitch, D., Narayanan, S., Panwar, S.: MRTP: a multiflow real-time transport protocol for ad hoc networks. In: IEEE 58th Vehicular Technology Conference, VTC 2003-Fall, vol. 4 (2003)
10. Pascucci, V., Laney, D.E., Frank, R.J., Scorzelli, G., Linsen, L., Hamann, B., Gygi, F.: Real-Time Monitoring of Large Scientific Simulations. In: Proceedings of ACM Symposium on Applied Computing, SAC 2003 (2003)
11. Rosenbaum, R., Schumann, H.: Progressive refinement - more than a means to overcome limited bandwidth. In: SPIE - Electronic Imaging 2009, San Jose/US, January 18 - 22 (2009)
12. Rosenbaum, R., Schumann, H.: Progressive imagery beyond a means to overcome limited bandwidth. In: SPIE - Electronic Imaging 2009, San Jose/US, January 18 - 22 (2009)
13. Shneiderman, B.: The Eyes Have It: A Task by Data Type Taxonomy for Information Visualizations. In: Proceedings of the IEEE Symposium on Visual Languages, pp. 336-343 (1996)
14. Taubman, D., Marcellin, M.: JPEG2000: Image compression fundamentals, standards and practice. Kluwer Academic Publishers, Dordrecht (2001)
15. Tian, D., Alregib, G.: BaTex3: Bit Allocation for Progressive Transmission of Textured 3-D Models. IEEE Trans. Circuits Syst. Video Techn. 18, 23–35 (2008)
16. Wattenberg, M.: Visualizing the stock market. In: CHI 1999: CHI 1999 extended abstracts on Human factors in computing systems, pp. 188–189. ACM, New York (1999)
17. Weiser, M.: The computer for the 21st century. SIGMOBILE Mob. Comput. Commun. Rev., ACM 3, 3–11 (1999)

A Java-Based Approach for Consistent User Assistance in Distributed Heterogeneous Environments

Johannes Weber and Andreas Rehkopf

TU Bergakademie Freiberg, Institut für Automatisierungstechnik
Lessingstr. 45, 09596 Freiberg
{johannes.weber,andreas.rehkopf}@aut.tu-freiberg.de

Abstract. In modern factory – or home automation environments it is increasingly important to be able to offer a consistent user interface to a variety of interconnected devices that may even use different communication interfaces. The devices usually have some form of user interface such as LEDs and buttons but almost certainly do not possess any mechanism to offer comfortable e.g. 3D-based user-guidance mechanisms. Besides, the devices' vendors do not directly cooperate with each other and they may not be willing to disclose the details of the communication protocol to the device. This contribution presents a novel Java-based approach that enables vendors to offer a comfortable GUI for their devices that can be run on a (mobile) management console that is connected in any form to the respective devices. This approach is based on the idea that a vendor may deploy a pre-compiled JAR file to be run on a management console while leveraging a framework that takes care of device-independent functions like communication channels, user access and role management or multi-language capability. The article furthermore discusses issues like security aspects, consistent integration of several devices' GUIs, framework functionality and possible alternative solutions. The approach presented has been successfully tested in a factory automation environment in the print industry.

Keywords: Remote operation, graphical user interface, Java, GUI distribution, JAR, device integration, user assistance.

1 Introduction

Many different environments today are characterized by a variety of heterogeneous devices that are somehow connected with each other. Such devices can vary greatly with regard to their complexity, ranging from simple, low-power microcontroller-based devices to systems incorporating a significant amount of processing power. Modern industrial production lines that are becoming ever more flexible in terms of lot sizes and variety of products to be manufactured are an example for such an environment. Such production lines are constantly changed by equipment upgrades or replacements which steadily enhance the production lines' capabilities. This may lead to heterogeneous production lines consisting of a variety of devices from different vendors and a mixture of rather old and very modern devices. Common to all devices usually is *some* interface to be able to communicate with other devices and systems.

D. Tavangarian et al. (Eds.): IMC 2009, CCIS 53, pp. 61–71, 2009.
© Springer-Verlag Berlin Heidelberg 2009

Modern devices may implement Ethernet-based communication protocols while older devices in the factory automation field likely possess a fieldbus-based interface.

To become ever more productive, operators need to overlook large production facilities including many different machines. In case of a steady production the operator's main focus is monitoring and data acquisition which can for example be conducted with today's SCADA (supervisory control and data acquisition) systems. However, if comparatively small lots of different products are to be produced, different machines might have to be reconfigured frequently. In this situation it increases an operator's effectiveness greatly to be able to setup all relevant machines from a single management console. Unfortunately, existing machines normally possess their own user interfaces, ranging from foil keyboards with small LCD panels to machine consoles, incorporating sophisticated 3D functionality with remote control capabilities. However, remote access is often limited; sometimes standardized for certain device classes it can by no means replace a user-friendly graphical user interface (GUI) but is merely able to complement it. New production equipment that is based on powerful embedded control systems with industrial Ethernet connections implement sometimes embedded web server technology for remote control purposes. However, all existing equipment is not going to be changed soon as lifecycles are long. Even modern equipment that do not need a lot of processing power and which only have e.g. fieldbus interfaces can hardly leverage modern techniques such as embedded web servers or the simple network management protocol (SNMP).

The concept described in this contribution is able to cope with existing hardware that is connected to some sort of communication infrastructure. Even if it uses Java infrastructure, this does not imply that the systems to be controlled need to be able to run a heavy Java virtual machine. It was originally developed for the digital production print industry. Here, production lines typically consist of several different machines from different vendors. As there is a trend towards shorter print run-lengths (otherwise you would choose offset printing anyway), the print line might have to be reconfigured for every new print job. On the other hand, the machines' capabilities are steadily increasing, leading to ever more complex configuration processes. Additionally, operators shall be able to work with many different machines with a minimum of education effort. Thus, it is very useful to have a (mobile) management console that supports the production line's operation. As it has proven to be not effective in the print industry to automate all possible machine settings using servo motors, the operator needs to setup at least parts of a machine manually. In this situation a management console that directs the operator in an interactive and user-friendly way through all necessary software switches (via GUI) and hardware settings (e.g. using a screwdriver) certainly helps preventing errors.

Some of the aspects mentioned can also be applied to a modern home automation environment. Here, there is also a number of interconnected devices of different complexity from various vendors that may not directly cooperate with each other. In such a situation a mobile management console is useful that allows it to operate all devices in a comfortable way. Such an universal remote control may hence form a container to run different vendors' GUI applications.

2 Remote Operation

2.1 Taxonomy and Overview

This section makes an attempt to sketch a taxonomy of remote-operating concepts and outlines some common techniques found in today's factory or home automation systems. Fig. 1 shows a remote-operating taxonomy that helps in comparing various approaches. It is structured according to a methodology for virtual laboratories which was applied and adopted to factory automation [1].

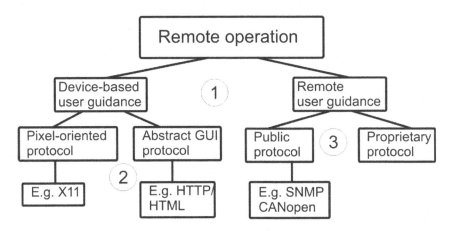

Fig. 1. Remote operation taxonomy

(1) At first, remote operating concepts can be distinguished between concepts that are characterized by the user guidance mechanism implemented on the embedded device itself and those which implement it on a control station. This means that menu structure, layout, colors or the user language etc. are defined either on an embedded device or remotely on a management console.

In general, a device vendor is more flexible if the user guidance is implemented on its device because in this case anything can be changed without having to worry about dependency issues. In practice, such problems can become very complicated because different customers may use different management console systems. Besides, implementing the user guidance on the embedded devices means somehow duplicated infrastructure because every device has to implement the complete GUI infrastructure itself.

Remote user guidance offers the advantage that a user can configure the remote operation mechanism once for all devices to be controlled. Typical customizations include e.g. language settings, access rules or changes in the menu structure. It also tends to use fewer hardware and software resources on the embedded device in comparison to device-based user guidance as for instance only the management console needs to deal with user interface-related graphics.

(2) In case of device-based remote control, the protocol between the remote operating console and the device can be pixel-oriented or it can be defined in a more

abstract manner. If it is pixel-oriented, virtually all GUI elements such as 3D elements can be implemented in a perfectly device-suited manner but even if compression is applied, a comparatively high bandwidth for the connection is necessary plus this approach normally only makes sense if the embedded device has plentiful hardware resources. Examples for this kind of protocols are e.g. X11 or VNC [2].

More abstract protocols tend to require less hardware resources on the embedded device but serving a fairly complex protocol can be very demanding in terms of needed software complexity. Depending on the used protocol it may be hard to implement a feature exactly as the embedded device's vendor would like to have it displayed (e.g. specific layout of some GUI elements such as sliders, bars or gauges). An example for such an approach apart from HTTP is described by Roman, Beck and Gefflaut [3].

(3) When it comes to remote user guidance, either a public or a proprietary protocol can be used for communication between the embedded device and the management console(s). A fairly typical setup consists of an operating panel PC that may stand directly next to the machine which talks to the device using a proprietary protocol and thus unburdens the embedded machine control from resource-intensive graphical representation tasks (see e.g. [4]). This proprietary protocol may be based on well-known communication abstraction layers such as for instance CORBA [5]. Although this type of GUI can be used remotely, it is difficult to integrate several such GUIs from different vendors into one management console system in a neat way.

On the other hand, using a public protocol suffers from the fact that a device vendor has almost no influence on the graphical representation of the remote operation facilities because these may be vendor-independent. Therefore to ensure user-friendly operations it is hardly possible to rely entirely on such a GUI concept without any other user interface for the device. Besides, the protocol is typically published which means that it may not be extended without notice for a specific device. We have also come across situations in practice where vendors did not want to publish which variable can be altered in order to prevent competitors from gaining valuable insight. However, as a means to be able to remotely control a few well-defined variables, e.g. SNMP or CANopen can be found in many real-world devices.

2.2 Embedded Web Servers

A common concept is it to include a web-server into an embedded to enable the user to control the machine using a web browser only. Modern web technologies such as AJAX allow it to implement a browser-based GUI that feels like a rich-client using a modern GUI framework. AJAX is essentially based on the idea that a HTML page includes placeholder sections that may be altered at runtime, including client-side scripts. With the help of client-side scripting, requests to the web server can be made that change the currently viewed web page without having to reload it. On the other hand developing a GUI that uses advanced web technologies such as AJAX or session management can be very time-consuming, especially with a limited embedded software infrastructure on hand.

Building a basic HTML operating interface is a lot easier but a bare HTML page without any active scripting (client or server-side) cannot immediately react to user inputs. Furthermore, a web server essentially only makes sense if the embedded device has an Ethernet TCP/IP connection although conceptually, it is possible to tunnel the HTTP protocol over other physical media. In addition, every device's web user interface looks and behaves differently; therefore it is hard to integrate several devices' user interfaces in a neat way within a management console.

As a consequence embedded web servers do hardly use the latest web technology in practice but merely offer basic GUI elements. Depending on the application this may well be sufficient but sophisticated GUIs with interactive user assistance are typically not implemented using a web server but rather based on well-known GUI toolkits such as .NET, Qt, Java or Gnome which talk over a proprietary protocol to the device.

2.3 SNMP-Based Remote Control

Another example for a commonly found remote control technology is SNMP which can be found in a variety of environments.

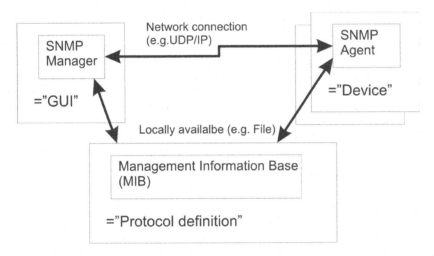

Fig. 2. Overview of a typical SNMP system as it can be found in factory automation systems

The GUI part is called SNMP manager and it is responsible for collecting data from one or several SNMP agents. Each SNMP agent is responsible for answering requests from SNMP managers. It thus fulfills the necessary operation on the device (e.g. set/get a certain variable) and acts as a bridge between the GUI and the embedded device control. Both, manager and agent have access to a typically locally available so-called management information base (MIB) that maps between SNMP addresses and a semantic meaning. These MIBs are typically standardized for various device classes. For instance a production printer typically implements the "printer MIB" (see RFCs 1759, 3805).

However, SNMP is not meant to support sets of variables to be set or retrieved that are proprietary for one specific device. As both the manager and the device need to have access to a common MIB it is usually not advisable to extend MIBs in a proprietary way. To remotely manage a device, any SNMP manager can be used as long as it supports the respective MIB. There are also generic SNMP managers available (called MIB browsers) that simply represent a given MIB as a tree structure. As a conclusion SNMP is great to manage and/or monitor a set of variables that is common to a class of devices but it is not very well suited to replace a device's GUI which may include functionality that is specific for only one device unless no proprietary SNMP manager shall be specifically developed.

2.4 Gateway-Oriented Remote Control

In order to deliver a remote control infrastructure in environments implementing various different physical interfaces and protocol gateway-oriented solutions are an obvious approach. Basically, the devices to be remote-controlled are connected with some sort of interface to a gateway that can translate between different physical layers and protocols. An example of such a Java-based gateway solution is e.g. described by Al-Ali and Al-Rousan [4]. In complex environments network hierarchies can be applied that consist of various gateways on different network abstraction levels (see e.g. [6], [7]). Depending on the application it may be efficient to use real-time capable interfaces between the gateways to ensure certain response-time requirements.

In real-world situations it is likely that a management console does not support all interfaces necessary to be able to communicate with all devices to be remotely controlled. Unfortunately using a gateway implies that without the gateway(s) up-and-running, a remote GUI cannot communicate with the respective devices. Therefore it might be sensible to consider a high-availability concept for all critical gateways employed in the system. In general, gateways might increase an overall system's complexity but are nevertheless a manageable part.

3 Novel Java-Based Approach

3.1 Overview

With regard to the mentioned approaches implementing a truly ergonomic embedded web-server-based GUI is demanding though possible (for powerful devices) but a seamless integration of several devices' GUIs into a management console is difficult. Whereas a solution based on a standard set of predefined variables is easier to implement and can be integrated into a management console but lacks flexibility and offers less graphical control capabilities. Additionally, standard protocols such as SNMP or CANopen are usually tied to a specific physical communication layer which is a problem in heterogeneous environments.

The basic idea of the approach presented here is that every device's vendor develops its own GUI in Java while relying on a unified framework that allows an easy integration of several GUIs. The compiled GUI byte code (no source needs to be distributed) then does not run on the device itself but only on a management console within a secured sandbox environment. All data necessary for the GUI to run, including images or multi-language text is included within one single JAR file. This JAR file can either be manually installed on the management console or automatically be transferred after device startup to ensure that the latest version is used. Common tasks such as communication, access control, user managements, logging etc. are handled by the framework. Thus some characteristics of this approach are:

- Weak microcontroller-based systems are supported as well because no computing-intensive graphics tasks are performed on a device while the communication physical layer is not fixed as long as the management console can communicate with a device perhaps using one or more appropriate gateways.
- Device vendors can use state-of-the-art GUI toolkits that allows them to efficiently create powerful and ergonomic GUIs .
- There are strong synergy effects between several different GUIs as they can be integrated into a management console while not having to perform common tasks. This further decreases development time while increasing versatility and ease of integration.
- There is no need for a vendor to publish the communication details between the GUI and the respective device. It is thus possible to change a GUI or its communication behavior whenever helpful and no information needs to be disclosed. The only congruence between different devices connected the same interfaces is the use of the same basic communication routines.

Existing works in this field include Marcos et al. [8] who have already suggested a Java-based approach although it focuses not on a management console to control several devices in a consistent manner but rather on a general architecture how to monitor a fieldbus-connected production line with client applications over the Internet. Besides, Kehr et al. [9] have described a JAR-based distribution scheme for middleware in the area of smartcard applications. However, our approach as a whole seems not to be covered by existing works.

3.2 Framework Components

The framework essentially consists of three major parts that share classes and interfaces between each other. The first part consists of interface classes that a GUI needs to implement to be able to run within a management console environment. Among others, important interfaces that may be implemented include the following functionalities:

- Menu tree node(s): All devices to be remotely controlled or monitored are displayed in a tree structure. Every device needs to implement at least a device root node and it may additionally implement one or more sub-nodes for different menu aspects.
- Toolbar information access: Common to all devices is a toolbar that presents important information about the device currently selected at the first glance. This toolbar can for instance be used to display the device's current status including any error conditions.
- Menu panel: Every (sub) menu of a device needs to implement this interfaces that for instance offers a panel to put the menu on.
- Event listener for global and toolbar-related events

- Defined initialization entry point: This interface may include functional-ity like receiving the user's selected language or getting the currently se-lected user role.
- Basic GUI and device information access: This may include functions such as get the management console version or get the device's firmware revision
- Access to the complete device configuration

The second part of the framework is formed by helper classes that may be used by the GUI developer. Functionalities include e.g.

- Tree menu infrastructure
- Easy-to-use communication interface: For most applications a rather simple communication protocol similar to SNMP functionality should be sufficient. This class ensures that communication requests to devices are tunneled appropriately if necessary. Of course, the device itself also needs to be able to handle the incoming requests or be able to send event mes-sages on its respective interface.
- Various templates such as generic event listeners/handlers or empty menus
- Multiple-access management: As there are potentially more than one management consoles wanting to simultaneously access certain device menu a ticket mechanism is provided to handle such situations.
- Configuration file infrastructure
- Complete placeholder GUIs as a reference and starting point
- Design patterns that handle the asynchronous communication between various menu parts.

The third part is the management console itself that runs on any PC having the appro-priate Java virtual machine installed and that possesses Java-accessible interfaces to the various devices. It contains a new class loader that is capable of running provided GUI JAR files if they implement the correct interfaces and if they contain all neces-sary resources.

3.3 Case Study

This approach was successfully tested in the digital print industry (see Fig 3) in a print production line. Such lines can produce more than 2.000 A4 images a minute and are for example used for on-demand book printing or bank statements.

In contrast to offset printing, production costs per page on digital printers are sig-nificantly higher but ideally there is no time-consuming manual setup effort necessary between different print jobs. To avoid production stops it is therefore very important to have a possibility to reconfigure all devices within the line as fast as possible. Fig. 4 shows an example of a management console controlling several devices within a print line that enables an operator to centrally configure the line. Not necessarily all devices can be controlled using the remote GUI since in the print line example there is not JAR GUI for every device. The physical layer communication in this case study is IEEE 1394 with a SNMP-like (=get/set/trap functionality) protocol on top of it. The

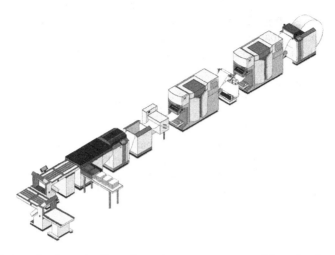

Fig. 3. Digital production print line where the concept presented here has been succesfully tested

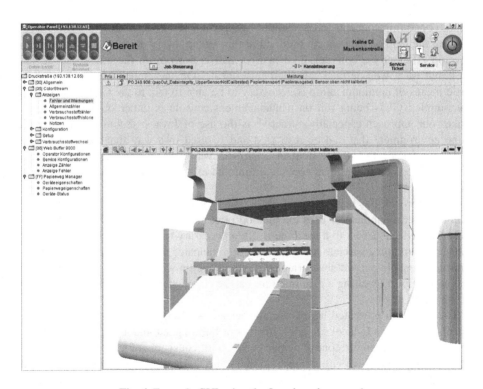

Fig. 4. Example GUI using the Java-based approach

tree structure on the left is used to select a device or a sub-menu. As soon as a node is selected, the upper toolbar shows general information regarding the selected device / menu. In case of a special event (e.g. error) the originating device is automatically selected and the operator thus informed about the problem.

This new remote operating approach has been proven to be especially useful with regard to operator guidance. Between different print jobs that are produced the operator may need to setup one or more devices in the production line. In these situations not all settings can be altered by software configuration only – some settings such as for instance the paper position needs to be set manually. As not all devices implement a user-friendly GUI, the Java approach helps to guide the operator through necessary setup steps in an ergonomic way. Currently only a fixed management console is used but conceptually this concept can also be applied to a mobile management console that can be placed next to the piece of equipment the operator is currently working on.

4 Conclusion

Today it is hardly possible to integrate several devices' GUIs from different not directly cooperating vendors into a consistent management console. Full-scale remote-operating concepts today seem to be typically vendor-specific.

With the help of the concept outlined in this article, every device vendor is able to develop efficiently a complex GUI in Java that is not run on the embedded device itself but on a well-defined management console. On the embedded device only a basic means of communication is necessary to be able to talk to the GUI. The idea of precompiled GUIs being run on a management console is rather obvious but what makes our approach especially attractive is the use of Java. It features a virtual machine environment that can be restricted and secured in a way that even malicious programs cannot alter the system in a harmful way (see e.g. [10]). Secondly, Java offers methods to integrate an application into an existing framework in a convenient way.

This approach has been successfully applied in the digital printing industry. One major printer manufacturer uses the method presented here as its main GUI concept. Because physical access to a machine is often necessary to resolve problems, the GUI can also be run on a wireless terminal that communicates with a gateway management console to enable e.g. fieldbus-oriented communication with a device. Thus, efficient operator support featuring e.g. animations can be supplied even for existing microcontroller-based devices.

The approach presented here is by no means restricted to an industrial context; it can also be applied to a consumer electronics or building automation context. Conceptually a universal remote control device can be built consisting of a hardware platform that is able to run a Java virtual machine like today's smart phones. With the potential help of one or more gateways which may even be included in a home appliance that is permanently running anyway such as a router, all interconnected devices can be operated in a consistent and user-friendly way. It is also possible to introduce abstraction layers by implementing e.g. a virtual device that integrates all building automation devices within one GUI.

References

1. Macedonia, M.R., Zyda, M.J.: A taxonomy for networked virtual environments. IEEE Multimedia 4(1), 48–56 (1997)
2. Corcoran, P.M., Papal, F., Zoldi, A.: User interface technologies for home appliances and networks. IEEE Transactions on Consumer Electronics 44(3), 679–685 (1998)
3. Roman, M., Beck, J., Gefflaut, A.: A device-independent representation for services. In: Proc. of the Third IEEE Workshop on Mobile Computing Systems and Applications, pp. 73–82. IEEE Press, New York (2000)
4. Al-Ali, A.R., Al-Rousan, M.: Java-based home automation system. IEEE Transactions on Consumer Electronics 50(2), 498–504 (2004)
5. Locher, H.N., et al.: Monitoring the Distributed Virtual Orchestra with a CORBA Based Object Oriented Real-Time Data Distribution Service. In: Meersman, R., Tari, Z., Schmidt, D.C. (eds.) CoopIS 2003, DOA 2003, and ODBASE 2003. LNCS, vol. 2888, pp. 1051–1062. Springer, Heidelberg (2003)
6. Kastner, W., et al.: Communication Systems for Building Automation and Control. Proc. of the IEEE 93(6), 1178–1203 (2005)
7. Hadellis, L., Koubias, L., Makios, S., An, V.: An integrated approach for an interoperable industrial networking architecture consisting of heterogeneous fieldbuses. Computers in Industry 49(3), 283–298 (2002)
8. Marcos, M., et al.: Object-oriented modeling for remote monitoring of manufacturing processes. In: Proc. IEEE International Conference on Emerging Technologies and Factory Automation, pp. 287–293. IEEE Press, New York (2001)
9. Kehr, R., Rohs, M., Vogt, H.: Mobile Code as an Enabling Technology for Service-oriented Smartcard Middleware. In: Proc. IEEE International Symposium on Distributed Objects and Applications, pp. 119–130. IEEE Press, New York (2001)
10. Pandey, R., Hashii, B.: Providing Fine-Grained Access Control for Java Programs. In: Guerraoui, R. (ed.) ECOOP 1999. LNCS, vol. 1628, pp. 449–473. Springer, Heidelberg (1999)

Service-Oriented University: Infrastructure for the University of Tomorrow

Raphael Zender and Djamshid Tavangarian

Chair of Computer Architecture, University of Rostock, Rostock, Germany
`firstname.lastname@uni-rostock.de`

Abstract. Challenged by an increasing use of IT, student as well as staff mobility, the introduction of assistive systems, and legal guidelines, todays universities have to rethink about their infrastructural organisation. The rag rug of stand-alone solutions reduces the university's flexibility and makes cooperations with other institutions difficult. This article examines the evolution of traditional universities to "pervasive universities" on the infrastructural level. It evaluates the service-oriented university as the next infrastructural step to the targeted pervasiveness, and suggests an infrastructure model for educational institutions. We look at the challenges and possibilities of such a model and show its benefit for the university of tomorrow.

1 Introduction and Motivation

As well as most other institutions, todays universities are challenged by an increasing use of IT. Internet-based communication, digital learning material, remote lectures, online conferences, assistive systems, and digital authentification, authorization and accounting are just a small subset of artifacts and mechanisms, that have to be handled by educational institutions. The 2009 Horizon Report [1] identifies and describes emerging technologies likely to have a large impact on teaching, learning, and research within learning-focused organizations. The report emphasizes main trends to be introduced over the next one to five years:

- *Integrative mobile systems (≤ 1 year)*: Smart devices that replace multiple other devices like cellphones, MP3 players, organizers, and internet access nodes
- *Cloud Computing (≤ 1 year)*: Ultra thin clients with everywhere remote access to distributed resources and services with well defined interfaces
- *Geo-Everything (2 - 3 years)*: Enrichment of data (e.g. documents, images) with geographic information (tagging)
- *Personal web (2 - 3 years)*: Individual online representations and content compositions (pushed by social web)
- *Semantic-aware applications (4 - 5 years)*: Applications that utilize the meaning of informations (e.g. search engines for natural language requests)
- *Smart objects (4 - 5 years)*: Physical objects, that are connected to a rich store of contextual information (e.g. museum exhibits, that are digitally linked to meta informations about themselves)

D. Tavangarian et al. (Eds.): IMC 2009, CCIS 53, pp. 73–84, 2009.

The report shows, that the realization of the tasks of universities, to combine education, research, and administration has to be modified. In accordance to the general evolution of computing [2], the context of education, research, and administration has changed [3]: The introduction of remote communication, fault tolerance, high availability, remote information access, and distributed security led to the *IT-based University*. Based on this, the extensive introduction of mobility breeds *Notebook Universities*. As well as current IT trends lead to pervasive computing, the evolution of universities likely results in *Pervasive Universities*, educational institutions that are enriched by mechanisms and artifacts of pervasive computing in a targeted manner [3].

The evolution towards pervasiveness in universities is driven by the technological evolution as well as guidelines and regulations by law. For example, the Bologna process makes demands on the mobility of teachers and students among universities worldwide. On the infrastructural level, this requires an IT-based communication independent from place and time, as pervasive computing promises [4]. On the organizational level, every university is additionally challenged by the cooperation with other universities on the one hand and the protection of its autonomy on the other hand.

The realization of the targeted pervasive university with regard to cross-university interactions is going to be quite hard and without a systematic and adaptive infrastructure it would lack in flexibility as well as usability. This article describes the potential infrastructure for the pervasive university of tomorrow, based on Service-oriented Architectures (SOA). A SOA-based infrastructure enables us to implement the main mechanisms and artifacts of pervasive universities. Thus, a *Service-oriented University* is the infrastructural basis of a pervasive university as the next section illustrates. We are going to highlight the potential of SOA for education, research and administration as well as the current SOA challenges. Section 3 gives a technical model of the required SOA-based infrastructure and also explains already implemented applications. This is followed by an use case, that exemplifies life at the university of tomorrow. Finally, section 5 draws a short summary with a view on future work.

2   Service-Oriented Architectures for Universities

SOA currently gains importance not only for selected eLearning systems [5] and eScience platforms [6] but also in general for university [7] and company infrastructures [8]. Every SOA is focused on real-life processes and their implementation by services. Basically, services are well-defined, reusable interfaces. They contain descriptions of their functionality in terms of their accepted input as well as expected output and optionally semantic meta information (e.g. Web Ontology Language descriptions and human-friendly descriptions). Services completely hide the specific implementations of their functionality. Thus, they are an infrastructural requirement for assistive systems, that spontaneously and proactively support users in their everyday work [9].

Universities have a wide range of possible services in every domain. **Educational services** are often about the provision of learning material for a lecture, the access to additional resources like digital books and multimedia, and the dissemination of lecture streams (audio and video). Furthermore, students and lecturers use collaboration services like chats and virtual worlds, as well as personal services like blogs and websites.

Scientific services partly overlap with educational services (e.g. knowledge services like digital books and multimedia) but also include services that are research domain specific. Good Examples are access to special equipment like compute clusters and simulators as well as the remote operation of special industrial machines and devices.

The **administrative services** of an university are the most pronounced. They cover the coordination of the universities physical infrastructure (e.g. room occupancy schedules), the general management of student lifecycles (e.g. online matriculations and monitoring of course assessments), the personnel and finance management (e.g. access to performance assessments and payroll), and several other administrative tasks (e.g. access to menu of cafeterias and university news).

Related work about university services focusses single services of one or two of these domains [10] [11], but lack a general, systematic infrastructure. If existing, not all of the mentioned services are "services" in terms of an SOA. Indeed, they are just implementations called "services". But today, several SOA frameworks support the encapsulation of implementations behind SOA interfaces as well as the handling of multiple consumers (reusability). Thus, the integration of many devices and applications into SOA can be realized in a short time.

Figure 1 exemplifies the roles and interactions of an SOA in the context of educational institutions like universities. Services are provided by a a device or application (*provider*), that is responsible for the service implementation. For instance, the provider of access to a lecture live stream is the recording device itself or a media control in the lecture room. Providers *publish* descriptions of their services at *brokers*. Brokers store the list of registered services. They are often simple lists of descriptions (similar to yellow pages) but sometimes databases with complex query syntax. *Consumers* (e.g. video player on students cellphones or laptops) are able to *find* services by requesting the broker (e.g. for registered lecture streaming services). The broker responds with a list of services, that match the request. In the next step, consumers select one or more services to use and *bind* them. Binding includes the connection establishment with providers a well as authentification (if required). If successfully bound, the service can be used (e.g. by playing the live stream on the students cellphone).

Even though services are also accessible for external use without a broker, the introduction of this instance dramatically increases the flexibility of service discovery. The consumers do not need a priori knowledge to address each available service, they just need the required service type and a broker address. Due to its high degree of agility and transparency, SOA is relevant especially in heterogeneous, dynamic environments like spontaneous assitive environments. Summarized, the SOA is characterized by:

- Loose coupling because of minimal interdependencies (interactions are independent from implementation details)

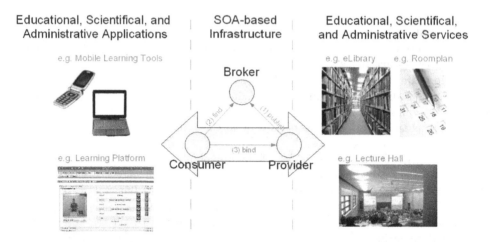

Fig. 1. Service-oriented Architectures are used for a highly flexible and scalable interconnection between university services and applications

- Content-based instead of resource-based addressing (search requests based on the nature of an object, not on its location)
- Late binding (service selection and invocation at runtime)
- Reflection of real activities (the architecture can be correlated with business processes [12])

These attributes together with decreasing device dimensions are the infrastructural basis for concepts like self-management and self-organization. Hence, SOA is the best applicable infrastructure for pervasive environments like the targeted pervasive university.

But there are problems with SOA, too. The most important is SOA heterogeneity: The SOA hype produced a large amount of different and incompatible technologies as well as runtime environments. Popular technologies are Web services, Jini, and Universal Plug and Play (UPnP). The consumer needs to use the same technology as the provider. Therefore, a student cellphone, that consumes web services can not natively consume video streams provided as Jini service. A mechanism that bridges between technology-separated SOA islands can significantly increase the spectrum of available services. We developed the so called General Purpose Access Point (GPAP) [7] to fullfill this task. Thus, the GPAP is part of our SOA university model, which is described in the following section.

3 Infrastructural Model for the Service-Oriented University

The basis of our infrastructural model are hardware resources and applications. Furthermore we concern about users like lecturers, students, and staff. Figure 2 illustrates, how these entities are related to each other. Humans use applications via user interfaces, and applications control or use hardware. Generally, the relations between applications and hardware can be divided into "hardware-focused" relations (applications that control hardware, like interfaces for industrial machines) and "application-focused" relations (applications that are hosted on hardware like web servers and office applications). In our SOA-based model, applications provide services. Corresponding to the two types of applications, there are two types of services: Services that control hardware (hardware services) and services that utilize software (software services). Nevertheless, all services are provided by applications.

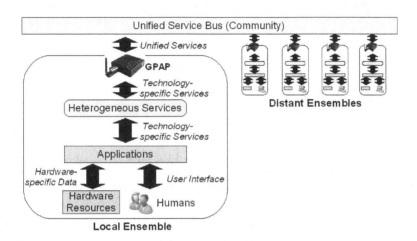

Fig. 2. The abstract model for service-oriented institutions uses a "Unified Service Bus" to interconnect ensembles (e.g. divisions, faculties, chairs) with communities (e.g. company, university)

As already mentioned, services can be provided in different SOA technologies. To afford a cross-technology service provision and consumption, we developed the GPAP. This multi-dimensional communication system enables pervasive communication on infrastructural level. On the one hand, the GPAP transparently interconnects devices, that use different network interfaces (e.g. Ethernet, Wi-Fi, Bluetooth) to communicate [13], but this is not in focus of this article. On the other hand, the GPAP is the translator between different SOA technologies. Therefore, it consumes technology-specific services and translates them into a meta format called *Service Technology-independent Language* (STiL). In turn, the resulting STiL services are used to create corresponding services in several other SOA technologies on plugin-base. From the organizational point of view, every GPAP is responsible for a dedicated *ensemble* [7]. Its local ensemble covers all applications that provide and use services in a specific physical or virtual area (e.g. division of a company, faculty of an university, or even a single room).

Beside SOA technology translations, STiL services are utilized to form a *Unified Service Bus*. The bus can be seen as a distributed broker. GPAPs provide

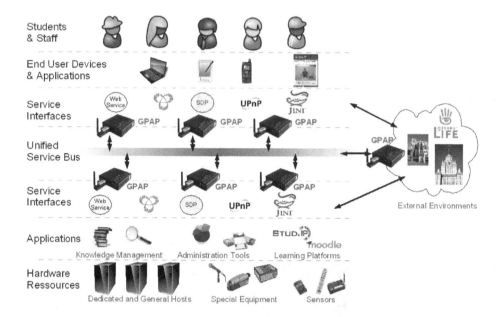

Fig. 3. The exemplified model for Service-oriented Universities illustrates the integration of different hardware resources and applications as well as end user devices and applications into a systematic, flexible, and high adaptive infrastructure

STiL services to the bus (if allowed by providers) and consume STiL services from the bus (to provide them in the local ensemble). In this way, ensemble members are able to find and use services from distant ensembles. From the organizational point of view, all ensembles that are interconnected by an Unified Service Bus build up a *community* (e.g. a company, a university, or collaborating universities). Furthermore, communities can be organized as hierarchy of Unified Service Buses to map hierarchic organizational structures to the infrastructure.

Figure 3 illustrates the mapping of our abstract model to the university context to build up the Service-oriented University. Like the abstraction our model integrates humans (students and staff) and hardware resources together with their corresponding applications. We already implemented applications on different levels to verify our concept. For reason of clarity, humans and hardware resources are widely separated in figure 3. The several layers will be presented in detail in the following sections.

3.1   Hardware Resources and End User Devices

Todays universities own a tremendous diversity of hardware. The spectrum ranges from high performance computing resources (e.g. fat servers and computing clusters) in the universities data processing center to special equipment for natural scientific experiments and beyond to small tags that identifies students and staff. Furthermore, many people use personal devices (e.g. cellphones, laptops, and smartphones) or common workstations to interact with the universities infrastructure. This section shows just a small subset of a university's hardware and the current challenges with them.

Dedicated and general host computers are essential in the infrastructure of every modern institute (e.g. for for personal and business websites, eMail, applications, and files). These systems are well connected to networks like the internet and the university's internal network. Therefore, the applications running on them can easily provide or consume services in an SOA, by the implementation of consumer and provider logic.

By contrast, special equipment often lacks in network connections. Thus, dedicated controllers are necessary to integrate the hardware into a network and to mediate between SOA and hardware. We already integrated our media lab (a special room with extensive equipment to realize eLearning scenarios) into the infrastructure to afford remote control and media consumption [14].

In particular, sensors are very important for pervasive environments. They measure and provide direct context information about the environment (e.g. humidity, light intensity, and temperature) and the user (e.g. identity, position, and speed). Usually, dedicated sensor nodes with extended resources are responsible for the integration of multiple sensors into larger networks. According to this, we implemented an integration of multiple SunSPOT sensor nodes into our infrastructure, by using a dedicated base station.

Beside these university owned hardware resources, students and staff use their personal devices and expect their integration into the university's infrastructure. Fortunately, todays personal devices are mostly well connected to the internet via different network interfaces (e.g. GPRS, UMTS, Wi-Fi) but there are still devices that use shortrange wireless technologies like Bluetooth. These heterogeneous network technologies are brought together by the network layer of our GPAP (if in range). Therefore, our applications benefit from interoperability on network layer.

3.2 Applications and Services

As well as hardware resources, modern universities utilize a lot of applications to support education, research, and administration. The main challenge on this layer is the extension of existing applications with SOA mechanisms. Traditional applications on the whole as well as their components have to be extended with SOA consumer and provider functionality to afford the targeted flexible, transparent, and adaptive interaction with remote entities. Many applications already suppport SOA (e.g. social platforms and blogs that provide Web Services).

Exemplary, we extended our media lab to provide services to control the different devices as well as to access the generated content in the media lab (e.g. live or recorded lecture streams). Furthermore, we extended the learning platform Stud.IP and the virtual world Second Life to consume these services. Thus, we realized remote participation to lectures via Stud.IP or Second Life. Beyond this, we implemented an SOA-based chat interface for cellphones as well as for Second Life to enable cross-environment messaging. Both implementations are first steps to a fusion of real and virtual learning scenarios [14]. The SOA-based approach assures the high flexibility, transparency, and efficiency of our fusion.

As already mentioned, SOA service interfaces exist for different SOA technologies. Our implementations use Web Services (media lab control and media access, Second Life control of the media lab, Second Life media consumption, Second Life messaging, and Stud.IP integration), the Bluetooth Service Discovery Protocol (chat service on cellphones), and Jini (access to sensor nodes). All these technologies are brought together by the service layer of our GPAP.

3.3   Service Layer of the General Purpose Access Point (GPAP)

The GPAP is our central component to realize interoperability on the network as well as on the services level. As the network level is described in other publications [13], this article focusses the service level. On this level, the GPAP architecture uses the XML-based *Service Technology-independent Language* (STiL) to transform technology-specific services into meta representations and vice versa. STiL is the result of a broad comparison of service descriptions from most spreaded SOA technologies. It presents attributes that all these descriptions have in common and is extendable for technology-specific properties.

A GPAP utilizes three different plugin types to perform this transformation in its local ensemble. Each plugin implementation is responsible for the syntactic translation of service descriptions into STiL as well as the consideration of the different interaction models of the targeted SOAs. Therefore, its development requires an excellent understandig about the specific technology and the STiL mechanisms. In return, each plugin is reusable on all GPAP nodes. There are three plugin types:

- An **x discovery plugin** discovers services of the local ensemble that are provided in technology x and transforms them into STiL.
- An **x provision plugin** searches for STiL services, transforms them into services of the technology x, and provides these services in the local ensemble.
- GPAPs with an **x broker plugin** act as broker of the technology x for the local ensemble. Local providers and consumers of x services use this broker to publish and find services. The plugin is an combination of discovery and provision plugin and is applied if we are able to control or modify a local SOA to introduce our "broker".

Currently, we are able to translate Web Services (discovery and provison plugin), Jini (broker plugin), Bluetooth SDP (discovery and provison plugin), and Bonjour (discovery and provison plugin) into STiL and vice versa. Thereby, all consumers and providers still use their original SOA technology. Therfore, STiL-based SOA transformation is a transparent and invisible interconnection between existing SOA technologies instead of a new technology, developers have to take into account. Compared with other SOA interoperability concepts, this approach requeires minimal adjustments for existing SOAs [7]. Nevertheless, not all services of all SOA technologies are transformable. In particular, our approach excludes services that extensively utilize the unique features of an SOA technology (e.g. Jini-based JavaSpaces).

The GPAP provides the generated STiL services to the Unified Service Bus. Currently, the bus is implemented as Peer-to-Peer (P2P) network and every GPAP is one peer. Therefore, other GPAPs (and consequently other ensembles) can find and use remote services. Thus, other rooms, floors, chairs, and faculities can work with services of the local room, floor, chair, or faculty. Moreover, the bus ensures the easy integration of other universities for cross-university scenarios.

3.4 Cross-University Integration

The main benefit of SOA is the easy and transparent integration of different IT environments and platforms (to work and exchange data) into each other. Thus, the integration of other universities (as external environment) into our infrastructure is as easy as the integration of applications into the ensemble or the interconnection of ensembles and communities. Therefore, two approaches are intended to integrate external environments:

1. **Applications of external environments as ensemble members.** In this case, the local university provides a dedicated ensemble for each external university or a common ensemble for all external universities. The external universities (or single external divisions) provide their services in a specific SOA technology directly to the dedicated ensemble. Furthermore, they find and use services of this ensemble. In particular for SOA technologies that do not have a global broker (e.g. Bonjour), we recommend the second approach.
2. **External environments as own ensembles.** The external university uses its own GPAP to connect to the Unified Service Bus. From the infrastructural point of view, the external environment is just another ensemble. It benefits from SOA interoperability as well as from the high scalable (because P2P-based) Unified Service Bus.

Every cooperation of one or more autonomous institutions raises privacy concerns. In our model privacy is currently considered at three different levels:

- **SOA technology-specific.** Some SOA technologies have their own mechanisms to prevent unauthorized service use (e.g. Web Service Security). These can be utilized by service providers. Unfortunately, our GPAP-plugins currently do not support those security-enriched services.
- **Scope of service provision.** The abstract STiL service descriptions allow to define a scope of service discovery (e.g. just in the own ensemble). The service cannot be found beyond this scope. The scope has been taken from the technology-specific service description (if possible).
- **Firewalled GPAP.** The GPAP can be configured to provide not all of the available services to the ensemble. For instance, the GPAP can be configured not to find services beyond the own IP subnet or beyond the own university network.

Our infrastructural model is the basis for further developments targeting the pervasive university as well as pervasive enterprise organizations. By the use of SOA, it provides a high flexible, adaptive, transparent, and scalable architecture. It can be used to implement context-aware applications (by using context services, e.g. from sensor applications), to breed new applications and services (by combining existing services), and to ensure user mobility as well as cooperation between separated institutions. The following scenario exemplifies the learning and living at an university that utilizes a service-oriented infrastructure.

4   Use Case: The University of Tomorrow

The following scenario happens at an service-oriented university: The student Alice has switched from university X to university Y and today is her first lecture at Y. Unfortunately, she lost her way to the lecture room, because she isn't yet familiar with the new city. The lecture already began, but that's no problem at a pervasive university. Alice uses her smart phone to search for a live video service in the university's community. She finds it and follows the lecture via live video stream. Furthermore, she finds a GPS-based navigation service, that leads her to the lecture room. When Alice enters the lecture room, the transmission stops, automatically.

In the lecture hall, Prof. Bob speaks in front of 15 real attending students as well as 20 remote participants. Some of them just follow the lecture stream, others participate in the discussions as well. This is possible because of the audio input service published to the whole university community. Remote participants use this service to send audio messages into the lecture hall. Prof. Bob is really happy about the discussing remote participants, because even if some students participate remote, the social presence still exists.

The poor utilization of the room has been sensed at the buildings administration office. Room manager Carry noticed that just 15 student tags are in the room and just two students currently use GPS to find their way to the lecture. Therefore, Carry assigns a small lecture room for the next lecture sessions. The on-site lecture participants automatically receive a location update message.

Next door to Carry's office, her colleague Dan recognizes the first login of Alice into the university's community. He uses the student finder service and identifies Alice as new student from university X. Dan permanently migrates Alice's user account to Y just by moving her student account service to the local university community. Welcome at your new pervasive university, Alice!

While some of the desribed services already exist (e.g. lecture via live video stream and messaging from/to lecture hall), others are work in progress or currently even visions driven by the 2009 Horizon Report [1]. Most of the services are or will be implemented as Web Services. But services like the "audio input service" are using SOA technologies like Blutooth-SDP because of the implementing device (e.g. Bluetooth-based speaker in the lecture room). Therefore, the lecture room needs its own GPAP component to transform between these different technologies and supply the resulting STiL services them into the university wide service bus. Because of its migratebility, the mentioned external "student account service" will assumed to be implemented as Jini service. GPAPs on both sides as well as a common Jini Broker can be utilized to migrate this service between two separated universities.

5 Summary and Future Work

The IT saturation of modern universities, the increasing mobility of students and staff, the upcoming introduction of assitive systems (as prognosed in the 2009 Horizon Report [1]), as well as the guidelines given by the Bologna process forces educational institutions to rethink about their infrastructure. Individual stand-alone solutions make cooperations with other institutions difficult and constrain the own flexibility. Furthermore, the current challenges are just the beginning. More and more emerging technologies find their way into education, research, and administration [1] and prove the change from traditional universities to pervasive universities [3] with own infrastructural requirements.

In this article, we introduced a high flexible, most adaptive, and transparent infrastructural model for pervasive universities, based on service-oriented architectures. The model is based on a division of the infrastructure into ensembles and communities and utilizes a unified service bus. We illustrated challenges, solutions, and possibilities for students and staff, hardware resources, applications, and as well for the cooperation between educational institutions. We exemplarily explained already implemented parts of the service-oriented university and verified our model but there is still a lot of work to do.

Our main infrastructural task is the modification of software towards service-orientation. Today, a lot of tools and frameworks exist to realize service-oriented architectures. Nevertheless, the modification requires a rethinking on the levels of management processes and software development. The main SOA problem, the heterogeneity of SOA technologies can be solved. For this purpose, we presented the General Purpose Access Point (GPAP) a multidimensional communication system, that enables interoperability between service technologies as well as different network solutions. This interoperability, together with basic SOA concepts and applications utilizing our infrastructure leads universities to communication everywhere and everytime as the vision of pervasive computing promises [4].

Acknowledgement

This research is supported by the German National Science Foundation (DFG, GRK1424).

References

1. Johnson, L., Levine, A., Smith, R.: The 2009 Horizon Report. The New Media Consortium (2009)
2. Satyanarayanan, M.: Pervasive Computing: Vision and Challenges. IEEE Personal Communications 8, 10–17 (2001)

 3. Tavangarian, D., Lucke, U.: Pervasive University - A Technical Perspective. IT - Information Technology 51/1, 6–13 (2009)
 4. Weiser, M.: The computer for the 21st century. Scientific American 09/91, 94–102 (1991)
 5. Allison, C., Nicoll, R., Bateman, M., Ling, B.: From Web To Grid: Evolution of a Learning Environment. In: Web Based Education, Grindelwald, Switzerland, pp. 461–472. ACTA Press (2005)
 6. Kuropka, D., Weske, M.: Die Adaptive Services Grid Plattform: Motivation, Potential, Funktionsweise und Anwendungsszenarien. Emisa Forum 26(1), 12–25 (2006)
 7. Zender, R., Dressler, E., Lucke, U., Tavangarian, D.: Meta-Service Organization for a Pervasive University. In: Proceedings of PerEL 2008, Workshop at 6th IEEE International Conference on Pervasive Computing and Communications (PerCom), Hong Kong, China, pp. 400–405. IEEE Computer Society, Los Alamitos (2008)
 8. Bosch, J., Friedrichs, S., Jung, S., Helbig, J., Scherdin, A.: Service orientation in the enterprise. Computer 40(11), 51–56 (2007)
 9. Kirste, T., Herfet, T., Schnaider, M.: EMBASSI: multimodal assistance for universal access to infotainment and service infrastructures. In: Proceedings of the 2001 EC/NSF workshop on Universal accessibility of ubiquitous computing: providing for the elderly, Alcr do Sal, Portugal, pp. 41–50. ACM, New York (2001)
10. Vossen, G., Westerkamp, P.: Towards the Next Generation of E-Learning Standars: SCORM for Service-Oriented Enviroments. In: Proceedings of the Sixth IEEE International Conference on Advanced Learning Technologies (ICALT), Kerkrade, The Netherlands, July 2006, pp. 1031–1035 (2006)
11. Schandua, H., Stiller, T., Emig, C., Abeck, S.: Integration of SAP Campus Management into a University SOA. University of Karlsruhe (2005)
12. Pasley, J.: How bpel and soa are changing web services development. IEEE Internet Computing 9(3), 60–67 (2005)
13. Dressler, E., Zender, R., Lucke, U., Tavangarian, D.: A new Architecture for Heterogeneous Context Based Routing. In: Proceedings of the 13th International CSI Computer Conference (CSICC), Kish Island, Iran, March 2008, pp. 526–534 (2008)
14. Zender, R., Dressler, E., Lucke, U., Tavangarian, D.: Pervasive Media and Messaging Services for Immersive Learning Experiences. In: Proceedings of PerEL 2009, Workshop at 7th IEEE International Conference on Pervasive Computing and Communications (PerCom), Galveston, TX, USA. IEEE Computer Society Press, Los Alamitos (2009)

Portable Real Time Needs Expression for People with Communication Disabilities

Lau Bee Theng

Swinburne University of Technology Sarawak Campus
Kuching, Sarawak, Malaysia
blau@swinburne.edu.my

Abstract. This paper discusses a research on biometrics information recognition in real time for expressing needs of the people with communication disabilities. They have facial expression ability and incomprehensible speech that can be interpreted to communicate their needs. We utilized the real time detected face features in the pattern recognition process. Their facial expressions for a specific need may not be identical but have some similarities that can be identified through pattern recognition and trained using artificial intelligence. EmoCom has achieved a recognition rate of 85% in both cluttered indoor and outdoor environment.

1 Introduction

Biometrics information of individuals can be recognized based on their physiological or behavioral characteristics. Face and voice features are the most commonly studied characteristics across computer vision and pattern recognition (Heisele et al. 2003, Zana and Roberto 2007, Zhao et al. 2003). According to psychologist, facial expression provides information about emotional states as well as cognitive activities (Ekman 2004). Furthermore, emotions are revealed earlier through facial expression than people verbalize or even realize their emotional state (Zhao et al. 2003). Some psychologists concluded that cognitive interpretations of emotions from facial expressions are innate and universal to all humans regardless of their culture (Zana and Roberto 2007, Zhao et al. 2003). Facial expression recognition is regarded as a non-intrusive method that captures human subjects' facial expressions through still images or video sequences in uncontrolled cluttered environment. This enlightens us with the use of biometric information of people with communication disabilities to communicate the needs ubiquitously, provide a better way to communicate and a new level of independence.

At the preliminary phase, we developed a prototype, EmoCom to detect and recognize the facial expressions of the people with communication disabilities in real time. EmoCom is portable as it is developed to work in a laptop, tablet computer or PDA that can be mounted on the wheelchair to go along with the disabled as shown in Figure 1. EmoCom is designed to perform both indoor and outdoor ambient context. EmoCom can also act as a monitoring system to track the activities of the disabled. When a real time 2D frontal face is detected, EmoCom perform the expression recognition process.

D. Tavangarian et al. (Eds.): IMC 2009, CCIS 53, pp. 85–95, 2009.
© Springer-Verlag Berlin Heidelberg 2009

If an expression is recognized and matched to a predefined need in the depository, a short message is sent to the caretakers through wireless technology that is Bluetooth. Bluetooth is used as it is not costly and sufficient to convey the message within 30ft. The predefined needs in depository are prepared by the caretakers or teachers. At homes and special schools, this could help to save the time, increase the mobility and productivity of the caretakers. When a caretaker is not around, any new one could substitute her easily without having to learn all the communication patterns of the individual disabled. Caretakers could monitor more than one person simultaneously.

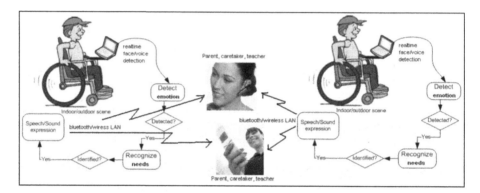

Fig. 1. Conceptual design of communication assistant, EmoCom

2   Real Time Needs Recognition

The foremost task in EmoCom is the needs recognition. Each disabled has a different way of expression for a need. Our defined disabled community has mobility constraints due to physical disabilities that restrict their arms and hands movements. On top of the physical disabilities, they also have communication disabilities. This makes their communication with computer and human impossible unless assistance and special devices are used.

2.1   Real Time 2D Frontal Face Detection

The success of needs our communication depends on how good the real time frontal face detection work. It is difficult to locate the disable people's frontal faces due to two main reasons. First, some of them could not coordinate their heads fully as part of their disabilities. Second, their ambient context, they stay indoor which may not have sufficient lighting or outdoor that is too bright in the day and too dark at night. They could not position themselves unless with some assistance as they also have physical disabilities.

Current real time detection systems employ techniques like Viola-Jone algorithms, Motion History Image (Huang and Lin 2008), Skin Color Model (Huang and Lin 2008), Support Vector Machine, SVM (Tistarelli et al. 2009) or Active Appearance Model, AAM (Datcu and Rothkrantz 2007). Most of the recent researches use only

Viola and Jones algorithm with some configurations to detect the face from the image (Yang et al. 2009, Geetha et al. 2009) and then utilize AAM to extract the face out of the background. Viola and Jones algorithm has a big drawback despite many advantages like against illumination condition and scale invariant that is it cannot detect rotated frontal face (Huang and Lin 2008).

From the testing we conducted, we decided to use our hybrid detection algorithm as it could detect the frontal faces under both indoor and outdoor conditions with mixed background objects. The hybrid algorithm combined Skin Color Model, Viola and Jones and Motion History Image. First, it scans the image until the face is located by the Viola and Jones Method. After that, it tracks the box which contains the face based on the CamShift algorithm. Finally, the face box is scanned by the Skin Color Model to check whether the box still contains the face. If not, the face is relocated using Viola and Jones.

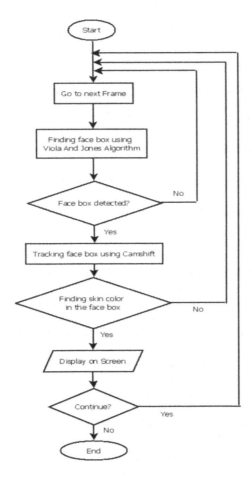

Fig. 2. Hybrid algorithm for 2D frontal face detection in real time

Fig. 3. Detecting face with Hybrid method under indoor condition with cluttered background

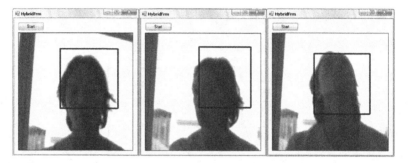

Fig. 4. Detecting face with Hybrid method under outdoor condition with cluttered background

2.2 Face Image Preprocessing

When a 2D frontal image is detected successfully, we perform face image preprocessing for the captured image. It is transformed into gray scale images. The centers of two eyes on each image are used as the centers for rotation, translation, scaling and cropping. Each processed image has a size of 256×256 pixels. The preprocessed images are then subject to contrast/illumination and histogram equalization. Contrast is a measure of the human visual system sensitivity. The face recognition process in different lighting conditions with different illumination and contrast has different level of efficiency and psychologically meaningfulness. Hence, for our needs recognition, all images are processed with same illumination and root mean square (RMS) contrast. The RMS contrast metric is equivalent to the standard deviation of luminance (Weyrauch and Huang 2003). x_i is a normalized gray-level value such that $0 < x_i < 1$ and x is the mean normalized gray level. With this normalization, images of different faces have the same contrast as long as their RMS contrast is equal. RMS contrast does not depend on spatial frequency contrast of the image or the spatial distribution of contrast in the image. All the faces are maintained with the same illumination and same RMS contrast where α is the contrast and β is the brightness to be increased or decreased from the original image f to the new image g as in Equation 2. On the other hand, histogram equalization is used to compensate the lighting conditions and enhance the contrast of the image. This is due to the face images may encounter poor contrast because of the limitations of the lighting conditions especially indoor.

$$RMS = \left[\frac{1}{n} \sum_{i=1}^{n} (x_i - \bar{x})^2 \right]^{\frac{1}{2}} \tag{1}$$

$$g = \alpha f + \beta \tag{2}$$

2.3 Eigenfaces

There are many algorithms for face recognition and most of them depend on the features on the face to locate the global position (the face) and also the local position (features on the face). Some algorithms are complex and unable to provide a universal solution and they require higher computational time. Some other solutions proposed a feature extraction module that estimates only the state of facial features. Then intelligent classifiers are designed to cater for the inherent uncertainty in the estimated facial features. Furthermore, in a fully unconstrained environment, frontal faces may be taken under different illuminations, from varying distances and directions, in cluttered backgrounds, and with unpredictable facial expressions (Raquel 1995). Our needs recognition system depends on the level of detail in facial features solely. The most suitable technique is projecting face images or sub images onto a low dimensional feature space using Principle Component Analysis (PCA). The face on the image can be represented by a vector containing the gray levels of the pixels and after that PCA is applied to capture the face space in a low dimensional space spanned by orthogonal eigenvector. A linear combination of Eigenfaces are computed from these eigenvectors and then used to represent the faces.   When a person makes an expression such as happy, angry or surprise; each point on the face has a relationship in distance corresponding to the emotions. By calculating the distance of every point on the face to others and comparing these distances with the distances of a neutral face, we can determine which expression is shown on a face.

2.4 Expression Training with Back Propagated Neural Network (NN)

For our expressions training, we proposed to use back propagated neural network. The rationale of utilizing artificial neural network is due to our target users do not show exactly same facial expressions at all time, variances occur within the same user's expression for a need. However, the variations are within a range that can be trained and modeled through artificial neural network. Hence, accurate needs recognition for all the disabled requires a set of facial expression images to be supplied to EmoCom as training data. We adopted a back propagation neural network to identify the similarities and variations. A set of trained facial expressions and non facial expressions is produced from the back propagation neural network.

We employed a multilayer perceptron back propagated neural network to train the expressions as in Figure 6. The input layer receives Eigen vectors detected as its input. The number of nodes in training layer equals to the dimension of the face features incorporating the Eigen vectors. The number of nodes in the output layer equals to the number of individual expressions the network is required to recognize. The number of epochs for this experiment was 10,000 and the goal was 0.01. The back propagated neural networking training algorithm is shown in Figure 5. In the initialization stage, all the weights and threshold values of the network are set to random numbers within $(-F_i, +F_i)$ where F_i represents the sum of neurons, i in the network. In the activation stage, the network is activated by applying the inputs $x_1(t), x_2(t),..., x_n(t)$ and the desired outputs $y_1(t), y_2(t),..., y_n(t)$. The actual outputs in the training and output layers are calculated. In the weight training stage, all weights are updated, and the errors associated with the output neurons are propagated backward. Iteration, t is increased by 1. If termination does not occur, then the back propagation iterates again.

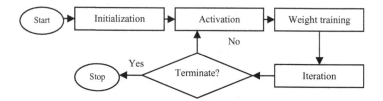

Fig. 5. Back propagation algorithm

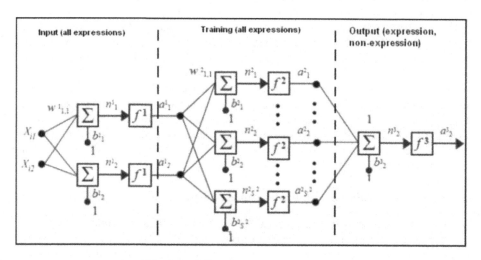

Fig. 6. Back Propagated Neural Network

3 Prototyping

Our prototype, EmoCom is developed with a training and detection interface. The training interface allows each user create their profiles of emotions. Our approach works for arbitrary user-defined expressions. However, for testing and evaluation purposes, we use the universal basic emotions. A profile is a set of images showing various emotions for a user to train the recognition. The prototype works under automatic or manual mode. For automatic detection, caretaker can set a time interval for each user. By default, the detection is at 50 frames per second. We assume a full frontal view of the face, but take into account our human subject dependent variations in head pose and framing inherent in video-based interaction. EmoCom is portable to detect the users' emotions by utilizing the built in camera on a laptop. It can be used at anywhere anytime as the illumination or lighting is not an issue for our face detection algorithm. EmoCom features an intuitive Graphical User Interface which allows the user's expressions to be detected with the caregiver's preset instructions. Figure 7 shows the main interface, where caretaker can start the expression recognition by clicking *Start EmoCom*. Then EmoCom will proceed until termination instruction is given by the caretaker again. It is using automatic detection without intruding the activity of the disabled child. *Start EmoCom* starts the webcam, retrieve frame from the webcam for processing. The processing of these frames includes 2D frontal face tracking and expression recognition. *Message Path* allows the caretaker to locate and set the Sound Clips that will be played when an expression is recognized successfully. EmoCom has a Training Module that trains a user's profile using digital images in the storage in common formats like BMP, DIB, JPEG, JPG, JEP, PNG, PBM, PGM, PPM, TIFF and TIF. Alternatively, Training Module also allows a user to train his profile using the webcam in real time.

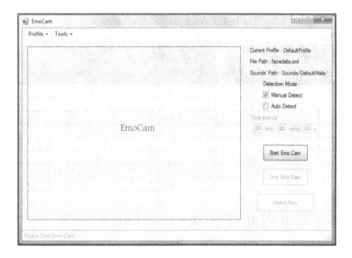

Fig. 7. Main interface of EmoCom

4 Pilot Test with Faces

The pilot tests aim to investigate the performance of our 2D frontal face detection algorithm, histogram/illumination preprocessing, Eigenfaces and Back-propagated Neural Network work well as an expression recognition system for commonly used face images. The two face databases are AT&T and JFFE before implementing on our targeted community in real time basis. AT&T has a total of 400 2D frontal face images from 40 human subjects. On the other hand JFFE has a collection of 200 2D frontal face images posed by 10 female human subjects on 7 facial expressions. The

AT&T database is tested first with our facial expression recognition using Eigen vector based back propagated Neural Network. AT&T database contains 10 different images of 40 distinct human subjects in 5 different illumination conditions. The image is resized to 256 x 256 pixels to maintain consistency to our second face database test. For some human subjects, the images were taken at different times, varying lighting, expressions and facial details (glasses/no-glasses). All the images are taken against a dark homogeneous background and the subjects are in up-right, 2D frontal position with a tolerance for some side movement. This mimics the context of our real environment setting where most of illuminations are due to sunlight and indoor lighting. A 10% of the 400 images in the database were used as a training dataset and the remaining images were used as probe images in the expression recognition. The AT&T images are fully tested for frontal face detection and facial expression recognition from database. The testing was performed with Pentium Dual CPU T3200 2.00GHz, 1.43 GB RAM, at the average running time for a face on an image to be detected and recognized (matched) is averagely 10 seconds for all the 40 human subjects tested. For JFFE face images, we tag each expression for each human subject with a need. Hence it simulates the recognition of an expression which triggers a message being sent to the respective caretaker through Bluetooth devices on the laptop and mobile phone. Table 1 shows accuracy of expression recognition from the two free face databases.

Table 1. Pilot test of face images

| Facial expressions class | AT&T | | JFEE | |
	Average recognition rate (%)	Standard Deviation	Average recognition rate (%)	Standard Deviation
Happy	96.1	0.54	96.5	0.52
Sad	95.8	0.52	96.1	0.49
Fear	96.5	0.46	97.0	0.50
Angry	95.6	0.51	96.1	0.51
Surprised	95.9	0.45	97	0.48
Worried	96.8	0.52	97.2	0.5
Frowned	97.6	0.49	96.8	0.52
Mean	96.3	0.5	96.7	0.5

5 Evaluation with Real Time Detected Faces

10 volunteers were invited to evaluate the real time EmoCom. Each of them displayed 5 distinctive expressions of anger, sadness, happiness, fears, worries, surprise and frown. The images of each volunteer were used to create his/her expression profile. The average detection time for a successful emotion is 13 ms using either automatic or manual detection mode. The real time frontal face detection was conducted in indoor and outdoor with cluttered backgrounds.

The success rate of detecting various emotions depends on the training images for a particular expression for each human subject. We found out that 20 images for training an expression would give the highest recognition rate. It is rather difficult and time consuming to obtain more images for training from the disabled. The main cause of lower recognition rate in real time with volunteers was due to insignificant expression for a particular emotion, lower frontal face detection rate, and insufficient training data being provided. The confusion matrices for various expressions show that

EmoCom uses hybrid recognition algorithm has higher recognition rate and lower confused recognition between classes of expression.

Fig. 8. Various expressions in a profile

Table 2. Expression recognition rate with 10 volunteers

Emotion	Average detection %	Standard Deviation
Happy	85	0.51
Sad	83	0.53
Fear	85	0.49
Angry	87	0.48
Surprised	88	0.55
Worried	84	0.53
Frowned	86	0.49
Mean	85.43	0.51

Table 3. Confusion matrices of recognition with 10 volunteers

Expression	EmoCom						
Angry	**.85**	.03	.00	.03	.00	.01	.03
Scared	.05	**.87**	.00	.00	.00	.01	.00
Happy	.00	.00	**.85**	.01	.03	.00	.00
Sad	.09	.00	.00	**.83**	.00	.01	.01
Surprised	.00	.00	.03	.00	**.88**	.02	.03
Worried	.01	.01	.00	.01	.02	**.84**	.02
Frowned	.03	.00	.00	.01	.03	.02	**.86**
	Angry	Scared	Happy	Sad	Surprised	Worried	Frowned

6 Conclusion

We utilize the state of the art of information communication technologies to develop EmoCom, a system to recognize their needs through expressions shown on the faces. EmoCom provides a flexible framework for the caretaker to configure the real time detection, train the recognition with static images for each profile, tag and store the needs with prerecorded voices, and receives expressions through speaker or short messages sent via Bluetooth wireless. It can be used in the care center, home and school. In the preliminary phase, EmoCom has successfully recognized the core needs of the community who have communication disabilities. We will work on recognizing more expressions of other daily needs like hungry, like, dislike, agree, disagree, games and movement.

Acknowledgements

We gratefully acknowledge the time, efforts and comments of the volunteers. Special thanks to Hii King Shii and Tran Cao Thai for allowing us to publicize their images in this paper.

References

1. AT&T Face Database (The ORL Face Database)
   http://www.cl.cam.ac.uk/Research/DTG/attarchive/pub/data/att_faces.zip (Accessed on December 31, 2008)
2. Boumbarov, O., Sokolov, S., Gluhchev, G.: Combined face recognition using wavelet packets and radial basis function neural network. In: CompSysTech 2007: Proc of International conference on Computer systems and technologies. ACM, New York (2007)
3. Datcu, D., Rothkrantz, L.: Facial expression recognition in still pictures and videos using Active Appearance Model. In: A comparison approach. ACM, New York (2007)
4. Ekman, P.: Emotions Revealed. Henry Holt and Company LLC, First Owl Books, New York (2004)
5. Ekman, P.: Facial Expressions. In: Dalgleish, T., Powers, M. (eds.) Handbook of Cognition and Emotion. John Wiley & Sons Ltd., Chichester (1999)

6. Geetha, A., Ramalingam, V., Palanivel, S., Palaniappan, B.: Facial expression recognition – A real time approach. Expert Systems with Applications 36(1), 303–308 (2009)
7. Heisele, B., Ho, P., Wu, J., Poggio, T.: Face recognition: component based versus global approaches. Computer Vision and Image Understanding 91(1/2), 6–21 (2003)
8. Huang, X., Lin, Y.: A vision-based hybrid method for facial expression recognition. In: Proceedings of the 1st international conference on ambient media and systems (2008)
9. Japanese Female Facial Expression (JFFE) Database,
   http://www.kasrl.org/jaffe_download.html
   (Accessed on December 31, 2008)
10. Lau, B.T.: Gabor Neural Network based Facial Expression Recognition for Assistive Speech Expression. In: Koeppen, M., Kasabov, N., Coghill, G. (eds.) Proceedings of 15th International Conference on Neural Information Processing of the Asia-Pacific Neural Network Assembly, Auckland, New Zealand. LNCS, vol. 5506–5507, Springer, Heidelberg (2008)
11. Lau, B.T., Low, T.K., Hii, K.S.: A Mobile Real Time Interactive Communication Assistant for Cerebral Palsy. International Journal of Computer and ICT Research 3(2), 1818–1839 (2009)
12. Raquel, A.R.: Real-time Face Verification. Thesis (M.S.) Massachusetts Institute of Technology, Dept. of Electrical Engineering and Computer Science (1995)
13. Tistarelli, M., Bicego, M., Grosso, E.: Dynamic face recognition: From human to machine vision. Image and Vision Computing 27(3), 222–232 (2009)
14. Weyrauch, B., Huang, J.: Component-based Face Recognition with 3D Morphable Models. In: Proceedings of 4th Conference on Audio- and Video-Based Biometric Person Authentication, pp. 27–34 (2003)
15. Wong, J.J., Cho, S.Y.: A local expert organization model with application to face emotion recognition. Expert Systems with Applications 36(1), 804–819 (2009)
16. Yang, P., Liu, Q., Metaxas, D.N.: Boosting encoded dynamic features for facial expression recognition. Pattern Recognition Letters 30(2), 132–139 (2009)
17. Zana, Y., Roberto, M.C.: Face recognition based on polar frequency features. ACM Transactions on Applied Perception (TAP) 3(1) (2007)
18. Zhao, W., Chellappa, R., Phillips, P.J., Rosenfeld, A.: Face recognition: A literature survey. ACM Computing Surveys (CSUR) 35(4) (2003)

Recommendation of Personalized Routes with Public Transport Connections

Bernd Ludwig, Bjørn Zenker, and Jan Schrader

Chair for Artificial Intelligence
Friedrich-Alexander-University Erlangen-Nuremberg
Haberstraße 2, D-91058 Erlangen
ludwig@cs.fau.de, bjoern.zenker@cs.fau.de, jan.schrader@cs.fau.de

Abstract. ROSE (ROuting SErvice) is an application for mobile phones, which suggests events and locations to the user and guides him to them via public transportation. Many different systems partly incorporating recommending and navigation features exist. However, no system exists which combines event recommendation and pedestrian navigation with (live) public transport support. In this paper we describe ROSE a mobile application which combines these features. Our motivation is to free the passenger from many tedious tasks, e.g. finding an interesting event and navigating to it. ROSE determines the best possible transport link and then accompanies the passenger throughout his entire journey. It reacts in real time to delays in the public transport system and calculates alternative routes when necessary. For route planning in this context, we will propose a $h_\epsilon u$-optimal algorithm for incorporating non-monotone multi dimensional user preferences in an A*-like algorithm. We also present an assignment of theoretical foundations to real world route planning problems.

1 Introduction

The development of mobile hardware has lead to a new variety of navigation systems. There are situations in which this is not the case, for example, tourists in unfamiliar cities can only use the navigation system, after they have looked up the places available to visit, e.g. a famous castle. Also city residents often do not know where to go or what to do. If they want to enjoy a jazz concert, they first have to look up when and where there is such a concert and then they have to plan the trip to it. For this, they have to use at least two different information sources: one to search for the concert and a navigation tool. In on-the-move situations this is not practical.

To ease the whole process of trip planning, we are developing ROSE which combines the recommendation of events and locations with navigation. To account for the weak hardware of mobile phones we use a client server architecture, where the ROSE server processes all data from different service providers like for example live public transport data, event and location directories or map services.

D. Tavangarian et al. (Eds.): IMC 2009, CCIS 53, pp. 97–107, 2009.

1.1 Combining Pedestrian Navigation with Event Recommendation and Live Public Transport Routing

We separated the system in three main parts:

Recommendation Part. To get a recommendation, the user enters a query, like 'eat pizza', into his mobile phone. The recommender then generates a list of suggestions based on the user input and the user preferences. In this example it would likely be a list of restaurants which sell pizza.

For recommendation we you use currently stemmed string matching, results are ranked using the Okapi BM25 measure [1].

The Okapi measure helps us normalizing documents of different length, because different event provider tend to send event descriptions of different sizes. Normally (without Okapi) the longer texts tend to score higher and shorter descriptions are getting unjustified penalized.

Route Generation Part. After the user chose one of the presented options, the system calculates a route from the current location to the selected goal. To consider a diverse set of user preferences in route generation, we propose a $h_\epsilon u$-optimal algorithm in section 2.

To ease the traveling, public transportation is also considered. The system calculates a route from the user's current position to the nearest public transport option, which means of transportation to take, where to change transportation and how to walk from the last stop to the goal location.

Navigation Part. Figure 3 shows, how the route is displayed on a map on the mobile phone. If the route includes public transport, the next possible departure time is shown and the user is informed, whether he has to hurry to catch a bus. The system also informs the user if he has to hurry to reach his goal. As map-data we are using OpenStreetMap.

All three parts can be loosely coupled: the results of the recommendation are the input (goals) of the route generation. The result of the route generation is the input (way) of the navigation service. Such a loose coupling lacks the flexibility needed in many special situations, especially when errors occur, or the user behaves in an unpredicted manner. For example, if the user misses a bus, the system has to decide what to do: wait for the next bus, take another line, or just walk. Another case occurs, when the user wants to get a recommendation for multiple events, a route which goes through these events respectively. Often, the events that match well with the user preferences are located too far away from each other. This illustrates, loose coupling of recommendation and route generation to be disadvantageous.

This is an example of the disadvantage of loose coupling of recommendation and route generation.

To address these problems, e.g. considering distance when recommending multiple events, we propose a closer coupling of recommendation, route generation and navigation. Close coupling results in a theoretical problem formulation, as it can be seen in Section 3.

1.2   Current State of the ROSE System

To address the limitations of mobile devices like limited computational power and slow and expensive Internet access, we constructed a client server-architecture. Expensive calculations are moved to the server and the transferred amount of data is minimized. The ROSE system consists of the ROSE server, a J2EE application which integrates different services from multiple service providers and offers them as web services to the ROSE client, as you can see on the left hand side in Figure 1. The connections to 3rd party data is shown on the right hand side. In the middle you can see the ROSE databases which contain preprocessed data from various providers.

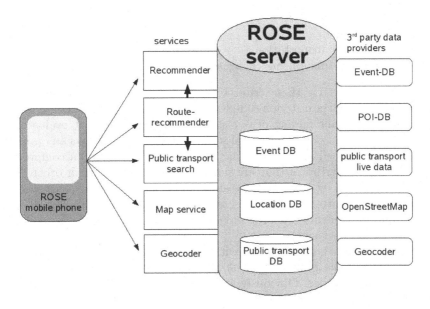

Fig. 1. Overview of the ROSE server

At the moment, we are developing two prototypes of the client, running on J2ME enabled mobile phones with GPS receiver and on Google Android.

The client sends the query over HTTP to the ROSE server. The server then gathers, based on the user's location, information from various providers, preprocesses it, and sends the result to the client. Routes, timetables, and live public transport data is obtained via VPN from a local public transport company.

On the client side, different localization services are integrated to cover a large number of devices and to allow navigation in various locations. As the start and end of a journey are often in buildings, and to support navigation also in subways a suitable indoor localization technique is needed. Therefore, we incorporate the Fraunhofer WiFi-localization module [2]. It is unique in that way as it works autonomously on the mobile terminal and does not need access to the WiFi access points. This protects user's privacy.

2   Algorithms for Comfortable Routes

Criteria for evaluating the quality of a route are limited mostly by formal constraints dictated by the algorithm used to find optimal paths. Efficient greedy graph search algorithms require the heuristic function to be monotone; A* even requires the heuristics to be optimistic, i.e. to never overestimate real costs of a path. In practice however, such constraints for heuristics are not adequate to reason about user preferences. In a survey conducted at our computer science institute among public transport users, the following criteria were marked as important by the test candidates:

- No long waiting time until departure
- Short duration of the trip
- Short foot walks
- Few changes of transportation
- No long waiting time during changes

Optimistic estimates for these criteria are just the function $f(x) = 0$; this amounts to omitting the criterion completely, which is an undesired consequence.

A second important finding of our study is that users do not evaluate the utility of a route on a one-dimensional scale (where there is always an optimum in a finite set or closed interval of utility values), but try to find a compromise between multiple attributes that are not comparable among each other. This finding is supported by investigations and studies in the field of psychology of decision making reported in [3,4,5]: Users accept locally sub-optimal proposals if they optimize the benefits of a proposal and minimize its risk globally (so-called noncompensatory decisions).

For example, somebody traveling with a lot of luggage accepts using a bus line that arrives some minutes later at the train station than the fastest one, but is much less crowded. Obviously, in this context, the comfort of the trip is valued higher than the duration. From an algorithmic point of view, this means that the standard shortest path approach cannot be applied successfully in order to satisfy the user needs as good as possible. However, searching according to a heuristic function that forces the search procedure to visit (almost) the whole search space is no attractive option for developing programs intended to run in real-time.

2.1   An $h_\epsilon u$-optimal Algorithm for Comfortable Routes

The key to an efficient solution that belongs to the same complexity class as A* and retains it's soundness and completeness is therefore to use a) a monotone heuristic function h for computing correct solutions and b) to incorporate a non-monotone, multi-attribute heuristic u for the user preferences into the search procedure.

In Fig. 2 you can see two paths from the start node s to a goal node g. g_i denotes the actual costs from s to the node which is currently being expanded, h_i the estimated costs to g according to the heuristic function h. u_i denotes the

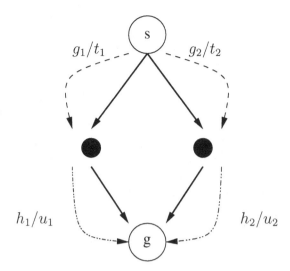

Fig. 2. $h_\epsilon u$-optimal Expansion of the Search Space

actual valuation from s to the node which is currently being expanded, t_i the estimated valuation to g according to the multi-attribute heuristic function u (user preferences).

If there is exactly one optimal successor state with $|g_1 + h_1 - g_2 - h_2| > \epsilon$, the search procedure works as usual. In the case of $|g_1 + h_1 - g_2 - h_2| \leq \epsilon$, both paths from s to g in Fig. 2 are undistinguishable in h.

In practical applications, if $|g_1 + h_1 - g_2 - h_2| \leq \epsilon$ then often other criteria become relevant for decisions in the sense of [5]. In order to explain the meaning of ϵ, let us consider the two public transport connections from s to g in Fig. 2: one takes 50 minutes, the other one 47 minutes. However, the first connection requires fewer changes of transportation than the second one. If the user dislikes changes, the first connnection is optimal according to the user preferences u under the assumption of an ϵ-tolerance $\epsilon \geq 3$ minutes.

In order to select a path that is both optimal in the sense of h given ϵ and in the sense of u, we compute the ranking $p_1 = t_1 + u_1$ and $p_2 = t_2 + u_2$ of both options. The vectors p_1 and p_2 represent all user preferences in u. Each dimension represents a single preference (cf. the list of criteria in section 2). As the preference space to which p_1 and p_2 belong is partially ordered, in general there is no unique minimal element. Therefore, we compute a pareto-optimal set which includes all paths which cannot be distinguished neither by h nor by u. The final selection of a path which is h_ϵ-optimal and u-optimal is performed by applying a decision procedure (as described in section 2.3). We call the result $h_\epsilon u$-optimal.

2.2   Approximation of the $h_\epsilon u$-Optimal Algorithm

Instead of implementing the $h_\epsilon u$-optimal algorithm directly, we simulated it's behavior by having the path search procedure compute the n-best list of solutions for a given destination. Each of these n solutions is evaluated according to the user preferences. The final set of $m < n$ solutions is the set of m routes which are $h_\epsilon u$-optimal.

In out first prototype, we implemented the n-best approach in order to obtain an evaluation platform as fast as possible. The algorithm works in two steps:

1. **Compute n best results**

   Just computing the n best routes using always the same heuristics often leads to proposals that only differ minimally among each other — in particular, if just one line serves as public transport to the destination. Therefore, it is better to compute n routes using n different (optimistic) heuristics and to compare the n resulting best routes. This observation has also been made by [6].

2. **Rank the n best lists**

   In order to get a global score for each user preference and each route, we sum up the contributions of each segment of the route to each criterion. The sum is called the rating of the route corresponding to the criterion under investigation. Finally, a total score is computed: The easiest approach to take multiple criteria into account is to compute a weighted sum of all criteria by multiplying each rating with the weight for the preference as entered by the user in the configuration dialog for the ROSE system (see Figure 1 *left*).

   A more elaborate approach is to compute a pareto-optimum for the rating of the n routes. Beyond that, it is possible in our system to apply other multi-attribute decision rules, as the *Take The Best* decision rule proposed by [7].

We have implemented the described approach in JavaME for a standard Nokia N95. Figure 1 *right* shows a screenshot for a calculated route in Nürnberg (Germany) town centre. On the average, the algorithm takes just a few seconds to compute at least five solutions for the user's request. The underlying public transportation network consists of about one hundred bus stops. There are ca. 20 bus lines, each of them departing from 5 to 10 times per hour. As a consequence, the memory consumption of the search procedure is high: the frequency of the bus lines leads to large open and close lists. To reduce the search space, we implemented a number of domain-dependent pruning strategies.

2.3   Multi-attribute Decisions

A common and often used decision rule for multi-attribute decisions is the weighted sum. As known from decision theory, weighted sums are problematic as incommensurable data is mapped onto a unique scale. For example, the duration of a trip and the amount of space in a bus available for a passenger's luggage do not have the same units. Therefore, just multiplying such values with a weight factor and adding it to some other weighted value makes it hard for the user to understand the system's decision. Anyway, it is difficult for the designer of such a system to improve the selection process by adjusting the weights, as it is impossible to state that the user always prefers one criteria over others, e.g. short waiting time is preferred over trip duration.

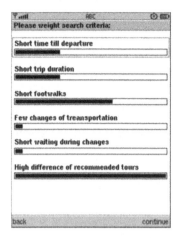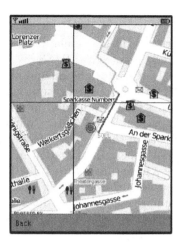

Fig. 3. *left:* Configuration Dialog, *right:* Calculated route on mobile phone (map from OpenStreetMap under CC-BY-SA)

In order to better model the way users take their decisions among several proposed routes, we implemented a module for multi-attribute decisions. Its basis is formed by a decision-oriented programming language. Figure 2 shows a code fragment for a decision in this language called MADL (Multi Attributive Decision Language). The decision named 'doWhat', using the pareto decision rule, consists of three alternatives, namely taking bus 293, waiting and taking bus 288 or walking. The goal is to minimize the three given attributes 'waiting Time', 'duration' and 'trip duration'.

The advantages of using MADL are: all decision specific information is stored in one designated place and easily understandable and adaptable by humans. It allows configuring the parameters that influence a decision and the strategy (decision rule) used to make a decision in a given situation. Furthermore, MADL allows combination and inheritance of decisions. It fosters the usage and evaluation of different decision rules, as they are already implemented and can be used out of the box.

```
ParetoDecision doWhat
{
    ALT [bus293]
    ALT [wait, bus288]
    ALT [walk]

    GOAL MIN!(waitingTime)
    GOAL MIN!(changes)
    GOAL MIN!(tripDuration)
}
```

Fig. 4. MADL decision

2.4   Comparison

Our algorithmic idea is similar to the approaches of various recommendation and navigation systems. COMPASS [8] and Magitti [9] employ different prediction strategies in recommendation and rate the yielded results based on user preferences. P-TOUR [10] uses a genetic algorithm to find different near-best solutions and presents them to the user in a k-means clustered overview, from which he can select his preferred route. RouteCheckr [11] employs a multi-criteria Dijkstra based algorithm, which remains limited to the usage of the weighted sum. As it is not using an estimation function, it does not have to cope with non-monotone and optimal criteria, but is presumably slower as an algorithm using such a heuristic. Hochmair [12] studies, which decision rules bicyclists utilize in route planning and discusses different decision rules. He concludes that a compensatory decision rule should be used, but he does not implement this concept in a new algorithm.

In contrast, PECITAS [6] is a mobile personalizable navigation system, which advices routes using means of public transportation. However, it does not include recommendation of events or locations and routes are restricted to one starting point and one destination point only. For user adaptation, PECITAS generates multiple routes by using different heuristics (e.g. fastest route, or not taking any bus) and ranks them according to user preferences (walking preferences, number of bus changes, arrival at destination, sightseeing).

Compared to these systems, the unique features of ROSE are:

- routing to multiple destinations,
- integration of recommendation and route generation with live public transport support and navigation
- usage of various compensatory decision rules.

3   Assignment to Theoretical Problems

The presentation of the ROSE system and its capabilities highlights the fact that applications such as ROSE should offer two modes of usage:

Single destination mode: The user wants to reach a single location or complete just one tasks and needs assistance in finding the appropriate location and a transportation link to it.

Multiple destination mode: The user wants to reach more then one location or complete several tasks. The locations or the respective tasks are partially ordered leading to some time constraints that have to be respected by ROSE when it recommends locations and transportation links.

In order to give an overview about the algorithmic complexity for the functionality that has to be provided by ROSE, in this section we sketch the graph theoretical problem for each (level of) functionality. The most fundamental problem finding the shortest path from one location to another is known as the shortest

Table 1. Assignment of route planning problems to theoretical problems

Route Planning Problem	Graph-Theoretical Problem	Most Efficient Algorithm
Single destination		
	Shortest Path	Dijkstra, A*
with public transport	Time-dependent shortest path (TDSP)	PFS [14] , Ding [13]
Multiple destination recommendation		
	Orienteering Problem (OP)	Fischetti, Salazar, Toth [15]
with time windows	Orienteering Problem with time windows(OPTW)	For an overview see [16]
with time windows and constrained attributes	Multi-constrained team orienteering problem with time windows (MCTOPTW)	Garcia et al. [16]
with public transport	Time-dependent orienteering problem (TDO)	Fomin, Lingas [18]
with public transport and time windows	Multi Path Orienteering Problem with Time Windows (MPOPTW)	Garcia et al. [19]

path problem and investigated in depth. It solves the problem of finding a transportation link without respecting a time table. An extension to this problem includes public transport. A theoretical definition of this problem is known as time-dependent shortest path problem (TDSP) and according algorithms can be found in [13] and [14].

A different extension is to find a best path between multiple, differently valued locations. This is known as the orienteering problem (OP) [15], which is NP-hard. Furtheron, considering opening hours of locations leads to the orienteering problem with time windows (OPTW). [16] gives an overview. This problem is extended for the tourist route recommendation context by [17] which takes multiple constrained attributes into account, e.g. a maximum price of the trip. [16] presents an iterated local search based algorithm which yields good results ('[...] below 2 seconds for problems with up to 100 locations [...]'). For our application scenario we need another extension to support public transport in route finding. As [14] shows, normal shortest path problems have little in common with public transport best path problems. [18] introduces the time-dependent orienteering problem (TDO) which adds public transport support to the OP.

By taking time windows into account, TDO is extended to the Multi Path Orienteering Problem with Time Windows (MPOPTW). [19] recently proposed an algorithm for this problem.

Table 1 shows an overview about some route planning problems, their corresponding theoretical problems and adequate algorithms.

4   Conclusion and Outlook

We introduced ROSE, a mobile system for recommending events and planning routes. For considering arbitrary user preferences when using A* like search, we developed a $h_\epsilon u$-optimal algorithm. Combined with MADL it allows easy integration of multiple criteria and different decision rules into its heuristic.

We studied mappings of different real world problems to theoretical problems and found out, that at the moment, no theoretical problem formulation for our scenario exists.

Our next steps are developing a suitable heuristic algorithm for solving the MPOPTW problem in our context and to conduct user studies to find criteria for the heuristic and more information about decision rules in the combination of recommendation and route finding.

Additionally, the impact of close and loose coupling of the recommendation and route finding services on the user satisfaction shall be researched. As we presume that the algorithmic complexity of close coupling is too big and that loose coupling is not satisfactory, we want to research, how an intermediate coupling between these extremes could be realized.

References

1. Singhal, A.: Modern information retrieval: A brief overview. Bulletin of the IEEE Computer Society Technical Committee on Data Engineering 24(4), 35–42 (2001)
2. Meyer, S., Vaupel Th. Haimerl, S.: Wi-fi coverage and propagation for localization purposes in permanently changing urban areas. International Journal of Information Technology and Web Engineering (2008)
3. Tversky, A.: Elimination by aspects: A theory of choice. Psychological Review 79, 281–299 (1972)
4. Tversky, A.: Choice by elimination. Journal of Mathematical Psychology 9, 341–367 (1972)
5. Kahneman, D., Slovic, P., Tversky, A.: Judgement under uncertainty - Heuristics and biases. Cambridge University Press, Cambridge (1981)
6. Tumas, G., Ricci, F.: Personalized mobile city transport advisory system. In: ENTER Conference 2009 (2009)
7. Gigerenzer, G., Goldstein, D.G.: Reasoning the fast and frugal way: Models of bounded rationality. Psychological Review 103, 650–669 (1996)
8. van Setten, M., Pokraev, S., Koolwaaij, J.: Context-aware recommendations in the mobile tourist application compass. In: De Bra, P.M.E., Nejdl, W. (eds.) AH 2004. LNCS, vol. 3137, pp. 235–244. Springer, Heidelberg (2004)
9. Bellotti, V., et al.: Activity-based serendipitous recommendations with the magitti mobile leisure guide. In: CHI 2008 Proceedings (2008)
10. Maruyama, A., Shibata, N., Murata, Y., Yasumoto, K.: P-tour: A personal navigation system for tourism. In: Proc. of 11th World Congress on ITS (2004)
11. Voelkel, T., W.G.: Routecheckr: personalized multicriteria routing for mobility impaired pedestrians. In: Proceedings of the 10th international ACM SIGACCESS conference on Computers and accessibility, pp. 185–192 (2008)

12. Hochmair, H.: Decision support for bicycle route planning in urban environments. In: Proceedings of the 7th AGILE Conference on Geographic Information Science. Crete University Press, Heraklion (2004)

13. Ding, B., Xu Yu, J., Qin, L.: Finding time-dependent shortest paths over large graphs. In: EDBT Proceedings (2008)

14. Huang, R.: A schedule-based pathfinding algorithm for transit networks using pattern first search. Geoinformatica, Greece 11, 269–285 (2007)

15. Fischetti, M., Salazar, J., Toth, P.: Solving the orienteering problem through branch-and-cut. Informs J. Comput. 10, 133–148 (1998)

16. Garcia, A., Vansteenwegen, P., Souffriau, W., Liniza, M.T., Arbelaitz, O.: Iterated local search applied to the multi-constrained team orienteering problem with time windows. Submitted to Computers & Industrial Engineering (to appear)

17. Vansteenwegen, P., Souffriau, W., Garcia, A.: Personalised tourist guide: Multi-constraint team orienteering problem with time windows. In: Proceedings of OR-BEL 2009, Leuven, Belgium (2009)

18. Fomin, F.V., Lingas, A.: Approximation algorithms for time-dependent orienteering, information processing letters. Information Processing Letters 83, 57–62 (2002)

19. Garcia, A., Albelaitz, A., Otaeguui, O., Vansteenwegen, O., Linaza, M.P.: Public transportation algorithm for an intelligent routing system. In: 16th ITS world congress, September 21-25, Stockholm, Sweden (to appear, 2009)

KopAL – A Mobile Orientation System for Dementia Patients

Sebastian Fudickar and Bettina Schnor

Institute of Computer Science, Potsdam University, 14482 Potsdam, Germany
{fudickar,schnor}@cs.uni-potsdam.de

Abstract. In the aging sectors of societies in the western world, dementia and its characteristics such as disorientation and obliviousness are becoming a significant problem to an increasing number of people and health systems. In order to enable such dementia patients to regain a self-determined life, we have developed a mobile orientation system with a focus on minimal operational costs and a speech based human computer interface. This system assists dementia patients in everyday problems, such as remembering appointments and staying on track within their familiar surroundings as well as informing caretakers in critical situations.

1 Introduction

Dementia manifests itself primarily in old age (particularly at age 72.3 and older), as stated at the multi-study of Clarfield A.M. et al. [2]. Normally (56.8% of the cases) dementia is caused by Alzheimers disease. Since 20.3% of the German population and 17.34% of the European population at or over age 65 in 2009 displays symptoms of dementia (CIA World fact book) [1], it is clearly becoming a severe problem in western societies.

Dementia patients suffer from disorientation even within their familiar surroundings and experience difficulty remembering appointments or people, for example. As a result, such patients lose a significant amount of self-determination because they must depend on caretakers. Further, when patients leave their familiar surroundings for an unaccompanied walk, it can lead to critical situations, including becoming lost. With our assistance system KopAL, we focus on supporting disoriented elderly people and their caretakers in an adequate speech-based manner.

One constraint determining our approach is minimal operational costs. Hence, our system is independent of central mobile network services like UMTS or GSM. Instead, we utilize the near field communication protocol IEEE 802.11 b/g WLAN [4] in a multi-hop manner. All communication (such as VoIP streams) and data management is decentralized, enabling a decentralized peer 2 peer infrastructure. As a result of the decentralized approach, our system can operate in any region, even in regions with very limited or non-existant wired or mobile communication infrastructure.

The paper is structured as follows: Section 2 gives an overview over related work. Section 3 introduces the use cases supported by KopAL. The concepts

D. Tavangarian et al. (Eds.): IMC 2009, CCIS 53, pp. 109–118, 2009.
© Springer-Verlag Berlin Heidelberg 2009

of KopAL are explained in section 4 from an architectural point of view. The article concludes with a summary and an outlook in section 5.

2   Related Work

In the research field of assisted living for dementia patients, three projects appear prominently: the Oatfield estate [14], the Fonium derButler [6] and Personalised Ambient Monitoring (PAM) [9]. In the Oatfield estate project, a (primarily wired) computing sensor infrastructure is integrated into an elderly people home. The patients are equipped with badges which frequently transmit their ID via RFID and Infrared to their surroundings, thereby localising the user. In an emergency, the badge can submit an emergency message to the system, if triggered by the patients. As a result, the mobile badges can neither react adaptively to the patients' demands nor interact with them. The mobility support of the system is also restricted, which limits the usage of the systems precise localization information. In addition, deploying the Oatfield estate system requires highly intrusive changes to the building infrastructure, since most sensors are wired. The patients' data is not processed on the patients' mobile nodes but on central computers, which increases privacy concerns. The system does not contain any mobile communication support.

The main component of the Fonium Butler is a mobile device, which includes services such as voice-based emergency calls, medication reminders, and localization. The system primarily utilizes a GSM network along with near field communication wireless transceivers. All communication between patients and caretakers occurs via the GSM network and thereby carries a monetary cost. The device is localized via GSM fingerprinting, which enables sufficient results in outdoor environments but is not appropriate for indoor localization; an inappropriate delay would occur when caretakers are warned that a patient has left their common surroundings.

The Personalised Ambient Monitoring (PAM) system is intended for people suffering from bipolar disorder. This illness is characterized by periods of depression or manic activity interspersed with stretches of normality. Some patients are able to manage this condition via their self-awareness that enables them to detect the onset of debilitating episodes and take effective action. PAM uses PDAs to collect different types of data and uses it to automatically issue alerts. PAMs monitored data types include location and activity (e.g. via GPS and accelerometers) and environment (e.g. temperature and light levels). Other types of sensors under consideration are passive IR sensors (within the home) and sound processing to log the audio "environment".

Since location based services are in the context of assisted living of gaining interest several approaches have been discussed and evaluated in literature. As shown, current approaches like GSM based fingerprinting, GPS (see for example [12]) and RFID based localization suffer from poor in-house localization precision or the necessity of large-scale installations (e.g. RFID scanners). An alternative approach is the localization via WLAN networks. The overall goal of this work is to predict the current location as precise as possible. A reliable, precise localization is simply necessary in several specific areas (critical regions) while in most areas a very coarse-grained localization is well suited.

3   KopAL Use Cases

This section summarizes the major use cases of the KopAL System, with specifications based on previous user surveys with caretakers as well as patients. Our resulting system focuses on the following scenarios:

1. Orientation assistance: When patients leave their surroundings, they are alerted and asked to request a caretaker to accompany them. If they continue walking, a caretaker is informed, including the direction (e.g. "Mr Meier is walking into the forest. To call him dial 222."). The caretaker can additionally talk directly to the patient via the devices, e.g. to ask if he or she is accompanied by friends.

2. Appointment management: Dementia patients often suffer from forgetting appointments. Even if patients remember appointments, they often loose a feeling for time and thereby miss events. The reminder of upcoming appointments thereby enables them to act in a more self-determined manner. Our system neither includes a visual representation of other participants, nor can the appointments be accessed by anyone other than the included patients and their caretakers - for privacy reasons. Upcoming appointments are read out to the patients by their mobile device. As a result, the patients can attend events on their own, which also reduces the workload of caretakers who do not have to inform all patients individually anymore. Instead they can focus on such, not coming on their own. To reduce the caretakers' workload in creating appointments, these can be created as recurring (such as meals, weekly events or birthdays) or non-recurring events (such as shopping). In addition the appointments can be generated for either individual patients or groups.

3. Emergency Service: Disoriented dementia patients tend to feel panic easily, even in common surroundings. In this case they can use an emergency button to speak to a caretaker. Since in most cases a caretaker would not be immediately present, our system includes a voice over IP (VoIP) system which enables a patient to call a caretaker by pressing the emergency button on the mobile device. The caretaker can talk with the patient and if necessary can go for assistance. Our system is furthermore applicable in emergency cases without the presence of caretakers, since we support internal calls as well as landline calls.

4   Concept of KopAL

To enable these scenarios KopAL includes several components which interact with each other. Essential parts of the KopAL system are a central server, stationary routers, mobile patient devices and mobile caretaker phones, as shown in Figure 1. Communication between the components is accomplished via WLAN channels in an ad-hoc manner. These components are described in detail below.

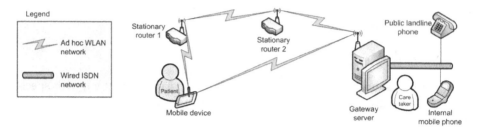

Fig. 1. The Components of KopAL

4.1   Components of KopAL

The **gateway server** acts as a gateway between the decentralized ad-hoc network of stationary routers and mobile devices and the in-house and landline telephone system, as shown in Figure 1. Additionally, it includes the web-based appointment management system.

Stationary routers act as relay stations and place marks. The stationary routers are necessary to achieve a minimum WLAN coverage of the supported area (e.g. a retirement home). This assures that the services are available in most cases. Further, the stationary routers are an essential component for the localization of the mobile devices.

The regions of our testbed, located at a nursing home belonging to LAFIM[1], are distributed as shown in Figure 2. In this installation we use five stationary routers.

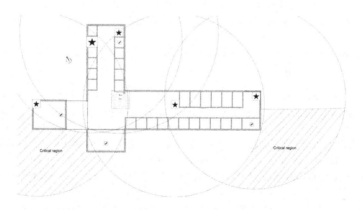

Fig. 2. The region distribution within the test bed

Two regions are critical, since the user that bypasses them could intend to leave the area. When the mobile device is localized in a critical region, the warning agent creates an adequate warning message which is rendered via the

---

[1] http://www.lafim.de

speech syntheses component. A precise description of the localization system can be found in section 4.4.

Mobile patient devices are carried by the patients and contain essential functionality, including the user interface. As a prototypical hardware platform, the Nokia N810 Internet tablet is used with the OS2008 running as operating system. The mobile devices connect with other components (each other, stationary routers, and the central server) via ad-hoc based WLAN multi-hop connections.

Mobile POTS caretaker phones: The caretakers are connected to the KopAL system via their given mobile POTS phones.

4.2 Architecture of KopAL

As shown in Figure 1, the KopAL system consists of the OLSRD, a localization component, a speech component, an appointment component, a session controller as well as the web-based manager. The cooperation of these components enable the features described in section 3. These components contain the following functionalities:

4.3 The OLSRD Component

The **OLSRD component** contains an implementation of the Open Link State Routing protocol (OLSR) [3], which is a proactive routing protocol for mobile multi-hop ad-hoc networks, and thereby is the essential component for routing

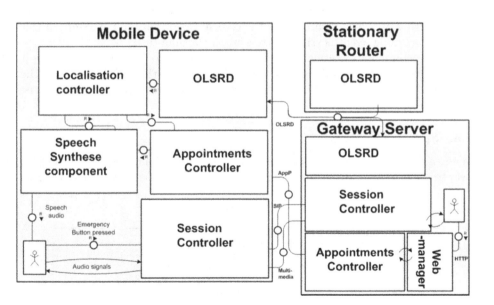

Fig. 3. The Architecture of KopAL

messages among the participating devices. All nodes can can calculate the topology of the network based on frequently generated Hello and Topology-Control (TC) messages. Based on the topology, each node decides which neighboring node is the appropriate next receiver when forwarding a package. Multi point Relays (MPRs) forward collections of TC messages and thereby reduce the message load during the topology calculation.

We extended the functionality of OLSRD with a Plug in that supports the KopAL system with condensed topology information (IP addresses, hop distance and quality values of all nodes) which is utilized by the localization controller as the basis for localizing of the mobile devices.

4.4   Localization Component

Localization is done using a **zone-based approach**. The **localization component** contains a representation model of the area in which the mobile device is deployed: the so-called **area table**. This is shown in a simplified manner in table 1. The area table is set up manually on system deployment, based on the position of the stationary routers and the measurement of their connectivity topology. By accessing the topology data of the OLSRD component, the topology manager can localize the mobile device within a region of the area.

The orientation system is based on an aggregation of the OLSRD component and the localization component and is placed within the mobile devices. To calculate the current position, a list of currently available stationary routers in one hop distance from the processing mobile device is requested from the OLSRD component. This list is combined with the representation model of the area table to calculate the specific area, in which the device currently is localized. The resulting area is compared with the critical regions in the next step. In this case, the warning agent is triggered to start a warning task.

If an upcoming appointment description contains information about where it is to take place, this is compared to the current area of the mobile device. If the mobile device is not yet within the area, the appointment is just read out by the mobile device.

4.5   Speech Component

When a message is to be read out on a mobile device, the message text is handed over to the **speech controller**, where it is queued. The speech controller triggers

Table 1. Area table of LAFIM

Region number	Name	IP Addresses
Region 1:	Critical forest region	192.168.2.22
Region 2:	Critical road region	192.168.2.66
Region 3:	Center Region	192.168.2.22, 192.168.2.33, 192.168.2.44, 192.168.2.55
Region 4:	North east region	192.168.2.44, 192.168.2.55 (either 192.168.2.33 or 192.168.2.66)

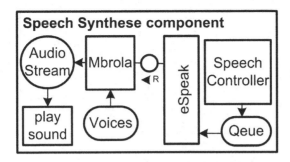

Fig. 4. The KopAL Speech Controller

the MBROLA speech synthesis framework [10] via the eSpeak library [5] to render a voice audio stream with the given message text. Since the MBROLA speech synthesis framework was not available as ARM compatible binaries, we ported them to the ARM hardware architecture. The resulting MBROLA ARM binaries are available via [11].

4.6 Appointment Controller

The appointments controller handles the decentralized, peer-to-peer-like distribution of appointments between devices and initiates the deployment of upcoming appointments on the mobile devices.

Appointments can be created or edited via a web front-end on the central gateway server by authorized users. The changes are then transferred hop by hop through all devices within the system.

A caretaker can set up the following parameters for a patient (hereafter referred to as "user"):

- The internal user name (e.g. FMeier@depah.net)
- The real name of the user (e.g. Mr Frank Meier)
- The number of his room (e.g. 121)
- The internal call number (e.g.1211)
- The department number (e.g. floor 1)

If the caretaker creates a new appointment, s/he can set the following parameters:

- S/he can either select an individual patient, or all users of a department.
- S/he can set the frequency of the appointment (once, weekly, several days of each week, monthly, yearly), the time the event begins and the validity time of the event (begin and end dates).
- The description text of the event.
- The place/zone of the event (optional).

All appointments are stored primarily in the **appointment database** on the gateway server. In case an appointment is edited, its version ID is incremented to keep track of whether the information is up to date.

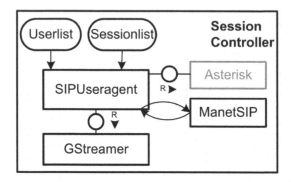

Fig. 5. The KopAL Session Controller

Each appointment controller contains an **Update Node List** of other devices which have updated their appointments within a given time period. When a mobile device which has not been recently updated enters the range of the gateway server, both update managers compare their current representation of the appointments. This comparison only includes appointments that occur within the next 14 days, due to the memory restrictions of the mobile devices. As a result, the mobile devices contain a limited view of all future appointments. If a discrepancy between the two representations exists, the edited or missing appointments are updated to the mobile device. In any case both devices update their local Update Node Lists with each other's IP addresses.

If two mobile devices whose IP addresses are no longer contained in each Update Node List come within direct communication range, their update managers compare their appointment representations with each other. In case a discrepancy exists, the appointments are updated. If an appointment exists on both devices but with different version IDs, the device with the lower version ID updates the appointment with the newer one. This mechanism assures that even devices which do not enter the range of the gateway server have an up to date representation of appointments.

In our approach, the devices must additionally contain the appointments for other users, since they are updated in a peer-to-peer manner.

The appointment manager regularly scans the appointment list for upcoming appointments (in our current implementation every 20 minutes). If an appointment takes place within this time period, the appointment is read out by the speech synthesis component if the mobile device is not already in the designated area.

4.7   Session Controller

An emergency call is initiated by pressing the emergency button, whereupon the **session controller** initializes a SIP [13] based session with the gateway server. For SIP user registration and session initialization, we utilize ManetSIP [7], a decentralized implementation of the SIP registrar, location and proxy service.

The appropriate phone number for the emergency call is determined within the gateway server and a POTS phone call is triggered via an Asterisk service. If the session was able to be established, a bidirectional voice communication between the mobile device and the gateway service is setup with GStreamer[8].

5   Summary and Outlook

In this paper we have presented KopAL, a mobile orientation system for dementia patients. KopAL enables dementia patients to achieve a higher degree of self-determined living by reminding them of appointments and offering them opportunities to protect them from or assist them in critical situations. To this end, KopAL contains VoIP communication channels for emergencies, voice based read-out of upcoming appointments and an orientation system that informs patients and caretakers when a patients leave their familiar surroundings.

We have set up a first test field in cooperation with a nursing home of the LAFIM organization and are currently evaluating the system. The evaluation is assisted by surveys.

We are currently integrating security aspects into KopAL. These include user authentication for appointment management and SIP based session establishment as well as the encryption of critical content streams (e.g. appointment update). A further focus lies on increasing speech quality, considering both speech synthesis and the VoIP media streams. In the latter, we are attempting to improve quality by reducing jitter and delay. The deployment in other areas implies a manual setup of the stationary routers and the resulting mapping table, as well as creating the set of patients and their appointments.

Acknowledgements

We would like to thank LAFIM, Florencehort, a nursing home, for its cooperation and for providing us with an ideal test ground. Further, we want to thank Prof. Dr. Neyer and his group from the Department of Psychology at the University of Potsdam for accompanying the KopAL project, especially in helping us to improve the usability of KopAL.

References

1. CIA World fact book,
   https://www.cia.gov/library/publications/the-world-factbook/
   (June 2009)
2. Clarfield, A.M.: The reversible dementias: do they reverse? Annals of Internal Medicine 109(6), 476–486 (1988)
3. Clausen, T., Jacquet, P.: Optimized link state routing protocol (olsr) (October 2003)
4. IEEE Project 802 LAN/MAN Standards Committee. IEEE std 802.11g-2003 further higher data rate extension in the 2.4 ghz band (2003)

5. Espeak, `http://espeak.sourceforge.net/` (June 2009)
6. Fonium GmbH, `http://www.fonium.de/`, `http://www.fonium.de/` (June 2009)
7. Fudickar, S., Rebensburg, K., Schnor, B.: Manetsip - a dependable sip overlay network for manet including presentity service, 2009. In: Proceedings of the Fifth International Conference on Networking and Services, ICNS, pp. 314–319 (April 2009)
8. GStreamer, `http://www.gstreamer.net/` (June 2009)
9. James, C.J., Crowe, J., Magill, E., Brailsford, S.C., Amor, J., Prociow, P., Blum, J., Mohiuddin, S.: Personalised ambient monitoring (pam) of the mentally ill. In: Proceedings of the 4th European Conference of the International Federation for Medical and Biological Engineering, pp. 1010–1013. Springer, Heidelberg (2008)
10. Mbrola, `http://tcts.fpms.ac.be/synthesis/mbrola.html` (June 2009)
11. Mbrola - Arm distribution, `http://www.depah.net/mbrolaarm` (June 2009)
12. Mundt, T.: Location dependent digital rights management computers and communications. In: Proc. of 10th IEEE Symposium on Computers and Communications, pp. 617–622. IEEE Press, Los Alamitos (2005)
13. Rosenberg, J., Schulzrinne, H., Camarillo, H., Johnston, A., Peterson, J., Sparks, R., Handley, M., Schooler, E.: Sip: Session initiation protocol (June 2002)
14. Stanford, V.: Using pervasive computing to deliver elder care. IEEE Pervasive Computing 1(1), 10–13 (2002)

Smart Home Challenges and Approaches to Solve Them: A Practical Industrial Perspective

Roland Eckl and Asa MacWilliams

Siemens AG, Corporate Technology, Software Architecture,
Otto-Hahn-Ring 6, 81739 Munich, Germany
{Eckl.Roland,Asa.MacWilliams}@Siemens.com

Abstract. Why are smart homes not successfully deployed on the market, even though there are many demonstrator systems in research and industry? Over the past years, we have built and improved one smart home platform ourselves and have been involved with many other comparable systems. In this paper, we share the problems we have come across, and present pragmatic approaches towards solving them.

Current smart homes tend to be too simplistic (limited in their application) or too complex (too hard to use or build or maintain). Many research-oriented systems disregard users' intent and make decisions for them, trying to "know better." Also, current systems require too high up-front investment in technology from owners, manufacturers and possible operators.

We suggest using a system architecture with centralized but subsidiary controllers, with open interfaces at software and network levels. Interaction should be based on different types of highly responsive control devices. Besides traditional interaction such as turning on lights, they should let the user select complex scenes, with unobtrusive assistance (prioritizing the presentation of scenes according to context).

We foresee the greatest chance for commercial success if market players work together to create the most valuable applications for end users, but keep their systems open for extension.

Keywords: Smart Homes, Pervasive Computing, Software Architecture.

1 Introduction

With the ever-increasing number of smart home demonstrators in research and industry, we would expect a greater market penetration of smart home technology. However, adoption of smart homes – by consumers and by manufacturers – has remained slow over the last years. Why is this so? In this paper, we analyze several of the problems that we believe make it hard to build successful smart homes, and suggest several possible solutions from our practical industrial perspective.

D. Tavangarian et al. (Eds.): IMC 2009, CCIS 53, pp. 119–130, 2009.

1.1 Our Background

As a corporate R&D group specializing in software architectures for pervasive computing, we have been involved in several real-world smart home installations and public-private research partnerships. One example is *ePerSpace* [1], a project funded by the European Union, which developed a highly extensible network-oriented service architecture to deliver multimedia smart home services to the residential and to the mobile user. Another is the *T-Com House* [2], a collaboration with Deutsche Telekom which involved building and equipping a single-family house in Berlin, which was occupied by test families for a year and half. At the same time, we have maintained two smart home integration laboratories at our Munich and Beijing research sites. From one project to another, we have re-used technologies and maintained hardware and software platforms for smart home devices. These projects gave us many insights and helpful feedback on user needs and technical stumbling blocks in such a complex evolving system.

2 State of the Art: Current Challenges

As we see it, current smart homes fall into three categories, each with its specific challenges (see Figure 1). On the one hand, there are optimized special-purpose niches. These are often *too simplistic* to be widely adopted in market. On the other hand, there are large platforms, which could support many different applications – but those are *too complex* – too hard to use, install or maintain. (We plead guilty to having designed

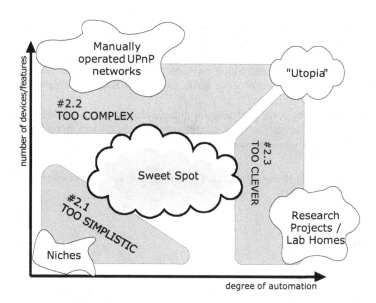

Fig. 1. Landscape of smart home solutions. Most current systems are too simplistic, too complex, or too clever, as described in sections 2.1-2.3

such systems ourselves.) As a third class, there are many research-oriented systems that disregard users' intent and make decisions for them, trying to "know better". These systems are *too clever* and fail to gain the user's trust. We believe that any system that tried to fully integrate all possible devices in a fully automatic fashion (labelled *Utopia* in the figure), would be *both* too complex and too clever for real use. Somewhere between all these mentioned systems lies a *sweet spot* – systems that users will actually find useful.

Almost all systems require *too high up-front investment costs* in technology from owners, manufacturers and operators. We will examine these challenges one by one.

2.1 Too Simplistic: Limited Application Scope

Especially many of the industrial smart home projects are too limited in their scope and serve specialized niches. For example, the serve@Home [3] system offered a powerful, commercially available remote control and monitoring solution for home appliances (refrigerators, dishwashers, ovens, washing machines). However, extending this system to other crafts (e.g. lighting, entertainment) was not part of any commercially available package. serve@Home was discontinued after several years.

Another class of smart home research projects focuses on optimal user interaction or algorithms of behaviour inference. Results are often very promising. Regarding wider dissemination, the tone is, "we demonstrated this on basis of these selected devices. It could easily be extended to any other." This sounds good in theory, but proves very difficult in practice.

Why are the results of these projects hard to transfer into large-scale real-world adoption? One problem is that they often assemble various devices and sensors into complex but inseparable units – extending the devices or replacing parts is difficult. Will prediction algorithms for adaptive environments, such as the MavHome [4], still work properly, or do they require some additional calibration or learning phase? Another is that they chose communication media and protocols that are optimal for a specific application or class of devices (e.g. Powerline for serve@Home), but then aren't extensible to others (e.g. Powerline for mobile devices).

2.2 Too Complex: Too Hard to Use, Build or Maintain

The second class of smart home research projects comes from the area of large distributed systems, e.g. hosted by network operators. One example is ePerSpace, which we participated in ourselves. These systems, as we are well aware, are often too general to be of real practical use. The tone is, "our system is so extensible that we will be able to integrate any kind of application in the future. Just describe these 250 parameters in XML." This leads to systems that are, for any specific application, too hard to use, to build or to maintain – so far such systems remained in Utopia or restricted themselves to a limited scope as described above.

Too Hard to Use
The key challenge to consumer acceptance (besides price) is usability. An interface has to be as simple as the classic light switch, but of course more powerful. Within an

extendible system the connected user interface can quickly become inherently complex, especially if the user should be able to control everything.

We have developed interfaces for full control (e.g. on a PDA or smart phone), and many users were intimidated. Some of our other approaches concealed parts of the complexity and were more popular with lab visitors.

An example where specifically tailored solutions can have higher usability than general ones is multimedia control. Multi-room media streaming solutions, e.g. from Sonos, Philips, or Apple, are optimized for their purpose, although they cannot control other devices such as lights.

One key factor for usability is responsiveness. Commands must have immediate effects, and immediate feedback on the interaction device. System architectures that involve several layers of marshalling, converting and dispatching events in a distributed network are at a challenge here (we built one of those).

Too Hard to Build

The more device types are included and the more a system is capable of, the more heavyweight it will become. The architecture of such a generic system becomes increasingly difficult for developers, making systems hard to build. Also, such generic systems consume more resources (production cost, electricity) than specialized ones. For example, adding even a simple service (a TV program guide) to the ePerSpace service management platform required hundreds of lines of hand-written XML.

Sometimes these hurdles are sourced out to gateways and bridges, which reduce complexity to a common denominator, in most cases according to protocol or service type. But systems that abstract all their devices in this fashion only defer problems to the gateways; they do not solve them.

The KNX electrical installation standard [5] is successful in commercial buildings, but not yet so in residential markets. Besides the price of the devices, commissioning costs are an issue. Programming KNX devices (which can be programmed to do almost anything) requires an expensive software tool, ETS, and a professional training in how to use it. Not many professional electrical installers are trained yet.

Too Hard to Maintain

The more complex a system is, the harder is it to maintain. In the KNX example, ETS is good for protecting the market share of trained electrical installers, but bad for end users who want to reconfigure their smart home themselves. These users would go for a system such as Peha Easyclick [6], which is less powerful, but more easily configured. Or for a media system based on DLNA [7], which does not leave much space for frustrating configuration, but is restricted to its specific field of application.

2.3 Too Clever: Trying to Know Better Than the User

Many research systems address the issue of inferring the user's intent and attempt to control devices accordingly, by use of sensors, rules, and learning techniques. As an example, the Neural Network House [8] claims to essentially *program itself*. This is done by observing the inhabitants and anticipating and accommodating their needs. Discomfort has to be expressed by overriding the environment's choice.

If such a system achieves 100% accuracy, it's wonderful. But when it doesn't (and no system does), users want to know why it is acting the way it is. This can be further complicated by conflicting strategies, e.g. saving energy and meeting the users' intention. "Smart" is fine for users, but "haunted" is not. In our experience, trying to infer the user's intent just leads to frustrated users. This effect has been observed before in other application domains, such as with Microsoft's Office Assistant [9].

Some problems do not occur until the experimental system leaves the lab. Most prediction systems are limited to a single domain. Others suffer from different calibration techniques and potential error rates. It is hard enough to transform original data from different research groups to a common basis – and this gets worse when data comes from different types of devices. Most researchers use only identical devices when testing their systems, neglecting real-world heterogeneous systems. But the less reliable and comparable a prediction system, the worse the result is, which leads to poor user experience. Thus, most users face prediction systems very critically.

2.4   High Up-Front Investment Costs

Users, manufacturers and operators want value for their money from smart home systems, and they want it quickly. But currently, up-front investments are prohibitive.

There are several cases of companies discontinuing their smart home activities. serve@Home was described above. More recently, in May 2009, Nokia discontinued its own smart home activities and licensed the previously developed Home Control Center technology to *There Corporation* [10].

Although reasons for these product discontinuations are rarely given, we suspect the high up-front investment costs for the companies as the root cause.

Investing in a System Architecture

For a system to be successful (not too simplistic), it has to be extensible. But up-front investment in system architecture for this and creating standards is expensive. Companies (both manufacturers and operators) will shy away from this investment until their own prospective market share is promising enough. But business models are still unclear at the moment, and these determine how a system has to be designed with regard to its extensibility and its ability to integrate further crafts or services.

Architectures differ according to who may extend a smart home's capability; the user, an operator, both or others? This covers considerations about frameworks such as OSGi [11] for dynamic service handling at a central point, or restricting the integration of new devices to those being controlled through a single communication path, e.g. per UPnP. Creating a flexible system that offers a good mixture of everything, or even allows cutting out only the components that are required for a given use case, is incredibly challenging.

Investing in a System

Consumers currently have to pay a very high price in adding smart home technology to their new homes. Unfortunately, this applies to new buildings and retrofit solutions, and to homeowners as well as tenants. New homeowners are often short on money, and will not want to increase the size of their mortgage. Existing homeowners will shy away from the effort of retrofitting wiring in the home. Tenants do not wish to invest in an apartment that does not belong to them. Thus, the technical solutions must make it easier for each of these groups of residents to invest in smart home technology (e.g. using easy-to-install wireless devices).

3 Approaches

Not claiming to have found the universal answer to all questions, we believe that the following six approaches can relieve of some of the above challenges. Of the six approaches, three affect the system architecture, two affect usability, and the final approach concerns business models.

As a running example to illustrate these approaches, we describe our current demonstration system installed in our labs in Munich and Beijing – either as it is, or as we now know it should be.

3.1 System Architecture with Centralized but Subsidiary Controllers

Whether to use a centralized architecture or one with distributed peer-to-peer controllers has been a matter of much debate in the past. Commercial systems often use a central *home server* or *home gateway* which controls all devices. Examples are Gira HomeServer [12] or the ePerSpace home gateway [1]. The advantage of a central server is that it provides a single point for implementing integrative applications.

Several research systems have suggested implementations based on peer-to-peer controllers, e.g. [13]. In principle, such systems can be more robust, since there is no single point of failure. In practice, manageability is a serious issue.

Our approach follows standard practice in building automation: the automation pyramid. A central home gateway or server runs a software platform for its applications, exposes wired and wireless IP network interfaces, and provides the central integration point. In our lab system, this is based on OSGi technology. Powerful devices supporting IP networking can be connected to it directly. In our case, this includes UPnP media servers and user interface clients. Other devices, i.e. ones that do not support IP networking, require a bridge or subsidiary controller. For example, in our lab installations, lighting and blinds control are automated by KNX, and a KNX/IP interface provides the necessary physical network translation between the wired KNX and wired Ethernet interfaces. The home gateway runs a software module that handles the KNX communication at IP level and exposes its functionality to the rest of the software platform.

In practice, many functions will not require intervention of the home gateway. For example, switching on light using a KNX switch is handled entirely on the KNX twisted-pair bus. The home gateway only observes the KNX actions for monitoring purposes, in order to keep its internal representation of devices' status up to date.

This principle of *subsidiarity* keeps the system simple. Our design rule is to use the simplest technology that will perform the task and allow further integration.

Of course, this principle applies to other technologies as well – DALI lighting automation, ZigBee wireless sensor nodes or LON devices. In each case, a subsidiary controller and network bridge is required, as well as an appropriate driver module for the home gateway.

For special-purpose markets, a home gateway (or a home server without additional networking functionality) can be built including hardware interfaces for KNX, DALI, ZigBee, etc. Since there are so many competing bus technologies on the market, this will only pay off once the installed base reaches a critical size.

The advantage of running controlling software on a central gateway is that it is always on and connected to the home IP network as well as the internet. This allows attractive business models for telecom operators. However, for business models that should be independent of telecom providers, the central software can run on any other embedded device in the home that is always on and connected to the home network.

The central home gateway and its connected devices are shown in Figure 2.

3.2 Open Interfaces at Software and Network Levels

No single manufacturer will be able to supply all components of a complete smart home system. Thus, interoperability is of the essence to succeed on the market. We suggest that interoperability be standardized at three different levels of interfaces. One is a software API level on the home gateway. The other two are network levels between devices. All of these are based on open standards, of which there are many in the smart home arena. A forthcoming ISO specification document [14] shows a taxonomy of standards in the smart home domain.

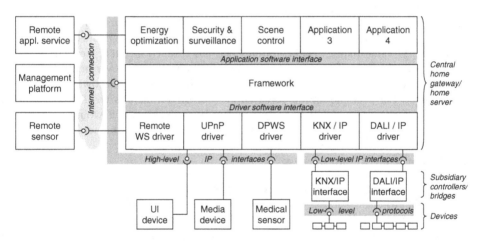

Fig. 2. Proposed smart home software and system architecture with example devices, drivers and applications. The different types of interfaces are shown in gray.

Software Interfaces: Application and Driver Interfaces

For APIs on the home gateway, we suggest standards based on a commonly accepted component platform such as OSGi or .NET. The software interfaces must cover at least two layers, shown in gray in Figure 2: an application interface, and a interface supporting different types of drivers. In our demonstration systems, we have created a family of OSGi-based *smart home* interfaces. Other research groups have done the same thing. Vendors such as Prosyst [15] have started creating their own implementations. Domain-specific standardization, e.g. within the OSGi Alliance, is required here.

High-Level Network Protocols Based on IP

Between devices, network-level integration standards are required. For the most general compatibility, these should be based on IP.

In our demonstration system, we use the UPnP family of standards (including DLNA extensions), which have become state of the art in industry and in the consumer market. Thus, the user (or technician) can easily add new crafts, as long as they support UPnP. Other emerging, sometimes competing standards here are DPWS (Device Profile for Web Services) or IGRS (Intelligent Grouping and Resource Sharing). In practice, a home gateway may well need to support several of these.

Subsidiary Control Networks: Low-Level Bus and Low-Level IP Protocols

Addressing each light in a house directly is prohibitively expensive, and raises scalability issues. Thus, subsidiary control networks, e.g. DALI for lighting, are still required, and as described above, different industry standards exist for low-level protocols. Device manufacturers should adhere to these, and they should be extended, where necessary, to allow better control and monitoring by central controllers. To connect subsidiary networks to the gateway, a bridge or controller must expose this protocol at least partially as IP. Some protocols, e.g. KNX, already support mappings to IP. These are generally distinct from the high-level IP protocols such as UPnP.

Better Inter-Standard Harmonization Needed

Unfortunately, different standards are governed by different internation bodies with different members and interests. Work between the standardization bodies, e.g. UPnP Forum and OSGi Alliance, has been done, and has resulted in interoperability standards such as the OSGi UPnP base driver specification [16]. However, more work is required here, since such inter-standard standards often end up as a lowest common denominator. For example, in the OSGi UPnP base driver, there is no standard "language mapping" between UPnP actions and Java methods, which would be fairly simple and could greatly improve the standard's usability for programmers.

3.3 Optimize for Responsiveness

Users want immediate response from devices in their homes; they're used to it from simple light switches. Turning on all lights in a house, for example, should be instantaneous. (For effect, dimming them on simultaneously might be even more pleasant, but reaction to user commands should still be instantaneous.)

Therefore, when choosing implementation technologies, one should optimize towards responsiveness. This means using lightweight technologies where possible; re-marshalling method calls from one XML format to another is likely to cause unnecessary delays, especially when operating on an embedded system. Commands should be sent concurrently instead of sequentially, if the target device or bus allows this. Even waiting for acknowledgments should be considered carefully.

For event handling, it means avoiding chattiness and optimizing for event bursts. In this context, event handling (e.g. from environmental sensors) is harder than one might think. On average, eventing is rather infrequent. But when the environment is modified, multiple devices have to be controlled, and this leads to a cumulative firing of events. For simple events (as they occur for example on the KNX bus) this may be easy to deal with. But for a real smart home, event types are more complex, carrying more detailed content. Batched events are beneficial here, that are sent to subscribed parties only. These should be compacted and allow parsing only details of interest.

An open question is the missing standard for such an eventing system. The eventing model of UPnP, as we have discovered ourselves, does not scale beyond several dozen devices. Thus, turning on 30 UPnP binary lights simultaneously was prohibitively slow in one of our demonstration systems and forced us to use non-standard UPnP device profiles. One interesting option would be a "smart home profile" or "industrial profile" for UPnP or DPWS, which would be backward-compatible, but specialized for scalability, just as DLNA is for multimedia purposes.

3.4 Interaction Principle: Intentionally Invoked Scenes, Prioritized by Context

In the effort to make increasing complexity manageable without trying to know better than the user, we chose the following control principle. We bundled all control possibilities into *scenes* according to recurring activities and typical environmental states. The user can manually invoke scenes ("dinner", "relax", etc.). Of course, in practice, a list of scenes can become very long. To make selection easier, we use prediction of what scenes will most likely be used next. This produces a weighting for all scenes, allowing the system to display only a clearly arranged number of scenes, emphasized in style to express the assumed probability.

In contrast to systems that act autonomously and assuming a user's intervention as training data only [8], we propose that the user makes a conscious choice. This may be simplified to an acknowledgment which starts the most probable scene, e.g. through a gesture. This follows the recommendation in [17].

Our concept also leaves room to fine-tune several elements of a scene through special devices. There can be knobs used to influence music's beat, or digital photo frames presenting photos according to tags placed on some kind of pinboard. This usually affects devices that would tend to become boring when simply replaying statically programmed properties any time a scene starts.

Our guiding mental model was that of polite butler. "May I serve the tea, or would you like the evening paper?" – "Tea please, James. But today I'd prefer green tea."

An open question remains: how to program these scenes easily? For the end user, we designed a *snapshot system* that can save devices' current state as a scene. More powerful programming, with sequences of control commands and conditional behaviour, require more complex tools. As few users want to program complex scenes themselves, a business model for technical support or remote service is needed.

3.5 Separate Control Devices with Differing Richness and Modalities According to Situation and User Expertise

The optimal interaction device for a smart home is a matter of much debate. One approach is the universal remote control, offered by several companies. Logitech offers remote controls with infrared and Z-Wave interfaces. Universal Electronics' Nevo series has additional Wi-Fi networking. Another approach is the set-top box or media PC as user interface, e.g. Microsoft's Media Center.

We contend that there is no such one-fits-all interaction device for smart homes; instead, users should be able to operate the home through various very distinct interfaces. This includes tangible devices (e.g. wall buttons, switches), gesture and voice control, small displays (e.g. integrated 1-line display on a refrigerator), mobile rich clients (universal remotes, smart phones) and integration into set-top-boxes and media PCs. The system should be able to interoperate with all control device classes, covering units for the different target group. The devices differ in modalities and richness, and with different devices, different sets of functionalities can be supported.

In our Lab system, we discovered that elderly people prefer to have only concrete and straightforward interfaces; interfaces with big display and keys but only a small choice of selection and a very few hierarchies are good candidates here. Seniors also liked speech control. On the other hand, technically affine people (especially the younger generation) favour the possibility of rich options, as long as they can also make simple and quick adjustments.

We developed interfaces for full control (e.g. on a PDA), and all but the most technical users were intimidated. We then developed other approaches with fewer options, but less complexity, optimized for use with the scene control system (see Figure 3) described in the previous section. These were more popular with lab visitors. This simplification is a two-edged sword – you must hide enough complexity without trying to know better than the user.

An open question remains: how to ensure consistent look and feel across such a range of devices?

Fig. 3. Scene cloud and display-enriched switch as different user interfaces for scene control in a smart home environment. The most probable next scene, *Lunch*, is highlighted.

3.6 Business Models: User Value and Extensibility

Beyond technical issues, getting the business model right has proven very difficult for smart homes. Different models have been tried – retail market, hosted operations, custom-built luxury homes, and various others. Perhaps the most advanced are emerging luxury markets with much new building construction. One example is Dubai, where integrators such as Smart Home UAE [18] offer custom solutions to the housing industry and to individual investors. However, regional markets such as Europe and the USA are very different, both regarding customer willingness to invest in different applications, and the relative value of new construction vs. retrofit solutions.

The only promising approach we see here is to focus on applications with concrete added value for the user, but to keep the systems open for extension. For example, one market study [19] shows that within Europe, end users show the highest willingness to invest in energy-saving and security solutions, as opposed to comfort systems. Thus, the key to market success is to offer a system for saving energy or an integrated security system, but to design this so that it uses the open standards described in Section 3.2. Then, once the system is installed, users will have the option of adding on additional applications such as for comfort or home healthcare.

Many new applications will require new collaborations between different market players. For example, smart metering and energy-saving solutions are currently bringing previously unrelated market players together, such as Google and electrical utility companies [20].

4 Conclusion

In smart homes, as everywhere else, there is no such thing as a perfect solution. However, we believe that smart homes are possible for the mass market in the near future, if a significant number of players in the market and in research act together, following the recommendations Section 3, and create valuable applications for end users while keeping their systems open for extension.

This cooperation of disciplines and of industry and academia is vital for success. On the industrial side, the lead role could be taken by one global player, but more likely, by a small consortium which can supply the home equipment, the back-end management infrastructure, and the services (e.g. security) adding value for the user. If, and only if, the system is kept open for extension, this can lead to widespread adoption and commercial success, with many other parties contributing device extensions or future services.

References

1. ePerSpace (Towards the era of personal services at home and everywhere). Integrated Project under the EU 6th Framework Programme (2006),
   http://www.ist-eperspace.org/
2. Pictures of the Future. T-Com House: At Home in the Future. In: PoF Fall 2005, Siemens AG (2005), http://www.siemens.com/pof
3. serve@Home Product Brochure. Siemens Electrogeräte GmbH, Munich (2006)
4. Cook, D.J., Youngblood, M., Heierman, E.O., Gopalratnam III, K., Rao, S., Litvin, A., Khawaja, F.: MavHome: An Agent-based Smart Home. In: PerCom 2003. LNCS, pp. 521–524. Springer, Heidelberg (2003)
5. ISO/IEC 14543-3. Konnex Association, Standard (2007),
   http://www.knx.org/knx-standard/
6. PEHA EasyClick: Electrical installations without miles of wiring,
   http://www.peha-elektro.com/Easyclick.aspx
7. Digital Living Network Alliance (DLNA), http://www.dlna.org/

8. Mozer, M.C.: The Neural Network House: An Environment that Adapts to its Inhabitants. In: Proceedings of the American Association for Artificial Intelligence Spring Symposium on Intelligent Environments, pp. 110–114. AAAI Press, Menlo Park (1998)

9. Bickmore, T.W., Picard, R.W.: Establishing and maintaining long-term human-computer relationships. ACM Transactions on Computer-Human Interaction (TOCHI) 12(2), 293–327 (2009)

10. There Corporation. Press Report from, May 29 (2009),
    http://www.therecorporation.com/,
    http://www.smarthomepartnering.com/cms/?p=100

11. OSGi Alliance. Specifications,
    http://www.osgi.org/, http://www.osgi.org/Specifications

12. Gira HomeServer3, Gira FacilityServer: Intelligent building management via KNX/EIB and TCP/IP. Order no. 1887 90 08/08 5. 16. Giersiepen GmbH & Co. KG, Duisburg (2008), http://download.gira.com/data2/1887900508.pdf

13. Turcan, E., Graham, R.L., Hederen, J.: Peering the smart homes. In: Proceedings of First International Conference on Peer-to-Peer Computing, 2001, pp. 103–104 (2001)

14. ISO/IEC PDTR 29107-1: Information technology, Intelligent homes, Taxonomy of specifications – Part 1: The taxonomy method. ISO/IEC JTC 1/SC 25 N 1652, Working document (2009)

15. Prosyst mBS Smart Home Extension. Prosyst Software (2009),
    http://www.prosyst.com/products/osgi_ext_smart.html

16. OSGi UPnP Device Service Specification, OSGi R4, Version 4.1. Service Compendium 111, pp. 253–280 (2007)

17. Intille, S.S.: Designing a Home of the Future. IEEE Pervasive Computing 1(2), 76–82 (2002)

18. Smart Home Automation Control, Digitcom Technology, Dubai, UAE,
    http://www.smarthomeuae.com/

19. Szuppa, S.: Marktforschung für komplexe Systeme aus Sach- und Dienstleistungen im Privatkundenbereich. Entwicklung und Überprüfung eines Vorgehenskonzeptes am Beispiel des Intelligenten Hauses. Ph. D. thesis, Verlag Dr. Kovac, Hamburg (2007)

20. Google Power Meter, http://www.google.org/powermeter/

A Generic Framework for Using Interactive Visualization on Mobile Devices

Marcus Hoffmann and Jörn Kohlhammer

Fraunhofer-Institut für Graphische Datenverarbeitung (IGD)
Fraunhoferstr. 5, 64283 Darmstadt, Germany
{marcus.hoffmann,joern.kohlhammer}@igd.fraunhofer.de
http://www.igd.fraunhofer.de

Abstract. The latest mobile devices are capable of displaying graphical content on larger screens and by increased CPU power offer possibilities for new interesting system approaches and technologies especially in the field of 3D visualization. This paper presents a generic framework for remote visualization on such devices. The presented framework focuses on increased portability and flexibility that goes beyond the results of previous work in this research area. On the server side, existing visualization applications can easily be integrated with and connected to mobile devices. On the client side, the utilization of current standard technologies assures a high portability over a variety of different mobile operating systems and devices.

1 Introduction

Driven by the growing mobility of the work force and ubiquitous data access, one focus of visualization these days is on mobile devices. The goal is to support the use of known visualization techniques interactively and in the same quality as on non-mobile devices. The main challenge in mobile computing is the limitation of mobile hardware resources. However, at the same time, data transfer rates have grown in recent years. It is now possible to establish affordable peer-to-peer data connections between mobile and non-mobile devices. Looking further into the future, we expect the use and acceptance of streaming data to mobile devices to grow in the coming years. Terminal server applications and proprietary remote visualization solutions tried to address these problems in the past. Nevertheless, these technologies aim for very specific solutions and have restricted flexibility when integrating and porting functionalities to mobile devices.

This paper presents a framework that allows the user to interact with high quality 2D and 3D graphical content on slim clients like Smartphones or PDAs. The visualization system is designed to connect to a variety of applications on the server side and to transmit pre-calculated visualization data to a mobile client. The user can then interact with the server-side application in real time. The application can use the entire hardware provided by the server to furnish the mobile client with visualization results of a very high quality. Thus, the visualization is limited only by the capabilities of the server application.

D. Tavangarian et al. (Eds.): IMC 2009, CCIS 53, pp. 131–142, 2009.

As an additional advantage of this approach, the framework will only transmit pre-calculated and rendered data over the network to the mobile device. This avoids the security risk that is created by transmitting data directly over networks. Especially for sensitive data sets, enormous effort is required to strictly secure data transmission via various encryption methods. Using this framework, the data is kept relatively safe behind firewalls and is only used by the application on the server side. The only data being sent to the client is the remote image data. The framework distributes this image data, created by the shared applications, to create interactive views, much like terminal-server solutions.

The framework presented here is completely independent of any specific software implementation or hardware-related implications. It allows generic connections of arbitrary applications with mobile devices and slim clients over different types of networks. This paper will provide examples, including highly dynamic 3D simulation environments, that go far beyond the computing capabilities of mobile devices, but are still interactively accessible. Other examples include 3D visualizations, as well as specialized visualization techniques for analysis or simple textual information.

This work extends the current related work in several ways, which will be described in detail in Section 2. The framework itself is thoroughly introduced in 3, including the server and client components, as well as the image capturing and encoding capabilities. Section 4 focuses on the specific communication structures that are necessary for the chosen approach. Section 5 will present several application examples to illustrate the benefits, using existing innovative applications. Section 6 will conclude the paper with a summary and an outlook to future work in this area.

2   Related Work

The field of mobile 3D visualization techniques can be divided into two major areas. The first one incorporates the calculation, rendering and visualization on the mobile device itself using specific frameworks like OpenGL ES [1]. In this paper, this approach will be called *direct mobile rendering*. The other major approach is to use a server to pre-render parts of or complete scenes and transmit the pre-calculated data to the mobile or slim device. Approaches of this nature will be called *remote rendering*. In recent years, a number of solutions were developed in both areas but a closer look at these solutions shows that most techniques require either special hardware or special software, including special integration procedures, to be successful. Our approach will present a generic alternative for connecting the visualization and the functionality of an arbitrary application with a slim client.

In the field of direct mobile rendering the approaches of Pulli et al [2] and Sahm et al [3] have achieved interesting results based on OpenGL ES. Nurminen [4] describes a good approach to rendering geographical information on mobile devices. An early approach to providing mobile users with 3D visualization content was presented by Schneider et al [5]. Their Network Graphics Framework provides adaptive transmission algorithms for 3D graphics over networks to enable visualization on slim devices. Other approaches utilize the Verse protocol [6] which can be used, to distribute 3D data between different clients in real-time. Here, a geometry compression was integrated to allow slim devices to render the data. However, all these approaches require special data formats and clients to enable remote visualization on slim devices.

In the field of remote rendering Stegmaier et al [7] and Engel et al [8] presented a remote visualization system and used CORBA to transmit the pre-rendered information to the client. On the server side the system was integrated directly into the 3D rendering pipeline of the captured application. While for this approach the framework must be integrated directly into the application, our solution does not require any integration effort. A hybrid approach with aspects of remote and direct mobile rendering is presented by Teler and Lischinski [9]. Here, parts of the 3D scene are pre-rendered on the server side and transmitted to the mobile client while other parts of the scene are sent directly to the mobile device. The mobile client then uses the raw data for rendering and adds the pre-rendered pieces to assemble the 3D scene on the mobile device. Other well known approaches in this area are SGI's VizServer [10] or Virtual network computing in general based on the work of Richardson [11]. The remote visualization solutions basically share the whole desktop environment or whole application window with remote users. Furthermore, VNC applications have no or only limited capabilities for grabbing OpenGL content. The approach described in our paper aims for a more sophisticated solution, which enables the user to select specific parts of the application to be shared, including their functionality.

3 Framework

The proposed framework consists of a client and a server component (see Figure 1). The server component is capable of connecting to an application and capturing the visual content of that application. The client component is the remote visualization tool that connects to the server and receives and displays the captured visualization data. Since the client simply displays continuously captured image data it runs on very slim devices. Today's mobile hardware is capable of decoding and rendering different image formats or videos. For example, the calculation effort of rendering a complex 3D scene lies completely on the server side, where the latest rendering hardware and CPU power can be used to achieve high-quality results.

The captured content on the server side will be made accessible for remote clients via a TCP network connection. The server captures the visualization data from Microsoft Windows' native handles using the Microsoft GDI+ API [12]. Since the server technology only requires handle IDs for the widgets to be captured for transmission, the integration effort to establish a remote connection to particular applications is almost non-existent. Basically, there is no need for the integration of special components into an existing application. The server will be started via command line options which will provide it with the necessary

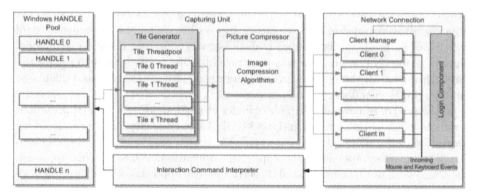

Fig. 1. System Architecture. The architecture of the overall system shows the the communication paths between the compontents of the framework.

information for capturing. The following chapters will describe the server and client components in more detail.

3.1   Server

The server works in two modes: a *listen mode* and an *application mode*. If the server runs in *listen mode*, it detects all applications running on the host computer. If a remote client connects, it will receive a list with all running programs that can potentially be captured. The client then chooses one of these applications, connects to it and receives the captured image data. When disconnecting, the connection to the server is closed and the server awaits new incoming connections. This mode allows the remote client to have remote access to different applications available on the server.

In *application mode* the server runs one particular application. The server is provided with the application's executable file name by a command line option when starting. The server starts the application if a client connects and then starts the capturing process. If the client disconnects, the server closes the application and waits for the next client to connect.

A third way to integrate the framework with an application is to start the server from the application. This method includes a small integration effort. The application starts the server and provides it with the application widget handles to be captured. The server then waits for client connections. If clients connect to it, the server starts to capture the handles provided by the application and transfers them to the connected clients.

Currently, the server component is designed to run on Microsoft Windows operating systems. The server is made up of three different components: a *window handle manager*, a *capturing unit* and a *network connection* module. The *window handle manager* contains and manages the list of all window handles selected for capturing and distribution to remote visualization clients. Since the widget handles are native system handles the server can only be run under Microsoft Windows. The following chapter describes the capturing process of the handles in detail.

Image Capturing. The *capturing unit* uses the handles and grabs the content from them. The window is split into tiles. Currently, the number of tiles is fixed to a number of 4x4 tiles. The tile-based approach is well known from MPEG4 and H.264 [13] encoding. For our first prototype, we used it as a simple way to parallelize the capturing process. In the future, more sophisticated methods of detecting changes, animations and movements inside tiles are planned.

This approach has several advantages. First of all, the image size of one tile to be captured, processed and transmitted is small compared to the size of a complete image containing the content of the entire application window. The second reason is the detection of changes inside the application. Most applications contain parts that very rarely change, but other parts - especially when talking about visualization applications - that change very frequently. For example, control buttons, menus etc. will not change very often, while a 3D visualization will change continuously. Currently, the server overlays the application with 4x4 tiles. It does not specifically determine where to set the tiles. When capturing and processing tiles in parallel instead of capturing one large image the server-sided performance can be improved. This is the third reason to subdivide the application area into tiles.

The static and dynamic parts of the application can be defined before or while starting the server and the tiles set accordingly. The result is a bandwidth reduction and more available processing power on the server side. If we split the application into tiles, we can check for changes inside each tile. Only if changes occur, then the new image is processed and transmitted to the client. This saves computing power and - even more importantly - bandwidth. The comparison of the previously captured tile and the current tile is a simple byte comparison. Each byte of both tiles is compared. If a pair of bytes is unequal, the newly captured image is used.

The simple byte comparison is very fast compared to other methods to detect changes between two images. In the worst case every byte of the image must be tested. For image comparison methods, even for a checksum test, all bytes have to be read out. In the best case - for a tile image which changes completely over time - the first byte comparison is sufficient to detect a change in the tile. In our current approach, an image is renewed if one pixel has changed. Potentially, more detailed comparison methods, based on the content of the tile image, can be used to get better compression and detection rates. In addition, predictions of changes inside the tiles can be calculated. Here, methods known from MPEG compression algorithms can be used. Furthermore, information can be processed after sending out the image to the client to rearrange or subdivide the tiles based on frequent changes inside the visualized area. The third advantage of the tiles is that the capturing process can be parallelized. The server starts one thread for each tile and asynchronously captures the tile's content. The synchronization processes are shown in Figure 2.

Encoding. In recent years, video compression algorithms and techniques like MPEG-4 or H.264 were developed and advanced to achieve very high compression ratios. Nevertheless, for our framework we use a simple image by image

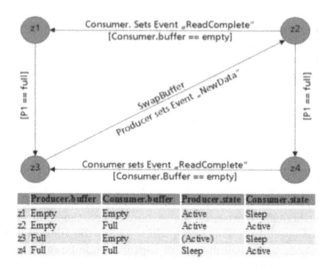

Fig. 2. Synchronization process for accessing the tiles. Every tile of the window handle is captured by an own thread asynchronously. z1-z4 are the states the capture processes can reach.

transmission for several reasons. The *first reason* is the ability of the mobile device to decode the image or video data for rendering. Decoding of video streams requires CPU power that is a scarce resource on mobile hardware. Especially when taking into account that the device not only has to listen to the incoming video stream, but also has to manage interactive commands from the user. This makes such a solution even less useful.

The *second reason* is a synchronization issue. This is the primary reason for deciding against encoded-video-stream-based visualization. Video streams with high compression rates typically consist of enclosed sequences of images. Within these sequences, single images are compressed using techniques that differ from format to format. But generally on the decoder side these sequence blocks must be decoded at once, because the individual images inside the sequence have certain dependencies on their parents. The current sequence has to be completely processed by the client before the client can react to the latest interaction. Therefore, the user would experience a delayed reaction of the remote visualization to her interaction requests. Especially when navigating through 3D scenes with fluid animations, it makes a huge difference if a camera movement occurs in real-time, as the user initiates it, or with a second's delay. In summary, an on-demand, single-image transmission is the best solution for our application scenario.

A *third reason* is the ability of the server side to encode video streams in real-time. MPEG or MJpeg software encoders available today require strong hardware ressources to achieve interactive framerates while encoding an image stream. Tests clearly show that a standard computer will not be able to encode a video stream in real-time from an image chain provided frame-by-frame. The best result reached frame rates of around 2 to 5 when using software encoders and the latest standard CPU hardware available. Even the use of multi-core CPUs does not influence the frame rate, because image compression for a network stream can not be parallelized to be more efficient. Even if the server-sided hardware would be able to achieve interactive framerates it would strongly require hardware ressources. Then, these ressources are no longer available for the application that should be captured itself leading to an overall lower performance.

Server-Side Client Handling. The *network connection* unit of the server handles the remote client connections. Every client that connects to the server is handled by the connection manager. The clients connect to the server using the TCP protocol. For remote visualization data reliability is a prerequisite, thus TCP can ensure that the image packages arrive correctly and completely on the client side. Additionally, to be able to determine which connected client sent interactive commands back to the server a one-to-one TCP connection is more useful than, for example, a connectionless protocol like UDP. Modern switching mechanisms like Microsoft's input output completion ports (IOCP) [14] allow very fast connection switching on the server side, which minimizes latencies when broadcasting image information to a large number of clients.

The network connection unit receives the captured visualization data from the capturing unit, encodes it into a stream able format and sends it to the related clients. Currently, all clients connect to the same application. In the future, client management will be done in a more sophisticated way, which will allow the use of one server to start multiple applications and connect different clients to different running applications.

3.2 Remote Visualization Client

The client is the part of the framework that runs on the slim device and visualizes the remote data. The client was developed using Adobe's Flash technology [15]. A major advantage of Flash lies in its portability. A large number of desktop and mobile computers have Flash players installed nowadays [16]. If a device has not installed it yet, the player is available online and can be installed quickly. Flash can be integrated into websites or run as a standalone application. With Flash Lite mobile phone users have the possibility to view Flash contents on mobile devices. Since Flash scales its content up and down when resizing the player, basic scalability issues have been addressed by the technology. For more sophisticated scaling regarding screen-size changes see Section 4.

The client is able to directly connect to the server using a socket connection for binary data transfer provided by Flash's Actionscript API. The client receives its encoded visualization data from the server through the socket connection. The incoming data stream from the socket is extracted by the client. The extracted image data is redirected to tile buffer accordingly. This buffer is constructed as a double buffer which is switched every time Flash redraws the images to the player's stage.

Basically, the visualization is updated continuously by the server application. As described above, if the server detects no changes in the tiles of the captured application, the client will not receive any image data to render. It keeps the last versions of the tile images for the visualization. Only when the captured graphics of the connected application change, will the server send new images to the client, which it can decode and draw. As discussed before, this tile-based capturing and visualization approach minimizes the required network bandwidth. Since the client only receives an image stream the computational effort for decoding and rendering is very low, which very slim mobile clients benefit from. Another performance issue to take into account is the tile based approach itself. Since the application's visualization is split into smaller images, the processing of each image requires less CPU power and can be rendered much faster than one large image containing the all rendered data from the server.

To be able to interact with the graphic content and steer the application from the remote client, the client itself registers all keyboard and mouse events and encodes them into Microsoft Windows keyboard and mouse codes. These system codes are packed into a network stream which is transferred to the server. The server unpacks the commands and sends them to the application handle the client is connected with. Additionally, the client has a very slim interface to connect to and disconnect from the server, as well as refresh all image data.

The feedback latency mainly depends on the network base latency and the time the application on the server side requires to render a frame. The commands sent back from the client to the server to signal mouse or keyboard interaction consist of simple 8 byte packets. Such small packets do not create additional latency when sent over network. For an application running on the mobile device at approximately 20fps connected using wireless lan with a base latency of 200ms the feedback latency of interaction commands usually is below 500ms which still can be considered as interactive. The additional 300ms up from the base latency are necessary to render, process and send the changed image from the server side to the client.

4   Scalability Discussion

There are two areas of scalability that must be taken into account. The first is the scalability with respect to the number of clients simultanously connected to one server instance. Here, the scenario, in which all clients connect to a single application, must be distinguished from the scenario, in which different clients connect to different applications using the same server connection. The second scalability issue is the challenge of scaling application windows from large screen sizes down to smaller screen sizes, like the screens of PDAs or Smartphones. This is a topic we want to address in the future to force the server to automatically adapt to the capabilities of the client.

Generally, when a large number of mobile users wants to access a large number of different applications hosted by the same server, the server will have to host an application instance for each independent user. An independent user in this case is a mobile user with access to an instance of an application provided by the server and not shared with others. This is, of course, hardly a new problem, but rather, a well-known issue that has been researched intensively by the network and service management community [17] [18]. Another scenario for this framework at present is to connect multiple remote clients to one application and to have collaborative views on the visualizations from those clients. Since the server buffers the tile images during the capture process, the connection of more clients in this scenario causes only a minor additional server load.

The bandwidth usage of the system mainly depends on the image size on the target platform and image compression algorithm on the server side. Using modern CPUs, the server-sided cpu load during the capturing and image encoding process can be disregarded. The image size for mobile devices does currently not exceed 640x480 pixels. For such image sizes, the size of each image compressed with e.g. a jpeg compression algorithm is about 20-30 kBytes. This data amount allows a framerate of approximately 15 frames per second using a HSDPA connection. For Wi-Fi connections the speed will boost up.

5   Results and Application Areas

Basically the server-sided component can be established on every Windows computer. The server is a standalone program. You can use it with whatever application you want to. You can capture every Windows-based program from the simple Windows Paint program up to an OpenGL 3D visualization. The following application examples focus on mobile and web visualization of 3D content rendered in OpenGL on the server side and transmitted to the mobile client.

5.1   Real-Time Visualization in Cloth Simulation Area

The visualization presented in Figure 3a shows an example of a GPU-based 3D cloth simulation rendering. The piece of cloth can interactively be dragged around the collision object using the touch display of the mobile phone. The remote visualization is running with frame rates of approximately 24fps. A GPU based 3D real-time cloth simulation running on a quad core and nvidia gtx280 on the server side. The image shows the mobile client with the interactive remote view of this high-quality rendering running at approximately 20fps.

The project SiMaKon utilizes this framework to seamlessly integrate a cloth simulation software within a web shop front-end and mobile usage of the 3D cloth simulation data. Within the project's architecture the simulator is mainly controlled bye a SOAP interface. This is done since most data is used as setup parameters for the simulation. These parameters cannot be controlled directly by user interaction and are generated by other programs like CAD cloth patterns. Therefore the framework only controls the interactive parts of the simulation's parameters and provides image feedback to the web front-end.

5.2   Visual Analytics Platform

Information visualisation and Visual Analytics technologies always have to deal with the problem of connecting different heterogeneous data sources to multiple

(a) Remote visualization of GPU-based real-time cloth simulation in very high quality.

(b) Visual analytics application for analysis of huge financial time series data sets.

Fig. 3. Application examples for remote visualization on mobile devices. The visualization techniques have special requirements for rendering: either they require strong hardware ressources (a) or need to be able to performantly discover huge datasets (b).

visualisation and data mining techniques. Moreover these different visualisations and data mining techniques have to communicate and to exchange data during the analysis of the data sets.

We identified this problem and developed an extensible Visual Analytics framework in the programming languages C++ and Java that standardizes the data import from sources like MySQL, ODBC, Access and CSV formats. Different visualisation techniques are connected via this unified interface. Due to its flexibility, other data source formats can easily be integrated into the framework. As one feature we provide a visualisation server that is capable of being integrated into the different visual analytics visualization applications and supports connections to slim rendering devices like browsers, mobile phones, PDAs and others. The major advantage of this framework is that multiple heterogeneous data can be analyzed by an expandable collection of different visualisation techniques using the framework described in this paper.

The visualization shown in Figure 3b shows an application example of this visual analytics framework. It is an OpenGL 3D visualization of financial market data. The very large data set itself is located inside a data base the application utilizes for its visualization. The mobile visualization runs at frame rates of approximately 23fps.

6   Conclusion

The goal of the work described in this paper was to establish an interactive connection between a server component running basically any application and a mobile client. In contrast to previous work we were able to achieve a server connection and remote client visualization to a variety of Windows applications without any integration effort. Previous work has produced several remote visualization frameworks that were able to be integrated only into a variety of special applications.

As a second goal, we wanted to improve the performance of the capturing process along with an optimization of the transmission of the image data. This could be achieved with the asynchronous and permanent capturing of multiple parts of the application's graphical content in parallel. Only altered content is re-captured and sent to the client. This saves computing time on the server side and bandwidth for the client connection.

A third goal was to achieve improved rendering performance on the mobile client, while keeping the flexibility to use the client on a variety of different systems and on different hardware. To achieve this goal the mobile client was developed in Adobe's Flash Lite. Flash Lite can be run on desktop computers as well as on slim devices like PDAs or Smartphones. We could achieve stable frame rates of 20 to 25 fps on clients from screen sizes of 400x200 on smartphones and up to 1280x1024 by embedding the client into a website.

6.1   Future Work

The tile generation in the current version of the server environment is encoded to generate 16 (4x4) tiles to capture for each application. This tile generation can be changed to adapt in a more sophisticated way to the captured application. For example, the analysis of changes during the capturing process at run-time, can identify more static and more dynamic parts of the application. This information could be used to reconfigure the tiles used for capturing to compress the overall size of data transmitted to the remote client more efficiently. Another interesting topic is the adaptation of applications from large screens down to very small screens sizes like those of smartphones. We hope to establish a semi-automated process for the adaption of visualization application controls to the very small screens of mobile devices, again working together in an interdisciplinary way with experience in the HCI arena.

Acknowledgements

Flash® and Flash Lite® are registered trademarks of Adobe Inc.

References

1. Bishop, L.: Opengl es 1.1, 2.0 and egl. In: SIGGRAPH 2006: ACM SIGGRAPH 2006 Courses, p. 3. ACM, New York (2006)
2. Pulli, K., Aarnio, T., Miettinen, T., Roimela, K., Vaarala, J.: Mobile 3D Graphics with OpenGL ES and M3G. The Morgan Kaufmann Series in Computer Graphics. Elsevier, Morgan Kaufmann, San Francisco (2008)
3. Sahm, J., Soetebier, I.: A client-server-scenegraph for the visualization of large and dynamic 3d scenes. Journal of WSCG, 1–3 (2004)
4. Nurminen, M.: M-loma - a mobile 3d city map. In: Proceedings of the eleventh international conference on 3D web technology (2006)
5. Scheider, B.O., Martin, I.M.: An adaptive framework for 3d graphics over networks. Computers & Graphics 23(6) (1999)

6. Brink, E.: The verse networked 3d graphics platform. In: Linköping Electronic Conference Proceedings. SIGRAD Conference, pp. 44–48. Linköping University Electronic Press (2006)

7. Stegmaier, S., Magallón, M., Ertl, T.: A generic solution for hardware-accelerated remote visualization. In: VISSYM 2002: Proceedings of the symposium on Data Visualisation 2002, Aire-la-Ville, Switzerland, Switzerland, Eurographics Association, p. 87 (2002)

8. Engel, K., Sommer, O., Ertl, T.: A framework for interactive hardware accelerated remote 3d-visualization. In: Proceedings of TCVG Symp. on Vis (VisSym), pp. 167–177 (2000)

9. Teler, E., Lischinski, D.: Streaming of complex 3d scenes for remote walkthroughs. In: Computer Graphics Forum, pp. 200–1 (2001)

10. Inc., S.G.: Opengl vizserver 3.0 - application-transparent remote interactive visualization and collaboration. Website (2003), http://www.sgi.com/ (visited on March 2009)

11. Richardson, T., Stafford-fraser, Q., Wood, K.R., Hopper, A.: Virtual network computing. IEEE Internet Computing 2, 33–38 (1998)

12. GDI: Microsoft windows gdi+. Website (2009), http://msdn.microsoft.com/en-us/library/ms533798VS.85.aspx (visited on March 2009)

13. Richardson, I.E.: H.264 and MPEG-4 Video Compression: Video Coding for Next Generation Multimedia, 1st edn. Wiley, Chichester (2003)

14. IOCP: Microsoft i/o completion ports. Website (2009), http://msdn.microsoft.com/en-us/library/aa365198VS.85.aspx (visited on March 2009)

15. Adobe: Flash lite. Website (2009), http://www.adobe.com/products/flashlite/ (visited on March 2009)

16. Robinson, S.: Flash lite-enabled handsets to top 1 billion cumulative shipments in q1 2009. Website (2009), http://www.strategyanalytics.com/default.aspx?mod=ReportAb-stractViewer&a0=4483 (visited on March 2009)

17. Foster, I.: The anatomy of the grid: Enabling scalable virtual organizations. International Journal of Supercomputer Applications 15 (2001)

18. Holma, H., Toskala, A., Ranta-aho, K., Pirskanen, J.: High-speed packet access evolution in 3gpp release 7. Communications Magazine, IEEE 45, 29–35 (2007)

19. Pulli, K., Aarnio, T., Roimela, K., Vaarala, J.: Designing graphics programming interfaces for mobile devices. IEEE Computer Graphics and Applications 25 (2005)

20. Chang, C., Ger, S.: Enhancing 3D graphics on mobile devices by image-based rendering. In: Chen, Y.-C., Chang, L.-W., Hsu, C.-T. (eds.) PCM 2002. LNCS, vol. 2532, pp. 1105–1111. Springer, Heidelberg (2002)

21. RDP: Microsoft remote desktop protocol. Website (2009), http://msdn.microsoft.com/en-us/library/aa383015.aspx (visited on March 2009)

22. Sun: Java platform, micro edition (java 2 me). Website (2009), http://java.sun.com/javame/index.jsp (visited on March 2009)

Speed-Dependent Camera Control in 3D Mobile Roadmaps

Timo Partala[1,2], Teemu Flink[2], Mika Luimula[3], and Ossi Saukko[3]

[1] Tampere University of Technology, Human-centered technology,
Korkeakoulunkatu 6, FI-33720 Tampere, Finland
[2] University of Oulu, Oulu Southern Institute, RFMedia Laboratory,
Vierimaantie 5, FI-84100 Ylivieska, Finland
`Timo.Partala@tut.fi, Teemu.Flink@gmail.com`
[3] CENTRIA Research and Development, RFMedia Laboratory,
Vierimaantie 5, FI-84100 Ylivieska, Finland
`{Mika.Luimula,Ossi.Saukko}@centria.fi`

Abstract. The aim of this study was to develop and experiment with methods for three-dimensional (3D) mobile roadmaps, which adjust the map view automatically based on the speed of a vehicle. A mobile 3D roadmap with no speed-dependent virtual camera control was compared to four mobile roadmaps, which automatically adjusted the following parameters based on the speed of the vehicle: 1) camera height angle, 2) camera distance from vehicle 3) camera height from ground level, and 4) both camera height angle and distance simultaneously. 13 subjects experimented with these implementations in real traffic. The results of the experiment showed that the developed implementations were evaluated highly in terms of navigation support. 9 out of 13 subjects preferred one of the implementations with speed-dependent camera control over the implementation with no speed-dependent camera control. The results suggest that automatic speed-dependent camera control can be a beneficial feature in 3D mobile roadmaps.

Keywords: Mobile navigation, 3D graphics, context-adaptive systems, viewpoint control.

1 Introduction

With the rapidly increasing popularity of different personal and professional navigation systems, location-aware mobile systems have become an important research area. However, most of the existing research has focused on technological issues such as solutions for positioning or real-time drawing of maps on mobile devices. Considering the popularity of mobile navigation applications among end-users, it is surprising that the related human-computer interaction research has been relatively sparse. Especially studies of car navigation conducted in real traffic are largely missing.

In a typical use context of a mobile navigation system, the user is on the move and can only pay a limited amount of attention to the system. An important branch of research concentrates on the question, how the location-based information of a mobile

D. Tavangarian et al. (Eds.): IMC 2009, CCIS 53, pp. 143–154, 2009.
© Springer-Verlag Berlin Heidelberg 2009

map should be presented to the user so that it is as useful as possible from the user's viewpoint. Some examples of existing studies on mobile maps have focused on different channels (e.g. auditory, spoken, textual, and visual) for information presentation [1]. In addition, it has been found that different easily perceptible features or landmarks [2] and overviews [3] can play an important role in mobile navigation. Different approaches have also been developed for the utilization of context information in mobile navigation. For example, Lee et al. [4] developed a system, which optimizes route instructions based on the vehicle's current route and to use appropriate amounts of user attention. Mooser et al. [5] presented a three degree-of-freedom control designed for viewing large documents and images on a mobile device by using recognition of mobile device movements using camera. They also applied their approach for zooming and panning in mobile two-dimensional maps. Partala et al. [6] suggested that automatic rotation of a mobile map based on heading of movement is a desirable feature in car navigation when using two-dimensional mobile roadmaps.

One of the most important recent trends in the area of mobile navigation is the introduction of 3D graphics. Many existing navigators offer 3D-like view constructed mostly based on 2D spatial data. Manufacturers of car navigation systems (e.g. Sony) have already launched navigators including 3D models of cities and providers of map materials (e.g. Tele Atlas, Zenrin) are in the process of modeling a large part of major cities worldwide in 3D. There is already some research focusing on human-computer interaction aspects of mobile 3D navigation. The majority of existing research on 3D mobile maps has concentrated on studying 3D maps in pedestrian navigation. In an early study, Rakkolainen and Vainio [7] studied using a 3D city model in mobile navigation and suggested that 3D city models help the users to recognize landmarks and find routes in a city easier than with a symbolic 2D map. In contrast, Oulasvirta et al. [8] compared manually controlled 2D and 3D mobile maps and found that 2D maps can outperform 3D maps in pedestrian navigation. These differences in findings can be explained in terms of different implementation solutions (e.g. street level vs. overall views) and the level of automation used (e.g. whether or not the map is automatically centered based on the location of the user). Overall, 3D mobile maps can be seen as a very promising application area provided that some of the associated challenges related to user interaction and information presentation can be solved.

A fundamental challenge in 3D navigation is the problem related to controlling degrees of freedom. Nurminen and Oulasvirta [9] suggested that movement in 3D mobile maps needs to be restricted and guided, yet enabling unrestricted access to all reasonable points of interest. In car navigation, the attentional resources that the users can typically pay to the system are limited and the need for manual control should be minimized. This highlights the need for systems, which control the virtual camera automatically in 3D mobile roadmaps. In automatic camera control, the goal is to use the available screen space in the most effective way possible, showing useful spatial information about the environment to the user at all times. This can be achieved by aligning the 3D view so that it is facing in the correct direction (typically the direction, in which the user is traveling) and also adjusting the view so that an optimal amount of spatial data about the user's environment is always displayed on the screen. The utilization of context information provides further possibilities for enhancing mobile 3D navigation. In car navigation, some of the most easily accessible sources of context information include location, heading of movement, and the speed of the vehicle. They can be easily calculated, for example, from standard Global Positioning System (GPS) signal.

One promising approach utilizes information about the speed of the tracked object (e.g. a vehicle or a pedestrian) to display the environment in a more optimal way to the user. Baus et al. [1] described a mobile system, in which a two-dimensional map is automatically zoomed in and out based on a pedestrian's speed (e.g. walking vs. running). Partala et al. [6] presented a study on automatic speed-dependent zooming in 2D mobile roadmaps. Their study was conducted in real traffic. The results showed that mobile roadmaps with automatic zooming based on the vehicle's speed were evaluated as higher in navigation support by the users when compared to similar roadmaps without automatic zooming.

To our knowledge, there are no published studies on systematically utilizing speed information in displaying 3D mobile roadmaps. Consequently, the aim of the current research was to empirically experiment with automatic speed-dependent camera control in mobile 3D roadmaps. A 3D mobile roadmap and four implementations for speed-dependent camera control were designed based on experiences of using 3D navigation systems. In all the implementations, automatic map rotation was used so that the orientation of the camera was always facing the heading of movement. Camera height angle, distance from vehicle, height from ground, and a combination of height angle and distance were selected as the variables to be manipulated based on the speed of the vehicle. Mobile 3D roadmaps with these four different implementations for speed-dependent camera control were compared to a mobile 3D roadmap with no speed-dependent camera control in real traffic.

2 System

2.1 System Platform and the 3D Graphics Engine

The 3D mobile navigation system used in the current study was built on top of the Locawe platform [10]. It is a platform for mobile location-aware systems developed at CENTRIA Research and Development, Ylivieska, Finland. For implementing context-aware systems using Locawe, there is support for sensors like positioning technologies, several telecommunication channels, and temperature and accelerometer sensors, both in indoor and outdoor use. Locawe provides features for conducting empirical research on location-aware systems. It has been used before in studying, for example, location-based communication and route history visualization [11,12]. The mobile 3D graphics engine used in the current experiment was built on top of the Locawe platform. The map materials included the urban area of a small town. The materials contained 3D information about buildings and trees in the target area. The 3D models of buildings closely modeled real size and color, but textures were not included. Different areas (fields, parks, paved areas and water areas) and roads were marked on the map with intuitive colors (e.g. blue for water areas). Street and place names were not shown to the user in the implementation used in the current experiment. The map materials were stored locally in a file, which contained all map materials, vertex coordinates, indices, and information about levels of details. Microsoft DirectX was used to draw to graphics on the screen of the mobile device. The system loaded dynamically visible objects to the memory if they were not there already. Nonvisible objects were removed from memory. After this, the virtual world matrix was set according to the camera position and objects were rendered.

The system used progressive transmission of vector data. This kind of procedure is a level of details approach. In the spatial database of the current implementation, each object has a level of details value. This value represents the priority of the object in drawing process. The objects which are less important are not drawn when the distance between the camera and the object is increasing over a critical value. Solid objects are drawn first and then transparent objects are drawn in order from the far-thest objects to the nearest. In the current experiment, the virtual camera viewpoints were selected so that all the important information could be drawn and displayed to the user in real time. The 3D map materials also covered a large area surrounding the experimental route in order to display the subjects a large amount of 3D information at all points of the route.

2.2 Speed-Dependent Camera Control

The most important concepts used in the current paper for describing speed-dependent automatic camera control are illustrated in Figure 1. In all the mobile 3D map imple-mentations developed for the current experiment, automatic rotation of the map based on the heading of the vehicle was utilized. Using this approach, the problem space of speed-dependent automatic zooming could be reduced to camera angles pictured directly from behind of the vehicle towards the heading of movement.

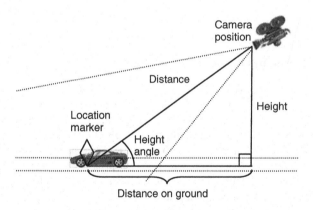

Fig. 1. An illustration of central concepts in the current approach for speed-dependent camera control in 3D mobile roadmaps

In order to calculate the position of the camera the needed variables were: the location of the vehicle, the heading of movement (these variables were calculated based on the GPS signal), camera height angle relative to the ground level, and the distance of the camera from the location of the vehicle. The distance between the vehicle and the camera on ground level (the lowest side of the triangle in Figure 1) was calculated using basic trigonometry. After that the coordinates for the camera position were calculated in real time based on the GPS coordinates as follows:

(1) camera.x = cos(heading angle) * distance on ground + gps.x
(2) camera.y = sin(height angle) * distance on ground + gps.y
(3) camera.z = sin(heading angle) * distance on ground + gps.z

Information about the heading angle (denoting the vehicle's direction of movement changed by steering the vehicle) was used for automatically rotating the 3D map so that it was always facing the heading of movement. Camera pitch and yaw were set so that the camera always faced straight towards the location marker. In many existing three-dimensional mobile navigation systems, the marker for the location of the vehicle is not centered on the screen, but it is lowered so that it is located vertically at about ¼ from the bottom of the map area. Similarly, in the current experiment the system adjusted the camera pitch angle so that the vehicle position marker remained vertically at ¼ from the bottom of the map area in all the automatic camera control implementations. Using this method the user sees more location-based information in the direction, in which he/she is travelling.

In the current experiment, the goal was to compare five different implementations for speed-dependent automatic camera control:

1. A mobile 3D map visualization with no speed-dependent camera control.
2. A mobile 3D map visualization with speed-dependent camera control manipulating camera height angle.
3. A mobile 3D map visualization with speed-dependent camera control manipulating camera distance from vehicle.
4. A mobile 3D map visualization with speed-dependent camera control manipulating camera height orthogonally from ground level.
5. A mobile 3D map visualization with speed-dependent camera control manipulating camera height angle and distance from vehicle simultaneously.

2.3 Preliminary Testing

The configuration values for the automatic zooming functions used in the experiment were determined by the four authors before the actual experiment. Each author experimented with automatic camera control functions in real in-town traffic. First, all the authors tried to find approximately the best values for a basic view (i.e. an optimal view with no speed-dependent camera control). They experimented with height angles using intervals of ten degrees (e.g. 30°, 40°, 50° etc.) and different distances of multiples of 25 meters (e.g. 75 m, 100 m, 125 m etc.). During this process the authors did not communicate with each other. After all the preliminary testers had determined their preferred values for the basic view, averages were calculated for height angle and distance and they were rounded to the nearest five degrees or ten meters.

Second, all the authors independently determined optimal values for the different speed-dependent camera control conditions. They experimented with different minimum and maximum values for height angle, distance, height, and the combination corresponding to driving speeds of 0-10 km/h and 40 or more km/h. The values determined by individual testers were averaged and rounded as in the first phase. All the preliminary testers agreed that the speed-dependent camera control functions should work so that at low speeds, the camera should be closer and/or higher, and at higher speeds the camera should be further away and/or lower. After the optimal values had been determined, the system was tested once more with those values. These values were then used in the final experiment.

2.4 Automatic Camera Control in the Experiment

The location of the vehicle was indicated by a diamond-shaped figure. The basic view with no automatic camera control was pictured from a 40 degrees height angle from ground level and the distance to the vehicle was 110m (Figure 2). The range of the optimal values determined by the authors in the preliminary testing varied from 30 to 45 degrees for the height angle and from 100m to 125m for the distance.

Fig. 2. The basic view

The functions used for speed-dependent camera control are presented in Table 1 and illustrated in Figures 3 and 4. For driving speeds between 10 km/h and 40 km/h, the camera was moved linearly between the values in Table 1. For example, when the speed of the vehicle was 25 km/h, the camera distance was 90 m, when automatic camera control was carried out based on distance. 40 km/h was chosen as the upper limit for the camera control functions, because the highest allowed speeds in the test area were either 40 km/h or 50 km/h at any points of the in-town route.

Table 1. The minimum and maximum values for the functions used in automatic camera control

	Speed 0-10 km/h	Speed 40- km/h
Height angle (°)	55	25
Distance (m)	60	120
Height (m)	100	40

The optimal minimum and maximum values determined by the authors in the preliminary testing ranged as follows: height angle, 0-10 km/h: 50-60 degrees; height angle, 40- km/h 20-35 degrees; distance, 0-10 km/h: 30-70m; distance, 40- km/h:

100-150m; height, 0-10 km/h: 60-120m; and height, 40- km/h: 30-50m. The condition based on the combination of height angle and distance used the same values as used in scaling the variables individually, but both variables were manipulated at the same time using those values. The images below were generated for illustrational purposes after the experiment. They illustrate a point on the actual route, in which a typical driving speed is about 40km/h.

Fig. 3. Left: Speed-dependent camera control based on height angle. (Left: 0-10 km/h; right: 40 km/h or more.) Right: Speed-dependent camera control based on distance (Left: 0-10 km/h, right: 40 km/h or more).

Fig. 4. Left: Speed-dependent camera control based on height. (Left: 0-10 km/h; right: 40 km/h or more.) Right: Speed-dependent camera control based on combination of height and distance. (Left: 0-10 km/h, right: 40 km/h or more).

3 Experiment

3.1 Subjects

13 volunteer subjects (six females and seven males, mean age 34.4 years) participated in the study. They evaluated their previous experience of using PDAs as moderate (average 5.6 on a 1-9 scale, 1 = very little, 9 = very much) and their experience of mobile navigation systems as relatively low (average 3.4 on a 1-9 scale, 1 = very little, 9 = very much).

3.2 Equipment

A HTC Advantage X7500 mobile computer running Microsoft® Windows Mobile® 5 Pocket PC Edition was used for displaying the 3D roadmap for the subjects in the experiment. The device had 256Mb of ROM and 128 Mb of SDRAM memory and its Intel® PXA270 processor with ATi™ Graphic Chip W2284was running at 624 MHz. The device had a 5" transmissive TFT-LCD display and the resolution used was 640x480. This mobile device was selected in order to simulate car navigation devices in the near future. The equipment was fast enough to display the 3D scenery in real time, however, there was a normal short delay of less than 1 s related to GPS positioning. The built-in GPS receiver of the mobile device was used for positioning. A Volkswagen Polo 1.9 SDi -00 was used as a vehicle in the experiments.

3.3 Procedure

The subject was seated in the front seat of the vehicle, next to the researcher, who drove the vehicle in the experiment. The purpose of using the researcher as the driver was to ensure that the driving route and the driving speed remained the same for the five conditions. This procedure also enabled the subjects to fully concentrate on the task at hand (following the visualizations and the environment) and to form a realistic conception of each speed-dependent camera control implementation. The mobile navigation system was introduced to the subject. The subject was told that during the experiment her/his task is to observe both the mobile 3D map and the environment closely during the trials. The basic ideas behind the different implementations for speed-dependent zooming and also the scales of the evaluation forms were briefly outlined for the subjects so that they could instantly focus on observing the correct aspects of the developed techniques in the light of the current study (instead of e.g. focusing on how the buildings were drawn on the map).

The experiment was conducted in the urban area of a small town. The driving route consisted of a start/end point, nine turns, in which the car was stopped or the driving speed had to be reduced near zero, as well as three bends, which could be driven with smaller speed reductions. For the straight parts of the route, the driving speed chosen by the driver was 40 km/h or more. The total length of the route was about 2.4 km. The presentation order of the implementations was randomized for each subject. Other traffic was relatively sparse during the trials.

After an implementation had been tested in traffic, the researcher gave the subject an evaluation form on paper. The subject evaluated the most recently seen implementation on six scales. First, he/she gave an evaluation of position knowledge: how well the visualization supported knowledge about where the vehicle was located at each time (position knowledge support: 1 = poorly – 9 = well). Second, the subject evaluated the implementation based on how easy it was to make associations between the objects seen on the 3D map (e.g. buildings) and the corresponding real objects in the environment (identification: 1 = difficult – 9 = easy). Using the third scale, the subject gave an overall evaluation about the navigation support provided by the implementation from 1 = poor to 9 = good. The questions from four to six evaluated the appropriateness of the views provided by the implementations at different speeds from 1= too narrow (does not show enough useful spatial information) to 5 = appropriate and 9 = too large (shows too much information at one time). Using the same evaluation scale, the subjects also evaluated the overall appropriateness at different speeds, in question five when stopped or at very low speeds (0-10 km/h), and in question six while driving at 40 km/h or more.

After the route had been driven five times (once using each implementation), the subjects were also presented with a final questionnaire. In this questionnaire, the subjects were asked to rank the five implementations into an order of preference from (1= I would prefer to use this implementation in real navigation to 5 = this is the least preferred implementation in my opinion). There were also three scales, in which the subjects were instructed to rate how much they used different map materials (roads and intersections, 3D buildings, and different areas) as sources of information in their navigation (1 = little, 9 = much).

3.4 Data Analysis

Friedman's rank tests were used to compare the evaluations of all five conditions for significant differences and Wilcoxon's matched pairs signed ranks tests were used in pairwise comparisons. These tests were selected due to the nonparametric (distribution-free) nature of the gathered data.

4 Results

The average ratings for the different conditions in terms of position knowledge support, identification of objects, and overall navigation support are presented in Figure 5. Overall, the evaluations were fairly positive averaging about seven on a one-to-nine scale. The differences between the different conditions were not statistically significant.

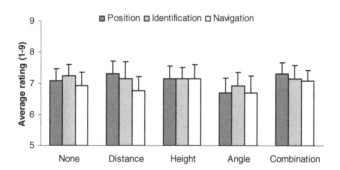

Fig. 5. The average ratings for the different visualizations in terms of position knowledge support, identification of objects, and overall navigation support (and standard errors of the means)

The average ratings for the appropriateness of the spatial information shown in the 3D view (1 = too small, does not show enough information – 5 = shows an optimal amount of information – 9 = too large, shows too much information) are presented in Figure 6 above.

Of these scales, statistically significant differences were found from the evaluations of the appropriateness of the views at low speeds (0-10 km/h) $\chi F2 = 12.8$, $df = 4$, $p < 0.05$. Pairwise differences were found between the evaluations for distance and none $Z = 2.7$, $p < 0.01$, distance and height $Z = 2.3$, $p < 0.05$, distance and height angle $Z = 2.1$, $p < 0.05$, height angle and none $Z = 2.0$, $p < 0.05$ and combination and none $Z = 2.3$, $p < 0.05$. Overall, however, the views were evaluated as near optimal in presenting a correct amount of information to the user.

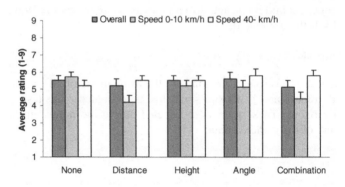

Fig. 6. The average ratings for the appropriateness of the amount of spatial information shown (and standard errors of the means)

The results concerning the subjects' ranks of preference are presented in Table 2. The number of choices given by the subjects is presented for each implementation and rank.

Table 2. The five implementations ranked by preference

Rank	None	Distance	Height	Height angle	Combination
1st	4	4	3	1	1
2nd	4	2	2	2	3
3rd	0	3	3	5	2
4th	2	1	4	3	3
5th	3	3	1	2	4

When asked which map elements they utilized in navigation, the subjects indicated that they used information related to roads and intersections (average score 7.5), as well as the 3D buildings (6.7) relatively much. Information about different areas (field, paved areas, water areas) was used slightly more rarely (4.9). These results confirmed that the subjects utilized the information provided by 3D buildings in navigation relatively much.

5 Discussion

In this paper, we presented a system platform for displaying 3D graphics on a mobile device augmented with features for implementing automatic camera control functions based on the current speed of the vehicle. Based on this system, an experiment was conducted, in which a view with no speed-dependent camera control was compared to four different implementations of automatic camera control based on the speed of the vehicle. These implementations were based on manipulating the camera height angle, distance, height, and combination of distance and height angle.

The results of the empirical experiment showed that the subjects evaluated the implementations highly in terms of their support of position knowledge, identification of real-world objects, and also gave high overall scores for the different alternatives as navigation aids. The evaluations were approximately on the same level for all the implementations. This indicates that none of the alternatives was clearly superior and the configurations specified in the preliminary testing were also at least relatively successful for all the alternatives. However, the results regarding the subjective preference measures showed an inclination towards the implementations using speed-dependent camera control. 9 out of 13 subjects chose one of the techniques with speed-dependent camera control as the most preferred technique, and ranked the basic view as inferior to one or most of these techniques. Of the speed-dependent camera control techniques, the techniques controlling the camera automatically by distance or height were the most preferred. In contrast, four of the subjects evaluated the basic view as the most preferred technique.

In the current experiment, the subjects were seated on the passenger seat, when they used the alternative mobile roadmap implementations. The purpose of this was to control variables that might have had a crucial effect on the results such as the experimental route, driving speed, and the amount of attention that can be paid to the mobile map implementation. A downside of this decision is that the ecological valid-ity of the experiment had to be compromised to some extent, because car navigation systems are typically used by drivers. However, we believe that when considering all aspects of validity, the current procedure as a controlled field experiment rates well because of being able to control the variables that might have influenced the results, while still being able to conduct the experiment in real traffic instead of a simulator.

Most of the existing research on 3D mobile navigation has concentrated on pedes-trian navigation and methods for manual techniques for controlling the map view. In the current study, we took a different approach and studied automatic techniques for car navigation. However, it would seem to be a good idea to mix automatic and man-ual camera control to some extent in car navigation. For example, the automatic camera control implementations presented in this paper could be augmented with manual control to rotate the view around the position marker. In this case, the system could switch between automatic and manual rotation so that when the user wants a view, which is not pictured from behind facing the heading of the vehicle, he/she could rotate the view manually into another viewpoint. When the user has finished examining the map by changing the viewpoint, the system could return to automatic camera control mode after a while or the user could lock the view to the manually selected viewpoint.

As a conclusion, the current results suggest that at least for some users speed-dependent camera control in three-dimensional mobile roadmaps can be more useful than a more stationary view such as the basic view of the current experiment. In the current experiment, the majority of the novice test subjects preferred a roadmap implementation with speed-dependent camera control, even though the basic view showed relatively much information due to the relatively large display and high resolution used. These results suggest that speed-dependent camera control would be a useful addition to 3D car navigation systems at least as an optional feature. Many navigation systems have smaller screens and display resolutions than in the device used in the current study. In those systems the benefits of speed-dependent camera control are likely to be greater. Different subjects of this experiment preferred different implementations of speed-dependent camera control, which suggest that it would be beneficial to offer different alternative implementations for the users to choose from. The current experiment was the first to study speed-dependent camera control in 3D mobile roadmaps. We believe that the current study and further research on speed-dependent camera control can help in satisfying the users' navigational needs in a more optimal way in the future.

Acknowledgments. The authors would like to thank all the test subjects, who participated in this research. This work was carried out within projects supported by EU Structural Funds, State Provincial Office of Oulu, Ylivieska Region, Ylivieska Town, and Pohjanmaan PPO.

References

1. Baus, J., Wasinger, R., Aslan, I., Krüger, A., Maier, A., Schwartz, T.: Auditory Perceptible Landmarks in Mobile Navigation. In: 2007 International Conference on Intelligent User Interfaces, pp. 302–304. ACM Press, New York (2007)
2. Aslan, I., Schwalm, M., Baus, J., Krüger, A., Schwartz, T.: Acquisition of Spatial Knowledge in Location Aware Mobile Pedestrian Navigation Systems. In: MobileHCI 2006, pp. 105–108. ACM Press, New York (2006)
3. Hornbæk, K., Bederson, B.B., Plaisant, C.: Navigation Patterns and Usability of Zoomable User Interfaces with and without an Overview. ACM Transactions on Computer-Human Interaction 9(4), 362–389 (2002)
4. Lee, J., Forlizzi, J., Hudson, S.E.: Iterative Design of MOVE: A Situationally Appropriate Vehicle Navigation System. International Journal of Human Computer Studies 66(3), 198–215 (2008)
5. Mooser, J., You, S., Neumann, U.: Large Document, Small Screen: A Camera Driven Scroll and Zoom Control for Mobile Devices. In: 2008 Symposium on Interactive 3D Graphics, pp. 27–34. ACM Press, New York (2008)
6. Partala, T., Luimula, M., Saukko, O.: Automatic rotation and zooming in mobile roadmaps. In: MobileHCI 2006, pp. 255–258. ACM Press, New York (2006)
7. Rakkolainen, I., Vainio, T.: A 3D City Info for Mobile Users. Computers & Graphics, Special Issue on Multimedia Appliances 25(4), 619–625 (2001)
8. Oulasvirta, A., Estlander, S., Nurminen, A.: Embodied Interaction with a 3D versus 2D Mobile Map. Personal and Ubiquitous Computing 13(4), 303–320 (2009)
9. Nurminen, A., Oulasvirta, A.: Designing Interactions for Navigation in 3D Mobile Maps. In: Meng, L., Zipf, A., Winter, S. (eds.) Map-based Mobile Services: Design, Interaction and Usability. Lecture Notes in Geoinformation and Cartography, pp. 198–224. Springer, London (2008)
10. Luimula, M., Kuutti, K.: Locawe: a novel platform for location-aware multimedia services. In: MUM 2008, pp. 122–129. ACM Press, New York (2008)
11. Haapala, O., Sääskilahti, K., Luimula, M., Yli-Hemminki, J., Partala, T.: Parallel Learning between the Classroom and the Field using Location-based Communication Techniques. In: ED-MEDIA 2007, pp. 668–675. AACE (2007)
12. Lehtimäki, T., Partala, T., Luimula, M., Verronen, P.: LocaweRoute: an advanced route history visualization for mobile devices. In: AVI 2008, pp. 392–395. ACM Press, New York (2008)

Heterogeneous Communication in Smart Ensembles

Enrico Dressler and Djamshid Tavangarian

University of Rostock, D-18059 Rostock, Germany

Abstract. Today's smart environments are characterized by small, inexpensive networking devices which support users in their everyday work in a proactive and intelligent manner. These devices utilize different network technologies varying in medium, range, latency and bandwidth. They build a heterogeneous network, wherein different IP-based and non-IP-based protocols are used for communication in specific application areas. Over the past years, service oriented communication gained importance in smart environments. Based on heterogeneous network technologies, service oriented communication results in using different mostly incompatible service technologies in a smart environment.

This paper presents an approach for a transparent bridging of different network and service technologies inside a smart environment. Therefore, devices are organized as members of cells with homogeneous network interfaces. A General Purpose Access Point (GPAP) combines these cells to a heterogeneous ensemble. An approach for service based communication between different network technologies, especially an interconnection of Bluetooth SDP (Service Discovery Protocol) and Web Services, is the focus of the paper and represents service proxying for a variety of other network and service technologies.

1 Introduction

Evolution in the area of wireless networks and integration has enabled small, inexpensive, flexible, and robust networking devices that interact with their environment through sensors, actuators and communication. Today, information processing can be integrated into every day objects which provide their abilities in terms of services and interact with their environment to support users in their everyday work. Thus, proactive and intelligent cooperation significantly change our environment that is associated with a widespread use of different wireless network and service technologies which are not compatible at all. Such a heterogeneous network, depicted in figure 1, allows devices in our environment to use a specific network and service technology for a certain task, but limits a communication between all devices.

Devices using wired Ethernet (like a printer or an embedded device) and devices using WLAN (like a laptop or a PDA) can be directly combined to an IP-based network und connected to the Internet by an IP router. Mobile devices using Bluetooth and ambient sensors using ZigBee can only communicate

D. Tavangarian et al. (Eds.): IMC 2009, CCIS 53, pp. 155–166, 2009.

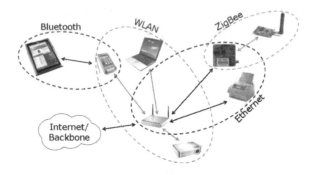

Fig. 1. Today's cell based communication inside an ensemble emerged by a smart pervasive environment

with devices equipped with the same network interface type. Thereby, the use of MAC-based communication protocols prevents an easy combination with IP-based network technologies like Ethernet and WLAN. Thus, different cells evolve, characterized as locally closed collections of devices interconnected by the same wired or wireless network technology. Wireless cells are typically dynamic because devices spontaneously enter or leave the cell's scope. However, wired cells are typically static.

A communication between members of directly overlapping cells is partially possible today, but not a communication between members of separated cells. For instance, a communication between a ZigBee and a Bluetooth device in figure 1 is not possible so that communication between any devices on network and service layer in a pervasive environment is still missing today.

At the beginning, this paper presents related work and current limitations in the area of communication in heterogeneous networks, especially inter-working of WLAN and WPAN technologies will be described. Thereafter, the paper introduces an approach for service proxying and heterogeneous addressing that expands related approaches and enables a communication between members of separated cells. The approach is based on a centralized General Purpose Access Point (GPAP) [1] and uses service proxying for Bluetooth SDP and Web Services to combine homogeneous cells (MAC- and IP-based cells) to a heterogeneous ensemble. The service proxying approach represents service proxying for a variety of other network and service technologies. The paper ends with a conclusion and future work.

2   Related Work

A key feature of heterogeneous communication in smart ensembles is the inter-working of various WPAN and WLAN technologies. Today, Bluetooth and ZigBee gain more and more importance within the WPAN operating space. Bluetooth is a robust, flexible, low cost, low power, and short-range communication standard with a medium data rate defined by the Bluetooth Special Interest Group (SIG) [3] and can be found in many consumer electronics such as cell phones, PDAs, and laptops. The main goal of Bluetooth is a simple cable replacement for a direct communication between mobile device.

The ZigBee technology is defined by the ZigBee Alliance [5] to ensure an integrated and complete solution for the market especially for sensor networking-based applications. It is designed for low-power devices and lightweight wireless sensor networks with a low data rate. Main advantages of ZigBee are the interaction with the local environment through sensors, lifetime requirements of months to a year and physical inaccessibility. ZigBee is fundamentally event driven, so reacting to changes in the environment (message arrival and sensor acquisition) is commonly used than communication driven by interactive or batch processing. Furthermore, ZigBee mesh networking enables an increased range, reliability (self-healing), and formation of ad hoc networks where redundant paths are provided.

Independence of infrastructure and required IP-addresses as precondition for communication is the main goal of Bluetooth and ZigBee. But especially the short range and direct communication turns out to be a limiting factor for Bluetooth application and makes a combination with IP-based technologies necessary. In heterogeneous networks, WLAN and WPAN technologies differ in terms of power consumption, coverage range, data rate, and costs, but they can be used to complement one another by different approaches to realize for example a communication between Bluetooth and WLAN enabled devices and between remote Bluetooth devices using a WLAN backbone.

A general approach for integration of Bluetooth devices into IP based networks is an all-over-IP issue. For this approach the Bluetooth SIG has published a native way for carrying IP traffic over Bluetooth by a protocol called Bluetooth Network Encapsulation Protocol (BNEP) [4], wherein unmodified IP packets are encapsulated in Bluetooth packets which are carried over Bluetooth links. This ability to communicate with a WLAN allows WPANs to take advantage of services such as printing, Internet access, and file sharing. Thereby, a network access point with a Bluetooth and a WLAN network interface is used to mediate between these network technologies. The connection procedure and setup time is extremely low and is for this reason a very attractive option, considering the high data rates of 11-55 Mbps in traditional IEEE 802.11 WLANs. This approach allows a communication between WLAN and Bluetooth enabled devices on the Internet layer of the TCP/IP model and above, displayed in figure 2. Current developments like BlueStar [13][14] enable such an all-over-IP approach of Bluetooth WPANs and IEEE 802.11 WLANs. They use a few Bluetooth Wireless Gateways (BWGs), which are also IEEE 802.11 enabled so that they can serve as access point to the IEEE 802.11 wireless network. BlueStar enables low-cost and short-range Bluetooth devices to access the global Internet infrastructure by utilizing WLAN-based high-powered transmitters. However, this approach leads to different drawbacks because the use of BNEP assumes an IP stack on every device. Thus, IP, gateway, and name server addresses must be

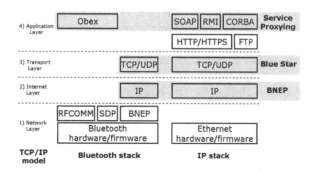

Fig. 2. Approaches for inter-working of LANs and WPANs

made available on all Bluetooth enabled devices (even less reasonable for ZigBee devices). Furthermore, the IP stack leads to a use of IP-based service technologies on Bluetooth devices so that adaptations of existing applications are now necessary for a service-based communication between Bluetooth devices. This assumption leads to software, protocol, and management overhead, typically unnecessary for common WPAN networks.

A second communication approach for heterogeneous networks combines Bluetooth and IP-based networks on application layer using service proxying, displayed in figure 2. The operation mode of this approach [15] uses an essential method of locating services in mobile Bluetooth ad hoc networks and utilizes proxies equipped with Bluetooth and Ethernet interfaces to connect remote Bluetooth networks. Thereby, proxies are searching for Bluetooth devices and available Bluetooth SDP services in the local network and offer them to nearby proxies which make them available in their local Bluetooth networks. Thus, proxies expand the service based communication through by-passing the communication over the IP network and make a set-up of communication links between remote Bluetooth devices possible. Applications on either end will communicate seamlessly and transparently with one another, unaware that the devices are not within radio range. So the communication range of Bluetooth devices can be increased by a large-scale IP-based backbone network. However, a seamless and transparent communication between Bluetooth SDP and IP-based Web Services is still missing.

In the next chapter, our advanced service proxying approach for combining Bluetooth SDP and IP-based Web Services will be explained. The approach is implemented by means of a middleware for a General Purpose Access Point (GPAP) and can be adopted as candidate for combination of a variety of other incompatible SOA technologies which have been established for dedicated application areas, like Open Services Gateway Initiative (OSGI) [6] for car and home automation, Jini [7] and Universal Plug and Play (UPnP) [8] for device use in IP-based networks, Bonjour [9] in particular for print services, and Web Services [12] especially for the business domain.

3   The General Purpose Acces Point Approach

An interoperable and efficient communication system is the base of a flexible and pervasive environment. Today's pervasive environments (e.g. Smart Homes) are characterized by heterogeneous network and service technologies which avoid a transparent integration of new devices. The General Purpose Access Point (GPAP), displayed in figure 3, is made up by a device with numerous network interfaces (e.g. Ethernet, WLAN, ZigBee, and Bluetooth) and has been developed to overcome the heterogeneity on both layers.

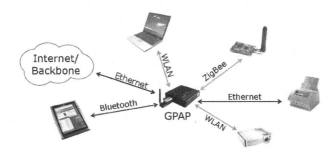

Fig. 3. The General Purpose Access Point (GPAP) combines homogeneous cells to a heterogeneous ensemble

The GPAP communicates directly with nearby devices equipped with the same network interface. Thereby, cells of locally, closed collections of devices evolve in the network wherein the same network and service technologies are used for communication. For example, the Service Discovery Protocol (SDP) is usual for a Bluetooth cell and Web Services for a WLAN cell. GPAPs are equipped with several network interfaces and thus members of different homogeneous cells. They can be used to combine homogeneous cells to a heterogeneous ensemble by a network and a service layer presented in figure 4.

A combination of several GPAPs leads to a community wherein GPAPs represent the interface between Ensemble and Community, and enable ensemble

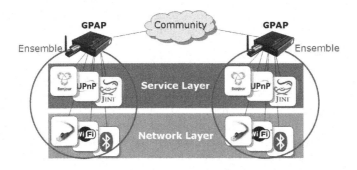

Fig. 4. Cooperation of the GPAP's network and service layer

members to communicate with each other independent of available network and service interfaces. The main task of a GPAP is the mediation between different technologies inside an ensemble as well as inside a community. Therefore, GPAPs provide gateway functionality for local devices by a network and a service layer, presented in figure 4 and explained in the following section.

3.1   Network Layer

The main goal of the network layer is a transparent addressing and communication between any devices inside an ensemble. Therefore, the network layer utilizes an enhanced version of our Heterogeneous Context Based Routing (HCBR) architecture [1] that permits the integration of all kinds of wired and wireless technologies. Additionally, the layer organizes homogeneous cells to a heterogeneous ensemble by bridging the communication between different cells and allows devices of different cells to communicate with each other. The central point of this layer is the HCBR core which supports a modular enhancement by a plugin concept to support new network technologies and functionalities. This core can be extended by two types of plugins: device plugins and HCBR plugins, and is also responsible for their collaboration.

For every new technology a device plugin is necessary to encapsulate special characteristics for arranging the communication with a specific network interface. Characteristics in data transport are treated as well. Thus, device plugins provide an intermediate layer to abstract from available wired and wireless network interfaces in the operating system.

HCBR plugins are used to enhance the HCBR core with new functionalities. The most important functionality is the realization of bridges between different homogeneous cells. To reduce the amount of necessary bridges, we use Ethernet as a basic technology and accordingly implement bridges between Ethernet and other technologies only. Thereby, we need bridges such as Bluetooth-Ethernet, ZigBee-Ethernet, but do not need bridges like Bluetooth-ZigBee implicitly (only for hard performance requirements), because this functionality can be composed by a Bluetooth-Ethernet and a ZigBee-Ethernet bridge as well.

Furthermore, plugins that gather and exchange information on neighbors, links, and network topology have been realized. This information is provided to other HCBR plugins, for example to a plugin which is responsible for routing in a heterogeneous network. This plugin can use the information to construct a smart metric for a routing table that uses the available network capacity of all sorts of channels inside the ensemble to significantly improve the overall capacity of the network. Hence, measurement based [16] and status based methods [17] could be used to realize multi-path routing. Furthermore, we implemented an info plugin that passes information from the HCBR core to a graphical user interface in order to allow analysis of network behavior.

Another plugin for collaboration between the network and the service layer has been realized that allows the service layer to use context information from the network layer and vice versa. Thereby, the network layer provides information of available routes in the network (latency, available bandwidth,...) that can be used on service layer to enrich service information with dynamic QoS parameters. In the other direction, service information can be used to optimize network routes for services with real-time requirements, for example in a heterogeneous video or audio chat.

3.2 Service Layer

The GPAP's service layer is based on the Service Technology Independent Architecture (STIA) approach [2]. This layer is responsible for mapping between different service technologies, for example between Bluetooth SDP services and IP-based Web Services. The service layer uses a Service Technology-independent Language (STiL) for translation between abstract and concrete services, and consists of three parts: the STiL Service Manager (SSM), multiple Service Technology Translators (STT), and multiple Service Technology Plugins (STP). Each of the plugins is used to discover and publish services of one specific service technology, like Jini or Web Services. Each STT is used to translate services, discovered by the service plugins, into a STiL Service description (e.g. a Bluetooth service provided by a mobile device). Thereby, context information from the network layer can be used to enrich the service description. Afterwards, the SSM uses the description to translate the service into other supported service technologies, using a specific STT (e.g. prepare an equivalent Web Service description) and publishes the service using the specific STP. The service transformation works in the other direction in the same manner. While using STiL for temporary service descriptions, the number of needed STTs can be reduced.

Thereby, services of an ensemble are not only translated into and provided for other service technologies inside an ensemble, but also provided in distant ensembles of the community. Therefore a P2P-based exchange of STiL service descriptions between linked ensembles is used to allow an inter-ensemble service-based communication between members of different cells.

4   Experimental Results with Service Proxying

For a heterogeneous service-based communication example in smart ensembles, we used the experimental set-up displayed in figure 5 with various end-user devices equipped with Bluetooth (2,1 Mbit/s maximal data rate) or rather Ethernet (100 Mbit/s) interfaces, and proxies with both interface types. To demonstrate and measure the service proxying functionality of our GPAP middleware we used a self-made Java chat application with a file-transfer function based on a Linux operating system, the BlueZ [10] Bluetooth stack and avetana [11] for BlueZ Java bindings. Two clients, a chat client for IP-based networks (using Web Services on the PCs) and a chat client for Bluetooth-based networks (using SDP services on the laptops) have been realized.

These clients enable a direct chat and file-transfer between devices with network interfaces of the same type using the same service technology. Thus a direct chat and file-transfer between the PCs as well as nearby laptops is possible without the proxies. To measure the bandwidth of a direct Bluetooth connection

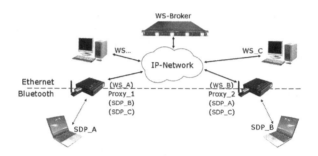

Fig. 5. Service proxying for Bluetooth SDP and Web Services

laptop A provides a service SDP_A that accepts files. Then laptop B searches for the service and uses a found service by sending a file to laptop A. Thereby, we measured a bandwidth of 154,2 kB/s of raw-file-data using a data-size greater than 10 Bytes per packet without header information and a used Bluetooth bandwidth of 158,0 kB/s with consideration of header information. The amount of the protocol overhead in this case is 2,5%. To submit a file using Web Services PC_C provides a service that accepts files and registers the service at a Web Service broker. Then, another PC requests the service at the broker und uses it directly to submit a file to PC_C. Thereby, we measured a bandwidth of 698,5 kB/s for raw-file-data and a used bandwidth of 996,5 kB/s considering SOAP protocol overhead. This measure shows an overhead of 43% while using SOAP as communication protocol for Web Services, and we noticed that using small data-chunks for data-transfers with SOAP causes an even worse use of available bandwidth.

Afterwards, we introduced the proxies to bridge between Ethernet and Bluetooth cells using service proxying between SDP and Web Services to transfer a file from a PC to a laptop. For this purpose, laptop A provides a local service SDP_A to accept files. Proxy_1 searches for local Bluetooth services periodically, finds service SDP_A, creates an equivalent Web Service WS_A and makes it available in the IP-based network. After searching for the service PC_C uses WS_A assistant for SDP_A and sends the data to Proxy_1 who forwards the data to the original service SDP_A. Thereby, we measured a bandwidth of 145,5 kB/s for raw-file-data.

In the last scenario we measured a file-transfer between two remote Bluetooth devices, device A and B. Therefore, service proxying between SDP and Web Services is needed twice, at Proxy_1 and Proxy_2. Once again, laptop A provides service SDP_A, Proxy_1 finds the service and makes it available as a Web Service WS_A in the IP-network. Simultaneously Proxy_2 searches for Web Services, finds WS_A and provides the service as a local Bluetooth service SDP_A which can be found and used by laptop B. A bandwidth of 111,4 kB/s has been measured for the raw-file-data in this scenario. Therefore, a bandwidth of 173,2 kB/s has been used for transmission in the IP network.

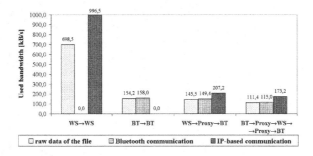

Fig. 6. Measurement results of a file-transfer using SDP and Web Services

The measured results, as depicted in figure 6, show that our middleware leads to efficient results in heterogeneous communication between SDP and Web Services as well as proxied remote SDP services. Thereby, the necessary overhead for Bluetooth communication is very small compared to the SOAP overhead of about 55,5% in the last scenario. These results support our approach to use a specialized service technology optimized for a special network technology and link between different technologies instead of using an all-over-IP issue using Web Services on Bluetooth enabled devices.

We had to observe that service usage on both sides, SDP and Web Services, is currently not applicable for applications with real-time requirements running on mobile devices. For example, a proxy needs more than 10 seconds to discover a new Bluetooth device and related services. So if a mobile device in range of Proxy_1 (figure 5) provides an SDP service, afterwards enters the range of Proxy_2 and leaves the range of Proxy_1, real-time requirements cannot be maintained during communication. Therefore, more support by the network layer and an approach for heterogeneous addressing is necessary to bypass the communication over the new proxy while subsequently updating service provision for new service searches. This approach will be introduced within the next section.

5 Heterogeneous Addressing and Mobility

Suppose a community with several ensembles combined by a backbone and overlapping communication ranges of their GPAP's Bluetooth interfaces. At the beginning, a PDA provides a Bluetooth service, a corresponding GPAP can find the service und provides it as a Web Service in the IP-based network. Thereafter, IP-based devices can use the service with the service parameters IP and port, both belonging to the GPAP. Now, when a mobile device enters the range of another GPAP and leaves the range of the previous GPAP, the new GPAP provides the PDA's Bluetooth service as a Web Service and the old GPAP stops the provision of the out-dated Web Service. In the IP network there is still a Web Service available representing the PDA's Bluetooth service, but the parameter IP changes while moving the PDA from a GPAP to another and service usage will be interrupted every time. This results in a frequently service search for IP-based devices which want to use the service (just a search needs more than 10 seconds). In order to circumvent the problem with the changing GPAP's IP in the service description, our network layer uses virtual IP addresses for Bluetooth devices in the IP network transparently for Bluetooth as well as IP-based devices. Therefore, a preparation phase shown in figure 7 is necessary before IP-based devices can communicate with Bluetooth devices using their corresponding virtual IP as depicted in figure 8.

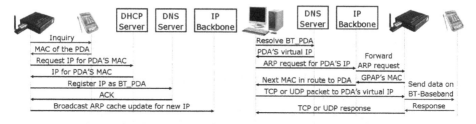

Fig. 7. Preparation phase   **Fig. 8.** Communication phase

In the preparation phase, a GPAP makes an inquiry to search for nearby Bluetooth devices. After receiving an answer which contains the MAC-address and the name of the Bluetooth device, the GPAP requests a virtual IP address for the PDA's MAC-address at a DHCP server. The GPAP stores the IP-MAC-name-set locally. Afterwards, the virtual IP and the name BT_PDA will be registered at a DNS server. The preparation phase ends with a broadcast for an ARP cache update in the IP network. Thus, we have a virtual IP address for every Bluetooth device, registered the name and the virtual IP, and published the new ARP information in the IP network.

Afterwards, a communication between an IP-based PC and a Bluetooth device can be realized as follows. The PC, only knowing the name of the Bluetooth device, requests the virtual IP of the device BT_PDA at the DNS server. Then, the PC broadcasts an ARP request into the IP network to get the next MAC of the route to the PDA. A GPAP, responsible for the virtual IP of the PDA, answers the request and sends his MAC back to the PC. Thereafter, a TCP or UDP communication can be organized by sending the packets to the virtual IP of the PDA. The GPAP transforms the packet and transmits the packet's data to the PDA using the Bluetooth baseband.

To return to the example of the mobile Bluetooth device moving from GPAP to GPAP, the so far implemented approach of using virtual IP addresses tends to a static IP address for corresponding Web Services, because they now contain the static virtual IP of the Bluetooth device and not the IP of the current GPAP which changes frequently. Thus, IP based devices using a corresponding Web Service of a Bluetooth device have not to search for the service and its IP address again. That's a main precondition for future service-based communication with mobile devices and further session handover mechanisms in heterogeneous networks that guides our ongoing implementation and evaluation.

6   Conclusion and Future Work

This paper presents a General Purpose Access Point which enables heterogeneous communication inside a cell, an ensemble of a smart environment, and inside a community which is characterized by devices using heterogeneous network and service technologies. We used the described service layer of the GPAP to combine Bluetooth and Ethernet cells using service proxying between Bluetooth SDP and IP-based Web Services and linked remote ensembles to a pervasive community to allow a service-based communication between members of different ensembles. An application for chat and file-transfer demonstrates our middleware and showed current limitations for mobile devices which could be circumvent with the heterogeneous addressing approach. The support of real-time requirements and handover for mobile devices and their services using the GPAP to bridge between heterogeneous network and service technologies guides our ongoing research.

Acknowledgment

This research is supported by the German National Science Foundation (DFG, GRK1424).

References

1. Dressler, E., Zender, R., Lucke, U., Tavangarian, D.: A new Architecture for Heterogeneous Context Based Routing. In: Appears in Proceedings of the 13th International CSI Computer Conference (CSICC), Kish Island, Iran (March 2008)
2. Zender, R., Dressler, E., Lucke, U., Tavangarian, D.: Meta-Service Organization for a Pervasive University. In: Proceedings of PerEL 2008. Workshop at 7th IEEE International Conference on Pervasive Computing and Communications, PerCom (March 2008)
3. Bluetooth Special Interest Group (SIG). Bluetooth specification, http://www.bluetooth.com
4. Park, W., et al.: Specification of the Bluetooth System (2007), http://bluetooth.com
5. ZigBee Alliance, http://www.zigbee.org
6. The OSGi Alliance. OSGi Service Platform. IOS Press, Amsterdam (2003)
7. Newmarch, J.: Foundations of Jini 2 Programming. Apress, New York (2006)
8. Microsoft Corporation. Understanding UPnP: A White Paper (2000)
9. Apple Inc. Bonjour Overview (2006)
10. BlueZ project. BlueZ, http://www.bluez.org
11. Avetana GmbH. avetana Bluetooth JSR 82 implementation, http://www.avetana-gmbh.de/avetana-gmbh/produkte/jsr82.eng.xml
12. Weerawarana, S., Curbera, F., Leymann, F.: Web Services Platform Architecture: Soap, WSDL, WS-Policy, WSAddressing, WS-Bpel, WS-Reliable Messaging and More. Prentice Hall International, Englewood Cliffs (2005)
13. Cordeiro, C., Abhyankar, S., Toshiwal, R., Agrawal, D.: BlueStar: Enabling Efficient Integration between Bluetooth WPANs and IEEE 802.11 WLANs. ACM/Kluwer Mobile Networks and Applications (MONET) Journal (2004)

14. Lim, Y., Kim, J., Min, S.L. Ma, J.S.: Performance Evaluation of the Bluetooth-based Public Internet Access Point. In: Proceedings of the 15th International Conference on Information Networking, ICOIN (2001)
15. Mackie, D.S.: Extending the Reach of Personal Area Networks by Transporting Bluetooth Communications Over IP Networks (2006),
    http://eprints.ru.ac.za/861/01/mackie-msc-tr07-23.pdf
16. Liu, K., Li, J., Huang, P., Fukuda, A.: Adaptive Acquisition Multiple Access Protocol in Wireless Multihop Mobile Ad Hoc Networks. In: Proceedings of the 55th Vehicular Technology Conference, VTC (2002)
17. Li, J., Haas, Z., Sheng, M., Chen, Y.: Performance Evaluation of Modified IEEE 802.11 MAC for Multi-Channel Multi-Hop Ad Hoc Networks (2003)

Location Based Logistics Services and Event Driven Business Process Management

Christoph Emmersberger, Florian Springer, and Christian Wolff

Senacor Technologies AG, Vordere Cramergasse 11, 90478 Nürnberg, Germany
{christoph.emmersberger,florian.springer}@senacor.com
University of Regensburg, 93040 Regensburg, Germany
christian.wolff@computer.org

Abstract. Location-based Services (LBS) [1] have already started their market penetration process and several platforms capable of running LBS are available. With the number of LBS increasing, the current development is targeting consumer applications, although LBS have a high potential for enhancing business processes in companies as well. Considering business process optimization, one concept recently discussed in the field of Business Process Management (BPM) [2] is *Event-Driven* Business Process Management (ED-BPM) [3], which combines Business Process Management (BPM) and Complex Event Processing (CEP) [4]. This paper introduces ED-BPM for LBS in the logistics field, exemplifying its potential use with an example for a logistics order process execution.

Keywords: ED-BPM - Event-Driven Business Process Management, LBS - Location-based Services, CEP - Complex Event Processing, GPS - Global Positioning System.

1 Introduction

This section provides an introduction to the concepts of Location-based Services (LBS) and Event-Driven Business Process Management (ED-BPM) in the context of logistics. It also gives an overview of the current market situation in the logistics industry sector. J. Schiller and A. Voisard define Location-based Services as "a recent concept that denotes application integrating geographic location (i.e. spatial coordinates) with the general notion of services" [1, page 1]. This means that LBS offer information related to their current location over a network, usually by using mobile devices. The fundamentals of LBS are based on military location systems (e.g. the *Global Positioning System* (GPS)) and mobile network communications. A wealth of applications that offer information related to the service users' actual position has been developed so far, e. g. restaurants and sights recommendation systems [5] or applications showing which friend is close to the user [1]). Compared to existing positioning systems (e.g. mobile navigation systems with deployed maps), the information is not statically installed on the mobile device but can be updated during the application execution upon a service request. Looking beyond consumer services, LBS obviously have a high potential for enhancing business processes as well. In this

D. Tavangarian et al. (Eds.): IMC 2009, CCIS 53, pp. 167–177, 2009.

paper we identify several services which could enhance current logistics order handling processes with more flexibility.

"The term Event-Driven Business Process Management is a combination of actually two different disciplines: Business Process Management (BPM) and Complex Event Processing (CEP)."[3]. BPM is seen as a management discipline to "support the design, enactment, management and analysis of operational business processes." [6]. This means that the business processes express each company's unique way of running their business which is their most valuable asset [3]. Processes are triggered by events; at the same time, they may publish events themselves during process execution. An event can be described as "anything that happens or is contemplated as happening" [7, page 5]. Events are sent over event processing networks (EPN) [7] where they can be filtered, routed, aggregated and may result in actions. These tasks are executed by middleware components with event processing capabilities (especially CEP engines).

The rest of this paper is organized as follows: In ch. 2 we give an introduction of current challenges for information processing in the logistics domain. Ch. 3 describes a common logistics process model and gives an in-detail description of selected processes, while ch. 4. presents an analysis of both, the processes' weaknesses as well as potential for optimization by introducing innovative LBS. Finally, ch. 5 discusses how location based services may be coupled with event-driven business process management.

2   Basic Characteristics of Logistics Companies

Basic concepts of current logistics have been established in the second half of the 20th century, although there is still no generally agreed-upon definition for "logistics" yet. In the literature the common understanding of logistics reaches from "simple" operations for transporting, handling, and warehousing of goods to more intricate management functions (*supply chain management* [8]): "Even when taking all the different opinions into account, a consensus exists [...] that the central function of logistics is the bridging of space-time disparities concerning goods and materials." [8, page 10]. To realize efficient goods and material logistics, an *adequate information supply* helps to provide a "(...) more precise picture of the sales development" [9] as well as to face the current market situation.

In this paper we highlight several LBS examples based on current logistics order processes for small and large logistics service providers (large package deliverers as well as smaller courier service providers). According to the Messenger Courier Association of America (MCAA), the difference in the business models is that the so called "big four" "DHL, UPS, FedEx and USPS [...]" of "[...] the delivery business [...] do not provide same-day delivery services uniquely designed to meet specific individual customer needs." [10, page 3]. The reason for that can be found in the order and shipment execution processes which have been originally designed for large throughputs. Fig. 1 shows the differences of large and small companies which becomes obvious when the delivery area covered, the number of employees, or the technical infrastructure typically used are considered.

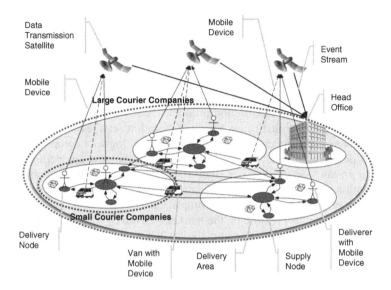

Fig. 1. Structural Differences of Small and Large Logistics Service Providers

Large logistics companies can be characterized by owning a global delivery network which is segmented into smaller pieces (i.e. regional distribution networks or delivery areas (Fig. 1)) to obtain the manageability of logistics complexity. The physical delivery process is not executed as a direct relation from the supply to the delivery node, and contains usually several steps over different distribution nodes.

Large companies already use several types of mobile devices (e.g. navigation systems or handheld scanners) to keep track of the state of their delivery processes. They operate on day-based, fixed-calculation production plans which can not be adjusted during their execution. Their business is optimized for delivering huge quantities of goods in small timeframes. The global quantity of delivered items is typically greater than 1 million items per day [14].

Small logistic companies or courier services work in small delivery areas like a city or a community instead of operating on a global delivery network. Therefore these companies usually can only offer their services within their own delivery area with the exception of cooperation with other service providers working in different delivery areas (Fig. 1). In comparison with big logistics companies, typically a single person is responsible for the whole delivery process from the delivery to the supply node including pick up, transport and delivery of packages. Small courier companies have to deliver their goods based on legal stipulations [15]. A stipulation is the traceability within the delivery process. Therefore several steps of the process have to be logged or journalized. While big logistics companies use hand scanners for this step, courier services often perform this manually and paper-based. In contrast to large logistics companies, small couriers deliver only a few hundred or thousands goods per day. They can act more flexibly, due to their size of typically about 25 employees [10]. In addition, the small amount of orders and the limited delivery area enhance flexibility and customer satisfaction for courier services.

Fig. 2 identifies four main parties that put pressure on the logistics domain. The first party is determined as customer's perspective: The increasing demand for time-definite [11] and end-to-end documented processes forces logistics companies to create faster, more flexible processes. Besides the demand for new products, customers own a huge bargaining power that results in decreasing margins.

The second force that puts pressure on the market can be identified as the threat of new competitors that create substitution products. A new competitor for the logistics industry is the IT industry that offers new collaboration services for information and document exchange which were formerly transported by logistics companies.

The third pressure party is closely connected with the new competitors, because they create a *product substitution* perspective: New products go beyond collaboration services mentioned above. Such services may provide online real-time information, which was formerly sold by the logistics companies.

The last party that puts pressure on the market is given by logistics suppliers which gain more and more influence, because the tendency of sourcing services to other companies encourages these companies to create more and new services. At the same time, it raises their bargaining power. This analysis should make clear that both, small as well as large companies need to improve their processes.

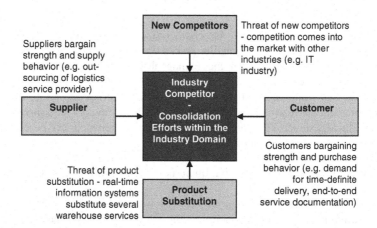

Fig. 2. Competitive Environment in the Logistics Domain derived from [11]

To exemplify the issues of small and large logistics service providers in more detail, the following section introduces state of the art logistics processes starting from a general logistics process model.

3   The Common Logistics Process in Large and Small Companies

Fig. 3 shows the simplified structure of a common logistics process model. The model can be applied to large and small logistics companies alike as well as to specialized customer-service providers. Similar process models can be found in [12] and [13].

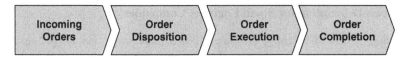

Fig. 3. Common Logistics Process Model

Based on the experience of the authors in several projects in the logistics domain, there is a large difference in executing the common logistics shown above process model depending on the business model. Based on the common model, the following section provides a more detailed process description for large and small logistics service providers. While it is idealized to a certain degree, we intend to explain the basic characteristics of current processes in logistics.

3.1 Process Description for Large Logistics Companies

1. *Incoming Orders:* Customers place their orders via e.g. internet portals, installed software, call centres or email. After the orders have been placed, package deliverers calculate their production plans based on the present order amounts and generate their work schedules (i.e. pickup, transportation and delivery). All items which have not been placed until a fixed time (e.g. 8pm) cannot be included in the task schedule.
2. *Order Disposition:* A logistics delivery process takes place between different nodes in the global network. There may be several nodes (hubs and distribution centres) between delivery endpoints that handle the routing of goods. Calculating work schedules is a complex task which be do not discuss here.

   After finishing the work schedule calculation the plans are distributed over the companies' local area network (LAN) to the mobile devices. The reason for the data transmission via LAN is the widespread delivery area with a partially missing area-wide mobile high speed network connection (e.g. UMTS) enabling the transaction of a large amount of data. After the initial load is finished, the deliverer can start with order execution.
3. *Order Execution:* During order execution, the deliverer approaches several nodes to pickup packages which have been pre-announced from customers by their order placement. At each node, packages labels are scanned to record their current order state. Besides the tracking of the order process, the scan is also used to confirm the transfer of risks and liabilities.

   During transportation, there can be several transit nodes where different distribution mechanisms occur (e.g. truck trailer exchange, manually sorting mechanisms, machine-based sorting). At these transfer nodes the packages need to be scanned again to throw state-change enabling tracking events. While the process is executed, a huge amount of events is collected from each single transported item.
4. *Order Completion:* At the package delivery node, the recipient confirms the successful transfer of perils by signing the order fulfilment form e.g. on a handheld scanner. The confirmation generates a final tracking event which is sent to the central information system. The order will be marked as successfully completed in the IT system and will be available for further processing in a financial services system, for example.

3.2 Process Description for Small Logistics Companies

1. *Incoming Order:* Currently, customers place there order via telephone, fax or email. The orders are directly placed in the company's head office or call center. An order for a courier service can be a pick up of an important compact disc (CD) with the layout of a flyer which has to be delivered to the printer or the transportation of a transplant from one hospital to another. Customers also place continuous orders where a courier has to pickup and deliver the daily post from the client.
2. *Order Disposition:* Depending on the priority of the order, staff decides manually and in many cases without software support on the point in time when the order has to be executed. High priority orders (express courier service) will be directly transmitted via cell phone to the responsible staff member. Orders with a lower priority (standard courier service) are collected and transmitted to the service staff on the next day or in a free time slot.
3. *Order Execution:* Before start of work the service staff gets a list of tasks to be executed during the working day. The execution of the schedules is sequentially except for high priority orders.
4. *Order Completion:* After a single order is completed, service staff starts with the tasks of the next order. Usually, service staff completes all assigned orders before the head office is informed about the order status.

4 Process Analysis: Weaknesses and Potentials

The difficult market situation forces logistics companies to optimize their business processes [16]. Based on the common process model, the main issues for large as well as small logistics companies are identified (Fig. 4).

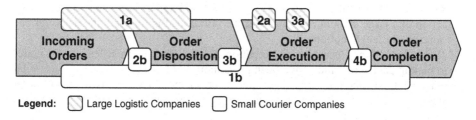

Fig. 4. Process Issues of Large and Small Logistics Companies

4.1 Process Issues of Large Logistics Companies

1a. Incoming orders that arrive after the deadline for order disposition cannot be considered for the next work schedule, even if the capacity utilization is not even close to 100%.
2a. Once the route schedules are calculated and pushed on the navigation systems, they are static and can not be adjusted according to current traffic and order situation.

3a. Due to the large amount of tracking events and the known limitations of mobile network connections, the actual state of the delivery process is an ex-post calculation. Adjustments based on past experience might mess up the ongoing delivery process. Enhancements in information supply can increase the flexibility for order disposition as well as enhance the resource efficiency.

4.2 Process Issues of Small Logistics Companies

1b. Due to manual (e.g. status report via cell phone) or paper-based journalizing approaches a real-time introspection of the order status is not possible. Automatically and electronically transmitted status responses, e.g. via special mobile devices have the potential to enable real-time insight and reduce the effort of the staff during the process. Insight about orders is also necessary to assure optimal order disposition.

2b. Currently, time- and cost-efficient order disposition is not possible: An overview of all orders and their respective status as well as the geographical position of service staff is needed to dispose tasks in an optimal way. This is primarily important for incoming, high priority orders which have to be executed immediately. The service staff has to be equipped with a mobile device that allows sending the geographical position as well as the order state.

3b. Assignment of orders from the head office to the service staff is currently done manually via cell phone calls. Modern mobile devices allow transmission of orders directly to the mobile device of the service staff.

4b. Currently, service staff has to take care of reaching the right destination in an efficient way. The reason for that is that the staff has no information about the actual traffic situation, etc. The taken route is in most cases not the optimal track. Modern navigation systems help resolving this issue.

Table 1. Location Based Services for Process Enhancement

	Courier Service Provider	Large Package Deliverer
Optimal Order Disposition based on Order State and Geographical Position	++	+
Electronically order Transmission depending on Geographical Position of the Courier	++	+|0
Rerouting of goods depending on the geographical position of the receiver	-	++
Effective Route Scheduling and Guidance by Using Different Event Sources	+	+
Potential process improvement and relevance:	++ very high + high	0: low - not relevant

4.3 Location Based Services for Process Enhancements

Based on the process issues identified above several LBS can be identified to improve the logistics companies' processes. Tab. 1 gives an overview of such LBS along with their relevance for small and large logistics companies. The suggestions will be discussed in more detail below.

4.3.1 Optimal Order Disposition Based on Order State and Geographical Position

To resolve one of the existing issues of the order execution process, a LBS for optimal order disposition based on real-time order-state confirmation was identified. Status information combined with the geographical position of the courier or service employee enables the logistics company to react on short term, high priority orders in the way of re-scheduling the order disposition. The re-scheduling occurs e.g. when a customer calls in, to place an order for an express shipping. The disposition of this order can be calculated based on the closest distance of a service employee to the customer. The second restriction which has to be considered for re-scheduling the order disposition is the capacity of the courier. These can be calculated based on the order-state information sent through mobile devices. Optimal order disposition has to be done centrally in the head office based on the transmitted status information of the couriers.

4.3.2 Electronically Order Transmission Depending on Staff Position

In order to enable an optimal order disposition, a mobile device needs the functionality of receiving the disposed data. The disposition has to be calculated based on the current position of the courier and needs to be published to the mobile device to provide the new information containing the changed working schedule.

In large companies this mechanism is currently not possible because of the non-availability of real time status data and missing area-wide network connections, in small companies it is executed manually via calls on the mobile phones. Recently released mobile devices and the growing network accessibility create the potential to extend the existing functionalities for enabling an automatic order transmission. This extension creates more efficiency by reducing manual task and enabling more process flexibility.

4.3.3 Rerouting of Goods Depending on the Geographical Position of the Receiver

The increasing mobility of people creates the customers' demand for receiving their packages at their current whereabouts. An extreme example for the increasing mobility is the life of business consultants who are usually working during the week at their customer's site and not in their place of residence. If they urgently need media (e.g. books, newspapers, magazines) they had ordered before they left, the order process needs to be adjustable to sending the goods to the place where they stay. That demand requires short term re-routing which can be realized as follows: After a package has been picked up at the delivery node, the receiver retrieves information via SMS or email about the beginning of the shipment. After the information has been delivered, the receiver can decide to which place he wants to get the package. If he likes to change the delivery address he needs to response to the SMS or email with an updated delivery address.

4.3.4 Effective Route Scheduling and Guidance by Using Different Event Sources

The inclusion of different event sources enables a more efficient delivery process: Such event sources may include a traffic message channel (TMC) which transmits current traffic information. The information can be used by correlating these events with the scheduled routes of the transportation vehicles to enable re-routing in case of traffic congestions. Other event sources in that context are e.g. weather, flight and train information to enable forecasting as well as avoiding delivery delays. A proof of concept that evaluates technologies for achieving this approach already exists [17].

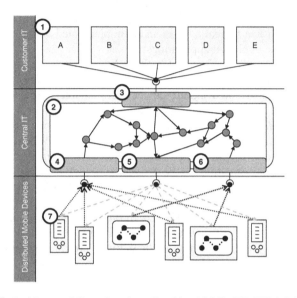

Fig. 5. Architectural Overview for a Combined LBS - ED-BPM Solution

5   Combining LBS with Event Driven Business Process Management

For realizing the proposed LBS that are designed to resolve the current issues in the logistics domain, the solution approach is comparable to existing ED-BPM reference models for other industry domains, like for example in the financial services domain [18]. Taking a look at the logistics context, the conceptual architecture has three layers (Fig. 5): The *"Customer IT"* layer, onto which the logistics company has limited influence only, the *"Central IT"* layer of the logistics company which hosts all applications that affect the logistics service provider and the *"Distributed Mobile Devices"* layer which is spread out over the delivery areas. The following enumeration explains the solution architecture of Fig. 5 based on the numbers posted in the overview diagram:

1. *Customers IT Systems:* Each customer has its own IT systems, which are realized on different technologies from different software vendors. These application systems need to be connected to the central IT systems of the logistics service provider to enable order placement and state-information reception.

2. *Event Correlation Engine:* The central component of the logistics companies' IT infrastructure is an *event correlation engine* or *complex event processing engine*. This component correlates information coming from customers, the mobile devices in the delivery areas and from potential other sources (e.g. traffic- and weather information) to provide a real-time insight in the ongoing processes. The correlations and aggregations are deposited as event patterns. If an event pattern matches, the engine is capable to send a new, complex event to the affected peripheral systems. The communication relation the surrounding peripheral systems is realized through so called event adapter.

3. *Event Adapter for Customers IT Systems:* The event adapter for customer IT systems is responsible for retrieving orders as well as sending state information to the customers. It is a logical adapter and is implemented on several technologies, depending on the deployed applications.

4. *Event Adapter for Receiving Order State Information:* The event adapter for receiving order state information is placed at the border between the central IT system and the distributed mobile devices. The adapter collects all information from the mobile devices related to the current state of an order.

5. *Event Adapter for Position Information:* The adapter for position information gathers the location information of the mobile devices. When using the global positioning system, the information is declared as longitude and latitude. Other possible position information can be derived from mobile transmission towers.

6. *Event Adapter for Distribution of Re-Scheduled Working Tasks:* If an event pattern that causes a re-scheduling of current tasks has matched in the CEP engine, the information needs to be published through a specific event adapter. This means that changes in existing route and working schedules are published to the mobile devices while they operate in the delivery areas resulting in dynamic real time adaptation of routes and schedules.

7. *Mobile Devices:* Mobile devices are used to support the order execution process. They route the deliverers to their next destinations and keep them informed about the orders they have to accomplish. Mobile devices enable the tracking of the current order state, the actual position of the packages and the employee's position for extending the existing order disposition and routing processes. To achieve this enhancement their functionality is extended by LBS as well as ED-BPM in combination with adequate data loading and distribution mechanisms.

6 Conclusion

This paper provides analyses current issues in process management in the logistics domain and discusses the coupling of location based services and event-driven business process management. Following the identification of current issues in the delivery process of large and small logistics service providers, we suggest four location based services for order scheduling and route planning and propose an architectural sketch for LBS / ED-BPM in logistics. While there are still major conceptual as well as technical problems that need to be resolved (e. g. area-wide mobile network coverage), the concept sketched above helps to understand how LBS may be applied in the daily business of a logistics company. The core issue of modeling and detecting relevant complex events in this model will be a key issue for further research in this area.

References

[1] Schiller, J., Voisard, A.: Location-Based Services. Elsevier the Morgan Kaufmann Series (May 14, 2004) ISBN: 1558609296

[2] Chang, J.F.: Business process management systems: strategy and implementation. CRC Press, Boca Raton (2006)

[3] Özsu, M.T., Liu, L.: Encyclopedia of Database Systems, 1st edn. Springer, Heidelberg (2009)

[4] Luckham, D.: The Power of Events: An Introduction to Complex Event Processing in Distributed Enterprise Systems. Addison-Wesley Professional, Reading (2002)

[5] Focus online Digital: Umgebung checken: Around me, http://www.focus.de/digital/handy/iphone/tid-14047/iphone-apps-umgebung-checken-around-me_aid_394119.html (Downloaded 2009/06/08)

[6] Aalst, W.v., Hofstede, A.t., Weske, M.: Business Process Management. In: van der Aalst, W.M.P., ter Hofstede, A.H.M., Weske, M. (eds.) BPM 2003. LNCS, vol. 2678, pp. 1–12. Springer, Heidelberg (2003)

[7] Luckham, D., Schulte, R.: Event Processing Glossary - Version 1.1. Event Processing Technical Society (July 2008)

[8] Deepen, J.M.: Logistics Outsourcing Relationships. Physica-Verlag, Heidelberg (2007)

[9] Dyckhoff, H., Lackes, R., Reese, J.: Supply chain management and reverse logistics. Springer, Heidelberg (2003)

[10] MCAA Messenger Courier Association of the Americas, Same-Day Delivery and the Messenger Courier Industry: A Profile of the Less than 24 Hour Delivery Industry and its Value, Washington DC (2006)

[11] Pfohl, H.-C., Dalquen, P., Deller, M., et al.: Güterverkehr - eine Integrationsaufgabe für die Logistik. Erich Schmidt Verlag GmbH (2003) ISBN 9783503074587

[12] Ordys, A.W., Uduehi, D., Johnson, M.A., Thornhill, N.F.: Process control performance assessment: from theory to implementation. Springer, Heidelberg (2007)

[13] Windt, K., Hülsmann, M.: Understanding Autonomous Cooperation and Control in Logistics: The Impact of Autonomy on Management, Information, Communication and Material Flow. Springer, Heidelberg (2007)

[14] Goldschmitt, W.: DHL Express Post beendet US-Abenteuer, Frankfurter Rundschau, (November 11, 2008), http://www.fr-online.de/in_und_ausland/wirtschaft/aktuell/1627600_Post-beendet-US-Abenteuer.html (Downloaded 2009/06/12)

[15] Regulierungsbehörde für Telekommunikation und Post (20.04.2002), http://www.kurier.com/sites/bdkep/doku/2df_Offermann-Thesen.pdf

[16] BdKEP - Bundesverband der Kurier-Express-Post-Dienste e.V., KEP aktuell - Dem KEP-Mittelstand gebührt Aufmerksamkeit (January 2009), http://www.kurier.com/2007-04-14/artikel/15-2009.pdf

[17] Springer, F., Emmersberger, C.: Event Driven Business Process Management taking the Example of Deutsche Post AG - An evaluation of the Approach of Oracle and the SOPERA OpenSource SOA Framework. University of Applied Sciences, Diplomarbeit (2008), http://www.citt-online.de/downloads/EmmSpr_Diplomarbeit_Final.pdf

[18] Ammon, R. v., Emmersberger, Ch., Ertlmaier, Th., Etzion, O., Paulus, Th., Springer, Fl.: Existing and Future Standards for Event-Driven Business Process Management. In: Proc. DEBS, Third Int'l Conference on Distributed Event-Based Systems, Nashville/TN (to appear, 2009)

My World – Social Networking through Mobile Computing and Context Aware Application

Keyur Sorathia and Anirudha Joshi

IIT Bombay
keyurbsorathia@gmail.com
anirudha@iitb.ac.in

Abstract. Social networking websites are being regularly used by individuals, groups, friends, colleagues etc. where they share information, communicate with each other by means of using websites like facebook, orkut, twitter, my space & many more.

Increasing internet connectivity and rapid adoption of mobile devices, social networking have migrated to mobile platform; which is accessible anywhere, anytime users' want. In this paper, we describe design of a new concept mobile application based on contact based social networking. In addition to this, it also describes how a system-aided application can enhance user experiences; helping users to understand other users' activity, help them navigate easily and encourage the use of this application. This application is focused on activity sharing, real time location sharing and media sharing between phonebook contacts.

Keywords: Interface design, mobile computing, 3G, social networking, system aided application.

1 Introduction

Social networking is group of individuals looking to share information, their experiences, develop friendship, professional relationship etc. People are part of different social groups and interact with different people in various situations and activities. Social networking websites bring individual and groups together to interact with each other through chat rooms and share personal information, ideas around the topic and to know unknown people. This means, although you are in India, you can make friends from other countries, know their culture, new languages etc. A number of websites and mobile applications are focused on making friends, profession contacts, mobile chat, photo-video sharing, instant messages, photo blogging, mobile games, interacting with family members, friends, colleagues etc.

Because of the technological evolution in recent years, mobile devices are pervasively connected to global network as well as to persons. The development of location based services and the rapid adoption of mobile devices such as cell phones, gaming machines and handheld computers by a wide variety of users, social networks have migrated onto the mobile platform. Social networking has tremendous jump in usage over the last few years, reaching Facebook and Myspace global user numbers to 115

D. Tavangarian et al. (Eds.): IMC 2009, CCIS 53, pp. 179–188, 2009.

million to 73 million respectively in April 2008 [1]. In mobile social networking segment revenues from mobile communication in 2007 were approximately US \$3.4B, which is expected to climb US \$28B in 2012 [2].

But, there is a gold feature that none have yet:

"System aided context aware application which understands users' need, physical presence detection and information exchange with other users"

This paper describes an opportunity to look forward to a system that can understand users' behavior, their activity and help them navigate through their social contacts. It also explores the possibility to understand new ways of social networking that encourages physical meetings & interactions between users through mobile phones. There are three main parts of paper describing the background and research studies, concept development and prototype section. Future work section will emphasize on future possibilities of this application, how it can be embedded more with context awareness and system behavior.

2 Background and Research Studies

The target demographic people of "My World" application are people aged 20-35 years old, who have lots of friends, meet them, go out a lot and socialize. A detailed research was commissioned to determine the principal ways of social networking, users' behavior, their experiences and habits. The idea is to know users' perception of social networking, how and what platform they use to socialize.

In general, their main engagement in a social network is to talk to their family, friends, colleagues and people around them. Here are some interesting sayings from users:

- I am always updated about what is happening in my friend's life, if someone has gone somewhere I am aware of it, if someone has done something I know what is happening, it is very interesting to know what is happening in other people's lives
- Social networking is a way one does a permanent small talk
- It is about connecting people even if I am at my private space
- When you are frustrated, when you do not want to work anymore then you chat, gossip, make fun, talk sense, talk non-sense, talk interesting things, hobbies and pass your time
- Social networking term is coming from human ability to make friends with each other. These days social networking helps us to make new friends, help finding our lost and old school friends.

3 Concept Development

Looking at the research studies done, the solution revolved around a touch based concept mobile application focusing on contact based social networking using 3G technology. We have divided them down into three categories.

- Activity Sharing
- Real Time Location Sharing
- Media Sharing

In addition to these three categories, a 3D phonebook was designed arranging phone-book contacts around a 3D cylinder in several layers – each representing a social network of the user. User can define what information to be shared with which social network. An intuitive user interface allows user to view several options like call, message, real time location, email, share, my access & more; just on a single tap.

3.1 Activity Sharing

"Imagine a system which helps you to understand your friend's activities like meeting, party, office etc. and helps you to behave accordingly"

In a real life situation, when you peep in a friend's office and find her busy in a meeting, you quietly close the door and leave. We do not do on the phone.

Activity sharing is a way to bring similar behavior on the phone. (which has a tendency to ring at critical times when one is seeking some privacy). This system behaves according to the activity shared by the user. For example, if user is in a meeting, system recognizes her activity and does not allow 'merely social' calls. Activity sharing is a system-aided application, helping user to understand other user's activities and encourages the behavior accordingly.

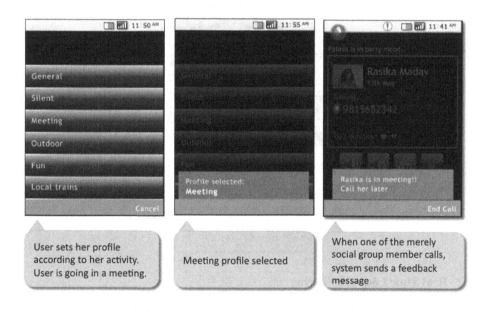

User sets her profile according to her activity. User is going in a meeting.

Meeting profile selected

When one of the merely social group member calls, system sends a feedback message

When user finishes her meeting, she changes her activity by selecting "General" profile

System sends a notification message about the user's activity

A single tap on notification calls the user

User can share other activities, which is displayed & create a topic of conversation

3.2 Real Time Location Sharing

"Imagine yourself walking into a conference, sea beach, party, bar, subway station etc. and seeing your friends around and physically meeting them"

You may have hundreds of friends on facebook/orkut etc., even thousands, but on a lonely Friday you cannot figure out which one is nearby.

Real time location sharing explores the idea of sharing real time location with your phonebook contacts. System understands user's location and shows orange circle on the top right corner of contact's photograph to describe user's presence in specified area. System allows user to directly send message or chat with other user. It is an attempt to encourage physical meeting and interaction between users through just a single tap.

Orange circles above the face represent contacts in user's area

Tapping on contact picture displays the menu, from where user taps on address

The map shows the contact's real time location. The user can explore the map to find other contacts.

Tapping on contact's picture opens up a chat box, from where the two users can start chatting

3.3 Media Sharing

"Imagine yourself going into someone's phone, taking a song or contact information without disturbing that person depending upon user defined privacy settings"

You know where your friend hides his home key (in a potted plant above the ledge) & a couple of times you have borrowed his vacuum cleaner by letting yourself in, yet you cannot access his MP3 without bugging him.

Media sharing allows user to share media contents like images, videos & music with single and multiple phone book contacts and groups. A simple navigation system helps user to share her family videos, vacations pictures and his favorite music to her contacts. It also includes a new feature called "my access" which helps user to navigate through other contact's phone and add media contents to her phone, depending upon the user's defined privacy settings.

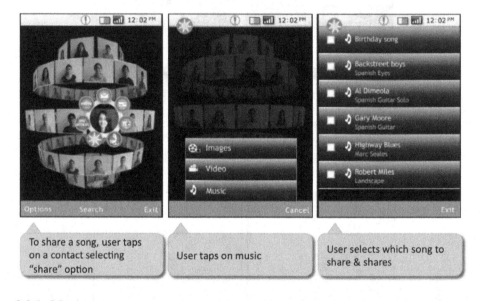

3.3.1 My Access

Why do I have to bug a friend to give me a great music collection? Do I always need to ask my friend if want to exchange a collection of group photos?

My Access understands user's defined privacy settings and allows permitted user to enter in other users' media contents and access certain amount of information. User can enter in to her friend's phone, find media contents like group pictures, favorite music collection etc., copy it and add to her phone. Here, the user can copy shared media content from their friend's phone to their phone.

3.4 D Phonebook

"Imagine yourself into a complete new paradigm of playing through your phone book, look at pictures of contacts instead of text, send a message, mail, call, view

real time location, share media contents & other relevant information on just a single tap"

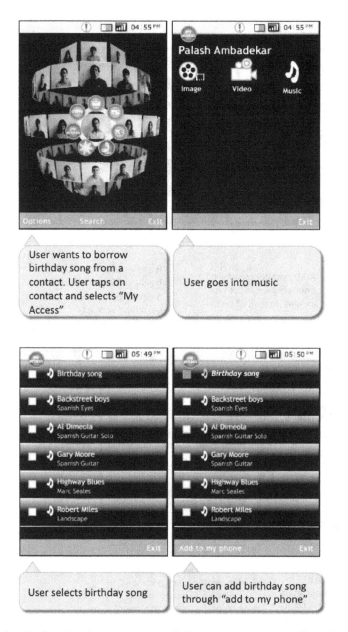

Conventional phonebook uses a textual format to present a list of phonebook contacts. 3D phonebook contacts are represented by a 3D cylinder-allowing user to play with the contacts represented through images. Here, 3D cylinder can be rotated in the space and customized according to the user's need. User can customize contacts according to the group or in alphabetical order. Just a single tap allows user to view 7 options including call, message, address, email, share, my access & more.

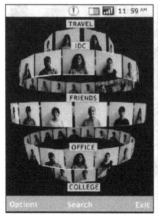

A 3D cylinder structured phonebook has contact images instead of text

It allows user to navigate freely in 3D space, which is a new & playful way of searching contact

Tapping on contact opens a menu consisting of 7 options, which allows user to view 7 features on just a single tap

Double tapping on contact image or tapping on "more" option opens more detail about the contact as shown

4 Prototype

Being a concept mobile application, "My world- social networking through mobile computing and context aware application" was prototyped using Adobe Flash CS4 (action script 3.0). Actual phonebook contacts of a user were taken as a reference to build the application and a 3D phonebook. Different social network like family, friends, colleague etc. of user were defined and presented in layers of 3D phonebook. Google Maps images were taken as reference to show real time location & address of the user. The prototype was build on a touch screen computer for a demo version and testing purposes.

5 Future Work

In particular, we are interested in developing an application that can reach up to a stage of complete context aware application, which would not only behave according to the location or user fed data, but it can also understand the context and the behavior of a user and act accordingly. In future, we would also like to investigate users' behavior, experiences and habits in different context, understand their social networking needs & behavior and design accordingly.

6 Conclusion

In this paper, we describe our conceptualized mobile application based on social networking using 3G technology. We offered three different domains of social networking through mobile computing. In addition to this, a complete new interface of phonebook allows interesting & intuitive navigation through contacts & several other features. It encourages users not only to meet virtually, but also encourages physical meetings & interaction between social contacts. This application can be a starting point of a system-aided application, helping user to understand the context & behave accordingly. We emphasized on playfulness & intuitiveness of the application. This application can also create new forms of behavior that fade the distinctions between virtual and real world interactions.

References

[1] Venture beat,
    http://venturebeat.com/2008/06/13/
    why-facebook-is-now-the-number-one-social-network-in-the-
    world-and-why-this-matters/
[2] Perey, http://www.perey.com/mobilesocialnetworking.html
[3] Dearman, D.: That does not tell me what I want. In: CHI 2006 (2006)
[4] Ziv, N.D., Mulloth, B.: An exploration of mobile social networking: dodge ball as a case in point. In: IEEE conference proceedings, MBusiness conference (June 2006)
[5] Mashable – a blog on social networking, http://www.mashable.com/
[6] Dogdeball, http://www.dodgeball.com/

[7] Social networking resource center,
`http://www.deitel.com/ResourceCenters/Web20/`
`SocialNetworking/tabid/1231/Default.aspx`

[8] Dearman, D., Hawkey, K., Inkpen, K.M.: Rendezvousing with location aware devices: Enhancing social coordination. Interacting with computers 17(5), 542–566 (2005)

[9] Schmidt, A., Gross, T., Billinghurst, M.: Introduction to Special Issue on Context-Aware Computing in CSCW. Computer Supported Cooperative Work 13, 221–222 (2004)

[10] Bassoli, A., Moore, J., Agamanolis, S.: tuna Local Music Sharing with Handheld Wi-Fi Devices. In: Proc. of 5th Wireless World Conference 2004, UK (2004)

[11] McKnight, L., Dajani, L.: Trends in mobile social networking for mainstream consumers and supporting technologies required. In: Barcelona, W3C workshop on social networking, Spain, January 15-16 (2009), `http://www.w3.org/2008/09/msnws/`
`papers/Nokia-Stratemerge.pdf`

[12] Juice Caster, `http://www.juicecaster.com`

[13] Mocoscope, `http://www.mocoscope.com`

[14] Mobimii, http://www.mobimii.net/

[15] Qeep, `http://www.qeep.net/`

[16] mobikade, `http://www2.mkade.com/`

Challenges in Content Based, Semantically Decoupled Communication on Neighbor-Relations

Henry Ristau

University of Rostock, Faculty of Computer Science and Electrical Engineering,
Institute of Computer Science, Information and Communication Services Group,
18051 Rostock, Germany
`henry.ristau@uni-rostock.de`

Abstract. Announcement/Subscription/Publication (ASP) is an approach for content-based communication, decoupled in time, space, threads and semantics. The idea behind ASP is to rely only on neighbor-relations and does not involve any communication infrastructure above the link-layer. This makes the ASP approach perfectly suitable for application communication in smart and ubiquitous environments. In this paper we analyze the process of implementing scenarios using the ASP approach. After specifying the necessary requirements for application interfaces and the behaviour of the middleware we identify circumstances where problems could arise and present our solutions to these problems.

1 Introduction

Future smart and ubiquitous environments emerge from the ad-hoc cooperation of different devices surrounding the user in her everyday life. The goal of such cooperation is to support the users in what they are doing e.g. by enriching her environment with information, controlling parts of her environment to suit her needs or providing her with services to support her daily routine.

A main requirement for this kind of cooperation is the ability of applications on these devices to exchange information. The aforementioned ubiquitous environments however often have a very heterogeneous nature in terms of devices and communication techniques. Furthermore their ad-hoc generated topology can not be expected to provide compatible communication protocols or even unique addresses. This results in the strong need for a middleware to support decoupled communication in space, time and threads [1][2][3].

Publish/Subscribe has emerged as a paradigm to support the distribution of information in a decoupled way. However especially in ad-hoc generated smart environment very heterogeneous applications are to be expected. Applications provide and seek for information in different formats and levels of aggregation. This often requires information to be aggregated and processed while it is delivered from source to sink and results in the need for decoupling in semantics as well.

D. Tavangarian et al. (Eds.): IMC 2009, CCIS 53, pp. 189–200, 2009.
© Springer-Verlag Berlin Heidelberg 2009

Announcement/Subscription/Publication (ASP) [4] is an approach to provide content based communication decoupled in space, time, threads and semantics. It is based only on neighbor relations between adjacent brokers and thus can perfectly adapt to heterogeneous environments even with a rather high degree of mobility resulting in a dynamic topology. ASP as a communication approach only provides a system architecture and a routing algorithm with some optional enhancements. In the task of implementing a scenario using the ASP approach a number of problems and challengers arise that need to be overcome to result in efficient communication. In this paper we will outline the most important problems and provide solutions to overcome them.

Therefore the paper is structured as follows. In the following section we present related work. In section 3 we outline the application interfaces and the routing requirements that provide the framework for an ASP implementation. Afterwards we analyze the three phases of ASP and the associated problems and explain, how we solved them. In section 5 we conclude our work and present ideas for future work.

2   Related Work

Publish/subscribe (pub/sub) provides the basis for decoupled communication between an information source and an information sink in time, space and threads [2]. Content-based routing (CBR) [5] implements the pub/sub paradigm in a fully distributed fashion by introducing a network of brokers. Between these brokers subscriptions are distributed in the form of filters that either match a publication or not. Using these filters each broker keeps a local routing table to allow for content-based routing of publications. CBR was enabled to work in mobile ad-hoc networks (MANETs) e.g. by [6][7].

Pub/sub especially for smart environments is provided by MundoCore [8], a modular middleware for the requirements of pervasive computing based on a microkernel design. It supports structured, hierarchical and single-hop strategies for routing resulting in high scalability and adaptability. It allows for channel and content-based subscriptions.

There are many algorithms for on demand routing in MANETs most common probably ad hoc on demand distance vector routing (AODV) [9]. The basic idea of such routing protocols is for a node N_1 to find a communication partner N_2 in a MANET on demand by sending a route request (RREQ). This request is flooded through the MANET until it eventually reaches N_2 which replies with a route reply (RREP). The RREP is send back on the shortest path to N_1 and a communication path is established. The main advantage of on demand routing is that a path is created only on demand and thus, no traffic is induced by nodes that do not communicate. Furthermore through the availability of unique (IP-)addresses and a homogeneous communication protocol (IP) throughout the MANET, these routing algorithms can be highly optimized. If such conditions can not be guaranteed as in heterogeneous ubiquitous environments, these algorithms are not applicable.

3   Requirements

In this section we outline the requirements for the ASP approach induced by its adjacent components which are the applications and the network.

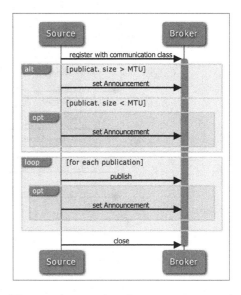

3.1   Source

A source application (source) provides information to other applications by message publication. The availability of these messages is to be distributed by the middleware and the messages have to be communicated towards interested applications.

A source's interface consists of four methods as shown in figure 1. Registration is done stating the communication class[1]. Afterwards an announcement is provided by the source. This is

Fig. 1. The interface between source and broker

optional if the size of messages is < MTU. At this time the source starts to send messages to the middleware. From that moment on the announcement can be updated anytime by the source. If the source does not send further messages, it closes its registration at the middleware.

3.2   Sink

A sink application (sink) consumes information from other applications by receiving messages from the middleware. Therefore it registers at the middleware with an optional filter to narrow the amount of received announcements. Based on the contents of received announcements it can

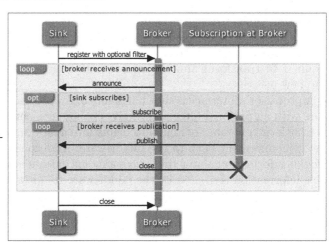

Fig. 2. The interface between sink and broker

---

[1] The taxonomy given in [4] divides scenarios in four communication classes by message size (one packet (< MTU) vs. fragmentation) and message frequency (one message vs. message stream).

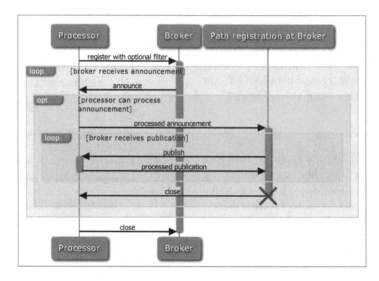

Fig. 3. The interface between processor and broker

subscribe to associated messages. The middleware then delivers all associated messages to this sink. The registration of the sink can be closed completely by the sink itself or partially by the middleware if no more messages are to be expected for the current announcements. The respective interface is shown in figure 2.

3.3 Processor

Processor applications (processors) are needed for message aggregation or processing on the path between source and sink if semantic decoupling is required. Since message processing can be one way in many scenarios, a processor is only required to transform announcements into new announcements and messages into new messages.

A processor's interface is shown in figure 3. A processor registers at the middleware with an optional filter and receives announcements afterwards. If it is able to transform a number of announcements into a new announcement, it sends the new announcement back to the middleware. Additionally, the processor has to provide information about the source announcements and the processing metric. This information is needed by the middleware to optimize paths from source to sink and to avoid communication loops. Later on, if needed, the processor has to transform messages associated to its source announcements into new messages and send these to the middleware. The processor's registration can be closed fully by the processor itself or partially by the middleware if no more messages are to be expected for the current source announcements.

3.4 Efficient Routing

In respect to the network the middleware has to distribute announcements among all brokers and find efficient paths between source brokers and sink brokers for message delivery. These paths need to involve the right processors if message aggregation or processing is necessary for the communication. The choice of processors needs to be optimized according to the following criteria.

If multiple processing steps are needed, the most efficient combination is to be selected. Efficiency thereby depends on the metric provided by the processors. If multiple equal processors are available, a single one needs to be selected for every path between a source and a sink to avoid unnecessary double processing of messages. If multiple aggregating processors are available, aggregation has to be done as early as possible to optimize network utilization. In the contrary, if processing enlarges the message size, late processing might be useful to again optimize network utilization.

4   ASP-Algorithm

As ASP works in three phases, we analyze each phase for its specific challenges to fulfill the aforementioned requirements.

4.1   Announcement Phase

An announcement is generated by the ASP middleware from the information provided by a source or processor. If generated or received, an announcement is to be distributed to all neighbors except the one this announcement has been received from and to all processors and sinks except for those that provided a filter that does not match the announcement.

Announcement Identifiers. By processing respectively routing through a processor, an announcement's content is changed. To avoid loops where an announcement is processed back and forth again and again and to detect duplicates after similar processing in different processors, announcements need to be compared based on their content. Additionally, announcements need to be referable by later subscriptions, publications and eventually other announcement. Therefore we generate a content based identifier for each announcement upon its generation in a source's or processor's broker using a hash algorithm. Comparison and recognition of an announcement therefore can easily be done by comparing the announcement's identifier.

Based on the implemented scenario, similar processing of an announcement in different processors can lead to slightly different announcements actually representing the same content. One example are arithmetics on floating point values that can lead to different results by rounding. Such announcements result in very different identifiers owing to the hash algorithm. If this can be the case for a scenario, we suggest to extend the source/processor-interface by providing a mask to the ASP middleware to allow the application to unmask the parts of the announcement that should not be used for hash generation.

Announcement Caching. A very efficient way of repairing broken paths in a stream scenario is for the source's broker to start a new announcement after it was informed of the path failure. Since this can happen before the initial announcement becomes invalid, multiple valid announcements for the same information can be circulating. In combination with announcement caching, where each broker caches all current announcements and forwards them to newly discovered neighbors, the number of announcements to cache and forward rises. In a dynamic scenario path failures can thus increase the network traffic which leads to more path failures and finally to parts of the network being overloaded.

In a scenario where the announcement for a given source and therefore its identifier does not change, this behaviour can be avoided by introducing a sequence number that is incremented on every re-announcement. Thus invalid announcements can be sorted out easily. If however the announcement changes frequently, its identifier changes as well. To recognize invalid announcements each re-announcement can be provided with a list of identifiers of invalidated announcements. This allows receivers of the re-announcement to immediately remove announcements that became invalid. Even the attachment of only the most current invalidated identifier to each re-announcement decreases the occurrence of the aforementioned network overloads to a minimum.

Path Metrics. To evaluate different paths in the process of announcement distribution a path metric is calculated from the link metrics on the announcement's path. These can be metrics of communication links or processing links. This leads to a number of requirements for such a metric:

1. There must be a metric to reflect the transmission costs between two adjacent brokers and a metric to reflect the costs of processing in a processor.
2. A path metric will most likely contain transmission costs and processing costs. Thus, there must be a method to compare or even aggregate them.
3. If processing involves data aggregation, multiple path metrics need to be aggregated as well. This process has to reflect the requirement, that aggregation should be done as early as possible to optimize communication costs.
4. To generate useful path metrics for the publication phase they actually need to reflect the costs of message transmission. Especially the size of a message can be very different from the size of the associated announcement and can largely influence the transmission costs.

In our experimental scenarios we identified time based metrics as very promising to fulfill the first two requirements. The basis for our metric is the expected transmission time (ETT) like in [10]. The ETT is therefore calculated in the network abstraction layer (NAL) [4] by monitoring the packet round-trip time and the number of necessary (re-)transmissions as this approach can easily be generalized for any kind of link layer communication and above. For announcement processing the processing time replaces the ETT as basis for the metric. Inspired by the parameter *willingness* in OLSR [11] we multiply the time with an effort factor to reflect additional criteria like power consumption, monetary costs or network respective CPU utilization. The effort for each connection is dynamically determined by the brokers NAL and the effort for announcement processing is provided by the processor itself.

The path metric P for a path with m links of either announcement forwarding or processing is generated from the connection respective processing metrics M by summation: $P = \sum_{r=0}^{m} M_r$.

This has two main advantages. Firstly an announcement only needs to carry one value to reflect the overall path metric. To append a new step to the path metric its connection or processing metric is added to the announcement's path metric before this step. Secondly, if n announcements A_i are aggregated somewhere on their path, the path metric of the announcement is summed up with the processing metric of their aggregation M to generate the new announcement's (A') path metric: $P_{A'} = M + \sum_{i=1}^{n} P_{A_i}$.

This procedure fulfills the third requirement. If possible, an earlier aggregation of two announcements on the same path will automatically result in a lower path metric for the resulting announcement given that the metric of the early aggregation is about the same as for the later one.

The fourth requirement results in a fundamental problem because the actual size of the message is not necessarily known at the time the announcement is distributed. However, we assume that a processor can estimate the size s' of a message after processing in relation to the size s_i of all n messages before processing by providing the growth factor G with $G = \frac{s'}{\sum_{i=1}^{n} s_i}$.

We propose to add a size factor S to each announcement. The initial value is $S = 1$. On a processing step involving n source announcements, the size factor of the resulting announcement A' is calculated as: $S_{A'} = G \times \sum_{i=1}^{n} S_{A_i}$.

This gives the following general equation for the path metric on each step.

$$P_{A'} = \sum_{i=1}^{n} P_{A_i} + M \times S_{A'} \tag{1}$$

$$= \sum_{i=1}^{n} P_{A_i} + M \times G \times \sum_{i=1}^{n} S_{A_i} \tag{2}$$

However, if a step only involves communication, there is only one source announcement ($n = 1$) and no change of size ($F = 1$) resulting in the following very simple equation.

$$P_{A'} = P_A + M \times S_A \tag{3}$$

The path metric using the size and growth factors should result in a more realistic path metric for the communication of the message afterwards because changes of message size from processing are reflected in the overall path metric of received announcements. Processing steps that enlarge (reduce) a messages size will result in a better overall path metric if performed late (early) in the communication path.

4.2   Subscription Phase

Based on the contents of a received announcement, a sink can decide to receive the associated message or message stream. The delivery of the message or message stream afterwards is channel based. We call this channel an active path. A path is activated by the sink's broker sending a subscription back to the source's broker.

Path Identifiers. The announcement's identifier is used to identify the contents to be delivered on an active path later. The active path itself needs another unique identifier to allow for multiple active paths for the same content that can be unsubscribed from or repaired independently of each other. Therefore we use a path identifier that is generated randomly by the sink's broker for each subscription it initiates.

In the unlikely event of two sinks generating the same random path identifier for the same contents, the second subscription will overwrite the first one. This results in all further publications being received by the second sink only. However this state will only last until the announcement becomes invalid and another one is initiated. Thereafter new path identifiers are generated by both sink's brokers and another collision is extremely unlikely.

Empty Announcements. The standard flooding algorithm results in the first announcement that is received being forwarded. This does not necessarily have to be the announcement with the best path metric. To find the one path with the best metric one can use an extension we called empty announcements [4]. An empty announcement contains only the announcement's identifier and the path metric and is used to inform a broker of a better path being available after the announcement has already been delivered. The utilization of empty announcements is only useful if very large messages or streams with a very large amount of data are to be delivered. Otherwise the costs of delivering all the empty announcements can easily outreach the gain of the best path.

Using empty announcements results in one announcement and eventually one or more empty announcements for better overall paths being received by a sink's broker. Since that broker never knows if one more empty announcement is to be expected, it would have to send a subscription for the first announcement. For each empty announcement it would have to send a subscription for the new path and afterwards unsubscribe from the old path. This can generate a large amount of unnecessary network traffic.

Our solution to this problem is for the sink's broker to react to the first received announcement with a subscription to assure that one active path exists as soon as possible. To optimize that path later on, the broker collects all empty announcements it receives for a not too small amount of time. After this time has passed it treats the last empty announcement with a better path metric than the ones before as the best path. If such a best path is available, a subscription for that path is initiated. Afterwards the broker unsubscribes from the initial path. This procedure is illustrated in comparison to the trivial approach in figure 4.

This procedure guaranties fast delivery of the first publications to decrease the initial latency. For the expected large amount of later publications the best possible path is used to unload the communication and processing infrastructure. The number of subscription rounds is limited to a maximum of two.

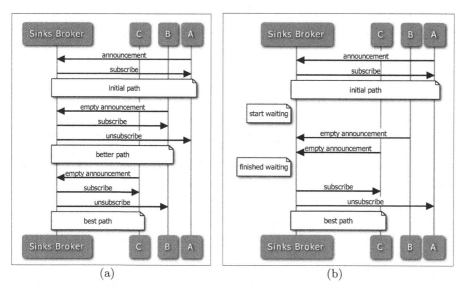

Fig. 4. Case where the sink's broker receives three empty announcements: Instead of adjusting the active path on every empty announcement (a), it waits to collect all empty announcements and adjusts the active path once (b)

4.3 Publication Phase

The purpose of the publication phase is the delivery of messages on every active path. Depending on the communication class, one message can be fragmented into multiple publications. Additionally multiple messages can form a message stream. If a message is fragmented into multiple publications, each publication must be delivered reliably because loosing one fragment would render the whole message useless. If multiple messages are to be transmitted as a stream, it is desirable to deliver as many messages as possible but we assume loosing single messages in a stream not as problematic. Developers of scenarios and applications for ASP have to choose their communication class carefully to reflect this assumption.

Publication Caching. According to the aforementioned behaviour, all publications that belong to a single message, are cached in every broker on the active path. This has two main advantages. On the one hand, this reduces network and CPU utilization. If a new subscription is initiated by a broker that results in an active path which overlaps with an existing active path the publications that have been transmitted on the existing active path do not have to be transmitted on that path again. Instead they can be forwarded immediately by the broker where both active paths stop to overlap. This also reduces the message transmission latency to the aforesaid subscribing broker.

On the other hand, publication caching is a major requirement for time decoupling. Especially if only one eventually fragmented message is to be transmitted the source might already be disconnected at the time when any subscriptions arrive. Only by caching the publications they can still be delivered towards the subscriber in this case.

5   Conclusions and Future Work

In this paper we analyzed the process of implementing scenarios using the ASP approach for content based decoupled communication based on neighbor relations. After specifying the necessary requirements for application interfaces and the behaviour of the middleware we identified six circumstances where the ASP approach could lead to problems and presented solutions how to solve these problems:

- different announcement identifiers for the same content,
- multiplication of invalid announcements through announcement caching,
- path metrics for optimal paths,
- path identifiers to keep active paths independent,
- a re-subscription algorithm to reduce subscription overhead if empty announcements are used, and
- publication caching to assure time decoupling.

In the following sections we present advantages and disadvantages of implementing a scenario in heterogeneous ad-hoc environments using the ASP approach.

5.1   Advantages

The only precondition for the network topology of a scenario to be implemented using ASP is that a bidirectional link-layer communication of any kind between neighboring nodes is available in a way that the nodes and communication paths form a connected graph. The degree of heterogeneity does not matter. Globally unique network addresses are not necessary.

Because of its decoupled nature, the ASP approach is very flexible in dynamic environments and therefore allows for mobility and ad-hoc topologies involving mobile components.

If a scenario is implemented using ASP, all applications - sources, sinks and processors - are fully decoupled from each other and the network in terms of location, availability and semantics. This enables independent development of applications. Another advantage is the resulting completely distributed infrastructure. Applications can be added, removed and even used in parallel at any time.

5.2   Shortcomings

Even though using ASP has many advantages we do not want to forget to mention its shortcomings. The most important one is probably that due to the utilization of flooding algorithms, ASP does not scale to arbitrary large networks. Boundaries for the distribution of announcements are necessary in a physical, an algorithmic and a logical way. Physical boundaries can be environments of limited size like smart or ubiquitous environments. Algorithmic measures are e.g. a time to live or context based means to limit the distribution of an announcement. With logical boundaries we refer to the fact that especially if algorithmic measures are taken the developer needs to understand that the availability of information is not distributed and thus known everywhere anymore.

Another disadvantage owing to the nature of the pub/sub paradigm might be that ASP is unidirectional. Content is delivered from the source to the sink only. In most scenarios especially for content based communication this is not a problem. However there might be the necessity for bidirectional communication. If bidirectionality is limited to a confirmation of reception the ASP approach could probably be extended without much problems to provide such a confirmation. But this would destroy the very idea of decoupled communication in time and especially in threads. Therefore we did not propose such an extension ourselves.

5.3   Future Work

For future research we plan to investigate three open questions: Can the ASP approach be extended to not only allow the implementation of single scenarios but to provide a toolkit for ASP based application developing?

Can the ASP approach be extended to provide more quality of service features for applications? Right now ASP allows for applications to provide a communication class to optimize communication which means it can select between optimization for small vs. large messages and optimization for single messages vs. a message stream. Features like reliability vs. load-efficiency or real time demands for applications could be very interesting as well.

Can ASP be extended to provide efficient bidirectional communication in heterogeneous ad-hoc environments? The availability of such bidirectional communication could allow for e.g. content based service announcement with subsequent channel based service utilization.

Acknowledgement

Henry Ristau is supported by a grant of the German National Research Foundation (DFG), Graduate School 1324 (MuSAMA).

References

1. Eugster, P.T., Felber, P.A., Guerraoui, R., Kermarrec, A.M.: The many faces of publish/subscribe. ACM Comput. Surv. 35(2), 114–131 (2003)
2. Aldred, L., van der Aalst, W.M., Dumas, M., ter Hofstede, A.H.: On the notion of coupling in communication middleware. In: Meersman, R., Tari, Z. (eds.) OTM 2005. LNCS, vol. 3761, pp. 1015–1033. Springer, Heidelberg (2005)
3. Aldred, L., van der Aalst, W.M.P., Dumas, M., ter Hofstede, A.H.M.: Dimensions of coupling in middleware. Concurrency and Computation: Practice and Experience (February 2009)

4. Ristau, H.: Announcement/subscription/publication: Message based communication for heterogeneous mobile environments. In: Mobile Wireless Middleware, Operating Systems, and Applications, Mobilware 2009, Berlin, Germany (2009)
5. Carzaniga, A., Wolf, A.L.: Content-based networking: A new communication infrastructure. In: König-Ries, B., et al. (eds.) IMWS 2001. LNCS, vol. 2538, pp. 59–68. Springer, Heidelberg (2002)
6. Baldoni, R., Beraldi, R., Cugola, G., Migliavacca, M., Querzoni, L.: Structure-less content-based routing in mobile ad hoc networks. In: Proceedings of International Conference on Pervasive Services, ICPS 2005, July 11-14, pp. 37–46 (2005)
7. Petrovic, M., Muthusamy, V., Jacobsen, H.A.: Content-based routing in mobile ad hoc networks. In: Mobile and Ubiquitous Systems: Networking and Services, MobiQuitous 2005, pp. 45–55 (2005)
8. Aitenbichler, E., Kangasharju, J., Muhlhauser, M.: Mundocore: A light-weight infrastructure for pervasive computing. Pervasive and Mobile Computing (2007)
9. Perkins, C., Belding-Royer, E., Das, S.: Request for Comments: 3561 - Ad hoc On-Demand Distance Vector (AODV) Routing. RFC (July 2003)
10. Draves, R., Padhye, J., Zill, B.: Routing in multi-radio, multi-hop wireless mesh networks. In: MobiCom 2004: Proceedings of the 10th annual international conference on Mobile computing and networking, New York, NY, USA, pp. 114–128 (2004)
11. Clausen, T., Jacquet, P.: Request for Comments: 3626 - Optimized Link State Routing Protocol (OLSR). RFC (October 2003)

Towards a Spatial Position Information Management System for Interactive Building Environments

Stefan Knauth[1], Rolf Kistler[2], and Alexander Klapproth[2]

[1] Stuttgart University of Applied Sciences - HFT Stuttgart
Schellingstr. 24, D-70174 Stuttgart, Germany
stefan.knauth@hft-stuttgart.de

[2] Lucerne University of Applied Sciences CEESAR - iHomeLab
Technikumstr. 21, CH-6048 Horw, Switzerland
rolf.kistler@hslu.ch, info@iHomeLab.ch
http://www.iHomeLab.ch

Abstract. Indoor localisation systems enable a variety of assistance services in commercial buildings and home environments. Applications in this area cover guidance, asset tracking, behaviour monitoring for smart assistance and alert systems, intelligent remote control, to name a few of them. It is desirable to employ a position information management system which collects, manages, offers and distributes such information. This paper focuses on how to design such a middleware which gathers position information from one or more localisation systems and provides this data to interested and authorised applications.

1 Introduction

Today there exists a variety of indoor localisation systems. Many of them allow the determination of spatial positions of persons or things, with system-dependent accuracy in the range of a few centimeters to some meters. The systems considered in this paper typically comprise objects whose positions shall be determined, and a fixed positioning infrastructure deployed in the indoor environment. The position of an object is typically calculated by determining ranges between the object and reference points given by the infrastructure, and/or determining angles between the object and reference points. For fundamental examples see [1,2,3,4,5,6,7,8,9]. In applications like goods tracking, robot control, navigation and logistics such systems are already marketed by several companies (references: [10,11,12,13]). Applications in the building and home automation sector are currently evolving. An obvious application is guidance in hospitals. Here patients receive a display device, for example a PDA. This device may visually and, if desired, also acoustically, guide a patient to destinations within the hospital and back to his room. Such systems may also be used in large scale office buildings. Also in this area lie the commonly used phone-like devices employed in museums or exhibitions, which provide location based explanation of exhibits.

D. Tavangarian et al. (Eds.): IMC 2009, CCIS 53, pp. 201–211, 2009.

Another example are universal remote controls, which may be dedicated physical devices or which may be implemented in software on a mobile device of the user. Such devices allow access to control functionality based on the position of the device. A popular example is the control of equipment in a presentation room. Here the blinds, lightning, sound volume and the beamer may be controlled by a presenter (see for example [14] and references therein).

In private homes such systems are yet quite uncommon. A typical resident may actually not have a need for such a system, especially if it costs money. Today one application focus of localisation systems for private homes and retirement- or nursing homes is the sector of assistance systems, in particular the topic "AAL" (Ambient Assisted Living). Main applications are fall detection, object localisation and data provisioning for behavioural monitoring systems. Such systems increase the subjective and objective security sentiment since the system can alert someone if the inhabitant is in a situation where he/she needs help but is not able to actually perform the alert.

In a future scenario, where such systems are installed at numerous locations, it is predictable that further, not yet thought-off applications will be demanded. A monolithic application which includes a localisation system, data analysis and some reaction and/or presentation mechanisms will not easily allow use cases like inclusion of new types of sensors or integration of new applications. In this paper we discuss a structure for a position related information management system for interactive building environments. We do not focus on the localisation system itself since this is not part of the management system. We assume that the underlying localisation system(s) provides spatial positions of subjects/objects. Systems which deliver relative positions or other information which is not directly convertible to absolute spatial coordinates (with respect to a local reference frame) are not considered at this stage of the project.

A proof of concept implementation is presented: The demonstrator comprises a generic position information management system, which collects position information from underlying indoor localisation systems and offers services to clients which implement the actual applications. The system also manages static spatial information like floor maps and interaction points to allow the applications to identify position dependent services available at the current spatial context. On the application side, 2d- and 3d visualisation and interaction points are demonstrated.

2   Requirements

For an integrated position information management system for buildings, be it in the residential or in the commercial sector, we assume that at least the following data should be managed:

- Reference grid and building map: This includes information which can be used by clients for visualization of rooms and routes, and to relate positions of goods and persons for example to a room context given by area identifiers.

- Static objects. The static objects can be on one hand used for visualisation purposes, and on the other hand as tracking points, for example to enable applications like "alert if someone crosses line".
- Interactive objects - The interactive objects are static objects which are enriched with a so called "interaction point" functionality. An application may sense for interaction points in the vicinity of a person and then provide a position-related "action menu" to a user. For example, a user who uses a client on his mobile phone, may be presented a menu to switch the light on, call an elevator, or open a door, according to the spatial context of the user.
- Dynamic subjects/objects, whose position shall be observed. The position of these items will be tracked by underlying localisation systems. Dynamic subjects represent people who use a guidance application or which are tracked for security reasons. Dynamic objects are typically goods which are tracked for finding them or for which an alert shall be generated if they leave a specific region.

The above identified items shall be made available to interested and authorized applications by the management system. The list has been defined by analysis of the data needed for the functionalities given in the following list:

- Guidance
- Behavioural observation based alert applications
- Object finding
- Fall detection
- Position based control / remote control
- General location based services

These functionalities may be provided by dedicated client applications. According to the description given so far, the principal tasks of a spatial position information management system shall include at least:

- Sensor input for a variety of modalities. Some examples are: position information from localisation systems, position information from proximity-based detectors like movement detectors, pressure-sensor equipped floors and light barriers. The sensor input must be processed by an underlying localisation system to generate spatial coordinates of objects, which are collected by the actual management system.
- Data management: This includes recording, storing, retrieving and deletion of position data of dynamic subjects/objects, map-related spatial information, the map itself and static objects as well as data and bindings for action points.
- Application interfaces: There shall be interfaces which provide the above mentioned data to applications. The interface shall provide static data and shall allow subscription for the client to receive information on dynamic subjects/objects.
- Interaction interface: The system shall forward services provided by action points to the clients registered at the system. Note: Besides keeping an identification and a binding to a service interface, it is not a task of the system

to itself provide high level services. In the case of action points, the system shall act as a broker rather than interpret the communication between an application and the services behind an action point.

- The system shall manage authentication and privileges at the service interface.

3 Related Work

Intelligent building and home automation systems are highly relevant research topics, and numerous groups perform research on integrated systems. We will here focus only on some particular projects which have reasonable overlap with our particular requirements. The "Mundo" [15] Project goal is to provide universal models, concepts, architectures, and frameworks for a ubiquitous computing world. The Mundo Vertical Architecture classifies the devices according to their primary function and shows their relationships. It is centred around a users personal device, called Minimal Entity (ME). Mundo comprises the "Indoor Scout - Local Positioning System (IRIS-LPS)" [4] which is an optical infrared local positioning system. The tracked objects carry active tags that emit infrared signals which are received by stationary mounted stereo-cameras.

Fraunhofer "Booth Staff Tracker" is an example of the Fraunhofer localisation systems portfolio [5], targeted to applications like Inventory Systems, Facility Management, Asset Management, Tracking of emergency responders or Anti-theft systems.

Some "early" indoor localisation systems were the Bat, Active Bat, Cricket, and Calamari projects [3,1,2]. Besides the comprehensive Mundo project, all of the above focus on the localisation technology. For most of them, the mentioned applications have been implemented. To our knowledge the applications were closely related to the particular localisation system, and technology independent position data management was not a main goal of the systems.

4 Experimental Implementation

4.1 System Overview

Fig. 1 explains the scope of the position information management system (PIMS) within a position based application infrastructure. The PIMS forms the center of the infrastructure. It receives position data, accesses a database and supports applications with position data. It also keeps binding information by which applications may access controllers by their spatial context.

Fig. 2 sketches an overview of the experimental Java implementation intended as a proof of concept. In the figure, the main components and interfaces are depicted. The core of the system is formed by the PIMS. A localisation system is connected via the LSI interface. This interface is actually implemented using Web Services. No UDDI Server is currently deployed. Instead connecting to a real world localisation system, the position data is generated by so-called

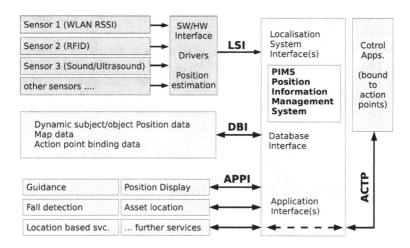

Fig. 1. Scope of the position information management system within a position based application infrastructure

PG (Position data generator) instances. The position data generator simulates objects which can be moved by user commands via CLI (Command line interface) or a GUI. Position data comprises the Cartesian coordinates of an object and the heading, which is an angle in the (x, y) plane and can either be interpreted as "direction of view" of the object or as movement direction. Position data is pushed to the server. The server stores this data and pushes it to registered applications. The applications subscribe to online position information on a per

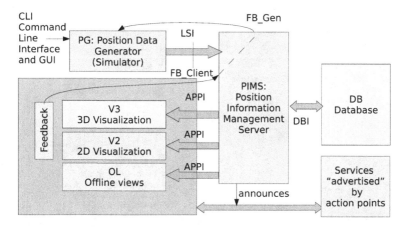

Fig. 2. Set up overview. The main blocks are: PG - Position data generator, PIMS - Position information server, DB - Database. The clients are grouped within the grey box. Arrows indicate flow of information. The feedback interfaces for simulation control are indicated by "FB...".

subject/object base. Additionally, applications may request map information, information on static objects and information on action points.

The usage of a "virtual positioning system", i.e. simulated position data, does not principally influence the validity of the implementation and results, since the localisation system itself is not part of the management system. Any localisation system can be connected via the LSI interface. Therefore typically a small tool needs to be created, which mediates between the given positioning system and the LSI interface of the management system (i.e. data format and interface modality conversion).

Currently implemented applications include 2d online visualisation, 3d online visualisation and offline visualisation, The latter requests previously recorded position data from the database via the PIMS.

4.2   PIMS: Position Information Management Server

The PIMS resembles the core of the system. It comprises 3 main interfaces. The LSI interface and the APPI interface are implemented using SOA. A "MySql" database (DBI interface) is accessed via ODBC/JDBC (Java "hibernate"). Fig. 3 lists the current database layout. For initial database setup and database maintenance like deletion of records a simple separate application has been created. The static information for the maps, the static objects and the action points is currently stored in an XML file. Its data structure is tailored to the needs of a building information system and contains among others information on boundaries like walls which are not traversable by subjects/objects, about visual objects like windows, tables, chairs, shelves, etc. These elements allow an

Fig. 3. Database structure

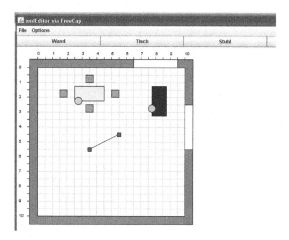

Fig. 4. Screenshot of the map tool. Rooms are easily created and edited by placing predefined objects on a canvas representing a particular area like one or some rooms or even a whole floor. Several such areas are related to each other by absolute coordinates with respect to a reference point in the building.

abstract visualisation of the area. It is not the aim of the map to give an optical exact representation of the room where the actual deployed interior is visible. Rather, since the system shall be easily deployable without having to render the real interior of a room, the map can be easily created and edited by a map creation tool using predefined visual components. An impression of the creation tool is shown in Fig. 4. The map data is actually not processed by the PIMS, but the PIMS provides this data to interested applications which themselves use the information for example for visualization or route planning. The application interface APPI is also implemented via SOA. Offered services are parsing the dynamic objects list, subscribing for position data of dynamic objects, delivery of this position data, retrieving of recorded data, retrieving of map and static data, and retrieving of action point locations as well as simple interfacing with applications bound to these action points.

To increase reliability of the system, it is possible to run several PIMS instances for a given region. All running PIMS receive the position information via the LSI interface in parallel. An application shall use services from only one of the PIMS instances at the same time. The database may be replicated, but the behaviour when recording position data to the database needs to be specified. Possible policies are to write it only to the currently accessed database and replicate it later by a regularly scheduled synchronisation service, or to perform the write operations to the databases simultaneously.

Given the above description, the main functionality of the PIMS is to act as an abstraction level between the position data sources and the applications, and to act as a central building data information system. No particular data processing is associated with the PIMS.

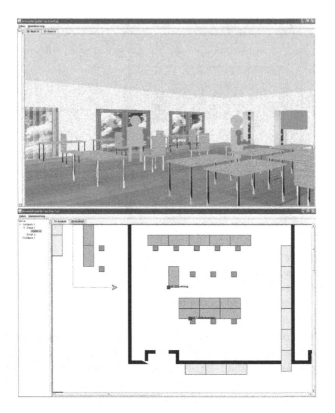

Fig. 5. Visualisation application screenshots. The two coloured squares (top) and rectangles (bottom) indicate interaction points.

4.3 Applications

Currently implemented applications are 2d- and 3d visualisation of dynamic subjects/objects in a 2d/3d building map context. The principal operation is as follows: A visualization client connects to the PIMS via web-services. He requests static data for a region (a floor or a room). Furthermore, the client parses the list of dynamic subjects/objects in the given region and subscribes to some or all of them. The subscription provides the client with regular position data updates. The client puts the received position data of dynamic subjects/objects into a spatial context by displaying a token for the object within a map (2d case) or a rendering (3d case) of the environment. The user can change the context (floor, area), viewport and the camera position interactively. Some screenshots (Fig. 5) give an impression of the visualisation application.

4.4 Position Sensing

The LSI interface provides the mechanism for receiving position information from underlying localisation systems/sensors. Such systems will push information into the PIMS. As mentioned, the current demonstrator does not use a real positioning system but uses object simulators, so called position data generators. These simulators simulate objects by reading trajectories out of a file or provide interactive online position manipulation via a GUI. This interactive manipulation can be performed directly via the visualisation client. A user who views an object, can directly manipulate the object position via keyboard commands, quite like in popular 3d virtual environments or computer games. This allows straightforward testing and evaluation of the system. The visualisation can be set in "objects perspective mode". Here the image screen rendered by the client directly simulates a persons view walking through the building. This enables applications like guidance to be tested on the system even without the need for the actual positioning system. At any stage, the position data generators can be replaced by a real localisation system not inducing any changes in the application.

4.5   Interaction Points

Applications are able to request information on "interaction points". The PIMS provides coordinates and binding data which links an action point with a dedicated control application. An action point may for example represent a light switch. When a person (a dynamic subject) is within a certain range of an action point, the current implementation of the visualisation shows a hint. The user of the visualisation application can then send a string to the action point object. The PIMS routes this information, enriched with the action point id and the object id, to the corresponding application. The application binding is stored in the database. This application is of particular use when run on a mobile device like a PDA (A PDA version is not currently implemented).

5   Conclusion

5.1   Current State

The paper has outlined a possible structure for a spatial position information management system for interactive building environments: The core component is a PIMS implementation, which provides applications with building data like maps and static objects and with position information for dynamic subjects/objects. For interaction, so-called "interaction points" serve as anchors for position-related building services typically in the automation and control domain. Some possible applications are outlined. Such a system can serve as generic platform for services and functionality for example in the sector of ambient assisted living.

A proof of concept of the PIMS and prototype applications have been implemented. Position information was not taken from an indoor localisation system but from so-called position data generators, which simulate dynamic subjects/objects.

A very simple interaction mechanism with building infrastructure has been developed.

5.2 Outlook

The analysis and implementation currently is at a very early stage. Interfaces and map- and object descriptions are very basic. Currently only position data and heading is taken as dynamic subject/object information. For a broader deployment, extension mechanisms should be included which allow for example inclusion of sensor information from acceleration sensors for fall detection, or manual sensor information like keys on a localisation tag for example for manual alerting or remote control. Also authorisation, privileges, safety and security needs to be addressed.

A next step will be to attach the PIMS to a real indoor localisation system like the iLoc [8] system at the iHomeLab, Lucerne [16]. Also more application prototypes shall be developed.

We think that the described approach may serve as anchor point for an open assistance framework for homes and smart homes providing assistance services for residents. We hope that the paper may stimulate fruitful discussions on what data and services such a system might provide.

Acknowledgements

The following B. Sc. candidates contributed to the the proof-of-concept implementation: Mathias Schwope, Frederik Rothe, Tobias Droste, Uwe Tartler, Victor Chernukhin and Tuan Nha Benjamin Luu implemented the PIMS functionality as well as the map editor. Dennis Ottenbacher, Nikolaj Burtasenkov, Daniel Roppelt, Alexander Moor and Jack Lee created the visualisation apps.

References

1. Smith, A., Balakrishnan, H., Goraczko, M., Priyantha, N.B.: Tracking Moving Devices with the Cricket Location System. In: 2nd International Conference on Mobile Systems, Applications and Services (Mobisys 2004), Boston, MA (June 2004)
2. Whitehouse, K., Jiang, F., Karlof, C., Woo, A., Culler, D.: Sensor field localization: A deployment and empirical analysis. UC Berkeley Technical Report UCB//CSD-04-1349 (April 2004)
3. Ward, A., Jones, A., Hopper, A.: A new location technique for the active office. IEEE Personal Communications 4(5), 42–47 (1997)
4. Aitenbichler, E., Mühlhäuser, M.: An IR Local Positioning System for Smart Items and Devices. In: Proceedings of the 23rd IEEE International Conference on Distributed Computing Systems Workshops (IWSAWC 2003), pp. 334–339. IEEE Computer Society, Los Alamitos (2003)
5. Fraunhofer IIS: Localization and Navigation,
   http://www.iis.fraunhofer.de/EN/bf/nl/index.jsp
6. Brüning, S., Zapotoczky, J., Ibach, P., Stantchev, V.: Cooperative positioning with magicmap. In: Workshop on Positioning, Navigation and Communication 2007 (WPNC 2007), Hannover, Germany (March 2007)

7. LaMarca, A., Chawathe, Y., Consolvo, S., Hightower, J., Smith, I., Scott, J., Sohn, T., Howard, J., Hughes, J., Potter, F., Tabert, J., Powledge, P., Borriello, G., Schilit, B.: Place lab: Device positioning using radio beacons in the wild. In: Gellersen, H.-W., Want, R., Schmidt, A. (eds.) PERVASIVE 2005. LNCS, vol. 3468, pp. 116–133. Springer, Heidelberg (2005)

8. Knauth, S., Jost, C., Klapproth, A.: i-loc: a localisation system for visitor tracking and guidance. In: Proc. INDIN 2009 7th International Conference on Industrial Informatics, Cardiff, UK, June 2009, pp. 262–266 (2009)

9. Knauth, S., Klapproth, A.: Indoor lokalisierung: Gesucht - gefunden. Design+Elektronik 1 (2007); WEKA Fachzeitschriften Verlag, Poing, Germany

10. Symeo GmbH: Symeo absolute positioning, http://www.symeo.com

11. CAIROS technologies AG: High resolution 3d positioning, http://www.cairos.com

12. Ubisense Limited, Cambridge, UK: Ubisense precise real-time location solutions, http://www.ubisense.net

13. Nanotron Technologies GmbH, Berlin, Germany: Robust, Reliable Wireless RF Products for Building Ranging and Location Solutions, http://www.nanotron.com

14. Kistler, R., Knauth, S., Klapproth, A.: An adaptive network architecture for home- and building environments. In: Proc. 12th IEEE Inter. Conference on Emerging Technologies and Factory Automation (ETFA 2008), Hamburg, Germany, September 2008, pp. 295–302 (2008)

15. Aitenbichler, E., Kangasharju, J., Mühlhäuser, M.: Experiences with MundoCore. In: Third IEEE Conference on Pervasive Computing and Communications (PerCom 2005) Workshops, Kauai Island, Hawaii, pp. 168–172. IEEE Computer Society, Los Alamitos (2005)

16. Lucerne University of Applied Sciences: iHomeLab-Denkfabrik und Forschungslabor für Intelligentes Wohnen, http://www.iHomeLab.ch

Modelling Device Actions in Smart Environments

Christiane Plociennik, Christoph Burghardt, Florian Marquardt,
Thomas Kirste, and Adelinde Uhrmacher

University of Rostock, Albert-Einstein-Str. 21, 18059 Rostock, Germany
firstname.lastname@uni-rostock.de

Abstract. Smart environments are places that contain numerous devices to assist a user. Those devices' actions can be modelled as planning operators. A problem when modelling such actions is the *persistent action problem*: Actions are not independent of one another. This is especially relevant when regarding persistent actions: An action that is being executed over a longer timespan may be terminated by a subsequent action that uses the same resources. The question is how to model this adequately. In dynamic environments with a high fluctuation of devices an additional challenge is to solve the persistent action problem with as little global information as possible. In this paper, we introduce two approaches: The first one locks resources which are being used by an action to prevent other actions from using the same resources. The second interleaves planning and execution of actions and is thus able to use software agents as "guards" for actions that are being executed. We furthermore compare the characteristics of both approaches and point out some implications those characteristics have on the modelling and execution of device actions in smart environments.

1 Introduction

Smart environments are places that contain numerous devices to help users accomplish certain tasks. Meeting rooms, for example, are typically equipped with projectors, canvasses, computers, cameras, and lights. In addition, users can bring mobile devices with them. What makes a smart meeting room smart is that it is able to integrate all those devices into one coherent ensemble that proactively assists the user, enabling her to focus on her core activities rather than on configuring the environment. For example, if the user has the intention to give a talk, a smart meeting room should relieve her of the tasks of manually connecting her notebook to the projector, adjusting the light level, etc. The device ensemble should perform these tasks for the user. Many researchers are concerned with the question how to enable such assistance [8,12]. One particularly promising approach is to assist users in smart environments using AI planning [7,1].

The key elements in classical AI planning are *operators*. These operators are actions that are described in terms of *preconditions* and *effects*. Preconditions

D. Tavangarian et al. (Eds.): IMC 2009, CCIS 53, pp. 213–224, 2009.

and effects are conjunctions of propositions that can be either true or false. For the action to be executed, its preconditions must hold. After the execution of the action, its effects hold. Consider the simple planning operator *CanvasDown*:

```
(:action CanvasDown
  :parameters (?c - Canvas)
  :precondition (not (CanvasDown ?c))
  :effect (CanvasDown ?c))
```

This operator is described in PDDL [11], a language widely used for planning problems. It describes the action of lowering a canvas. It has a single precondition which states that the canvas must not be down for the action to be executed. After execution the world state will have changed: now the canvas is down.

A planning problem consists of a domain description, a set of objects, a set of true conditions specifying the initial world state (all conditions not mentioned are assumed to be false) and a set of conditions specifying the goals of the planning process. The domain description is a set of operators. Objects are used to instantiate planning operators: All variables in operator descriptions are bound to an object. The variable *?c* in the operator description of *CanvasDown* is instantiated with all objects of type *Canvas* defined in the problem description. Thus, for each *Canvas* object one instance of the CanvasDown operator is generated. To solve a planning problem means to find a sequence of instantiated operators (a *plan*) which transforms the initial world state into the goal state. A comprehensive introduction to planning is beyond the scope of this paper, but can be found in [14].

The possible actions of devices in smart environments can be modeled as planning operators. This has the advantage that user assistance can be very flexible. Whenever a new user goal becomes apparent, a planner can consider all possible actions of all devices in the ensemble and search for a sequence that fulfills the goal. The action sequences need not be precompiled by a domain expert. Every device can carry descriptions of all its possible actions. Upon entering a new environment, it can provide these descriptions to the devices already present. This way, the device ensemble is constructed of modular pieces and can be dynamically extended. This is key for smart environments which are typically characterized by a high fluctuation of devices, yet it poses a special requirement on the planning domain: It should be modeled in a way that avoids global knowledge as much as possible. In other words, device actions should need as little as possible information about other planning operators. A naive way of modelling a smart environment is the following domain *smartenvironment-naive*:

```
(define (domain smartenvironment-naive)
  (:requirements :strips :equality :typing)
  (:predicates (Pointing ?c - Canvas ?p - Projector)
               (CrossbarIn ?n - Notebook)
               (CrossbarOut ?p - Projector)
               (DocShown ?d - Document ?c - Canvas)
               (isDown ?c - Canvas)
```

```
                (Hosts ?d - Document ?n - Notebook)
                (isMax ?d - Document ?n - Notebook)
                (Connected ?n - Notebook ?p - Projector))

(:action CanvasUp
  :parameters (?c - Canvas)
  :precondition (isDown ?c)
  :effect (not (isDown ?c)))

(:action CanvasDown
  :parameters (?c - Canvas)
  :precondition (not (isDown ?c))
  :effect (isDown ?c))

(:action MoveProjector
  :parameters (?c1 - Canvas ?c2 - Canvas)
  :precondition (and (Pointing ?c1 NEC-MT1065 )
                (not (Pointing ?c2 NEC-MT1065)))
  :effect (and (not (Pointing ?c1 NEC-MT1065))
          (Pointing ?c2 NEC-MT1065)))

(:action SwitchCrossbar
  :parameters (?n - Notebook ?p - Projector)
  :precondition (and (CrossbarIn ?n)(CrossbarOut ?p))
  :effect (forall (?x - Notebook)(when (= ?x ?n)(Connected ?x ?p)
          (not (Connected ?x ?p)))))

(:action Maximize
  :parameters (?n - Notebook ?d - Document)
  :precondition (and (Hosts ?d ?n))
  :effect (forall (?x - Document)(when (= ?x ?d)(isMax ?x ?n)
          (not (isMax ?x ?n)))))

(:action ShowDoc
  :parameters (?n - Notebook ?p - Projector ?d - Document ?c - Canvas)
  :precondition (and (Connected ?n ?p)(Pointing ?c ?p)
                (isMax ?d ?n)(isDown ?c))
  :effect (forall (?x - Document)(when (= ?x ?d)(DocShown ?d ?c)
          (not (DocShown ?d ?c)))))
```

The domain *smartenvironment-naive* models a smart meeting room containing two notebooks (NB1, NB2), two documents (Doc1, Doc2), eight canvasses
(LW1, LW2, LW3, LW4, LW5, LW6, VD1, VD2), three fixed projectors that
can each point to one fixed canvas (EPS3, EPS6, Panasonic), and one steerable
projector (NEC-MT1065) which can point to any of the eight canvasses. This
domain can be used for solving the planning problem *presentation*:

```
(define (problem presentation)
  (:domain smartenvironment-naive)
  (:objects NB1 NB2 - Notebook
```

```
          Doc1 Doc2 - Document
          LW1 LW2 LW3 LW4 LW5 LW6 VD1 VD2 - Canvas
          EPS3 EPS6 Panasonic NEC-MT1065 - Projector)
(:init (Hosts NB1 Doc1)
       (Hosts NB2 Doc2)
       (CrossbarIn NB1)
       (CrossbarIn NB2)
       (CrossbarOut EPS3)
       (CrossbarOut EPS6)
       (CrossbarOut Panasonic)
       (CrossbarOut NEC-MT1065)
       (Pointing LW4 NEC-MT1065)
       (Pointing LW3 EPS3)
       (Pointing LW6 EPS6)
       (Pointing VD2 Panasonic))
(:goal (and (DocShown Doc1 LW3)(DocShown Doc2 LW1))))
```

The goals of the planning problem *presentation* are to show document Doc1 on canvas LW3 and document Doc2 on canvas LW1. Using the domain description *smartenvironment-naive*, a planner could generate the following plan:

```
(CanvasDown LW1)
(CanvasDown LW3)
(Maximize NB1 Doc1)
(Maximize NB2 Doc2)
(SwitchCrossbar NB1 NEC-MT1065)
(MoveProjector LW4 LW3)
(ShowDoc NB1 Doc1 NEC-MT1065 LW3)
(SwitchCrossbar NB2 NEC-MT1065)
(MoveProjector LW3 LW1)
(ShowDoc NB2 Doc2 NEC-MT1065 LW1)
```

In this plan, the steerable projector (NEC-MT1065) is used to show both Doc1 on LW3 and Doc2 on LW1. In the real world, this is not possible, of course. A single projector cannot be used to show two documents on two canvasses simultaneously. Hence, the modelling of the domain is inadequate. Lowering a canvas, for example, is a very short action. In contrast, showing a document is an action that persists over a longer timespan. We thus call this a *persistent* action. We need to express somehow that if a projector shows a document, it is occupied. As soon as we maximize another document on the same notebook screen, connect the projector to a different computer via the video crossbar, or move the projector to another canvas, the first document is not visible anymore. Hence, the effects of the first *ShowDoc* action are not valid anymore. Thus, there is a dependency between the actions. We call this the *persistent action problem* because it applies to actions that persist as long as no other action is carried out on the same resources. This paper addresses the question how the persistent action problem can be solved. The additional challenge in smart environments is that we want to solve it with as little global information as possible. The remainder of this paper is structured as follows: In the next section we review some approaches that try to express dependencies among actions in planning. In Sections 3 and 4 we introduce two approaches that solve the persistent action problem. The first locks resources which are being used by an action to prevent other actions from using the same resources. The second interleaves planning and execution of actions and is thus able use software agents as "guards" for actions that are being executed. In Section 5 we point out some of the similarities and differences of the two approaches and discuss their implications for the modelling and execution of device actions in smart environments before concluding the paper in Section 6. In a nutshell, this paper makes the following contributions:

- We identify the persistent action problem.
- We describe and compare two approaches that solve the persistent action problem without requiring global knowledge.
- As a by-product of our work, we provide an example domain description that shows how smart environments can be modeled in PDDL.

2   Related Work

For decades, the planning community has strived to extend the classical planning paradigm to better express dependencies among actions. In the early problem solver Hacker [15], Sussman incorporated a protection mechanism for already achieved subgoals. Hacker employs a primitive backward chaining mechanism: It first chooses an action X that fulfills a goal. As long as action X has an unfulfilled precondition, it goes on to select an action that can fulfill this precondition. This process is repeated for every action that has open preconditions. If an action Y has been selected because it can fulfill one of action X's preconditions, this means that action Y must be executed at some timepoint prior to action X. Action Y now adds an expression called a *purpose comment* to a comment repository stating that action Y fulfills a precondition for action X. This purpose comment is kept in the repository until action X is executed. Whenever another action Z is chosen during this interval, the comment repository is checked to see if action Z's effects conflict with the purpose comment. This means that action Z would be executed after action Y, but before action X, and that action Y undoes the precondition action Y has achieved for action X. Should this occur, the process backtracks to avoid the violation. This protection mechanism resembles the concept of causal links introduced by McAllester and Rosenblitt [10]. Unfortunately, both mechanisms only protect conditions shared by two subsequent actions. Hence, they do not solve the persistent action problem.

A number of researchers have incorporated linear logic into planning. Linear logic allows to handle resources: Any precondition of an action that is not in an effect of the same action is "consumed" upon execution of the action, i.e. unlike in classical planning, it is not valid anymore. This allows to easily block certain (unwanted) actions that use the same resource. Chrpa [5] demonstrates how this can be used e.g. in the BlocksWorld domain: before performing the action *(PickUp ?Box ?Slot)* the condition *(canPut ?Box ?Slot)* is true (i.e. the action is allowed). Performing *(PickUp ?Box ?Slot)* renders the condition *(noPut*

?Box ?Slot) true, i.e. it blocks the inverse action *(PutDown ?Box ?Slot)* – once picked up, the box cannot be put back into the same slot, it must be moved. In our domain, however, this concept is not applicable because we would not only have to block inverse actions, but several instantiations of the same action with different parameters. For example, to prevent that the action *(Maximize Notebook1 Document1)* is undone, we would have to block *(Maximize Notebook1 Document2)*, *(Maximize Notebook1 Document3)* and so on. This would lead to an explosion of effects. Furthermore, it requires global knowledge.

Another approach to better represent dependencies among actions is to extend classical planning with temporal logic. Weld and Etzioni [16] introduce two kinds of *safety conditions*: *dont-disturb* constraints and *restore* constraints. Dont-disturb constraints are conditions specified in the initial state of the planning problem and must not be violated by the plan at any timepoint. Restore constraints are somewhat weaker. They may be violated, but must be restored by the end of the plan. Safety conditions do not solve the persistent action problem, however. We cannot specify which conditions must not be violated in the initial state because they are not known at this point. They arise in the course of planning. A more expressive language is MITL (Metric Interval Temporal Logic) by Bacchus und Kabanza [3]. Using certain formulas one can e.g. specify that a robot should only open a door if it intends to move through the door, and that the next action after moving through the door must be to close it: If it opens the door at timepoint t, it must pass through the door at timepoint t+1 and close the door at timepoint t+2. Thus, one can specify conditions that must hold at a certain timepoint or during an interval relative to another fixed timepoint, not only relative to the initial or goal state. A similar approach is TAL (temporal action logics) by Doherty and Kvarnström [6]. Control formulas allow to specify which actions may or may not be executed if certain conditions are fulfilled. For our domain this means that e.g. if at timepoint t something is projected onto a canvas, at timepoint t+1 this canvas must not be raised and the projector must not be moved: [t] (DocShown ?d ?c) ∧ (Pointing ?c ?p) ∧ (IsProjecting ?p) → [t+1] (CanvasDown ?c) ∧ (Pointing ?c ?p) In other words, this forces the planner to terminate the projecting activity before moving the projector or raising the canvas. This would be expressive enough to solve the persistent action problem. However, MITL, its predecessor TLPlan [2] and TAL all suffer from one serious drawback: They need domain dependent search control knowledge (that is, the control formulas) to be able to solve practical problems. These control formulas must be written by a domain expert who has global knowledge. Hence, it is not applicable in our domain because the developers of our operators do not have global knowledge – they do not know which other operators will be present at the time of planning.

3   Planning: The Locks Approach

One possibility to solve the persistent action problem in classical planning is to introduce certain conditions which we call *locks*. During the planning process, locks prevent chains of actions from being "destroyed" by conflicting actions that use the same resources. Consider the following domain *smartenvironment-locks*:

```
(define (domain smartenvironment-locks)
  (:requirements :strips :typing)
    (:types Notebook Document Projector Canvas - Device)
    (:predicates (isLocked ?d - Device)
                 (isActive ?d1 ?2 - Device)
                 (isConnected ?d1 ?d2 - Device)
                 (Hosts ?d - Document ?n - Notebook)
                 (isDown ?c - Canvas)
                 (CrossbarIn ?n - Notebook)
                 (CrossbarOut ?p - Projector)
                 (Pointing ?c - Canvas ?p - Projector))

  (:action CanvasUp
    :parameters (?c - Canvas)
    :precondition (and (not (isLocked ?c)) (isDown ?c))
    :effect (not (isDown ?c)))

  (:action CanvasDown
    :parameters (?c - Canvas)
    :precondition (and (not (isLocked ?c))(not (isDown ?c)))
    :effect (isDown ?c))

  (:action Maximize
    :parameters (?d - Document ?n - Notebook)
    :precondition (and (Hosts ?d ?n)(not (isLocked ?n)))
    :effect (and (isLocked ?n)(isActive ?d ?n)
            (isConnected ?d ?n)))

  (:action Unlock-Maximize
    :parameters (?d - Document ?n - Notebook)
    :precondition (and (isActive ?d ?n)(isLocked ?n))
    :effect (and (not (isActive ?d ?n))(not (isLocked ?n))
            (not (isConnected ?d ?n))))

  (:action MoveProjector
    :parameters (?c1 - Canvas ?c2 - Canvas)
    :precondition (and (Pointing ?c1 NEC-MT1065)
                   (not (Pointing ?c2 NEC-MT1065))
                   (not (isLocked ?c1)))
    :effect (and (not (Pointing ?c1 NEC-MT1065))
            (Pointing ?c2 NEC-MT1065)))

  (:action SwitchCrossbar
    :parameters (?n - Notebook ?p - Projector ?d - Document)
    :precondition (and (not (isLocked ?p))(isActive ?d ?n)
                   (CrossbarIn ?n)(CrossbarOut ?p))
    :effect (and (isLocked ?p)(not (isActive ?d ?n))
```

```
            (isActive ?d ?p)(isConnected ?n ?p)))

(:action Unlock-SwitchCrossbar
  :parameters (?n - Notebook ?p - Projector ?d - Document)
  :precondition (and (isLocked ?p)(isActive ?d ?p)
                (isConnected ?n ?p))
  :effect (and (not (isLocked ?p))(isActive ?d ?n)
          (not (isActive ?d ?p))(not (isConnected ?n ?p))))

(:action ShowDoc
  :parameters (?p - Projector ?c - Canvas ?d - Document)
  :precondition (and (not (isLocked ?c))(isActive ?d ?p)
                (isDown ?c)(Pointing ?c ?p))
  :effect (and (isLocked ?c)(not (isActive ?d ?p))
          (isActive ?d ?c)(isConnected ?p ?c)))

(:action Unlock-ShowDoc
  :parameters (?p - Projector ?c - Canvas ?d - Document)
  :precondition (and (isLocked ?c)(isActive ?d ?c)
                (isConnected ?p ?c))
  :effect (and (not (isLocked ?c))(isActive ?d ?p)
          (not (isActive ?d ?c))(not (isConnected ?p ?c)))))
```

We omit the problem description here as is the same as in the problem *presentation* described in Section 1, except for the goal statement, which is now
(:goal (and (isActive Doc1 LW3)(isActive Doc2 LW1)))

Three locks are required for every persistent action: The first one locks the resource in question *(isLocked ?d)* such that no other action can use this resource. Thus, the set of locked resources states which resources are currently parts of chains of persistent actions. The second lock *(isConnected ?d1 ?d2)* states which two resources are used consecutively in a chain of actions. This is important if a new goal is to be fulfilled and this requires that an action sequence previously generated must be unlocked. We will get back to this in Section 5. The third lock *(isActive ?d1 ?d2)* always denotes the current end of the chain (the *tail*). During the planning process, this lock is propagated through the action sequence. Consider e.g. the *ShowDoc* operator: It has *(isActive ?d ?p)* as a precondition. Its effects include *(not (isActive ?d ?p))* and *(isActive ?d ?c)*. I.e., when *ShowDoc* is selected, the tail moves from *(isActive ?d ?p)* to *(isActive ?d ?c)*. Because every persistent action (apart from *Maximize* which is the head of the chain) has such a lock as a precondition, the chain can only be manipulated at its tail. Hence, the chain of actions cannot unintentionally be "destroyed" by a conflicting action. With this domain description, planners generate correct action sequences like the following:

```
(CanvasDown LW1)
(Maximize Doc2 NB2)
(MoveProjector LW4 LW1)
(CanvasDown LW3)
(Maximize Doc1 NB1)
```

(SwitchCrossbar NB2 NEC-MT1065 Doc2)
(SwitchCrossbar NB1 EPS3 Doc1)
(ShowDoc NEC-MT1065 LW1 Doc2)
(ShowDoc EPS3 LW3 Doc1)

Note that we added a corresponding *unlock* operator for every operator that locks a resource. This enables the planner to unlock the chain starting at its end if new goals are to be fulfilled.

4 Action Selection: The Guarding Approach

The persistent action problem can also be solved if we do not employ planning, but another approach that draws its principle from nature: action selection. In contrast to planning, action selection does not construct an explicit plan, but at every timepoint selects the action that is most likely to lead towards an open goal. This selection is based on the current world state and the goals to be fulfilled. The selected action is then executed right away. This resembles the way animals decide what to do next. Well-known action selection algorithms are those by Brooks [4] and Maes [9].

Particularly Maes' algorithm is feasible for smart environments as it can easily be distributed [13]: Each device carries descriptions of its possible actions. Each of those action descriptions is assigned a software agent that communicates with the agents of other actions. It takes part in the action selection and keeps track of the world state. The agents of all devices in an ensemble form a network at run-time. This network can easily be adapted if devices join or leave the ensemble, and it requires no central controlling component.

Action selection interleaves planning with execution: Every action selection step is followed by an execution step which changes the world state. This makes it possible to solve the persistent action problem in a fundamentally different way: One can employ the agent of a persistent action A as a "guard" for that action. Guarding means that as long as A is active, A's agent monitors whether any effect of a subsequent action B that is executed is the opposite of one of A's preconditions. In this case, it sends a message to all other agents stating that A is not executed anymore and its effects become false. Should one of A's effects be a precondition of another persistent action C which is currently executed, this process continues: C's agent will notice that C is not executed anymore, etc.

As an example, reconsider the erroneous action sequence generated by the planner in Section 1. This action sequence cannot be generated if we use the guarding approach: Consider the point in the action sequence when the action *(SwitchCrossbar NB2 NEC-MT1065)* is executed. This renders the condition *(Connected NB1 NEC-MT1065)* false. One precondition for the action *(ShowDoc NB1 Doc1 NEC-MT1065 LW3)*, which is currently active, requires the same condition to be true. This is noticed by this action's agent. It notifies the rest of the ensemble that the action is not active anymore and its effects become false. The goal *(DocShown Doc1 LW3)* is now open again and can be fulfilled once more. Hence, the action selection algorithm cannot generate an action sequence that uses the steerable projector NEC-MT1065 to show Doc1 on LW3 and Doc2 on LW1 simultaneously. This means the world state in the model of the world does not become inconsistent to the actual world state in the real world. Thus, the guarding approach enables us to model the domain as in Section 1.

5   Comparing the Two Paradigms

In Sections 3 and 4 we introduced two paradigms which both solve the persistent action problem. In this section, we elaborate in more detail on the similarities and conceptual differences between the two paradigms. We also point out some of the implications those differences have on modelling and execution of devices' actions in smart environments.

Both paradigms have in common that actions can be modelled without global knowledge. Each action description can be written using only knowledge about conditions that must be fulfilled before the action can be executed and conditions that will be true after the action is executed. Of course, it is preferable that the developer of an action description has an idea e.g. which other actions might rely on the effects of the action. This guides the developer's decision which effects to consider for inclusion in the action description. However, the developer need not have knowledge about the complete domain.

One difference between the two paradigms is the cognitive model they resemble: The locks paradigm can be described with the concept of data flow. In the example action sequence shown in Section 3, the following *isActive* locks become active one after another:

```
(isActive Doc2 NB2)
(isActive Doc1 NB1)
(isActive Doc2 NEC-MT1065)
(isActive Doc1 EPS3)
(isActive Doc2 LW1)
(isActive Doc1 LW3)
```

Doc1 can be seen as data flowing from a source (notebook NB1) over an intermediate station (projector EPS3) to a sink (canvas LW3). Likewise for Doc2. In contrast, the agents in the guarding approach resemble the concept of guards that are positioned along a line to the goal, each monitoring whether its assigned persistent action is still being executed. This comes along with a fundamental difference in the approach to solving the persistent action problem: In the locks approach, we prevent conflicting actions from being executed. Thus, the developer has to be careful to add the appropriate locks to the action descriptions of persistent actions. Furthermore, for every operator describing a persistent action, a corresponding unlock operator must be added. This also implies that the overall number of operators is higher. In the guarding approach, on the other hand, we do not prevent conflicting actions from being selected. Instead, for every action A, we monitor whether a conflicting action B terminates

A's execution. The developer of an operator for a persistent action must only mark the action as a persistent action. The rest is managed by the action selection algorithm.

Another difference manifests itself if an action sequence has been generated and a new goal is to be fulfilled. Consider the point where the action sequence in Section 3 has been generated and the following new goal arises (the former goals are now not valid anymore): (:goal (isActive Doc1 LW1)).

This requires the locks approach to execute a number of unlock actions before the new goal can be fulfilled. A planner generates an action sequence such as:

```
(Unlock-ShowDoc NEC-MT1065 LW1 Doc2)
(Unlock-ShowDoc EPS3 LW3 Doc1)
(Unlock-ShowDoc NB2 NEC-MT1065 Doc2)
(Unlock-ShowDoc NB1 EPS3 Doc1)
(SwitchCrossbar NB1 NEC-MT1065 Doc1)
(ShowDoc NEC-MT1065 LW1 DOC1)
```

The existing chain of actions has to be unlocked backwards to the point where necessary actions to fulfill the new goal (*SwitchCrossbar*, *ShowDoc*) can be executed. This is the kind of scenario we need the *(isConnected ?d1 ?d2)* lock for: without it, the planner could not figure out which predecessor an action has and would thus not be able to unlock an existing sequence correctly. The guarding approach does not perform any unlock action in order to fulfill the new goal, it just executes *SwitchCrossbar* and *ShowDoc*. This is both a blessing and a curse. On the one hand, of course, less actions have to be executed. On the other hand, existing action sequences can unintentionally be "destroyed" by conflicting actions because there is no mechanism to protect them.

6   Conclusion

In this paper, we have motivated that it is feasible to model device actions in smart environments as planning operators. We have then introduced the *persistent action problem*: If a persistent action is active and another action is being executed that uses the same resources, the effects of the first action become invalid. We have suggested two ways to solve this problem: In planning, one can model actions using locks, thus explicitly preventing conflicting actions from being executed. Another approach which is applicable if one uses an action selection mechanism instead of planning is to assign an agent to each persistent action which monitors if any conflicting action destroys the preconditions of the persistent action when it is active. We have furthermore compared the characteristics of the two paradigms. Both have their benefits and shortcomings, yet both are suited for modelling device actions in smart environments because each has two key features: First, they solve the persistent action problem, and second, both allow to model the domain without global knowledge. As we have pointed out, the second feature is extremely important in highly dynamic environments.

Acknowledgement

Christiane Plociennik, Christoph Burghardt and Florian Marquardt are supported by a grant of the German National Research Foundation (DFG), Graduate School 1424 (MuSAMA).

References

1. Amigoni, F., Gatti, N., Pinciroli, C., Roveri, M.: What planner for ambient intelligent applications? IEEE Transactions on Systems, Man and Cybernetics - Part A 35(1), 7–21 (2005)
2. Bacchus, F., Kabanza, F.: Using Temporal Logic to Control Search in a Forward Chaining Planner. In: Proc. EWSP, pp. 141–153. Press (1995)
3. Bacchus, F., Kabanza, F.: Planning for temporally extended goals. Annals of Mathematics and Artificial Intelligence 22(1-2), 5–27 (1998)
4. Brooks, R.A.: A robust layered control system for a mobile robot. In: Artificial intelligence at MIT: expanding frontiers, pp. 2–27 (1990)
5. Chrpa, L.: Linear Logic in Planning. In: Proceedings of Doctoral Consortium of ICAPS, pp. 26–29 (2006)
6. Doherty, P., Kvarnström, J.: TALplanner: A Temporal Logic-Based Planner. AI Magazine 22(3) (2001)
7. Heider, T., Kirste, T.: Supporting goal based interaction with dynamic intelligent environments. In: Proc. ECAI, pp. 596–600 (2002)
8. Issarny, V., Sacchetti, D., Tartanoglu, F., Sailhan, F., Chibout, R., Levy, N., Talamona, A.: Developing ambient intelligence systems: A solution based on web services. Automated Software Engg. 12(1), 101–137 (2005)
9. Maes, P.: Situated Agents Can Have Goals. In: Maes, P. (ed.) Designing Autonomous Agents, pp. 49–70. MIT Press, Cambridge (1990)
10. McAllester, D., Rosenblitt, D.: Systematic Nonlinear Planning. In: Proceedings of the Ninth National Conference on Artificial Intelligence, pp. 634–639 (1991)
11. McDermott, D.: PDDL – The Planning Domain Definition Language. Draft (1998)
12. Mozer, M.C.: Lessons from an adaptive home. Smart Environments: Technology, Protocols, and Applications, 273–298 (2005)
13. Reisse, C., Kirste, T.: A Distributed Action Selection Mechanism for Device Cooperation in Smart Environments. In: Proc. IE (2008)
14. Russell, S., Norvig, P.: Artificial Intelligence: A Modern Approach, 2nd edn. Prentice-Hall, Englewood Cliffs (2003)
15. Sussman, G.J.: A Computational Model of Skill Acquisition. Technical report, Cambridge, MA, USA (1973)
16. Weld, D., Etzioni, O.: The first law of robotics (a call to arms). In: Proc. AAAI, pp. 1042–1047 (1994)

SPARK Rapid Prototyping Environment – Mobile Phone Development Made Easy

Robert Adelmann[1] and Marc Langheinrich[2]

[1] ETH Zürich, Clausiusstrasse 59, 8092 Zürich, Switzerland
adelmann@inf.ethz.ch
[2] Università della Svizzera italiana, Via Giuseppe Buffi 13, 6904 Lugano, Switzerland
marc.langheinrich@usi.ch

Abstract. Over the past few years mobile phones have evolved into attractive platforms for novel types of applications. However, compared to the design and prototyping of desktop software, mobile phone development still requires programmers to have a high level of expertise in both phone architectures and their low-level programming languages. In this paper we analyze common difficulties in mobile phone programming and present SPARK, a publicly available rapid prototyping platform that allows programmers without prior mobile programming experience to create advanced mobile phone applications in a fast and easy way. SPARK currently supports Symbian S60 devices and enables developers to quickly design, test, upload, monitor, and update their applications. We also present the results of a case study, where 70+ students used SPARK to develop mobile applications as part of a graduate course on distributed systems.

Keywords: Rapid prototyping, mobile phone, toolkit, PyS60.

1 Introduction

Mobile phones are increasingly becoming a very attractive application platform: They are ubiquitous, highly mobile, provide significant computing power, and often offer an abundance of built-in sensors. Especially in the field of pervasive computing, these devices show a lot of potential when it comes to bridging the often described gap between the real and the virtual word. Concrete projects use mobile camera phones to recognize 1D or 2D bar codes that link information to retail products [1], use the phone's built-in GSM, GPS or WLAN modules for location based services [2], do "reality mining" through Bluetooth sightings in order to map social networks and everyday activities [3], or to generate noise-maps of environments with the help of the built-in microphone [21].

However, despite today's abundance of feature-rich mobile phone hardware and powerful software platforms, creating applications that leverage the platforms' potential is still a time consuming process that challenges non-expert developers by requiring in-depth know-how [19]. This is especially true for applications that require full control of the device and its sensors. The limited API of JavaME [6], the Java runtime available on many mobile phones, severely restricts in-depth phone control, which

D. Tavangarian et al. (Eds.): IMC 2009, CCIS 53, pp. 225–237, 2009.

forces many application designers to delve into low-level programming languages such as C++ Symbian [7] (used on the majority of today's smart phones) or Objective C [26] (used on the iPhone). While a number of scripting languages are available for mobile phones, there is usually a drawback involved. Either they are still in early development (Lua [27], Ruby [28]), run on top of the phone's Java runtime and thus fair no better than Java ME (Hecl [30]) or allow only limited device control (Flash-Lite [29]).

One notable exception is the Nokia-initiated Python for S60 (PyS60) [10][4], as it is implemented in native Symbian C++, officially supported by Nokia, offers direct access to most available phone functions, and is extensible through C++ Symbian modules. However, PyS60 development is also not without difficulties, since its Symbian heritage requires programmers to be comfortable with the typical Symbian development process, e.g., how to package an application for distribution, or how to sign an application in order to gain access to sensors like GPS (which includes understanding the complex *Symbian Signed* [5] process and obtaining the appropriate certificates). Last but not least, any application development on mobile phones – be it low-level, Java-based, or scripted – faces three additional challenges when it comes to general development issues: a) since programming is typically done on a desktop or laptop computer, developers must repeatedly upload, debug, and update their software on the actual devices – a process that is often time consuming and fraught with errors; b) programmers must ensure that the software runs on different device types, and c) developers might need to update already deployed applications, e.g. for bug-fixing.

The goal of our system is to provide an easy and fast development environment for mobile phone applications, in particular for developers not familiar with mobile phone programming. This is achieved by providing a rapid prototyping environment that leverages the strengths of the existing PyS60 eco system and systematically addresses the remaining problems of mobile phone prototype development. Section 2 first describes the remaining difficulties of the PyS60 development process in particular and of application design for mobile phones in general. Drawing from these challenges, section 3 then presents the SPARK architecture and its implementation. Section 4 compares SPARK with existing solutions and discusses alternative application development options. SPARK is already used in a number of our research projects, in teaching, and in several larger projects with industry partners. Section 5 discusses an example case studies – a 70+ student class on distributed systems.

2   PyS60 Application Development

Based on several PyS60 projects conducted in the past, we identified a number of general areas in which application development for mobile phones challenges the design and implementation process. These areas are especially problematic for beginners, who face a steep and frustrating learning curve even when using PyS60 instead of Symbian C++. More general issues arise in application scenarios that target large user deployments and frequent code updates, e.g., as part of an early adopter rollout or during long-term user studies.

2.1 Beginner's Issues

When teaching colleagues and students on how to use PyS60, we noted three main obstacles for beginners: application signing, application packaging, and setting up a working development environment:

Application Signing: With Symbian OS v9, Symbian introduced a security system that is based on application *capabilities*[1] and certificates [5]. Getting access to certain features (for example the GPS module or GSM cell information) requires users to choose or compile the Python interpreter and PyS60 modules with the required capabilities and sign them with a certificate covering these capabilities. Getting used to the complex Symbian Signed processes, obtaining software modules that have been compiled with the appropriate capabilities as well as obtaining certificates that grant more capabilities is a time consuming and complex task.

Application Packaging: In order to distribute an application on more than one device, all application files have to be packaged as an SIS[2] (Symbian Installation System) file. This not only requires the above mentioned application signing, but also choosing a matching application identifier, creating the SIS file, and providing an appropriate application icon in a special SVGT format.

Development Environment Setup: Compared to other programming alternatives (especially C++ Symbian), PyS60 drastically simplifies the process of programming. However, even though PyS60 comes with a range of tools to support this process, getting to know what components and tools are required and available for what kind of Symbian version (e.g., there are significant differences between the 2nd and 3rd edition), as well as setting them up, is non-trivial and may differ across desktop operating systems. Preparing, e.g., a homework assignment involving PyS60 that covers all possible combinations of student hardware and software is still prohibitively time consuming.

2.2 General Issues

Even after users became familiar with PyS60 programming, three general issues continued to make the application development process tedious: the need for on-device testing, the variety of available devices, and managing software updates:

On-Device Testing: Emulators are no substitution for on-device testing of applications. They do not behave exactly like real hardware (e.g. regarding stack size, handling of low-memory situation, or timing), nor do they support all features (e.g. camera support). This requires the developer to ultimately test the application on actual devices, including the time consuming task of copying and executing all updated application files on the phone, resulting in long and tedious "code, edit, execute"-cycles.

---

[1] Capabilities control access to various sensitive features of the phone (17 in total), e.g., the current location of the user. If a developer wants a PyS60 program to query the current location, its calling shell must have been registered with this "capability" and subsequently digitally signed with a capability-enabling certificate.
[2] SIS files package application files for installation.

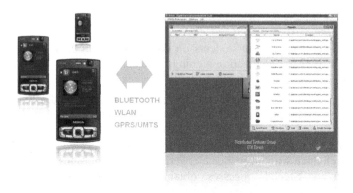

Fig. 1. Multiple mobile phones with the SPARK client software can be connected to a SPARK environment instance running on a PC

Multi-Device Support: Despite common programming platforms (such as Symbian S60 or even Java ME) every phone model has its differences. Mobile phone applications therefore need to be tested practically on every single device (including different firmware revisions) that they should be deployed on, in order to ensure proper operation. Given the above-mentioned lengthy "code, edit, execute" cycles, testing each program modification on all supported devices is a time consuming task.

Remote Application Updates: Large-scale and/or long-term application deployments invariably come to the point when critical updates or missing features need to be rolled-out to all handsets. A deployment such as the MEA application [11] used in the Metro future store, which allow users to scan products with their phone in order to perform self-checkout, has 100 registered users and around 30 in-store devices – fixing a bug or adding new features would require all users to bring in their mobile phone for servicing, as a typical user would not be able to easily install a provided SIS file on their mobile phone themselves. Developers would be equally challenged by manually updating over 100 devices with a new software version.

3   Rapid Prototyping with SPARK

In the following sections we will present the SPARK architecture and describe its implementation. SPARK specifically focuses on removing the above mentioned obstacles to PyS60 programming, in order to lower the barrier of entry for programmers that are unfamiliar with mobile phone architectures, and to simplify the general development cycles in order to support the development and deployment of large-scale, real-world applications.

The SPARK rapid prototyping environment is an OS independent software that facilitates the easy and fast creation, testing, deployment, and maintenance of arbitrary PyS60 applications. It builds upon the available PyS60 resources [4] and extends these with features that address the six previously identified problems (section 2). The environment comes in an easy to install single package and requires no prior

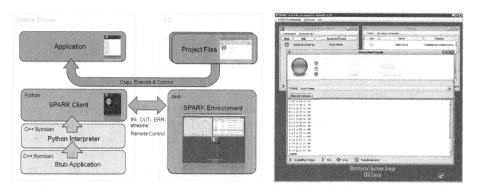

Fig. 2. Left: System architecture. Right: Screenshot of the SPARK environment with three open windows: The left showing all currently connected mobile phones, the right containing the list of projects and the middle being the remote control window for a connected phone showing the current program output.)

knowledge about mobile phone programming or PyS60. With only a basic knowledge of Python, developers can start creating applications within minutes.

Specifically, the design of SPARK followed four basic principles:

- **Low entry barrier:** Application creation should require no prior knowledge about mobile phone programming, and should take a minimal amount of time.
- **No application restrictions:** There should be no restrictions placed on the type of applications that can be created.
- **Fast application creation:** Setup should be fast, "code, edit, execute"-cycles should be quick, and application deployment simple.
- **Ease of use:** Non-expert developers should be able to create powerful applications by abstracting from complex tasks.

The SPARK system consists of two parts: A mobile phone application (SPARK client) as well as a desktop Java application (SPARK environment). Each mobile phone application is represented as a *project* in the SPARK environment. A project is simply a directory on the user's PC that contains all application files. These typically include one or more Python source code files and additional resources like images.

The SPARK *environment* allows users to manage (create, copy, delete) projects, to install and execute projects on connected phones, and to package projects into distributable SIS files. The SPARK *clients* act as containers on the mobile phones that provide a connected SPARK environment with remote access to the device. Multiple SPARK clients (and therefore multiple mobile phones) can be connected to a single SPARK environment (cf. Fig. 1). SPARK supports USB, Bluetooth, WiFi, and GPRS/UMTS connections between an SPARK environment and its clients.

In order to allow novel users to start quickly with development, installation has been designed to be very simple: A prepackaged SIS file must be installed on each development phone, and a single installer file (e.g., EXE for PCs, or an OS independent JAR) needs to be installed on the desktop computer. The SPARK client's SIS file contains all necessary resources needed for PyS60 development on Symbian9 3rd edition smart phones (e.g., the Nokia N73, N95/8g, or business phones like the E61)[3] and thus requires no other software to be present.

3.1 SPARK Environment

The SPARK environment provides several services that apply to the currently connected mobile phones (SPARK clients) and the list of managed projects.

For each connected phone, developers can open a window providing remote access to this device. A remote control window displays basic information about the phone (model, IMEI[4] number), provides a remote Python console with syntax highlighting, and allows the execution of all of the installed projects on the phone by simply pressing a button. The remote console provides developers with a very direct and interactive way to explore PyS60, to test code found on the web (by simply pasting it into the console), or for inspecting parts of their own application.

If multiple (potentially different) mobile phones are connected to the SPARK environment, developers are able to execute projects in parallel on multiple selected phones, and can also monitor their output in real-time, which allows for the easy detection and correction of application problems occurring only on some phone models.

Creating new projects is supported by a wizard dialog, allowing users for example to use application templates as a starting point for own applications. Available templates can easily be changed and extended with user generated ones.

Project management in the SPARK environment is very lightweight. There is no internal Python editor or file manager for managing project files – developers can choose their preferred editor and file manager instead. The SPARK environment simply keeps track of the main project directories, offering various actions for each of them. A typical "code, edit, test"-cycle is as follows: The user makes some changes to one or more project files (e.g., code or images). After saving the changes, she presses the "Copy & Run" button on the SPARK remote console window. The SPARK environment will: determine what files have changed; copy only the changed files to the mobile phone; and then run the updated project directly on the phone through the SPARK client. The application's output can then be monitored on the remote console. This allows for very agile development, as saving changes with "Ctrl-S" and then pressing the "Copy & Run"-button usually requires less than a second.

Once an application is ready to be deployed (i.e., installed as a standalone application), the "application packaging" dialog (see Fig. 3) provides a very simple way of doing this. It allows the generation of SIS files that contain all necessary project files, plus any additional software that might be required for the application to run, e.g., the Python interpreter or any of the third party C++ extension modules shipping with SPARK.

One important feature of SPARK is its auto-update mechanism, as this can significantly help in large-scale deployments. Developers can configure the generated standalone mobile phone applications in such a way that they will periodically monitor for changes in their original project files, and automatically update themselves without the need for end-user interaction. This makes changes to already deployed applications

---

[3] See www.s60.com/life/s60phones/browseDevices.do for a full list of devices.

[4] IMEI, the "International Mobile Equipment Identity", is a worldwide unique number for practically every mobile handset.

Fig. 3. Screenshots from the SPARK client application and the SIS creation dialog

very easy. The "application packaging" dialog allows for the configuration of "When?" and "How?" this updating happens.

3.2 SPARK Client

The SPARK client software allows the SPARK environment to remotely access a device. It also acts as a container for projects that should be executed on the mobile phone. It is a stand-alone application written in PyS60.

Fig. 3 on the left shows the main screen, the options dialog and console view displaying the current program's output. The main screen lists information about the contained projects (name, icon, and versioning information) and indicates whether the SPARK client is currently connected to an SPARK environment instance. Connections to an environment can be established using Bluetooth, WiFi, or the UMTS/GSM network. While WiFi and UMTS connections tend to be very responsive, we have found Bluetooth to provide the shortest delays when working with the interactive console. STDOUT and STDERR messages from executed applications can be viewed not only remotely on an SPARK environment, but also locally (i.e., on the phone) on a console. Once a project has been copied to an SPARK client, the project can also be started directly, without the need for a connected SPARK environment.

4 Related Work

A number of projects have recognized the need for providing rapid prototyping tools for mobile phone development. In this section we will cover prior work on rapid prototyping platforms for mobile phones (section 4.1), discuss alternative options for mobile phone programming (section 4.2), and contrast SPARK with existing tools that specifically target PyS60 programming (section 4.3).

4.1 Rapid Prototyping Platforms

The MakeIt [13] system by Holleis and Schmidt allows for the creation of application interfaces for mobile phones using (state, action)-graphs. MakeIt specifically targets the gap between IDEs and paper prototyping. One of its key features is the fact that created applications can be simulated and analyzed according to the KLM model. The main difference to SPARK is the fact that the system's focus is on interface creation, and that it allows only for the creation of Java ME templates. This requires developers to additionally use a Java ME development environment and limits the prototypes' functionality to what the Java ME supports.

Campaignr [14] is a C++ Symbian software for mobile phones that supports data collection from a larger set of sensors. It can be used to get both continuous and triggered audio, video and location information from the device, allowing also non experts in C++ Symbian to easily access and use this information. In a similar manner, the MyExperience [31] system also supports the collection of data from users, with the specific feature of allowing users to enrich the data gathered with subjective information that focuses on the user's activities, e.g. "working" or "biking". Compared to SPARK, both Campaignr and MyExperience are specific applications that can be configured using XML files. They are specialized to create customized data-collection applications and do not support other application types.

The ActivityDesigner [32] by Li and Landy allows users to create activity driven prototypes using a visual designer, and to test and deploy these applications on multiple devices, including mobile phones. This platform is similar to SPARK in so far as it targets non-experts, and that it allows for the very simple and fast creation of applications suitable for prolonged real-world usage. However, ActivityDesigner focuses much more on the design process, and only supports mobile phone deploy-ment as part of a JavaScript-based application that runs within a phone's browser.

ContextPhone [15] is a prototyping platform consisting of C++ Symbian modules that can be customized to sense and store data on a mobile phone, and to communicate data between a phone and a "sink" application. While ContextPhone can significantly ease and accelerate application creation for mobile sensing applications, it is not an "out-of-the-box" solution, but a collection of C++ Symbian components that require users to be familiar with C++ Symbian development, which renders it not usable for non-expert developers [19]. The same holds for the rapid application development system presented in [17] that provides a framework for C++ Symbian development, which eases GUI creation, data access and communication.

4.2 Mobile Phone Programming Options

Today's smartphones support an abundance of different programming options. We focused our work on the Symbian S60 platform, as it is still the most prominent platform by far [22], with the largest number of available devices. While the iPhone has recently attracted significant interest and momentum as an open development environment, it requires the use of Objective C. While certainly a powerful language, Objective C is hardly suitable for prototype creation by non-experts. Scripting languages, on the other hand, are currently not supported on the iPhone due to license restrictions from Apple. There are also additional restrictions that make prototype development on iPhones difficult: It supports no background processes, access to the camera's video images is restricted, and the development requires Apple hardware.

Java ME [6] is in general a good programming option for non-experts, featuring extensive tool support and documentation. There is a large set of frameworks that simplify and accelerate application development, e.g., J2ME Polish [23]. The BaToo toolkit [18] falls into the same category, being mainly a Java ME framework that supports the creation of services to retail products, based on 1D barcode recognition. However, as we pointed out in the introduction, Java ME offers only a very limited set of APIs, and the lack of extension options like the Java Native Interface (JNI) in MIDP [6] severely restricts application capabilities. Examples for restrictions include the lack of support for newer sensors like 3D accelerometers, lack of support for accessing video images from the camera for image recognition tasks, allowing only access to single images, or lack of control of Bluetooth scanning processes.

C++ Symbian offers speed as well as full control of devices, but it features a very steep learning curve, mainly due to the sub-optimal tool support and lack of documentation. Also, the unique Symbian language concepts like ActiveObjects, Descriptors, or Resource files are very complicated to use [19]. For the envisioned fast prototype creation of non-expert developers, C++ Symbian is not really an option.

4.3 PyS60 Related Tools

Python for S60 has been introduced by Nokia in 2006 and has since then gained a lot of attention by developers, which is due to several reasons: It is a very easy to learn and use, it features a large set of APIs (especially compared to Java ME), it is extensible through C++ modules, it features an open source license, and there is already an abundance of demo applications for numerous tasks available [24][25].

Due to the popularity of PyS60 there are also tools available that address some of the shortcomings that we identified in section 3.1 above. PUTools [8], as well as the PythonShell application contained in the standard PyS60 Python distribution [4], feature a remote Bluetooth console that allows users to remotely execute commands on the mobile phone. The SPARK implementation of this feature offers an easier setup by completely encapsulating Bluetooth connection setup – a process that needs to be done manually by the developer when using PUTools or the PythonShell. SPARK also supports WiFi and GSM/UMTS for remote connections, e.g. when the desktop machine has no Bluetooth hardware, or when access to the phone is required in "the field". The latter feature is complemented by allowing SPARK developers, e.g., to inspect devices by taking remote screenshots. Additionally, SPARK provides syntax highlighting and persistent logging, and the Bluetooth console is integrated into the remote console dialog described in section 3.2, offering further features.

PUTools also provides a command line tool for copying files to the mobile phone. SPARK in contrast offers this feature by seamlessly integrating it into the SPARK environment, allowing the developer to copy and execute project files using a single button press. SPARK also simplifies application execution, which is not covered at all by PUTools. Whenever a new version is uploaded to the phone, SPARK automatically ensures that the old module version is unloaded so that the new version will be considered upon execution. Using SPARK, the developer is also relieved from the micro management of where to store her application during development and deployment. SPARK ensures that all Python source code files and resources are always found and properly managed.

Table 1. "How useful do you think are the following features of the SPARK environment?"

	Easy setup (Phone and PC software)	Having a remote console	Edit project files on PC and execute them on the phone	Package files and create distributable SIS files	Test programs parallel on different phones	Already included extension modules
▪ Highly useful	8	14	22	11	5	13
▫ Useful	18	8	5	8	7	7
▪ Somewhat useful	1	5	0	3	2	4
▪ Not useful	0	0	0	0	0	1
▫ N/A	0	0	0	5	13	2

Ensymble [8] is a development project offering a set of command line tools for packaging PyS60 files into standalone SIS applications. SPARK uses the Ensymble tool set and extends it with additional features to reduce the amount of know-how required by the developer. In addition to providing a GUI to Ensymble, SPARK adds the following features: Choosing modules that have the appropriate capabilities and have been signed using the right certificate; choosing a correct application UID; icon creation; code parser for recommending external modules to include; and the auto-update mechanism (cf section 3.1).

5   Use Case: Use in Teaching

We used the SPARK rapid prototyping environment in the fall of 2008 as part of a lecture on distributed systems. The course had 73 enrolled graduate students, all from computer science. The topic "mobile phone programming" was not covered in the lecture, and students were not required to have had prior courses in mobile phone programming. Instead, the idea was to have students explore some of the concepts of distributed systems in a hands-on manner by programming a few applications on a mobile phone. Students had 3 weeks to design and implement a project using PyS60. Students were given access to the SPARK environment, but were free to use it or not (and instead rely on the standard PyS60 tools). Due to the limited time available for the two exercises, students were given a 30 minute introduction to PyS60/SPARK. They were then asked to form groups of two to work on the exercises. We had 50 Nokia N95/8g at our disposal[5], so each group was given one or two devices. Students were free to take the devices home during the exercise period. Feedback was gained in multiple ways: After the end of the second exercise, students were asked to present their applications to their peers (and to us). We also encouraged students to approach us with questions during the exercises, and asked them to fill out an online questionnaire with 26 questions about PyS60, and the SPARK rapid prototyping environment at the end of the course. We received 30 answers to the anonymous questionnaire (36% return rate). Last but not least, all SPARK environments by default logged all system events and user interactions with the software into a simple text file. Participants were informed about this logging, had the chance to review this data, and were

---

[5] 30 devices were graciously sponsored by Nokia.

asked to provide us with this file on a voluntary basis. 25 students sent us these log files. Here we can only briefly summarize the results. The full questionnaire and the results can be accessed from <removed for blind review>. All respondents (n=30) ended up using SPARK and only 2 students also used alternative methods (non-SPARK based) to develop their PyS60 application.

Entry barriers: Users were asked how easy it was for them to get started with PyS60 development using SPARK. The majority of them found it very easy (51.9%) and easy (44.4%). We also asked students for installation problems with the SPARK environment. 15 students answered this optional question, with 13 stating they had no problems and 2 stating that they had Bluetooth issues on Windows Vista and Linux.

SPARK features: Table 1 presents how useful students rated the various features of SPARK for their project. Support for automated SIS package generation and for concurrent development on different device types were rated as being not that important. Since these features address problems occurring in real-world deployments, this comes as no surprise. Asked to tell us what kind of features they missed, most students stated that they lacked a real PyS60 debugger (77.8%).

General Feedback: The majority of students found the SPARK environment highly useful (66.7%) or useful (25.9%) for realizing their project. All students indicated that they would use the software again and that they would recommend it to colleagues. Answers to the open question about what they liked most about the software included: "Easy to use; good looking; worked instantly", "It makes the development very easy and fast.", "The time you need to deploy and test the code is very short.", "Easy, simple, fast, reliable, free to use". Things that students disliked about SPARK were: "Bluetooth problems" and "Missing built-in help".

6   Conclusion

There is a growing gap between the emerging mobile phone platforms with their sophisticated capabilities, and the expertise among non-expert developers to control them. This gap cuts off an important source of creativity, as many might be inspired to create novel types of mobile applications using the phones' increasing power, but only few have the time and energy to dig into the intricacies of low-level mobile device programming. In this paper we presented a comprehensive overview of current rapid prototyping tools for mobile phones and identified PyS60 as an attractive choice that combines ease of use with flexibility. However, PyS60 development environments still pose considerable barriers for the rapid prototyping of applications, especially for novel users and when targeting large-scale, real-world deployments. We identified these barriers and presented the SPARK tool that targets non-expert users, supports fast development cycles and differs from related tools mainly by its very low entry barriers, making it a prominent choice for student projects and in teaching. We also presented the results of a large case study in which SPARK has been used – a graduate course on distributed systems, in which 70+ students used SPARK to develop mobile applications, with the large majority reporting the tool to be highly useful. SPARK is available as a free download at http://people.inf.ethz.ch/ adelmanr/spark.

References

1. Adelmann, R.: Mobile Phone Based Interaction with Everyday Products - On the Go. In: Proc. of NGMAST 2007, pp. 63–69. IEEE Computer Society, Los Alamitos (2007)
2. LaMarca, A., et al.: Place lab: Device positioning using radio beacons in the wild. In: Gellersen, H.-W., Want, R., Schmidt, A. (eds.) PERVASIVE 2005. LNCS, vol. 3468, pp. 116–133. Springer, Heidelberg (2005)
3. Nicolai, T., Yoneki, E., Behrens, N., Kenn, H.: Exploring social context with the wireless rope. In: Meersman, R., Tari, Z., Herrero, P. (eds.) MONET 2006. LNCS, vol. 4277, pp. 874–883. Springer, Heidelberg (2006)
4. Python for S60 Open Source Project,
   http://sourceforge.net/projects/pys60
5. Symbian Ltd. Symbian Signed User Guide,
   http://www.symbiansigned.com/app/page
6. J2ME Java 2 Micro Edition, http://java.sun.com/javame/index.jsp
7. Harrison, R.: Symbian OS C++ for Mobile Phones. Wiley, Chichester (2003)
8. The ensymble developer utilities for symbian os,
   http://code.google.com/p/ensymble/
9. Python utility tools for pys60,
   http://people.csail.mit.edu/kapu/symbian/python.html
10. Laurila, J., Tuulos, V., MacLaverty, R.: Scripting Environment for Pervasive Application Exploration on Mobile Phones. In: Fishkin, K.P., Schiele, B., Nixon, P., Quigley, A. (eds.) PERVASIVE 2006. LNCS, vol. 3968, Springer, Heidelberg (2006)
11. Metro group MEA application, http://www.future-store.org/fsi-internet/html/de/7803/index.html
12. BlueCove library for Bluetooth (JSR-82) implementation,
    http://www.bluecove.org/
13. Holleis, P., Schmidt, A.: MakeIt: Integrate User Interaction Times in the Design Process of Mobile Applications. In: Indulska, J., et al. (eds.) PERVASIVE 2008. LNCS, vol. 5013, pp. 56–74. Springer, Heidelberg (2008)
14. Joki, A., Burke, J.A., Estrin, D.: Campaignr: A Framework for Participatory Data Collection on Mobile Phones. Center for Embedded Network Sensing. TR 770 (2007)
15. Raento, M., Oulasvirta, A., Petit, R., Toivonen, H.: Contextphone: a prototyping platform for context-aware mobile applications. Pervasive Computing, IEEE 4, 51–59 (2005)
16. Forstner, B., et al.: Supporting Rapid Application Development on Symbian Platform. In: Proc. of EUROCON 2005, pp. 72–75. IEEE Computer Society, Belgrade (2005)
17. Long, S., et al.: Rapid prototyping of mobile context-aware applications: the Cyberguide case study. In: Proc. ofMobiCom 1996, pp. 97–107. ACM, New York (1996)
18. Adelmann, R., et al.: Toolkit for Bar Code Recognition and Resolving on Camera Phones – Jump Starting the Internet of Things. In: Proc. MEIS 2006, pp. 366–373 (2006)
19. Huebscher, M., et al.: Issues in Developing Ubicomp Applications on Symbian Phones. In: Proc. FUMCA 2006, pp. 51–56. IEEE Computer Society, Los Alamitos (2006)
20. Card, S.K., Moran, T.P., Newell, A.: The Keystroke-Level Model for User Performance Time with Interactive Systems. Comm. of the ACM 23(7), 396–410 (1980)
21. Mohan, P., Padmanabhan, V.N., Ramjee, R.: Nericell: Rich monitoring of road and traffic conditions using mobile smartphones.. In: Proc. of SenSys 2008, pp. 323–336. ACM, New York (2008)
22. Gartner Report on Smartphone Sales,
    http://www.gartner.com/it/page.jsp?id=827912

23. J2ME Polish, `http://www.j2mepolish.org/cms/`
24. Forum Nokia Python Resources,
    `http://wiki.forum.nokia.com/index.php/Category:Python`
25. Scheible, J., Tuulos, V.: Mobile Python: Rapid Prototyping of Applications on the Mobile Platform. Wiley, Chichester (2007)
26. Objective C,
    `http://developer.apple.com/documentation/Cocoa/Conceptual/ObjectiveC/`
27. Lua for S60 devices, `http://luaforge.net/projects/luas60/`
28. Ruby for S60 devices, `http://ruby-symbian.rubyforge.org/`
29. FlashLite, `http://www.adobe.com/products/flashlite/`
30. Hecl – The Mobile Scripting Language, `http://www.hecl.org/`
31. Froehlich, J., et al.: MyExperience: a system for in situ tracing and capturing of user feedback on mobile phones. In: Proc. of MobiSys 2007, pp. 57–70. ACM, New York (2007)
32. Yang, L., James, A.L.: Activity-based prototyping of ubicomp applications for long-lived, everyday human activities. In: Proc. of SIGCHI, pp. 1303–1312 (2008)
33. Fielding, R.T.: Architectural Styles and the Design of Network-Based Software Architectures. Doctoral Thesis. UMI: AAI9980887, University of California, Irvine (2000)

Rapid Prototyping and Evaluation of Intention Analysis for Smart Environments

Christoph Burghardt, Stefan Propp, Thomas Kirste, and Peter Forbrig

University of Rostock, Albert-Einstein-Str. 21, 18059 Rostock, Germany
`firstname.lastname@uni-rostock.de`

Abstract. The development of smart environments is cumbersome and time-consuming compared to traditional software, since lacking a standard development process and according tool support. Smart environments are termed "smart" due to pro-active user assistance: User behavior is anticipated by an "intention analysis" software employing machine learning algorithms. In this paper we present a tool that facilitates the development of intention analysis by guiding the domain expert through the development process. Initially, the tool allows the user-centered design of HCI task models, without taking care of implementation details. Subsequently annotated task models are transformed into low level models, which are applied within the machine learning inference engine. We support both evaluation at early and later development stages. At early stages we evaluate designed models with expert-generated scenarios to simulate artificial low level sensor data. At later stages we evaluate a physical environment on the basis of real sensor data. A comparison between observed behavior and defined expectation allows identifying usability issues. A close connection between development and evaluation should further ensure rapid software changes and reevaluation to access improvements.

1 Introduction

A smart meeting room should assist its users *proactively*. It monitors user interactions with sensors and tries to infer the most probable action given the observations. We call this software "intention analysis" [2]. The core of the intention analysis are machine learning techniques like Hidden Markov Models (HMM). The development of these statistical models requires the knowledge of an model expert who often lacks knowledge about the target domain that an usability expert can provide. To bridge this gap, we present in this paper a rapid prototyping tool that facilitates the creation of a HMM for intention analysis by a usability expert. It integrates design, test and analysis of intention analysis of smart environments. The tool assists the designer by giving him the possibility to describe scenarios by task models in a familiar and intuitive language (CTT) [14]. The task model is annotated with further knowledge (e.g. location information and task priority values) and subsequently transformed into an HMM description language. The HMM toolkit translates the description into the final

D. Tavangarian et al. (Eds.): IMC 2009, CCIS 53, pp. 239–250, 2009.

intention analysis software that can be executed within the room. This process is depicted in figure 1.

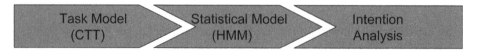

Fig. 1. Model transformation from task model into intention analysis

The rapid prototyping tool that we present in this paper assists the designer further with testing and evaluation of the built intention analysis software, enabling him to make rapid changes to the model and do a fast re-evaluation. This technique saves time and money as errors are caught earlier in the development process [13].

2   Related Work

The problem of development and evaluation of smart environments is well recognized. During our research we identified two important use cases, the design as well as the evaluation of the resulting HMM. Therefore the review of the related work covers both aspects.

Much work has been done in facilitating the use of machine learning algorithms for a broader community. One well-done and successful example is *d.tools* from Hartmann et. al [7]. d.tools is a design tool that embodies an iterative-design-centered approach for prototyping physical UIs. These UIs are state-chart based. d.tools offers great support for evaluation and testing the devices. The developer can choose between software evaluation and working with the real prototype. d.tools automatically generates annotation time stamps for later video analysis and enables site-by-site comparison of video output and the current state of the state-chart based model. However, this state-chart based prototyping model differs from the scope of intention analysis in two important aspects: the state-charts and their transitions are deterministic. Second, in state-chart based models there is no need for inference unlike in HMMs that try to derive the most probable state of a system, given a number of observations. In a smart environment, the "real" goal state of the persons cannot be observed and is hidden in the users mind. Therefore, the techniques from d.tools are not directly applicable.

Maly et al. [10] developed the tool *USEd* (User Scenario Editor) for creating and evaluating user interactions in ambient environments. They recognized the need to adapt usability testing to the special requirements of an ambient environment. USEd supports both scenario creation and evaluation by recreating the scenario in a virtual 3D environment. Besides the possibility to generate low - level sensor data, privacy concerns from users are an argument to create virtual environments. The scenario could be fed finally into *Sitcom* [4] (Situation Composer for Smart Environments) which bootstrapped a discriminative "meeting state detector" consisting of a c4.5 decision graph or a Bayesian network to learn the function between observation data and meeting state. Using a discriminative model has several disadvantages compared to an generative approach: these models are not able to predict the most probable future event. Their use in ad-hoc environments is also delimited, as they have to be retrained when the input space changes and because of the "black-box" nature of discriminative models USEd cannot give advice how to change the model input when the expected output differs from the output of the meeting state classifier.

Modie [9] employs task models for designing distributed interfaces for ambient environments. Context constraints for performing a certain task are formulated on the basis of an ontology. These annotations provide a deterministic description of task performance. A simulation environment allows visualization and interactive adaptation of underlying task models. The aim of Modie is similar to our approach: the gap between HCI design and development should be lowered. In our work we want to ease the development of statistical models for task recognition at runtime and exploit task models for intuitive design to combine advantages of both worlds.

Siafu [11] is a large scale context simulator developed by Martin et. al. It was inspired by the need to test the functionality of group services and applications before performing user evaluations. Furthermore, this tools enables the developer to generate test data as realistic as possible in order to test machine learning methods that support group awareness. In contrast to simulators like e.g. UbiReal [12], that want to simulate the environment including dynamic interactions as close as possible to generate appropriate input for low-level sensors Siafu can also deliver high-level context. While it is an advantage for Siafu to be generic and applicable to a wide range of scenarios, it has a number of disadvantages from the view of a designer: The applied language is complex and unfamiliar for usability experts. It is difficult to create low-level context data, like realistic movements of people. Because Siafu is lacking any knowledge about the underlying machine learning techniques, it cannot help in creating or diagnosing errors in the machine learning algorithm.

3   Designing Human Behavior Models

The intention analysis is the component in a smart environment, that makes the environment smart. While there are numerous designs for such an intention analysis available, HMMs are especially suited for such a task, as they can cope with missing or noisy sensor data and are able to take uncertainty into account. Given a number of observations, the aim of the intention analysis is to find out the most probable meeting state. Generative probabilistic models like HMMs are especially suited for this kind of task. In order to generate an HMM we need to define five information: A set of states s, a set of observations o, the transition matrix T_s that defines the probability of a transition $P(s_{t+1}|s_t)$ between two consecutive states and the observation matrix T_o that defines the probability of an observation in a certain state $P(O_t|S_t)$. The problem when creating such an HMM are the adjacency matrices T_s and T_o that grow exponentially with the number of states s and observations o. Therefore we want to facilitate the creation of such HMMs for the domain expert. In order to generate the HMM, the experts defines the following information that are equivalent to the parameters of the HMM:

1. A set of tasks and their temporal dependencies. These are equivalent to the states s and the transitions matrix T_s.
2. A preference of certain tasks over other alternatives. This changes the probabilities in the transition matrix and allows the designer to express situations when people prefer e.g. a moving along the windows over other possible movement alternatives to reach the presentation area.
3. The duration of tasks.
4. The context of tasks.

The context depends on the available sensors in the room and can describe e.g. a Position, Used Devices, the Transport Modality (car, foot, bike, bus) or a User Modality (walk, sit, stand, lie). To exemplify our development process from a task model to a intention analysis software we want to discuss the following scenario: Three users A, B and C are conducting a meeting in a smart environment. The requirements analysis discovers further that all of them should present in an arbitrary order, followed by a discussion and the exit of all participants. After having elicited these facts, the designer models a task model. A result in a CTT-like notation is depicted in figure 2. Nodes represent tasks, like "Presentation A" or "Discussion", or temporal operations, like "order independence" or "enabling". A further annotation at each task marks the user's preference of one task over another. For instance if an agenda suggests the sequence of presenters A, B and C. The priority of "PresentationA" can be set to 90, while "PresentationB" is 9 and "PresentationC" is 1.

The resulting task model (2) annotated with priorities is the starting point for automatically deriving a statistical model [6]. The resulting directed graph connects an initial state with transitions to the generated states and to a final state. Each performed task at runtime causes a transition from one state to another. Annotations at each transition mark the probability, which is derived out of priorities annotated at the task model's tasks. This HMM graph can be represented as adjacency matrix T_s.

To enrich the process of HMM generation we suggest to annotate further context information about the required context to perform a certain task. The context depends mainly on the devices installed into the room and what can be observed by the ambient environment. The following list are detailed examples for typical a-priory knowledge from the domain-expert and that can influence the parameters of the intention analysis:

– Duration of a task - If the expert has knowledge about the minimum, median or maximum duration of a specific task, s/he can annotate this information to the task. This annotation is kept and used in the HMM description

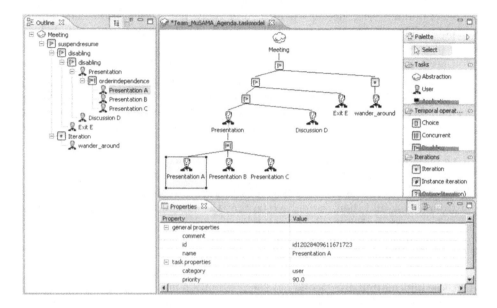

Fig. 2. A simple task model for the scenario

languages which finally modifies the structure of the underlying HMM. For more details about how to model timing information with stationary HMMs, the interested reader is referred to [1].

- Place or Location of a task - In outdoor scenarios the global positioning system (GPS), in indoor scenarios a local positioning systems (LPS) like Ubisense can determine the location of a person with a certain accuracy. When such systems are installed in the environment and the experts know which task require people to move throughout the environment or have to be at a certain place in order to execute a task, this prior knowledge about possible user movements can be encoded into the HMM as well. As an HMM works in a probabilistic fashion, it is advisable not to describe the places as deterministic bounding boxes as usually done by an usability expert, but rather as a probability density functions (PDF). The tool assists the designer by displaying a floor plan of the environment so s/he can deviate the most probable movements. When the designer has gathered some movement data, either created artificially or recorded from some case studies, the tool can deviate the optimal parameters of a Gaussian mixture model by fitting the points from the example data [5].
- Involved Devices - We can fit the user or his devices with a RFID reader. Patterson et. al. [15] found that the objects touched by the user are a good indicator for the task the user is executing and developed probabilistic models that try to infer the current user activity from object usage. When the expert knows which devices can be used during a task, s/he can annotate this information to the task. The probability of observing the RFID reading of a

laser pointer is e.g. higher when the user is giving a presentation than taking notes. The information about the object usage during a task is encoded as a discrete PDF and attached to the task.

- User Modality - If a user is fitted with accelerometer, Hein [8] used classifiers to infer the current modality of the user like sitting, standing, running or lying. The output of the classifier that detects the current user modality is modeled as a discrete PDF, so the domain expert can express uncertainty about how the user bridges two destinations by either moving or running.
- Task preference - If the user has a choice between alternative tasks and the domain experts knows that e.g. a user is twice as much showering than bathing,s/he can express this fact by giving showering a execution preference of 2. These factors are multiplied with the number of possible transitions from a task and then normalized so that the sum of the probabilities is one.
- Other Context that can be "sensed" with software, e.g. the state of a devices like a canvas or whether a document is shown. These values can be encoded as a probability density function.

All these information are encoded as the observation matrix T_o. The type of context that can be observed of course depends on the sensors installed in the final smart meeting room. When all these information is together, we can generate a HMM and transform it into a representation for a concrete HMM Toolkit.

Different Toolkits have different capabilities. How the information is transformed depends on the capabilities of the HMM-Toolkit and the type of sensor installation in the room. The toolkit we use for inference is based on C++ and describes the transition matrix in a graph-based way like:

```
States {
        PresentA : PDFvStruct(NSTREAMS,ARITY,PresentA_obs,1),
        PresentB : PDFvStruct(NSTREAMS,ARITY,PresentB_obs,1),
...
Transitions {
        PresentA
                -> @
                -> PresentA_PresentB 8e-04
                -> PresentA_PresentC 0.0002909091
                -> PresentA_Discuss 0.0003636364
...
```

The file describes the states and the corresponding observations as well as each state and the transition probabilities. The complete definition for the activity recognition HMM is more complex and gets translated by the HMM - Toolkit into executable software that can output the most probable state given a number of observations. In order to make use of the described HMM we describe in the next section how to generate training data, apply the HMM on the training data and compare the output of the HMM with the expected output from the domain expert.

4   Evaluation of Human Behavior Models

According to the "1:10:100 rule"[13] the costs for fixing defects increase with the progress of a project. A defect identified in a later development stage causes significantly more effort than in an earlier stage. Hence we aim at integrating development and usability evaluation, to ensure evaluation of artifacts at the different stages of development. During early stages the designed models are animated to allow usability experts to interactively walk through these models. During later stages progress within the physical environment is visualized as a 2D view of the environment, accompanied by videos and sensor data.

In this section we focus on the evaluation of designed models. Our goal is to identify model inconsistencies, before the physical environment is set up. A usability expert animates user interactions on a model level, which are fed into a HMM. Tasks recognized by the HMM are displayed to allow a comparison between actually performed user tasks and recognized tasks. Divergences indicate issues within the recognition engine, which have to be further examined.

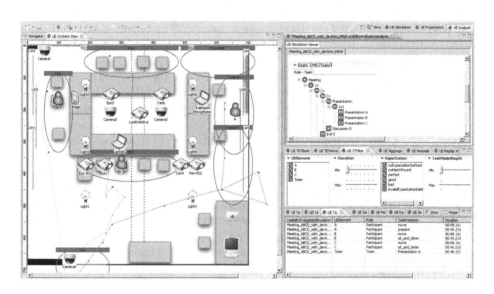

Fig. 3. Context animator to create user interactions

The animation tool is depicted in Figure 3. The screen is divided into four areas: (1) The left view contains a bird's view of the environment, comprising graphical representations for physical entities: users, devices (e.g. projectors, projection screens and laptops) and furniture (e.g. chairs and desks). Elliptical shapes mark locations to indicate e.g. the presentation zone or the room's exit. Users can be moved freely to feed expert generated location values into the HMM and attaching devices to users delivers RFID sensor values. (2) The upper right view visualizes runtime instances of task models which reflect the recognized progress of task execution. (3) The lower right view contains captured interactions, comprising performed tasks, location sensor values and information about devices carried by users. (4) Finally the middle right view provides controls for filtering logged data.

To systematically evaluate the designed models, an expert animates user interactions to replay different scenarios. To ensure authentic behavior we consider two sources. On the one hand during requirements analysis scenarios were elicited, which reflect requested actions and system reactions from a user point of view. On the other hand often an uninstrumented environment is already available which is in use. Captured videos of real-world situations allow insights into user behavior, which can be transcoded into interaction within the context animator. An expert animates user and device icons accordingly. A particular focus lies on testing context parameters which are associated with certain tasks. It has to be investigated whether the HMM recognizes task performance as specified by context annotations. In contrast to real persons moving within a room, a designer can animate only one user moving at the same time. When creating a certain meeting constellation it is sometimes sufficient to have minor time lags between different interactions. When a completely synchronized behavior is required, we start with animating a single person. The other persons are animated subsequently, while interactions of already captured persons are replayed to ensure synchronization.

If the animated model behaves in an unexpected way, for instance predicting a task erroneously, the expert is provided with different views on the underlying sensor data. For interactively exploring the current state, location information, available devices and predicted task progress are shown, with a particular focus on the required context for each task. Playing sensor data forth and back allows to identify precisely the error situation. Comparing the actual context with the required context, which is taken by the HMM to predict, a task have to be compared. To give an example: let us consider user "A" approaching the modeled location "presentation zone" while carrying a device "laptop". In this situation we expect the prediction of a task "presentation of A". If the HMM delivers a wrong prediction, we can check the shape of the modeled location. In this case the location was modeled too narrow and dislocated from the projection screen. Hence the location has to be remodeled. The context animation tool allows graphically editing locations directly within the animation view. A replay of the sensor data against the revised model discovers whether the prediction is now correct. Updating the animated context, in terms of locations, required devices and other sensors, is directly supported during animation, which allows rapidly changing the model and checking prediction quality.

5   Evaluation of the Physical Environment

After the physical environment is set up, further aspects introduced in the real-world setting can be evaluated. These aspects comprise for instance erroneous sensor values, practical issues with handling of devices, malfunctioning devices, issues with slow response times of devices and further uncontrollable context parameters (e.g. bright sunlight).

We aim at replaying and visualizing sensor data to support the error recognition process. When capturing real meetings there are often privacy issues, leading to the need of anonymizing actors and the meeting content. An overwhelming amount of details might distract the view on the relevant details. Hence a visualization should focus on the details necessary for evaluation. Further details have to be provided on demand, following the principle "overview first, zoom and filter, details on demand" by Card et. al [3].

Keeping these requirements in mind, we have enhanced the tool presented in section 4 to load and replay sensor data from our smart environment. Figure 4 depicts the tool. The left view gives a 2D view of the environment with persons, devices and furniture, while the upper right view contains the already known animated task models. The middle right view allows to load sensor data and replay it in real time, or with increased or decreased speed. The lower right view contains captured videos from the different cameras.

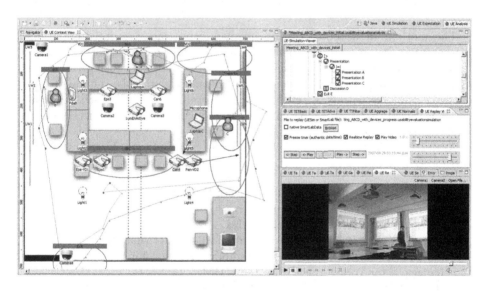

Fig. 4. Replay of captured data from physical environment

Arbitrary sensor data can be incorporated. Currently we are working with the following data, which is automatically captured: location values (UbiSense tags), applied devices (RFID tags), video streams (cameras), recognized tasks (HMM), video connections between devices (video BUS software) and activity states of devices (like on/off state of lights and projectors). Further observations can be annotated manually. To cope with the vast amount of data, particularly when a meeting is repeated several times we allow to specify expectations by a usability expert. From the development stage each task contains an annotation with context conditions which have to be met in a general meeting situation. When considering a specific test case, only a subset of these possible meeting situations is valid, for instance because certain functions have to be tested. While a usability expert defines a test case, he has already an idea of some ideal sequences of interactions to fulfill the test case. This implicit knowledge is made explicit with specifying the expectation annotations for tasks. During evaluation tasks progress, which is differing from the expected behavior is marked. Filtering these tasks allows to focus particularly on those identified candidates for usability issues. For filtering log data, it is sufficient to simply select icons within the bird's view of the environment. The selection of users, devices and way points of performed tasks allows filtering the according log entries. To provide a better overview of user interactions, we provide some visualizations [16], like timelines reflecting task progress. The related tool d.tools also contains visualizations. Their developers mentioned [7] that a vast amount of data sometimes causes a confusing number of graphical elements, stating the need of some intelligent filtering. We have a solution for this problem particularly focused on task models. We apply a semantic lens adapting the level of detail in a way that a selected area of interest is shown in detail, lowering the level of detail around.

The method of usability testing involves capturing user interactions and further annotate observations, which allows computer-aided exploration of user behavior to identify usability issues and typical situations causing this issues. When considering separate evaluation and development tools, the annotations are only available within the evaluation tool itself. In our approach we closely combine both tools to exploit the annotated context as parameter for the intention recognition models.

After the evaluation method is described, we want to briefly state the categories of potential issues and give avenues for solutions:

1. Observation: a task isn't included within the current task set.
   Reaction: Enhance the task model with the newly identified task, which introduces new states within the HMM.
2. Observation: a task was performed in another order than modeled.
   Reaction: Revise the task model's temporal relationships, which introduces changes of the transitions within the HMM.
3. Observation: a task was performed in a different context than defined.
   Reaction: Revise the context constraint annotated at the according task, which changes the observation matrix within the HMM.
4. Observation: user behavior differs from the specified expectation within the current test case.
   Reaction: Conduct a video analysis and visualize sensor data at the time where the divergence occurred to find the reason, which may comprise physical issues, intention analysis issues and room's strategy synthesis for steering devices. Depending on the individual issue, task model, HMM or the hardware configuration are adapted.

6   Conclusion and Future Work

In this paper we presented a method and a tool for rapid development and evaluation of software designed for activity recognition in smart environments. Previously suggested approaches required a developer to create statistical models for prediction of user behavior. Setting the huge number of model parameters, like states, probabilities and sensor constraints, was a tedious and time consuming task. To overcome these problems, we presented a model-based development process, starting with an HCI task model, enriched with annotations, subsequently transformed to an HMM and finally to executable software applied in the physical environment.

Another aspect was strengthening the evaluation methodology. To identify issues as early as possible, we described an integrated, iterative development and evaluation process. Created artifacts at each development stage are evaluated. At early stages an expert interactively walks through designed models. These expert-created interaction traces of the evaluation are further applied as training data to set initial model parameters. We presented tool support for the model-based development process and the graphical evaluation environment.

The presented method is applicable to a broad range of applications. Among our research are activity recognition in smart environments and for elderly support. Incorporated aspects are user interactions described by task models, handled devices and other objects referenced by particular tasks and movements described by a location model. Graphical tool support is provided to edit these models, perform model transformations and evaluate the created artifacts.

Further research work comprises the further exploration of experiences from real world examples within our smart environment laboratory.

Acknowledgment

This work was supported by a grant of the German National Research Foundation (DFG), Graduate School 1424 MuSAMA.

References

1. Bilmes, J.A.: What hmms can do. IEICE - Trans. Inf. Syst. E89-D(3), 869–891 (2006)
2. Burghardt, C., Kirste, T.: Inferring intentions in generic context-aware systems. In: MUM 2007: Proceedings of the 6th international conference on Mobile and ubiquitous multimedia, pp. 50–54. ACM, New York (2007)
3. Card, S.K., Mackinlay, J., Shneiderman, B.: Readings in Information Visualization: Using Vision to Think (The Morgan Kaufmann Series in Interactive Technologies). Morgan Kaufmann, San Francisco (1999)
4. Cuřín, J., Fleury, P., Kleindienst, J., Kessl, R.: Meeting state recognition from visual and aural labels, pp. 24–35 (2008)
5. Fraley, C., Raftery, A.E.: Bayesian regularization for normal mixture estimation and model-based clustering. Journal of Classification 24(2), 155–181 (2007)

6. Giersich, M., Forbrig, P., Fuchs, G., Kirste, T., Reichart, D., Schumann, H.: Towards an integrated approach for task modeling and human behavior recognition, pp. 1109–1118 (2007)
7. Hartmann, B., Klemmer, S.R., Bernstein, M., Abdulla, L., Burr, B., Robinson-Mosher, A., Gee, J.: Reflective physical prototyping through integrated design, test, and analysis. In: UIST 2006: Proceedings of the 19th annual ACM symposium on User interface software and technology, pp. 299–308. ACM Press, New York (2006)
8. Hein, A.: Echtzeitfähige Merkmalsgewinnung von Beschleunigungswerten und Klassifikation von zyklischen Bewegungen. diploma thesis, Universität Rostock (2007)
9. Luyten, K., Van den Bergh, J., Vandervelpen, C., Coninx, K.: Designing distributed user interfaces for ambient intelligent environments using models and simulations. Computers & Graphics 30(5), 702–713 (2006)
10. Maly, I., Curin, J., Kleindienst, J., Slavik, P.: Creation and visualization of user behavior in ambient intelligent environment. International Conference on Information Visualisation 0, 497–502 (2008)
11. Martin, M., Nurmi, P.: A generic large scale simulator for ubiquitous computing. Annual International Conference on Mobile and Ubiquitous Systems 0, 1–3 (2006)
12. Nishikawa, H., Yamamoto, S., Tamai, M., Nishigaki, K., Kitani, T., Shibata, N., Yasumoto, K., Ito, M.: UbiREAL: Realistic Smartspace Simulator for Systematic Testing, pp. 459–476 (2006)
13. Pandian, R.C.: Software Metrics: A Guide to Planning, Analysis, and Application. AUERBACH (September 2003)
14. Paterno, F.: Model-Based Design and Evaluation of Interactive Applications. Springer, London (1999)
15. Patterson, D.J., Fox, D., Kautz, H., Philipose, M.: Fine-grained activity recognition by aggregating abstract object usage. In: ISWC 2005: Proceedings of the Ninth IEEE International Symposium on Wearable Computers, Washington, DC, USA, pp. 44–51. IEEE Computer Society, Los Alamitos (2005)
16. Propp, S., Buchholz, G., Forbrig, P.: Task model-based usability evaluation for smart environments, pp. 29–40 (2008)

Use Cases and Task Models as Driving Forces to Identify Requirements in Smart Environments

Maik Wurdel and Peter Forbrig

University of Rostock, Department of Computer Science
Albert-Einstein-Str. 21, 18059 Rostock, Germany
{maik.wurdel,peter.forbrig}@uni-rostock.de

Abstract. Smart environments have made the way from an abstract idea to prototypes. Assistance through smart environments can be provided for narrow scenario nowadays. From our point of view the crucial issue for those technologies is the user needs. User-centered requirements engineering can narrow the gap between technology driven smartness and those needs. Within the paper we propose a special requirements engineering process to identify the desired functionalities to implement a smart system with respect to the user. Additionally we give an outlook how design can be started based on the requirements engineering process.

Keywords: Requirements Engineering, Task Models, Use Cases, Smart Environments.

1 Motivation

In recent years ubiquitous and pervasive computing environments have made the step from science to industry. These systems consist of an enormous amount of devices surrounding the user to support everyday tasks. Even though ubiquitous and pervasive systems entered the markets "smart" systems are still challenging to develop. In this context smart is considered as a property of system which is able to offer services personalized to the user needs, adaptable to users over time and potentially act on their behalf [1].

Building those systems has been mostly treated as technical challenge. However user needs are often disregarded. Obviously this is a major shortcoming since smart systems are still used by ordinary users. A clear understanding of users' characteristics, their expectations and requirements about an envisioned system is essential to build a usable and intuitive system as it is claimed in requirement engineering. During requirement engineering phase the envisioned functions of the software system under development are specified in accordance with the end-user.

In this paper we examine two techniques to apply requirements engineering to smart environments. First we explain each technique separately including its assets and drawbacks. Then we compare their applicability for smart environments with respect to the stage of requirements engineering. In Section 4 we propose a requirements engineering process which is based on use cases and task models for smart

D. Tavangarian et al. (Eds.): IMC 2009, CCIS 53, pp. 251–262, 2009.

environments. We also give an outlook how such a process con be continued to perform design and implementation. The section is accompanied by a running example illustrating how the process can be applied successfully. Finally we conclude and give an outlook for future research avenues.

2 Background Information

Requirements are understood as descriptions of the services provided by the software system under development and capture the user needs to accomplish a goal using the system [2]. The process of analyzing and specifying these descriptions is called requirements engineering. This step in the software engineering cycle is crucial for the success of the whole development effort since the highest risk for a software project is to develop just the wrong system with respect to the user needs.

Different taxonomies for requirements exist. The most common one is the distinction between functional and non-functional requirements. Functional requirements document how a system should behave, which function it should offer and what components it should consist of. In contrast to that, non-functional requirements make statements about quality, performance, usability, etc. This distinction is rather smooth in practice.

Specifying requirements is performed on different levels of abstraction. Starting off with user goals, functions and workflows are derived in later steps. Different techniques to identify requirements exist. They differ in level of formality, phase of application, type of requirement to elicit, etc. Therefore one distinguishes between techniques which are only used to elicit requirements, such as user stories, interviews, card sorting, and techniques which are usable for requirements elicitation and documentation for design stage, such as use case, task models, and UML (unified modeling language [3]) models.

In this paper we focus on user-centered requirements engineering to gain insight about the way users performing tasks in smart environments. The requirements engineering process is therefore driven by use cases and task models. These techniques are introduced in the following paragraphs.

2.1 Use Cases

Throughout industry use cases have become state of the art to specify requirement. Originally invented by Jacobson [4] they have been extended and adapted over the years. They are a part of the UML since decades which is the de facto standard modeling language for software engineers.

Basically use cases serve as vehicle to document and communicate the envisioned behavior of a software system. They are mostly considered as contract between software engineer and stakeholder how the system under development should behave and react on input. They are the result of the requirement engineering process, and thus the input of the design stage of software engineering.

Essentially specifying use cases is about writing text however use cases diagrams are used to give an overview of the interrelation of different use case and the involved actors.

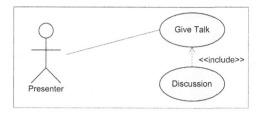

Fig. 1. Simplified Use Case Diagram for Meeting Situation for Presenter

In Fig. 1 a simple use case diagram is shown. First, it shows the actor "Presenter" with its assigned use case "Give Talk". Second, the use case "Give Talk" includes the use case "Discussion". A use case diagram can consists of the entities given in Table 1. Please note that the UML also defines the *generalization* relationship but it is very uncommon to use since the semantics is not clear defined.

Table 1. Entities used in Use Case Diagram

Entity	Description
Actor	One distinguishes between primary and secondary actors. The primary actor triggers the use case and/or gets the value from the system through the use case. Secondary actors only help to complete the use case of a primary actor.
Use Case	A use case specifies a certain function, its flow of event according to the inputs, the involved actor, the outputs and conditions.
Include Relation <<include>>	The *include* relation specifies a use case which is imported into another. The include use case and its flow of events is imported at a certain point within the including use case.
Extends Relation <<extends>>	If a certain flow of event of use case is particular it might be a good idea to factor that one out. This makes the use case more understandable and keeps the flow of event in the extended use case simple.
Actor-Use Case Relation	The relation defines that a certain actor is involved in the addressed use case.

As already pointed out use case diagrams serve as outline of requirements. The body of each use case is much more important. Different formats and guidelines exist but the most central principle when writing is: keep it simple. Use cases are meant to be understandable for stakeholders, who are usually not software engineers. Using natural language and a simple flow of events keeps the use case readable and thus a good vehicle to transmit knowledge about the envisioned system implementing the use case.

In requirements engineering one has to consider the existing and the envisioned situation. Even that use cases are able to specify both situations they are mostly used to specify the envisioned interactions. The body of a use case is defined using natural language and has different section. Different styles of writing use cases exist. Still, there is a common set of necessary fields which are mandatory for a use case. The style used here is based on [5]. Table 2 gives an overview of the different sections of

Table 2. Elements of the Use Case Body

Section	Description
Name	Very brief description of the purpose of the use case
Id	Unique identifier
Scope	Defines the scope of the use case and its boundaries in terms of involved entities in the use case (such as actors and system).
Level of Detail	Shows whether a use case is modeled rather high or low level. Cockburn introduces sea-level, cloud-level, underwater level [5]. The level applies for all fields in the use case.
Primary Actor	The participant who calls on the system to deliver the service implemented by the use case.
Goal	The goal the primary actor pursues through the use case.
Preconditions, Triggers & Guarantees	Preconditions needs to be fulfilled when the use case is started. Triggers specify events which let the use case start. Guarantees define both the minimal and success result of the system with respect to the result of the use case (fail or success).
Main Success Scenario	The core part of the body of the use case. Here the most common successful scenario (run through the use case) is specified. It should be easy to understand and must not contain alternatives. All other runs through the use case are defined in the extensions section. A scenario is specified by a set of action steps.
Extensions	Specifies all other scenarios in addition to the main success scenario. An extension consists of a condition under which it is relevant and the set of actions to rejoin the main success scenario.

the body a use case. An example of a use case is given in Fig. 2 specifying how a talk may be given using software system under development.

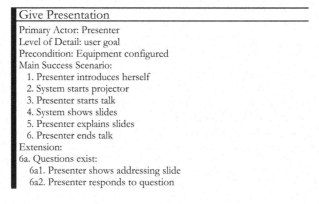

Give Presentation

Primary Actor: Presenter
Level of Detail: user goal
Precondition: Equipment configured
Main Success Scenario:
   1. Presenter introduces herself
   2. System starts projector
   3. Presenter starts talk
   4. System shows slides
   5. Presenter explains slides
   6. Presenter ends talk
Extension:
6a. Questions exist:
   6a1. Presenter shows addressing slide
   6a2. Presenter responds to question

Fig. 2. Use Case "Give Presentation"

2.2 Task Models

Task analysis and task modeling is a well-established research field in HCI (human computer interaction). It is performed to gain insight about the task world of users.

This technique can be applied on different levels of abstraction and throughout the whole requirements engineering process.

The idea of task model-based processes is to deliver a more usable system by analyzing how tasks are performed before starting development of the new system. Such a model of the existing work situation can be used to derive an improved version which is used as foundation to build the envisioned system. A task model represents a normative description of the tasks a user needs to accomplish to achieve certain goal.

Various notations for task modeling exist. Among the most popular ones are GOMS, HTA, GTA, and CTT [6]. They assume the following common tenet: tasks are performed to achieve a certain goal. Moreover, complex tasks are decomposed into more basic tasks until an atomic level has been reached. CTT, the most popular notation, and similar ones offer temporal operators to restrict the task execution order (sequence, choice, etc.). Tasks are classified according to the responsibility of execution and abstraction level (user, interaction, application or abstract). Besides their application within user centered requirements engineering they have been successfully established in the model-based UI development process as model to start of development.

In Fig. 3 an example of a task model is given. It specifies how a presenter gives a talk using the currently set up application within our meeting room. First the presenter introduces herself or configures the equipment (both have to be performed but in arbitrary order denoted by the *order independence* operator |=|). "Configure Equipment" is further decomposed into the sequence of "Connect Laptop to Projector" and "Start Projector" (the task type *application* denotes that the system performs the corresponding tasks). Then, the next task "Give Talk" can be started. It is decomposed into "Start Talk", "Show Slides", "Explain Slides" and "End Talk". After performing "Give Talk" the last task "Discussion" is enabled. By performing this task the goal "Give Presentation" is reached.

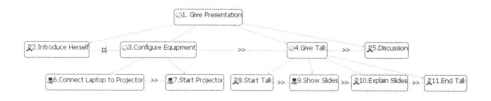

Fig. 3. Example Task Model for "Give Presentation"

The semantics of a task model is defined by the scenarios it produces. Such a formal semantics can be used to verify certain properties with respect to other modeled artifacts or derived models. In the example given above the following scenarios are valid (please note that we use the prefixed numbers instead of task names):

$$<2,6,7,8,9,10,11,5>,<6,7,2,8,9,10,11,5>$$

Since task models offer a precise semantics they can be interactively animated. Such a walkthrough is very helpful to explore the model. In Fig. 4 one can see a screenshot of our tool during animation mode of the previously shown model.

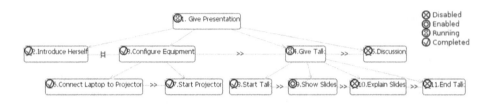

Fig. 4. Given Task Model in Animation Mode

3 Comparing Use Cases and Task Models

As already pointed out both techniques are able to specify requirement in a user-centered way. In this Section we highlight the assets of both techniques as well as their drawbacks with respect to the other. This assessment will serve as foundation for the process guided by both techniques presented in Section 4.

3.1 Level of Abstraction

Both techniques can be used on different levels of abstraction. Use cases explicitly support modeling on several level of abstractions through the field *Level of Detail*. The same use case can be specified on different levels of abstraction and can be gradual refined during the life cycle of the project. This is particularly useful during early stages of analysis in which fine-grained modeling only hampers the requirements engineering process. The same applies for task models. Even though there is no explicit concept gradual refinement can be performed easily by extending task models. Tasks can be further decomposed or on the contrary details can be hidden. On the one hand adaptation may result in improved models, one the other hand inconsistency can be introduced. Therefore we introduced an extension to task models which allows for verifying that certain structural and behavioral properties of the task model are still valid after adaptation [7].

3.2 Modularization

Use cases can be referenced using the *include* and *extends* relation. However, these relations are not supposed to be used very often. The semantics of the *extends* relation is also often misunderstood. However, the *include* relation is very useful to modularize use cases. Moreover, the use case diagram offers an overview of the different use cases and their interplay by the use case diagram.

Modularization in task model has been tackled on different level of abstraction. Our notation supports placeholder tasks which refer to task model fragments from other task models. In contrast to use cases task models do not offer a diagram to get an overview about the set of development artifacts even though such a diagram has been proposed [8]. In addition, task models offer only one relation (comparable to the *include* relation of use cases).

3.3 Formality

Given that use cases are specified by means of natural language they do not incorporate formal semantics. However, by formalizing the action steps and relations (*extends, include*) semantics can be defined [5, 9]. Fundamentally, use cases are used on high level of abstraction to elicit and specify requirements. Since they are rarely used to design systems a formal semantics is not very important. When specifying use cases one should focus on understandability and requirements to be specified not on formal correctness. Albeit, checking consistency is still expedient.

Most task model notations are based on process algebras. Therefore a clear semantics is inherently defined using traces and/or scenarios [10]. Each task model, or task model fragment, can be translated to a process. Due to this task models are used in later steps of requirements engineering when the envisioned behavior can be specified more precisely.

3.4 Hierarchy

The decomposition of tasks or processes is common way to reduce complexity. Use cases support decomposition by the *include* and *extends* relation. Hence, a use case may consist of a set of subordinate use cases. This high level hierarchy is very useful as already illustrated above. However, the decomposition of action steps is not supported.

The continuous decomposition of tasks into sub task until an atomic level has been reached is one of the major assets of task models. Hierarchical decomposition is a natural way of reducing complexity for human beings and as such fosters understandability.

3.5 Executability

During modeling executability of models is for several reasons helpful. First, when adapting an artifact early feedback through an interactive walkthrough helps improving the artifact. Second, trying to use an artifact as runtime model needs executability as well. For doing so an unambiguous semantics is needed. This applies for task models as shown in Fig. 4. Based on such an animation engine more sophisticated prototypes can be derived [11]. Due to the informal semantics of use cases execution is not directly possible.

3.6 The Main Success Scenario

Use cases are specified using a single line of events/ actions with extensions to be easily understandable. This is very helpful to highlight the most often run through the use case. When reading a use case the main success scenario becomes clear at the first glance. In contrast, task model do not distinguish between the induced scenarios. From our point of view this is a major drawback.

The relevance of a scenario of such a model (use case or task model) helps setting priority on the implementing functions and delivered user interface. Therefore we extended task models to integrate the main success scenario. It can be specified using our tool support by animating a model and setting the created scenario as main success scenario. In Fig. 5 a task model annotated with the main success scenario is depicted. Please note that this visualization does not show the order of execution.

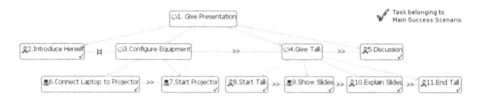

Fig. 5. Task Model Visualization with Annotated Main Success Scenario

4 Applying RE for Smart Environments – The Process

After introducing the different techniques to be applied for requirement engineering in smart environments we describe the process in which these techniques are applied. The requirement process needs to incorporate several entities relevant in smart environments. We consider actors, stationary and personal devices according with their interplay and additional constraints (e.g location and domain information) as most relevant. Thus, the result of such a process is a specification describing the interaction between actors and their devices. Based upon the previous sections and experimental modeling we found the three phases depicted in Fig. 6 of particular importance. The process starts by creating a text written scenario which describes the actors, their dependencies and the envisioned behavior of the system under development on a high level of abstraction. Next, use cases can be specified using the created scenarios. In the last phase task models are created based on use cases. Each phase is explained in detail in the following sub sections. To show how the process can be applied we accompany the explanations by a running example addressing our currently set up meeting environment equipped with several projectors and other stationary devices.

4.1 Start-Off Phase

Scenarios are a helpful technique for brainstorming the first high level use cases. These text written examples of the envisioned way of using the software system under development help to get a first idea to work with. Scenarios are supposed to be very concrete using names of persons. Based upon the developed scenarios the first high level use case can be derived. Since scenarios specify particular sequences of actions abstraction is needed when moving to the second phase. The first use cases should comprise the scenario they are based as main success scenario to truly reflect them. Hence, in contrast to scenarios use cases specify the interaction with the smart environment with respect to a certain actor.

4.1.1

The session chair Dr. Smith introduces herself and defines the topic of the session. Afterward she gives the floor to the first speaker who sets up her equipment, the laptop switches to presentation mode and the speaker starts with the talk. During the presentation the audience accesses additional information related to the talk using their personal devices. After finishing the talk the chairman asks for questions from the plenum which are answered by the speaker. Eventually the chairman closes the talk and announces the next one. Subsequent talks are given in the same manner until the chairman encourages an open discussion, wraps up the session and closes it.

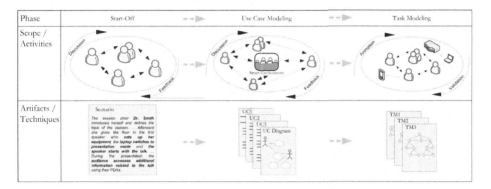

Fig. 6. Proposed Requirements Engineering Process. The Running Example – Scenario.

4.2 Use Case Modeling

Use case modeling is performed on different levels of abstraction. We distinguish between three levels of detail: user goal level, summary level, fully-dressed level. In the beginning user goal use cases are specified. Later on these use cases are gradually refined until an appropriate level is reached. Well written use cases call for stakeholders' and end users' discussion. Based on feedback modeling decisions can be revised and artifacts are improved. After agreeing on a set of use cases the level of details is increased. Thus a new iteration is triggered.

In general in our process use cases should specify the interaction of an actor with the smart environment. Technical details and concrete device dependencies are not supposed to be modeled in phase two. However, devices constituting to the smart environment can be named in the use case if they are relevant. In Fig. 2 an example of a potential first user goal use case implementing the scenario is given. On this level of detail the goal of the actor involved in the use case are specified. Such a use case should contain the interaction of the actor with the software system on an abstract level. The flow of events specified on this level. Next the use cases are further detailed. The summary level use cases are created based on the prior specified user goal use cases. The purpose of those use cases is the same but the level of detail is increased. Thus gradual refinement is applied.

The last type of use cases specifies the interaction with the smart environments on lowest level of abstraction. Here, steps are further refined with respect to the prior type. Again, gradual refinement is taking place. In Fig. 7 on the left hand side the use case diagram is depicted. It gives an outline of the use cases and their interplay. On the right hand side the use case "Give Presentation" is given. It specifies the flow of events on the summary level for giving a presentation for the actor "Presenter".

4.2.1   The Running Example – Use Case

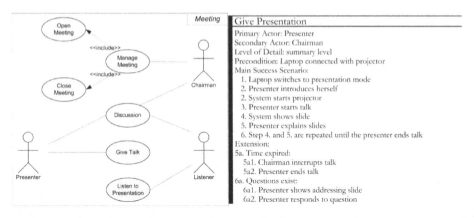

Fig. 7. Use Case Diagram and Use Case "Give Presentation"

4.3   Task Modeling

The input of this phase is a set of interrelated, fine-grained use cases. They are to be realized by task models. In this phase additional facts are taken into account. In contrast to use cases task models are used to specify the concrete interaction with the devices constituting to the smart environment. In order to be able to do so the potential interaction of user and devices needs to be analyzed according to the scenario and the use cases. Based upon the flow of events defined in the most detailed use cases the task models are derived. Previously defined steps in use case are further refined into tasks implementing these steps. Additionally types for tasks are defined expressing the responsibility of execution.

As already pointed out task models are executable. An interactive animation can help to illustrate the model artifact and its behavior. Therefore task models can be improved based on feedback given through animation. Thus, task modeling is an iterative phase which calls for stakeholders' and users' feedback.

In the end of this stage the high level interaction of users and devices as part of the smart environment is specified. The task model specifies all potential scenarios (runs through the task model) supported by the smart environment. On this stage all participants of the requirements engineering process should agree on the set of task models specifying the interaction of the user with the smart environment.

In order to support the user with respect to the scenario and use cases she is assumed to behave according to the specified task model. If this is not the case the user needs to use the technical devices in the ordinary way. Assistance cannot be provided. Thus, task models are understood as contract between all participants of the process. In Fig. 3 a task model for giving a presentation is depicted. It is based on, and further refines, the use cases of Fig. 7.

4.4   Moving to Design

When moving from requirements engineering to design new lower level models are of interest. In our currently set up meeting environment we use annotated labeled transition systems (LTS) to implement the specified requirements. They can be derived from task models. Basically those LTSs specify the set of scenarios defined by the task models and serve as input for our intention recognition module of our environment. At runtime, during the meeting, those annotated LTS specifications are combined with sensor data to derive the currently executing task of the users.

Fig. 8. LTS Diagram used as Input for Intention Recognition Module for "Give Presentation

In Fig. 8 an example of such an LTS is given. It is automatically derived from the task model given in Fig. 3. Please note that the state names only contain the prefixed number of the task names due to reasons of brevity. The initial state of the model is on the leftmost side. Transitions are labeled with the task names representing their execution. The state names are based on the already executed tasks. Please note that executed sub trees are aggregated.

5   Conclusion and Future Work

In this paper we proposed a user-centered requirements engineering process based on different techniques, namely use cases and task models, to identify desired behavior of smart environments. Technology driven prototypes have shown that user-centeredness is often disregarded. To satisfy user needs is the most important objective for smart environments. Therefore thoroughly performed requirements engineering is crucial to build those systems. In particular, the process is driven by use cases in early stages which are built upon scenarios. In later steps task models are derived which can even be used in design by translation to annotated LTS specifications.

We have introduced the idea of the "main success scenarios" into task models and provided the corresponding tool support. Moreover we have shown that the creation of task models can be guided by use cases. However, the formal semantics of task models can also help to show the dynamics of use case implemented by a task model. In this vein executables use case are realized.

However, such a process needs to be validated. Currently the phases are based upon software engineering knowledge and experimental modeling. Therefore a user study may lead to additional insights which can be used to further optimize the process.

Additionally, when moving from one phase to another consistency checks might be useful to verify that defined requirements are truly implemented in the subsequent stage. This is particular of interest in later stages (use case, task models). Verification algorithms have been developed for task models as well as for LTS diagrams.

References

[1] Aarts, E., de Ruytera, B.: New research perspectives on Ambient Intelligence. Journal of Ambient Intelligence and Smart Environments 1, 5–14 (2009)

[2] Sommerville, I.: Software Engineering: (Update) International Computer Science, 8th edn. Addison-Wesley Longman Publishing Co., Inc., Boston (2006)

[3] UML, Unified Modeling Language, http://www.uml.org/ (accessed May 10, 2008)

[4] Jacobson, I.: Object-oriented software engineering: a use case driven approach. Addison-Wesley u.a., Wokingham u.a. (1992)

[5] Cockburn, A.: Writing effective use cases. Addison-Wesley, Boston u.a (2001)

[6] Limbourg, Q., Vanderdonckt, J.: Comparing Task Models for User Interface Design. In: Diaper, D., Stanton, N. (eds.) The Handbook of Task Analysis for Human-Computer Interaction. Lawrence Erlbaum Associates, Mahwah (2003)

[7] Wurdel, M., Sinnig, D., Forbrig, P.: Task Model Refinement with Meta Operators. In: DSV-IS 2007, Kingston, Canada (2008)

[8] Sinnig, D., Wurdel, M., Forbrig, P., Chalin, P., Khendek, F.: Practical Extensions for Task Models. In: Winckler, M., Johnson, H., Palanque, P. (eds.) TAMODIA 2007. LNCS, vol. 4849, pp. 42–55. Springer, Heidelberg (2007)

[9] Sinnig, D., Chalin, P., Khendek, F.: Common Semantics for Use Cases and Task Models. In: Davies, J., Gibbons, J. (eds.) IFM 2007. LNCS, vol. 4591, pp. 579–598. Springer, Heidelberg (2007)

[10] Roscoe, A.W., Hoare, C.A.R., Hoare, C.A.R., Richard, B.: The Theory and Practice of Concurrency, p. 561. Prentice Hall PTR, Englewood Cliffs (1997)

[11] Reichart, D., Forbrig, P., Dittmar, A.: Task models as basis for requirements engineering and software execution. TAMODIA, pp. 51–58 (2004)

Creating AI Planning Domains for Smart Environments Using PDDL

Florian Marquardt and Adelinde Uhrmacher

University of Rostock, Albert-Einstein-Str. 21, 18059 Rostock, Germany
fm@informatik.uni-rostock.de, lin@informatik.uni-rostock.de

Abstract. One corner stone for user assistance in smart environments is service composition, which can be reached using AI planning. Therefore it is required to formulate the current environment as planning problem, which can than be solved with an AI planning algorithm. However, some characteristics of smart environments conflict with the strict requirements of classical AI planning as well as with the limitations of PDDL, which is the state of the art representation language for planning domains and problems. These interferences are uncovered in a bottom up manner by reviewing smart environment scenarios from literature. The scenarios were realized as planning problems in PDDL, consisting of operators, an initial world state, propositions, and goals. Possible problems and ways to avoid the respective hurdles are given.

It is concluded if AI planning based user assistance is suitable to solve the crucial challenges of the respective scenario and to what extend AI planning is able to contribute to the problem of service composition in smart environments in general.

1 Introduction

Smart environments are a vision right now. Research on this topic was done in different fields of application, e.g. for Smart Houses [3], Smart Health Care [1], Smart Laboratories [22] and Smart Rooms [14]. Thereby, the term "smart" refers to services that are offered to the user in an unobtrusive manner. The term "environment" refers to a dynamic ensemble of devices responsible for offering the services. This kind of "smartness" typically requires the cooperation of several devices based on intentions of the user, which are identified by observing the user and taking into account the context.

One possibility to provide this cooperation is AI planning based service composition [5,24]. Therefore a smart environment has to be modeled as a planning problem, which is a discrete state transition system. To solve planning problems different planners are available. In addition, numerous extensions of the classical AI planning problem are available. Many of them require additional modeling effort for the respective scenario.

The main contribution of this work is a set of requirements that should be fulfilled in order to use AI planning for service composition. The requirements are introduced to guide the modelling of smart environments as planning problems

D. Tavangarian et al. (Eds.): IMC 2009, CCIS 53, pp. 263–274, 2009.

in general and in addition chose suitable planning extensions when needed. The requirements cope the strict restrictions of classical planning, such as the static and finite state space [18,13]. It is shown that smart environments conflict with these restrictions. The requirement of AI planning to have a finite state space implies, that during a planning run the number of states is fixed and limited. As we want to represent the real world, the number of possible states is unlimited in the first place. The static state space implies that during a planning run entities may not be created or destroyed, thus the creation of files or information as outputs of information providing services in general can not be modeled directly. We present a possible workaround to handle this problem. In classical planning the execution of an operator, which represents a certain service in our setting, is timeless. I.e. the result of the operator is produced instantly. However, the execution of services takes time. We show that it is possible to abstract from these durations and, if necessary, list planning extensions to be used to express the duration of service execution. Planning problems usually are modeled a priori, hence make use of global knowledge about the involved operators and predicates. In contrast using planning for service composition in smart environments, requires ad hoc creation of planning domains. We show how this can be reached and which problems arise, if no global knowledge is allowed.

It is important to carefully handle the mentioned modelling issues. Therefore we describe a general guideline that helps to cover important issues. The requirements are derived bottom up based on the modelling of example scenarios from literature. The scenarios were encoded using the Planning Domain Definition Language (PDDL) [12], which will be introduced in the next section.

2   Introducing Example

An AI planning algorithm requires three inputs, the current state of the world, the available operators, and the goal description. In smart environments the current state of the world is given by the information from sensors and other information sources, which can be subsumed as context. The available operators are given by the descriptions of services which reside on the devices available in the environment. Goal descriptions are provided by an intention analysis component that is able to infer intentions of the user [4]. A more detailed description of this mapping and a general composition architecture that realizes this mapping is given in [17]. All information that relates to the planning problem are collected at runtime. Hence the PDDL domain and problem definitions have to be assembled at runtime, too. Afterward a planning algorithm is incorporated to solve the problem.

To describe AI planning for service composition as well as the syntax of PDDL in detail a simplified scenario from the project EmBASSI [14] is used. To the best of our knowledge this is the only project that incorporates PDDL for service composition in smart environments so far. Although the behavior in the original scenario is more elaborated and specialized, we simplified it to depict the usage of AI planning based service composition for user assistance in smart environments better. Initially a narrative description of the desired behavior is given.

An unnamed user is watching TV and would like to increase the brightness of the display. As the TV is already set to maximum brightness, the environment should reduce the ambient light, by closing the shutter and dimming the lamp, thus increasing the perceived brightness of the TV.

As PDDL is based on Lisp it uses the prefix notation. Variables are indicated with a question mark, e.g. *?x*. A planning scenario consists of a domain and a problem description. We will first describe how a PDDL domain looks like. It starts with a header containing the name of the domain and a list of requirements that are posed to the algorithm that should solve the problem. The requirement ":strips" states that the planner have to support the basic features of planning and thus is mandatory for most scenarios.

```
(define (domain brightenTV)
   (:requirements :strips)
   (:constants MAX HIGH LOW)
```

Here the measurements *MAX*, *HIGH*, and *LOW* are defined as constants. As planning is state based, predicates defining the state of world, are needed. The predicates (also called propositions) reflect aspects that can be accessed and/or changed by the operators. An alternative way to express the constants above would be to introduce different propositions, e.g. *(maxBrightness ?tv)*, *(lowLuminosity ?lamp)*, or *(highLuminosity ?lamp)*.
The predicates we used in our example are:

```
(:predicates
   (brightness ?device ?value)  ;The brightness of a device, e.g. TV
   (luminosity ?lamp ?value)  ;Representing the luminosity of a lamp
   (dimmable ?lamp)  ;Stating if a lamp can be dimmed
   (isOpen ?shutter)  ;Stating if the shutter is currently open
```

After the definition of constants and propositions a PDDL domain contains several operator descriptions. An operator represents a executable service in the smart environment. Each operator consists of a name, a list of propositions called precondition and a second list of propositions called effect. To be applicable all propositions in the preconditions of an operator must be true in the current state of the world. After execution the propositions in the effect list are applied to the current world state. Preconditions and effects describe the semantics of an operator. For clarification one have to differentiate between planning operators and planning actions. Operators as described below contain variables whereas actions are grounded instances of an operator and represent the concrete state transitions. Therefore operators are included in the domain description and the result of a planning run is a sequence of actions. The following operators are given to cope the scenario.

```
(:action dim-down ;A service to reduce the luminosity of a lamp.
   :parameters (?x)
   :precondition (and (luminosity ?x HIGH)(dimmable ?x))
   :effect (luminosity ?x LOW))
(:action closeShutter ;This service closes a shutter.
   :parameters (?x)
   :precondition (and (isOpen(?x)))
   :effect (and (not(isOpen(?x)))(luminosity(?x LOW))))
```

Definitions of predicates and operators are the main contents of the domain description. Now the problem description for the given scenario will be described. The head of a PDDL problem definition includes the name of the problem and the name of the according domain

```
(define (problem brightenTV-problem)
   (:domain brightenTV)
```

First the objects were defined. They represent the devices in the environment.

```
(:objects TV SHUTTER LAMP)
```

After introducing the objects the initial state of the world is given. It consists of several initial assignments to the propositions of the domain.

```
(:init
   (brightness TV MAX)
   (luminosity LAMP HIGH)
   (dimmable LAMP)
   (isOpen SHUTTER))
```

As AI planning tries to generate plans of actions, which fulfill a given goal based on an initial state of the world, finally the goal must be defined in the problem description. The planner, that is given the problem then searches for a sequence of actions that makes all propositions true in the goal state based on the initial world state.

```
(:goal (and (not (isOpen SHUTTER))(luminosity LAMP LOW)))
```

Having a PDDL domain and problem description a planner can search for a plan, that solves the given problem in the corresponding domain. A suitable plan for the current scenario is given below.[1]

```
0  (DIM-DOWN LAMP)
1  (CLOSESHUTTER SHUTTER)
```

In addition to the given domain, in the original scenario from Heider and Kirste *axioms* (also called *derived predicates*) were used. They are very useful means to keep operator descriptions simple and possibly more domain independent. In their scenario a first axiom infers the overall brightness of the room. In an additional axiom it is furthermore described that the brightness of the TV increases if the brightness of the surrounding environment decreases. Given the goal *(brighter TV)* the environment can thus automatically infer that dimming the surrounding light makes the TV appear brighter for a human observer. This is a very elaborated but also very specialized service composition behavior. To be able to reach this special behavior the authors make use of ":equality", ":quantified-preconditions", and ":derived-predicates" as PDDL requirements in their domain

---

[1] The used planner generates partial-ordered plans, which may contain parallel actions. The number in front of the actions shows the time step when the action is to be executed. Actions having the same index do not influence each other and can be executed in parallel.

(see [7] for further information). Furthermore in the original scenario global operators like *lights-out* were used. This type of operator conflicts with the ad hoc nature of smart environments. Without preparation, no device would be able to offer a service that switches off all lights together, unless there is a room-control unit connected with all available lights in the room and in addition it would be forbidden to bring additional lamps into the room. Both requirements are not acceptable for smart environments in general.

After the introducing example three further scenarios based on different visions and at different levels of detail will be reviewed to shade some light on the process of domain modelling and to uncover pitfalls. The chosen set of scenarios represents nearly one decade of visions for smart environments. Therefore some of the scenarios are near to reality right now, others still seem to be more fictional. As most of the scenarios are rather high level descriptions the liberty was taken to specify them at a suitable level of detail. Furthermore, just one possible problem representation that fulfills the scenario description is presented. Different approaches might be possible.

3 Scenarios

Most of the reviewed publications are not interested in service composition or strategy synthesis in particular but concerned with more general or overlapping questions. Thus, just the compositional challenges of the respective scenarios are picked no matter of their additional requirements.

Looking at the compositional challenges many scenarios in literature appear rather one-dimensional. Involved devices are mostly just used once. However, the reuse of devices and their services during one planning run is more challenging. Furthermore planning is only meaningful if plans are expected that contain sequences of actions that depend on each other. In the Project UbiREAL [19] an example for a smart environment is given where only stimulus response actions are needed. To this end it very much correlates to the one given in Brumitt et al. [3]. The services do not depend on each other, thus no action sequences are needed and all devices and/or services can act simultaneously. The focus of these scenarios is not on dynamic device cooperation but rather on seamless reaction to the user according to fixed rules with presumably hard wired devices. These kind of scenarios are not suited for planning.

Due to lack of space the operator descriptions presented in this publication are shortened and not exactly standard conform to PDDL. The definitions of preconditions and effects were left out, furthermore the syntax of the operator's parameter definitions was changed. The given operators are augmented with a description of its correspondent real world service. All described scenarios were completely modeled in PDDL and run successfully using the planner LPG-td1.0 [11].

3.1 Tom's Route Planning – Project Amigo [9]

Unlike in the example in the last section we will use typed variables and typed objects in the following scenarios. Using typing is indicated by adding *:typing* as

PDDL requirement to the header of the domain description. A typed predicate e.g. indicating, that a device is switched on, is encoded in PDDL like this: *(isOn ?d - Device)*. The name of the variable is followed by "-" and the type's name. Types must be declared in the head of a PDDL domain description. Typing the objects makes reading domain definitions more comfortable and furthermore allows for better performance optimization during planning. The current scenario furthermore shows the problem of the static state space.

> *Tom wants to automatically print out the route from its home to a new restaurant he found on the web. He won't bother about details like getting the address from the restaurants' website or accessing a route planner.*

Based on the description of this scenario it is not clear how Toms desire to get the route is expressed and what is known in the first place. It is therefore assumed that a voice recognition is able to infer the goal from Toms verbal input. Furthermore it is assumed that Tom's address is available and can be accessed by the planner.

Operators:

```
getAddress(?url − Data) ;A web service capable of collecting addresses
getRoute(?a1 ?a2 − Location  ?d − Document) ;A route planning web service
;returning an image of the calculated route
switchOn(?p − Printer) ;Switching on Tom's printer
printDocument(?d − Document) ;The printer service
```

Goals: (and (isRoute DOC TOMSADDR RESTAURANTSADDR)(isPrinted DOC))

Initial world state:

```
(isEmptyDocument DOC)
(isAddress TOMSADDR)
(isStart TOMSADDR)
(isURL RESTAURANTSADDR)
(isDestination RESTAURANTSADDR)
```

Plan:

```
0  (GETADDRESS RESTAURANTSADDR)
0  (SWITCHON TOMSPRINTER)
1  (GETROUTE TOMSADDR RESTAURANTSADDR DOC)
2  (PRINTDOCUMENT DOC TOMSPRINTER)
```

Planning time: 30ms

Remarks: This scenario reveals the general problem of AI planning that during planning runs no new objects can be created. Thats why no new document containing the found route can be created as an effect of the *getRoute* operator. A modeling workaround is to introduce an empty document and augment *getRoute* with another parameter, which would accept empty documents, that can be changed into non-empty documents containing a route as effect. This workaround must be known by all involved devices and their services. E.g. the operator *printDocument(?d - Document)* should contain a precondition *(not (isEmpty ?d))* otherwise it will possibly print non-existent documents. Empty documents are a kind of binary resources, which can be coped with simple locking predicates. Another problem of this scenario is hidden in the goal definition. Propositions that are used in the goal description can only become true by operators effects.

As services in smart environments do not know about each other until they join in an ensemble, they may not include global knowledge. Hence a printer can just have the general effect *(isPrinted ?doc)* but not the special effect *(isPrintedRoute ?from ?to)*. Therefore the intention analysis has to solely use propositions that are available in the effects of the services' operators.

3.2 Jane's Email – Project Aura [10]

The following scenario is of interesst, because it can only be solved with operators that include human actions.

Jane is at an airport waiting for her flight at gate 12. She wants to send a quite large email. Unfortunately the WLAN at gate 12 is overloaded, thus she would not be able to finish the upload until her boarding is closed. At gate 5 the WLAN connection is better and it is not too far away from gate 12. Jane would be able to go to gate 5, upload the email, and go back to gate 12 fast enough to not miss the boarding of her flight.

Operators:

```
connectWLAN(?l – Laptop ?loc – Location ?t – Thruput); A service located
;on a laptop which is able to establish a wireless connection as well as
;measure the thruput of the current connection
sendMail(?e – Email ?l – Laptop ?t – Thruput) ;A mail client able to send
;emails and infer if the current online connection is suitable, in terms
;of duration, for the size of the email
move(?from ?to – Location ?l – Laptop) ; This action models Jane's movement
checkIn(?l – Laptop ?loc – Location) ; This is the check in action
```

Initial world state:

```
(at  GATE12 JANESLAPTOP)
(isMovable  JANESLAPTOP)
(requiredThruput JANESEMAIL HIGHT)
(availableThruput GATE12 LOWT)
(availableThruput GATE5 HIGHT)
```

Goals: (**and** (mailSent JANESEMAIL)(checkedIn GATE12))

Plan:

```
0  (MOVE GATE12 GATE5 JANESLAPTOP)
1  (CONNECTWLAN JANESLAPTOP GATE5 HIGHT)
2  (SENDMAIL JANESEMAIL JANESLAPTOP HIGHT)
2  (MOVE GATE5 GATE12 JANESLAPTOP)
3  (CHECKIN JANESLAPTOP GATE12)
```

Planning time: 20ms

Remarks: As we assume Jane never letting her laptop alone, just her laptop was modeled in this scenario for additional simplification. Nevertheless, the used operators *move* and *checkIn* can not be implemented as services anyhow, because they include actions of a person. Jane can just be given the hint to move to gate 12, hoping she will do. Generalized one can say, as soon as acting of people is needed in an operator, the outcome of a planning run should rather be regarded as suggestion for acting, than as complete plan for execution of services [20]. Thus, this scenario can not be solved by service composition alone.

The proposition *(isMovable ?laptop)*, which is made false by the operator *checkIn*, was required in this scenario, as it had to made explicit that after boarding Jane can not move to any other location. Otherwise the planner would first chose the *checkIn* operator and then move her to gate 5 to send the email.

This scenario reveals another drawback of pure classical planning. Without enhancements it is not possible to express durative actions. For this reason the problem was simplified, by leaving out all durations, e.g. the walk from gate 5 to gate 12 as well as the duration of sending the mail.

Besides, this scenario shows that it is very tedious to model all possible effects of an action. Furthermore assuming just local knowledge it becomes nearly impossible. For example moving the laptop from one gate to another inherently disconnects its recent WLAN connection.

3.3   Bart's Order – Project Daidalos [23]

Bart is at home and watches the news on TV when his boss calls him via VoIP. The call is directed to Bart's PDA. During the call the news cast on TV is paused. His boss orders him to pick up a client from the airport. After the call the news are continued. When Bart enters his car the news were played as audio stream from his car radio. Arriving at the airport the navigation system of his car changes into an flight information service, so he is able to see when his client is landing.

This scenario describes an iterative process and should be divided into several parts. In each of the parts new goals must be fulfilled or new world states must be taken into account. Each part would be handled as an own planning attempt. A first goal is to receive the call from Bart's boss. The second goal is to pick up the client from the airport. As a third goal Bart should be able to receive the news cast during his movement from the living room at his home to his car and finally to the airport. The problem here is to find a way to update the goals and world states according to the events happening. E.g. after the call from his boss it must be inferred somehow, that Bart's new goal is now to pick up the client. Even more than in the scenario "Jane's Email", the focus here is on real world action planning with humans involved rather than service composition.

The most substantial service composition aspects in this scenario are changing the car radio into a flight information system and transferring the news cast to Bart's car radio. Whereas the first is straight forward from the service composition point of view, the second has its pitfalls and is therefore discussed. Assuming the news show is an ordinary cable broadcast, pausing it requires some record functionality of the TV. This can be achieved with current technologies (e.g. a HD-recorder). Nevertheless transferring the recorded news to the car radio requires either the news cast to be finished and the remainder of the news cast copied to the car radio afterward, or an existing network connection between the TV and the car so the buffered news cast can be forwarded. As unfortunately the scenario description gives no indication which of both is meant, the latter was assumed and the scenario was extend as described below.

Bart has just received the call and stepped into his car to drive to the airport, the TV at his home is showing the buffered news cast. As the car radio can only play audio streams the video stream containing the news cast must be converted to audio. Fortunately his PDA is able to do so.

Operators:

```
(startStream ?dev − Device ?s − Stream ?f − Format)  ;start a stream
(stopStream ?dev − Device ?s − Stream ?f − Format)  ;stop a stream
(accessStream ?src ?dest − Device ?s − Stream ?f − Format)  ;A service
;that can access a currently running stream on a distant device.
(connect ?dev1 ?dev2 − Device)  ;This service establishes a network
;connection between two devices.
(convertData (?d − Data ?fFrom ?fTo − Format ?dev − Device)  ;A service
;able to convert data from one format to another on a specific device.
```

Goals: (and (isActive CarRadio RecordedNews Audio))

Initial world state:

```
(supportsFormat Audio PDA)
(supportsFormat Video PDA)
(at Home TV)
(supportsFormat Video TV)
(isAvailable RecordedNews TV)
(hasFormat Video RecordedNews)
(isActive TV RecordedNews Video)
(isLocked TV)
(supportsFormat Audio CarRadio)
```

Plan:

```
0   (CONNECT PDA CARRADIO)
0   (STOPSTREAM TV RECORDEDNEWS VIDEO)
1   (CONNECT TV PDA)
2   (STARTSTREAM TV RECORDEDNEWS VIDEO)
3   (ACCESSSTREAM TV PDA RECORDEDNEWS VIDEO)
4   (CONVERTDATA RECORDEDNEWS VIDEO AUDIO PDA)
5   (ACCESSSTREAM PDA CARRADIO RECORDEDNEWS AUDIO)
```

Planning time: 20ms

Remarks: If converting services are needed, all information relating to the data types to be converted have to be modeled as propositions. Different PDDL-types (e.g. AudioStream or VideoStream) may not be used, as the type of an object can not be changed during planning time. The operator *startStream* contains three parameters, the device, the stream and the format of the stream. Knowing that a stream can just have one format makes it obsolete to use both parameters (stream and format) in an operator, as the latter could be inferred from the first. In planning this would be possible by using *axioms*. The truth value of a derived predicate is inferred from that of some basic predicates via axioms. Although omitted in the definition of PDDL 2.1[8], axioms are a powerful and reasonable mean to reduce domain complexity and planning effort [21] and returned in the definition of PDDL 2.2 [7].

4   Requirements

Modelling requirements which result from the examples above are summarized and listed in the following.

1. **All operators must solely represent one certain service.** As a result of the planning process a sequence of service invocations is expected, thus only operators that relate to available services may be used.
2. **Human actions may not be included in effects of operators.** In section 3.2 human acting is required to fulfill a plan. In that case planning may only create suggestions for acting rather than sequences of services for automatic execution. To remain in the problem space of service composition it has to be ensured, that planning operators may solely represent services that are available in the current environment. In case human acting is included in operators a decoupled planning, scheduling and execution is unavoidable.
3. **Operator's effects must not include global knowledge.** The domain descriptions are assembled at runtime, and were defined independently. Hence, they can only include knowledge referring to their own service or device. Requiring global knowledge is forbidden.
4. It is required that **the intention analysis may solely use propositions that are available in the effects of the operators or in the initial world state.** This implies that every time the configuration of the environment changes, the intention analysis must be updated.
5. **The resulting plans should be executable without further knowledge.** However, as the plans are generated using PDDL operators, the syntactical mapping from PDDL to a common service description language has to be provided.
6. **Creation of objects is not possible.** Because of the static state space of AI planning, creating new objects in operator effects is not possible. In section 3.1 a workaround that uses dummy-objects with an associated proposition is given.
7. **Using axioms is beneficial.** Already in the first scenario (section 2) some indications for the benefit of axioms are given. In addition the scenario "Bart's order" (section 3.3) reveals the need of domain axioms (or derived predicates). Axioms can only be part of service descriptions and as such have to be shipped with the devices carrying the services. This is an additional requirement to the service description. Unfortunately our experience shows, that current planner implementations do not seem to support derived predicates in conjunction with typing sufficiently.
8. In the scenario in section 3.3 we encountered binary and continuous resources. **Binary resources can be modeled using locking propositions** as for instance *(isLocked ?o)*. Continuous resources needs extensions like described by Koehler [15].
9. In section 3.2 Jane moves around carrying her laptop with her. **Moving objects that include other objects requires conditional effects for sufficient solving of the problem** [2]. Operators that include movement mostly implies that people are involved in the scenario, who carry the devices with them. However, this would conflict with the requirement to not include human actions in operators. Although one can imagine small robots moving around with mounted devices, these situations are rather rare in ordinary environments up to now.

10. In section 3.3 data streams must be converted. From a programmers point of view one would simply change the type of an objects by some kind of casting technique. However, **casting is not possible using PDDL**. This requirement also stems from the static state space, where objects are not allowed to change its type. However, propositions related to an object may change. Therefore, if conversions are needed types must be made explicit using e.g. a predicate like (hasFormat ?data ?format).

5   Conclusion

Modeling service composition in smart environments as AI planning problems is not straight forward. Various restrictions, like the static state space of AI planning, have to be considered carefully. The introduced requirements are a very useful mean to cope with this restrictions. Their usage allows to successfully model service composition in smart environments as AI planning problems.

One of the given requirements is to only use local information for operators precondition and effects, to enable their independent definition. Nevertheless, used propositions must have the same meaning for all involved operators. This unavoidably leads to usage of common ontologies. Although there is research done regarding ontologies for smart environments (e.g. [6]) no common ontology, which is comprehensible enough, exists up to now.

Evaluating the introduced scenarios it becomes obvious that AI planning service composition is more benficial the more actions a resulting plan exhibits. I.e. the more the services depend on each other the more planning becomes beneficial. It has been shown that performance of state of the art planners is suitable to solve artificial generated service composition problems in smart environments [16]. All of the scenarios reviewed in this work were no challenge for recent planning algorithms, too.

Acknowledgment

This research is supported by the German Research Foundation (DFG) within the context of the project MuSAMA (Multimodal Smart Appliance Ensembles for Mobile Applications).

References

1. Agarwal, S., Joshi, A., Finin, T., Yesha, Y., Ganous, T.: A pervasive computing system for the operating room of the future. Mob. Netw. Appl. 12(2-3), 215–228 (2007)
2. Anderson, C.R., Smith, D.E., Weld, D.S.: Conditional effects in graphplan. In: AIPS, pp. 44–53 (1998)
3. Brumitt, B., Meyers, B., Krumm, J., Kern, A., Shafer, S.: Easyliving: Technologies for intelligent environments. In: Thomas, P., Gellersen, H.-W. (eds.) HUC 2000. LNCS, vol. 1927, pp. 12–29. Springer, Heidelberg (2000)

4. Burghardt, C., Kirste, T.: Inferring intentions in generic context-aware systems. In: MUM, pp. 50–54 (2007)
5. Carman, M., Serafini, L., Traverso, P.: Web service composition as planning. In: Workshop on Planning for Web Services, Trento, Italy (June 2003)
6. Chen, H., Perich, F., Finin, T., Joshi, A.: Soupa: Standard ontology for ubiquitous and pervasive applications. In: International Conference on Mobile and Ubiquitous Systems: Networking and Services, August 2004, pp. 258–267 (2004)
7. Edelkamp, S., Hoffmann, J.: PDDL2.2: The Language for the Classical Part of the 4th International Planning Competition. Technical report, Fachbereich Informatik, University of Dortmund (2004)
8. Fox, M., Long, D.: Pddl2.1: An extension to pddl for expressing temporal planning domains. Journal of Artificial Intelligence Research 20 (2003)
9. Fujii, K., Suda, T.: Dynamic service composition using semantic information. In: ICSOC 2004: Proceedings of the 2nd international conference on Service oriented computing, pp. 39–48. ACM, New York (2004)
10. Garlan, D., Siewiorek, D.P., Steenkiste, P.: Project aura: Toward distraction-free pervasive computing. IEEE Pervasive Computing 1, 22–31 (2002)
11. Gerevini, A., Serina, I.: Lpg: a planner based on local search for planning graphs. In: Proceedings of the Sixth International Conference on Artificial Intelligence Planning and Scheduling (AIPS 2002), Toulouse, France. AAAI Press, Menlo Park (2002)
12. Ghallab, M., Howe, A., Knoblock, C., McDermott, D., Ram, A., Veloso, M., Weld, D., Wilkins, D.: PDDL - the planning domain definition language (July 1998)
13. Ghallab, M., Nau, D., Traverso, P.: Automated Planning, theory and practice. Morgan Kaufmann, San Francisco (2004)
14. Heider, T., Kirste, T.: Smart environments and self-organizing appliance ensembles. In: Mobile Computing and Ambient Intelligence (2005)
15. Koehler, J.: Planning under resource constraints. In: ECAI, pp. 489–493 (1998)
16. Marquardt, F., Uhrmacher, A.: Evaluating AI Planning for Service Composition in Smart Environments. In: Proceedings of the 7th International ACM Conference on Mobile and Ubiquitous Multimedia, Umea, Sweden, December 2008, pp. 48–55. ACM, New York (2008)
17. Marquardt, F., Uhrmacher, A.M.: An ai-planning based service composition architecture for ambient intelligence. To appear in Proc. AITAmI 2009 (July 2009)
18. Nau, D.S.: Current trends in automated planning. AI Magazine 28(4), 43–58 (2007)
19. Nishikawa, H., Yamamoto, S., Tamai, M., Nishigaki, K., Kitani, T., Shibata, N., Yasumoto, K., Ito, M.: Ubireal: Realistic smartspace simulator for systematic testing. In: Dourish, P., Friday, A. (eds.) UbiComp 2006. LNCS, vol. 4206, pp. 459–476. Springer, Heidelberg (2006)
20. Simpson, R., Schreckenghost, D., LoPresti, E., Kirsch, N.: Plans and planning in smart homes. Designing Smart Homes, 71–84 (2006)
21. Thiébaux, S., Hoffmann, J., Nebel, B.: In defense of pddl axioms. Artificial Intelligence 168(1-2), 38–69 (2005)
22. Thurow, K., Göde, B., Dingerdissen, U., Stoll, N.: Laboratory information management system for life science applications. Organic Process Research & Development 8, 970–982 (2004)
23. Yang, Y., Mahon, F., Williams, M., Pfeifer, T.: Context-aware dynamic personalised service re-composition in a pervasive service environment (2006)
24. Zhao, H., Doshi, P.: Haley: A hierarchical framework for logical composition of web services. In: IEEE International Conference on Web Services, ICWS 2007, pp. 312–319 (2007)

Finding Stops in Error-Prone Trajectories of Moving Objects with Time-Based Clustering

Max Zimmermann[1], Thomas Kirste[2], and Myra Spiliopoulou[1]

[1] Otto-von-Guericke-University of Magdeburg, Germany
{max.zimmermann,myra}@iti.cs.uni-magdeburg.de
[2] Dept. Computer Science, Rostock University, Germany
thomas.kirste@uni-rostock.de

Abstract. An important problem in the study of moving objects is the identification of *stops*. This problem becomes more difficult due to error-prone recording devices. We propose a method that discovers *stops* in a trajectory that contains artifacts, namely movements that did not actually take place but correspond to recording errors. Our method is an interactive density-based clustering algorithm, for which we define density on the basis of both the spatial and the temporal properties of a trajectory. The interactive setting allows the user to tune the algorithm and to study the stability of the anticipated *stops*.

1 Introduction

There is an increasing number of applications on moving objects e.g. satellites or RFID that require reliable tools to discover patterns and analyze trajectory structure. Recent technological improvements allow capturing and recording huge data volumes on moving objects. Each moving object is represented by a large number of space-time points. All points connected along time give a trajectory which represents the path of an object. Thus, an efficient method for mining trajectories is necessary to get knowledge out of such data.

We are particularly interested in the analysis of trajectories that reflect human behavior, such as the activities of a person who suffers from a chronic disease, the route of a truck transporting products, the movements of RFID-tagged clothes in a department store etc. There are two problems that make trajectory mining in those applications more difficult. First, human activity is not predictable not even for the types of activity as assumed e.g. in the hierarchical activity models of [LFK07]; the movement of a person attempting to steal an RFID-tagged apparel in a store is such an example. Furthermore activity is influenced by external factors, expressed e.g. in the form of unexpected transportation modes. The data recording may be partially unreliable, for example when persons move through areas that distort signals.

For the first problem, consider the trajectory of a person who spent some time walking and some time driving. The search for *stops* should not misinterpret movement at walking pace as *stops*. Moreover, assumptions about location of *stops* should be avoided, since the person may abandon predefined pathways.

D. Tavangarian et al. (Eds.): IMC 2009, CCIS 53, pp. 275–286, 2009.

The second problem may occur when receiving signals from satellites, e.g. in GPS devices. Current GPS technology may not work reliably inside buildings or in areas where sky view is obscured by trees [KLK+02]. Various dysfunctions may appear such as transcription errors or misleading recordings. In our experiments, we use a trajectory that contains such artifacts, namely recordings of motion when the GPS device was indoor and not moving.

Our paper presents a clustering and visualization approach for the discovery of *stops* in a trajectory, including *stops* masked as motion due to artifacts. Our method is based on OPTICS [ABKS99], a density-based interactive clustering algorithm that we extend to capture temporal proximity of data points on the basis of elapsed time and speed of motion. Our new method further incorporates a visualization utility that depicts both the motion and the duration of a *stop*.

The rest of the paper is organized as follows. In the next section we describe related work on mining trajectories. Section 3 describes our spatio-temporal trajectory model. In section 4 we present the methods for discovering and visualizing *stops* on the basis of this model. We describe our experiments on a trajectory containing *stops* and motion artifacts in section 5. The last section concludes our study and provides an outlook.

2   Related Work

In recent years, there is a proliferation of research advances on trajectory mining. A typical mining task is to discover crowded areas like airports [PBKA08]. We distinguish between two categories of methods: those that analyze a single trajectory [PBKA08] and those that derive patterns from multiple trajectories [NP06]. Our work belongs to the first category.

The algorithm SMoT which has been described by [ABK+07], divides a trajectory into *stops* and *moves*. It needs, however, a priori information for finding *stops* which is a big disadvantage. A derivation of SMoT called CB-SMoT has been presented in [PBKA08]: it needs no a priori information but can exploit such information CB-SMoT uses a speed-based method for detecting clusters and associates each cluster with a *stop*. For clustering it uses a variation of DBSCAN [EKSX96], a well known density-based clustering algorithm that even discovers unrecorded *stops*. However, it has difficulties in discovering *stops* after motions at different speeds, e.g. different transportation modes, since it relies on a global parameter that defines the size of the considered space to compute the speed in a certain area. Figure 1 depicts a counterexample: there is much variation of speeds; the speed changes at A-D are *stops*. The *stops* B and D would not be discovered by CB-SMoT if the speed parameter value were set below B and D. Thus, the accuracy of CB-SMoT is affected by the value of the speed parameter.

DBSCAN is a density-based clustering algorithm, especially designed to be robust towards noise [EKSX96]. It has a local notion of proximity and is sensitive to the order of reading the data points. These properties make it particularly appealing for trajectory mining, since the recordings of motion are ordered. Indeed, DBSCAN and its interactive follow up OPTICS [ABKS99] are often used for trajectory mining [Han05], [ZLC+08].

Our variation of OPTICS works with the model proposed in [SPD+08]: Spac-capietra et al. capture *stops* and *moves* in a trajectory, whereby a *move* captures the semantics of fast movements such as acceleration, driving a car, while a *stop* reflects slow motion as in a traffic jam, complete absence of motion as stopping at a traffic light or being indoor. We extend their model by incorporating temporal information in the definition of density. Differently from CB-SMoT, our method uses an duration threshold as a parameter instead of a global parameter to find *stops* and *moves* of a trajectory.

By using this threshold it can find *stops* associated with different speeds. In figure 1 it is sufficient to set the threshold at the height of B to discover all *stops*. Additionally the results of our method can be used to explore unpredictable behavior or technical dysfunctions.

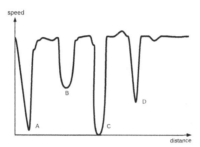

Fig. 1. Stops of different speeds

3 Spatio-Temporal Modeling of Trajectories

In the following, we describe the model of trajectory. We then describe the properties of OPTICS. In subsection 3.3 we introduce our notion of time-based neighborhood, on which our new version of temporal OPTICS is based.

3.1 Stops and Moves on a Trajectory

In this section we give a definition of a trajectory and the semantic properties of the model from [SPD+08]. Both of them takes an important role of our approach and will be used in the remaining of the paper.

A trajectory consists of *stops* and *moves*. A *stop* is a sub-trajectory confined to a certain area and characterized by very low speed.

Definition 1. *(trajectory)*
Let P be a list of space-time points, p_i be a point at (x_i, y_i, t_i) where $x_i, y_i \in \Re, t_i \in \Re^+$. A trajectory is an ordered P for $i = 0, 1, ..., N$, and $t_0 < t_1 < ... < t_N$.

To compute the speed it requires a geometrical and a time aspect. For the geometrical aspect we use a maximal length parameter that defines the allowed distance between two consecutive points to be in a *stop*.

The time aspect is captured by considering a *stop* as a set of points that are recorded within a time interval. Suppose a car driver has to slow down because of a red traffic light and the minimal speed has been defined as 10 km/h. Then, a *stop* starts if the driver reaches a less than 10 km/h and ends when the driver accelerates over 10 km/h.

Definition 2. *(stop)*

Let T be the trajectory, S be a sub-trajectory of T for the the time interval $[t_i, t_{i+n}]$ with temporal disjoint points and $\lambda_{distance}$ be the minimal length of the stop. Then, S is a stop if $\{p_i = (x_i, y_i, t_i), p_{i+1} = (x_{i+1}, y_{i+1}, t_{i+1}), ..., p_{i+n} = (x_{i+n}, y_{i+n}, t_{i+n})\}$, where $distance(p_j, p_k) \leq \lambda_{distance}$ for $[i, i+1, ..., j, j+1, ..., k]$ with $j \neq k$.

If a point does not belong to a *stop*, it is part of a *move*.

Definition 3. *(move)*

Let S_i and S_j be two stops of a trajectory T with the length of n and m, respectively, with $i + n < j$. Then, a move can appear in the following intervals, $[t_k, t_{i-1}]$, $[t_{i+n+1}, t_{j-1}]$ or $[t_{j+m+1}, t_l]$ for $k \geq 0$ and $l > (j + m + 1)$.

Note: each *move* can become a *stop* if the minimal speed is set to a larger value. To distinguish between *moves* and *stops* we propose a time-oriented version of OPTICS. The next subsection will give a short introduction to OPTICS.

3.2   Core Points and Density in OPTICS

OPTICS is a interactive density-based clustering method [ABKS99]. The basic idea of density-based clustering is that each object of a cluster must have at least *minPts* many points within a given radius *eps* (neighborhood). It has been shown [ABKS99] that density-based clustering discovers clusters of arbitrary shape in noisy areas. As human behavior has no explicit structure the noise tolerance of arbitrary shapes is a unavoidable feature.

The output of OPTICS is a cluster-ordering; the left upper picture of Table 1 depicts the cluster-ordering for $eps = 100$ meters. To order the points to a list, the OPTICS describes a point only by two values: the *core-distance* and the *reachability-distance*. Both of them depend on [EKSX96] definition of a *core point* and the ε-neighborhood, introduced in the following.

Let p_i be a point from a dataset P with the length N, $d(x, y)$ be a distance function and let ε be the threshold. The ε-*neighborhood* of point p_i is defined as

$$N_\varepsilon(p_i) = \bigcup_{n=0}^{N} \{p_n \mid (d(p_i, p_n) \leq \varepsilon \wedge p_i \neq p_n\}.$$ A point is a *core point* when

its ε-neighborhood contains at least *minPts* points, i.e. $N_\varepsilon(p_i) \geq minPts$. Then, this point also belongs to a cluster. $\varepsilon/minPts$ gives the minimal dense that a region must have to be part of a cluster.

Based on the ε-neighborhood and *core point*, we define the point values for OPTICS. The *core-distance* of a point p is the distance to the *minPts* closest point so that p becomes a *core point*. The second value that OPTICS uses to describe a point is the *reachability-distance* from a point p_i to a point p_j. If p_i is further away than the *minPts* neighbor of p_j, the *reachability-distance* is the normal distance from p_i to p_j. Otherwise it is defined as the *core-distance* of p_j if p_j is a *core point*. If not, the *reachability-distance* between p_i and p_j is ∞.

OPTICS uses the *reachability-distance* as follows. Initially a random point p_0 is chosen. Then, we iterate over all unvisited points and choose at each iteration step i, the point as next that has the smallest *reachability-distance* of all unvisited *core points* with respect to p_{i-1} as point. The iteration *stops* when all objects of the data set have been considered.

The result of the OPTICS may be a 2D reachability plot with the visiting order of the points on the abscissa and the *reachability-distance* of each corresponding point on the ordinate. A high reachability value means that all the successors have a high distance to all the predecessors. Hence, areas surrounded by high values of reachability may be defined as dense areas.

Table 1. Results for two runs of T-OPTICS (minTime=10 and 50) with alpha=70

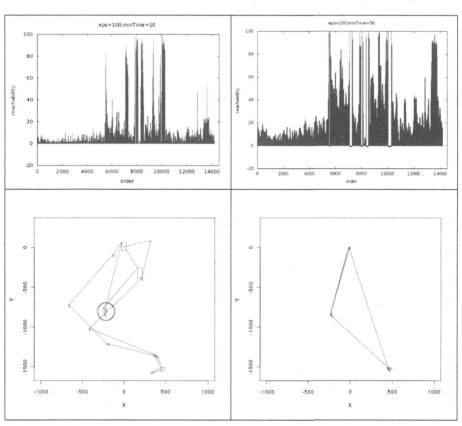

3.3   Spatio-Temporal Neighborhoods

Our OPTICS variation is supposed to distinguish between fast and slow areas. According to definition 2 a candidate *stop* describes areas of a trajectory where the object moves slowly. To define a *stop* we have to establish a relation between space and time. Hence, we also consider temporal proximity when we define neighborhoods, thus ensuring that data points that are spatially close but have been visited temporally far apart do not become part of the same neighborhood. We define this formally below and then proceed to describe our extension to OPTICS.

In a simple 2D environment, the distance between two points is their geographical distance. To compute the distance of two points p_i and p_j on a trajectory we must consider the path connecting them and must also take account of the time elapsed for going from one point to the other. The geographical distance may be computed by any known L-norm. In our examples we use the Euclidean distance $d()$ to compute distances in a 2D space.

Definition 4. *(trajectory-distance)*
   Let p_i and p_j be two distinct points of a trajectory. We define their distance

$$as\ Tdistance(p_i, p_j) = \begin{cases} \sum_{n=i}^{j-1} d(p_n, p_{n+1}), & if\ \{t_i < t_j\} \\ \sum_{n=j}^{i-1} d(p_n, p_{n+1}), & else \end{cases}$$

We use this new notion of distance when defining the term *core point*. We consider two kinds of neighborhood, one capturing only the spatial aspects of the trajectory, the other capturing also time.

Definition 5. *(trajectory neighborhood)*
   Let T be a trajectory of length N, p_i a point in the trajectory and let eps denote the radius of a neighborhood around a data point p_i, similarly to the ε in the original OPTICS. Then, the trajectory neighborhood of p_i is defined as
$$TNeighbourhood(p_i, eps) = \{\ p_n \mid (t_n > t_i \wedge Tdistance(p_i, p_n) \leq eps)$$
$$\vee (t_i > t_n \wedge Tdistance(p_n, p_i) \leq eps)\ \}$$

where we ensure that the trajectory neighborhood of a data point contains data points that were reached before or after p_i.

We now restrict a trajectory neighborhood to contain only data points reached within a specific elapsed time.

Definition 6. *(core neighborhood)*
   Let p_i be a point in trajectory T, eps be the geometrical aspect and minTime be the time aspect. Then, the core neighborhood *is defined as*
$$CNeighbourhood(p_i, eps, Mintime) = \{\ p_n \mid p_n \in TNeighborhood(p_i, eps)$$
$$\wedge |t_i - t_n| \leq Mintime\ \}$$

Definition 7. *(core point)*
   Let p_i be a point in trajectory T and TN its neighborhood. Then, p_i is a core point if $CNeighborhood(TN, minTime) \neq \emptyset$.

Contrary to OPTICS we define a *core neighborhood* by having at least one neighbor in its *core neighborhood* (Def. 6). That property ensures a slight influence by missing points. We can illustrate this by two kolmogorov axioms [Kol33].

Assume we have a set A consisting of a point p_i and one core neighbor of the p_i *core neighborhood* and a set B with all core neighbors of the p_i *core neighborhood* so that $A \subset B$. In addition to it, the probability that a point is being missed is for all points equal. Let us look for the following probabilities,

$$P(a\ point\ of\ A\ is\ missing) = P(A)\ \text{and}\ P(\ some\ point\ is\ missing) = P(B).$$

Since A is a subset of B we can use the second and third kolmogorov axiom. This results in $P(B) = P(A) + P(B \setminus A)$ and it follows that $P(A) \leq P(B)$.

Using the new notion of neighborhood (Def. 6) that captures space and time, we next introduce our algorithm for the discovery and presentation of *stops*.

4   Stop Discovery and Visualization

We come now to describe our approach for stop discovery. We designed stop discovery as an interactive process, for which we devised *T-OPTICS*, a variation of OPTICS [ABKS99] for time-based neighborhoods, and a visualization utility.

We first specify the notion of cluster; a cluster corresponds to a *stop* on the trajectory. The interactive clustering algorithm is presented thereafter. In the last subsection we describe the visualization of the discovered *stops*.

4.1   Cluster as Stops

To use clustering for stop discovery, we (re)define the notion of reachability to capture areas of slow motion. For a data point p_i, we define the length of its *core neighborhood* (Def. 6) on the basis of the trajectory distance (Def. 4). Similarly to OPTICS, we compute the reachability values of all points and define a cluster as sequence of points among two high reachability values. These data points are temporally proximal (by Def. 6) and are spatially close (by Def. 5). Thus, they correspond to an area of slow (or no) motion - a *stop*.

Definition 8. *(trajectory-core-length)*
Let $p_i \in T$ be a data point and CN its core neighborhood. *Its trajectory-core-length is the maximum trajectory distance within CN, if it is non-empty:*
$$tcorelength(p_i) = \min\{\max_{p_j \in CN} Tdistance(p_i, p_j), \infty\}$$

Equally to the reachability distance of the original OPTICS, we define the *reachability-length* of a data point p_j with respect to another data point p_i.

Definition 9. *(reachability-length)*
Let p_i and p_j be points of a trajectory, such that $t_i < t_j$. The reachability-length of p_j from p_i is defined as the maximum between the trajectory core length of p_i and the trajectory distance between the two points:
$$reachlength(p_i, p_j) = \max\{tcorelength(p_i), Tdistance(p_i, p_j)\},$$
implying that if p_j is in the core neighborhood *of p_i, then reachability-length of p_j w.r.t p_i is the trajectory-core-length of p_i.*

Similarly to OPTICS, a cluster is a sequence of points that are close to each other and surrounded by points that exhibit very high reachability values. A threshold α is used to specify when a reachability value is large enough to serve as a cluster's margin. More formally:

Definition 10. *(α-Cluster)*
Let $T = \{p_1, \dots, p_N\}$ be a trajectory and let R be the ordered list of reachability values for points in T. Let $r_i, r_j \in R$ be values with $0 \leq i < j - 1$, so that $\min\{r_i, r_j\} \geq \alpha$ and $\max\{r_{i+1}, r_{i+2}, \dots, r_{j-1}\} \leq \alpha$. Then, the set $\{r_{i+1}, r_{i+2}, \dots, r_{j-1}\}$ constitutes a cluster to α, also denoted as α-cluster.

For example, in figure 2 we show the reachability values (y-axis) of more than 14000 data points. Each horizontal line corresponds to a certain α and results in different clusters. The lowest threshold is at 4: it produces a large number of clusters that correspond to many small areas of slow motion. For $\alpha = 14$, we get fewer clusters, some of which cover large areas; the first 5500 objects would constitute one big cluster. For $\alpha = 28$, we get a very small number of clusters.

In the next subsection we describe how the parameters for the clustering are computed, how neighborhoods are built and data points are ordered.

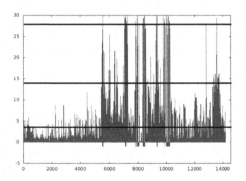

Fig. 2. Illustration of cluster constellations for different values of the threshold α

4.2   Interactive Cluster Construction

The pseudo code below depicts our algorithm `StopFinder` at a very abstract level. The algorithm consists of four steps. We explain the first three steps on stop discovery here. The visualization is described in subsection 4.3.

Algorithm 1. StopFinder

1: estimate *eps* and *minTime*
2: invoke T-OPTICS (*eps, minTime*)
3: extract potential *stops* on the ordered list for different values of α (interactively)
4: invoke visualization method

In the first step (line 1) we estimate the spatial parameter *eps* and the temporal parameter *minTime* for the specification of neighborhoods. To this purpose, we perform a first approximation of eps by computing the trajectory-distance from p_1 to p_N and averaging it over the number of data points N. We similarly approximate $minTime$ by averaging the duration of the trajectory over N. We then compute the ratio of those computed values $\overline{eps}$ and $\overline{minTime}$ and use it as basis for the specification of eps and $minTime$.

We might use $\overline{eps}$ and $\overline{minTime}$ directly as values of $eps, minTime$. However, the computation of the ratio allows us a more elaborate tuning. For example, if the ratio $\overline{eps} : \overline{minTime}$ is 1 : 3, then the average time needed to go from data point p_i to the next one p_{i+1} is 3 units. Since a data point requires at least one member in its *core neighborhood* to be a *core point* (cf. Def. 6 and Def. 7), setting $minTime$ to less than 3 units (for $eps = 1$) may yield too many data points unreachable from most others. The smaller eps, the smaller becomes the trajectory neighborhoods and with them the likelihood that a *core neighborhood* will have one member. In contrast, for a bigger eps the ratio may be smaller (e.g. 100 : 50) as the likelihood of having one neighbor increases. Hence, by using the ratio, we can derive one parameter if the other is specified.

In the second step (line 2), T-OPTICS uses our new concepts for trajectory distance, *core point*, trajectory-core-length and reachability-length when building neighborhoods, identifying *core points* and computing the reachability of each data point. A crucial difference between OPTICS and T-OPTICS is in the ordering of the data points. For OPTICS, the ordering does not need to reflect the sequence of the points in the trajectory. For T-OPTICS, there is no re-ordering; the data points appear in the same order as in the trajectory, but are now associated with reachability values. These values allow the identification of the clusters (line 3), subject to the threshold α (cf. Def. 10).

Once identified, the *stops* must be mapped in terms of the original trajectory (see e.g. a trajectory in Table 2 left picture and its three *stops* as ends of a triangle in Table 1 lower right). For a α the third step computes the cluster in the way that has been described in section 4.1. The visual representation of the *stops* should encompass more than their spatial coordinates, though: the duration of each *stop* contributes much to understanding the semantics of the *stop* and the behavior of the object. The visualization mechanism (line 4) described in the next subsection allows the inspection of the spatio-temporal properties of the identified *stops*.

4.3   Visualization Method

After extracting clusters from T-OPTICS, we must visualize them in such a way that the observer associates the clusters with locations of the trajectory. We use a rectangular representation of clusters. In the following we explain this process.

Def. 10 defines a cluster as accumulation of points that are spatially and temporally very close. To accumulate the points of a cluster, we consider each cluster as separate data set with 2 attributes: x-dimension and y-dimension. Then, for each attribute we compute mean and standard deviation. With this we obtain the four sides of a rectangle as it can be seen in Table 2 (right picture). Side b yields from the line $[Y_{stddev} Y_{mean} + Y_{stddev}]$ and side a from $[X_{stddev} X_{mean} + X_{stddev}]$.

To model the temporal aspect of a cluster, we should keep in mind that points in the same cluster are temporally very close. Hence, it is sufficient to connect each rectangle with the next one in terms of time: the result is a rough representation of the trajectory, consisting of the *stops* and lines that connect them. For example, the edge $r_1 \rightarrow r_2$ on Table 2 (right picture) indicates that cluster r_1 occurred before cluster r_2. Two rectangles may be unified if the corresponding clusters share a certain percentage of intersection, the percentage is defined by a threshold; e.g. the value 70 means that two rectangles which intersect more or equal to 70 % will be represented by a unification.

Through this we obtain on the one hand a condensed illustration of areas in the trajectory that are temporal different but spatial pretty close. This could be the daily errand to the supermarket, which can be in the morning or in the evening. Our visualization joins this to one rectangle with different edges in time. On the other hand the threshold helps us to distinguish dense and less dense clusters. Two rectangles that intersect less than the threshold are probably no daily habits of the recorded object. Rather, it allows us the interpretation of cluster, e.g. as an artifact.

In the next section we show the evaluation of our `StopFinder`.

Table 2. Left: original GPS trajectory; right: two clusters, represented as rectangles and connected across the time axis

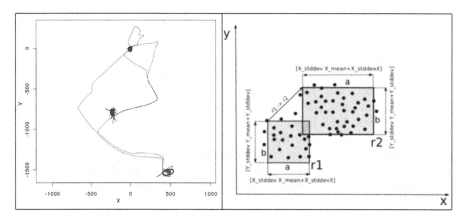

5   Experiments

In this section we study the behavior of our `StopFinder` on a trajectory that contains artifacts. At first we describe the experimental data; then we present the chosen parameters. We present the results for the real data set at the end and show an example for the interpretation of our rectangle visualization.

The trajectory used in our experiments contains recordings of a person's movements for two consecutive days with the different transportation modes walking, cycling and driving a car. At the first day we were recording five hours and on the second day it has been two hours. The recording device was a customary

GPS device. In Table 2 (left picture) we see the trajectory. Three potential *stop* areas are visible. Among them, the motion at center is actually an artifact; there has been no motion, so this is in fact a *stop*.

The data set that we use for our experiments includes no information about *stops* or artifacts. It consists only of spatio-temporal points that describe the trajectory; every 1-4 seconds the longitude and latitude of the human position has been recorded as a spatio-temporal point. Thus, finding all *stops* and distinguish between *stops* and artifacts is the aim. Because of the advanced knowledge about the trajectory we have a ground truth for the evaluation.

For our experiments we invoke the `StopFinder` with the described data set. The estimation of parameter *eps* and *minTime* yields to the ratio 1 : 3. As we know roughly the variety of transportation, we bound a *stop* to a radius of 100 meters (*eps* = 100) and to a *minTime* of 10 and 50 seconds. The upper left picture and the upper right picture of Table 1 show the reachability values computed by T-OPTICS. for In both pictures we see two valleys, one at the start and one at the end. They are clearly clusters and are extracted as such.

For extracting potential *stops* from the reachability values we set α (cf. Def. 10) to 70. The two lower pictures of Table 1 show the *stops* with our rectangle visualization. By depicting a cluster as a rectangle rather than a single point, we acquire better insights. For instance, the black surrounded area of the left lower picture of Table 1 shows two overlapped rectangles. We see that the the artifact is captured by overlapping rectangles, while the two other *stops* that contain no motion are captured by a single rectangle. In general, short edges of the rectangle indicates that there has been actually very dense movement. In this trajectory, this corresponds to the artifact motion that is actually a *stop*.

We see that our StopFinder has identified all three *stops* of the trajectory. We also see the impact of large vs small *minTime* values: as *minTime* decreases, we see more *stops*. Keeping in mind that a *stop* is actually a very slow motion, small *minTime* values capture short *stops*, as for direction change. Large values of *minTime* result in fewer *stops*, whereby the artifact (slow motion that IS a *stop*) is recognized in all cases. Through the variation of *minTime* we can identify *stops* resulting of different transportation modes.

6   Conclusions

In this paper we proposed an interactive density-based clustering algorithm, aimed at discovering *stops* in a trajectory that contains artifacts of motion and different transportation modes. We augmented the density with the spatial and the temporal properties of a trajectory. We have further designed a visualization mechanism that depicts both the spatial and temporal properties of the *stops* identified by the clustering algorithm. The first experiments with our approach show that we can discover *stops* despite the existence of movements at different speeds and that we can even identify artifact motions.

There are several opportunities for future research. Our estimations rely on mean and standard deviation; the mean is sensitive to outliers, though. So, we intend to study more robust methods for the estimation of our parameters such as confidence intervals. Distinguishing between *stops* that persist for different values of *minTime* and those that are just very slow motions, is another subject of future work. Another ongoing work yields from adding more features to T-OPTICS, as for instance an angle change rate for regarding direction changes. Zheng et al. [ZLC⁺08] have shown that this is a promising option.

References

[ABK⁺07]   Alvares, L.O., Bogorny, V., Kuijpers, B., de Macêdo, J.A.F., Moelans, B., Vaisman, A.A.: A model for enriching trajectories with semantic geographical information. In: GIS, Seite 22 (2007)

[ABKS99]   Ankerst, M., Breunig, M.M., Kriegel, H.P., Sander, J.: Optics: Ordering points to identify the clustering structure, pp. 49–60. ACM Press, New York (1999)

[EKSX96]   Ester, M., Kriegel, H.P., Sander, J., Xu, X.: A density-based algorithm for discovering clusters in large spatial databases with noise. In: Proceedings of the 2nd Conference on Knowledge Discovery and Data Mining, pp. 226–231. AAAI Press, Menlo Park (1996)

[Han05]   Han, J.: Data Mining: Concepts and Techniques. Morgan Kaufmann Publishers Inc., San Francisco (2005)

[KLK⁺02]   Kalkusch, M., Lidy, T., Knapp, M., Reitmayr, G., Kaufmann, H., Schmalstieg, D.: Structured visual markers for indoor pathfinding (2002)

[Kol33]   Kolmogorov, A.N.: Grundbegriffe der Wahrscheinlichkeitsrechnung. Springer, Berlin (1933)

[LFK07]   Liao, L., Fox, D., Kautz, H.: Extracting places and activities from gps traces using hierarchical conditional random fields. Int. J. Rob. Res. 26(1), 119–134 (2007)

[NP06]   Nanni, M., Pedreschi, D.: Time-focused clustering of trajectories of moving objects. J. Intell. Inf. Syst. 27(3), 267–289 (2006)

[PBKA08]   Palma, A.T., Bogorny, V., Kuijpers, B., Alvares, L.O.: A clustering-based approach for discovering interesting places in trajectories. In: SAC 2008: Proceedings of the 2008 ACM symposium on Applied computing, pp. 863–868. ACM, New York (2008)

[SPD⁺08]   Spaccapietra, S., Parent, C., Damiani, M.L., de Macedo, J.A., Porto, F., Vangenot, C.: A conceptual view on trajectories. Data Knowl. Eng. 65(1), 126–146 (2008)

[ZLC⁺08]   Zheng, Y., Li, Q., Chen, Y., Xie, X., Ma, W.-Y.: Understanding mobility based on gps data. In: UbiComp 2008: Proceedings of the 10th Int. Conf. on Ubiquitous computing, pp. 312–321. ACM, New York (2008)

Goal Understanding and Achievement for Humanoid Assistive Robots

Peter Nauth

Fachhochschule Frankfurt a.M. – University of Applied Sciences
Nibelungenplatz 1, 60318 Frankfurt, Germany
pnauth@fb2.fh-frankfurt.de

Abstract. Nowadays robots can recognize their environment in a limited way. Future robots designed for operations in a natural environment and for communicating with humans in a natural way must understand the goals a user wants to be met, navigate in a natural environment and develop a strategy to achieve the goals.

By means of intelligent sensors for speech recognition, proximity measurement, colour measurement and image processing an intelligent robot has been developed. The robot understands the name of an object a user has told the robot to take and searches for it by means of a smart camera and other sensors. After it has found and identified the object, it grabs it and brings it to the user.

Keywords: Interactive Assistive Robots; Goal Understanding; Intelligent Sensors; Sensor Fusion.

1 Introduction

Robots of the next generation such as assistive robots or rescue robots must be able to solve complex tasks which up to now only human beings can handle. They will act autonomously in a natural environment and will communicate in a natural way with those people they are supposed to support. Key technologies for these intelligent autonomous robots are Embedded Intelligent Systems [7] which analyze and fuse comprehensive sensor data and derive execution strategies in order to accomplish a goal.

In the Laboratory for Autonomous Systems und Intelligent Sensors at the Fachhochschule Frankfurt a.M., Germany, first a stationary intelligent robot with visual and auditive sensors has been developed. It understands spoken instructions and acts accordingly by grabbing the respective object [4]. Now, this technology is being transferred to an autonomous humanoid robot.

Algorithms for robot control and navigation have been developed by several research groups [5]. This paper focuses on the understanding of a goal a user has spoken to the robot, strategies to achieve the goal and on sensing and navigating in the users natural environment. The advantages over other systems [3] are among other things the reasonable deployment costs. This allows the user to adapt the number of robots according to the budget available and the kind of goal to be achieved for a complex task might require the cooperation of multiple robots.

D. Tavangarian et al. (Eds.): IMC 2009, CCIS 53, pp. 287–294, 2009.

2 System Architecture

An autonomous robot needs to know the goal to be accomplished, situation awareness and the ability to plan and perform actions depending on a situation. This requires the following functions [9]:

- Sensing by means of multiple sensors in order to acquire all necessary data about the environment. It includes getting to know the goal to be met, e.g. by understanding a spoken instruction.
- Fusion of the data acquired from intelligent sensors (intelligent sensor data) in order to assess the situation.
- Planning how to achieve the goal and
- Execution of the necessary steps by controlling the robot motors.

A distributed data base provides reference information e.g. for the pattern recognition algorithms in intelligent sensors, for strategies to fuse data or for setting an optimal execution plan. It is important that the data base can be adapted to new situations by methods such as learning algorithms. A robot embedding the features described above can be regarded as intelligent because it can perform tasks depending on a goal in a complex environment and can adapt to new situations by learning.

If a robot alone cannot acquire all environmental data or achieve a task by itself it is necessary to communicate with other robots in order to get help.

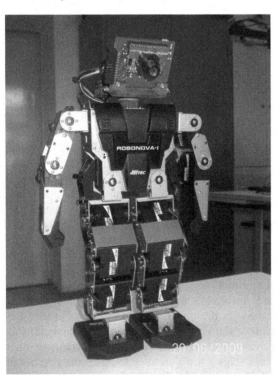

Fig. 1. Autonomous Humanoid Robots

We use the Movit MR-999E as a platform for our research on stationary robots and the Robonova 1 (Fig. 1) for humanoid robot development. As for the Movit, the sensor fusion, the control of the actuators and the coordination of all components are executed on a 32-Bit controller STR912FW44 (ST Microelectronics). The Robonova embeds the 8-Bit Atmel ATMega 128L for these tasks.

Depending on the area of activity the robot is equipped with some or all of the following sensors (Fig. 2):

- Speech   Recognition Sensor
- Proximity Sensor
- Colour Sensor
- Smart Camera.

The signal processing for speech recognition is implemented on

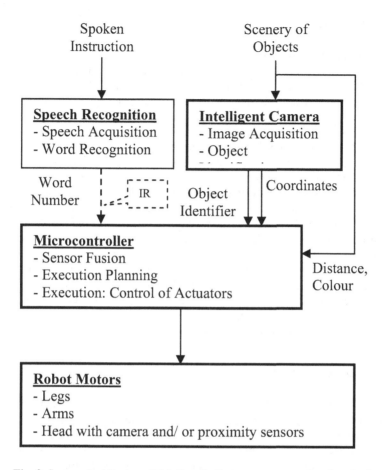

Fig. 2. System Architecture (thick lines indicate parts mounted at the robot)

the DSP-based module Voice Direct 364 (Sensory Inc.). The image processing algorithms run either on the 16-Bit microcontroller Infineon C165 of the Grabb Modul (Phytec GmbH) or the smart colour camera POB-Eye (POB Technologies) with an embedded 32-Bit controller ARM7TDMI. It is mounted on the neck of the humanoid robot and can be turned left and right as well as up and down.

In order to cope with new situations, the speech sensor can learn new words and the vision sensor can learn shapes and colours of new objects.

In order to measure the distance to an object, proximity sensors (laser beam triangulation method) are used for the near range from 4 to 24 cm and the far range from 15 to 80 cm. It can be mounted on the moveable head of the robot in order to scan the environment in 2 dimensions.

The colour sensor currently just differentiates between blue und non blue objects and is activated only if the robot is not equipped with the smart camera.

3 Goal Understanding

The intelligent speech recognition enables the robot to understand spoken instructions. These are either single words or a sequence of words which are spoken without breaks in between. After data acquisition, the algorithm divides the signal into segments and calculates the frequency spectra out of each segment. Next, frequency parameters are calculated and classified by means of a neural network. As for the training phase the user speaks a word and repeats it. If the frequency parameters from the first and the repeated word are similar, the word is accepted. The weighting factors of the classifier are being and adapted to the word's frequency parameters and assigned to a word number. Then the training can be continued with the next word.

During the recognition phase the speech sensor asks by saying "Say a word" the user to speak the instruction. If the classifier detects a high similarity to one of the previously learned words, it sets a respective pin to High. An additional controller SAB 80535 turns the spoken word into a word number by monitoring the state of the pins and transmitting a bit sequence via an infrared (IR) LED to the robot. The sequence corresponds to the pin number set to high and therefore to the word number recognized by the speech module. This enables the user to command the robot remotely.

The robot controller receives the bit sequence via an infrared detector and decodes the word number. For each word number is assigned to an instruction, the robots now knows its task, i.e. which object to search for.

4 Environment Sensing

For the recognition of the demanded object and for obstacle avoidance during the search phase the intelligent camera and the proximity sensors are used.

The algorithms we have developed for the smart camera converts the acquired RGB – image into the HSL – space, segments the image [1] by means of an adaptive threshold (histogram analysis of Hue) algorithm and extracts the form factor F

$$F = U^2 / A \tag{1}$$

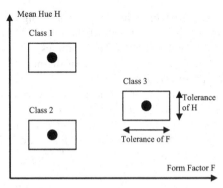

Fig. 3. Parameter Space

from the area A and the circumference U as well as the mean hue – value H out of each object detected [6]. By means of a box classifier each object is assigned to an object identifier which represents the class (Fig. 3). Given the extracted parameters, objects and obstacles can be differentiated regarding shape and colour.

Additionally the coordinates of each object are calculated. The object identifier and the respective coordinates of all objects found are transmitted to the robots microcontroller.

New objects can be learned by a supervised learning algorithm: Typical examples of each object class are shown to the camera and the learning algorithm assigns the mean values of each parameter to the class these objects belong to. The tolerances which define the size of the classification box of each class equal 1.5 times the standard deviation calculated during the teach-in procedure.

Proximity sensors supplement the camera information by sensing the distance between the robot and the object. Additionally proximity sensors can be used to provide parameters for object differentiation themselves, especially for obstacle detection [2]:

Given that the proximity sensors scan the environment in two dimensions, the distance $z (\alpha, \beta)$ is a function of the vertical angle α and the horizontal angle β. We are developing algorithms to apply this distance function $z (\alpha, \beta)$ for the differentiation of the obstacles "wall" and "stairs" from objects to be grabbed.

- In order to differentiate between objects and a wall the proximity sensors are turned horizontally. The system decides for the class "wall" if $z (\alpha, \beta=const.)$ is a steady function. It decides for the class "object" if unsteady parts have been calculated. This rule is based on the assumption that objects are smaller than the scanning range.

- In order to differentiate between objects and stairs the proximity sensors are turned vertically. The system decides for the class "stairs", if $z (\alpha=const., \beta)$ has at least 3 peaks (resulting from the edges of the stairs). It decides for the class "object" if less than 3 peaks show up. This rule is based on the assumption that the objects to be grabbed have a smooth surface.

A teach-in algorithm which adaptively assigns $z (\alpha, \beta)$ to a class is currently under development.

5 Goal Achievement

By fusing the auditive, visual and proximity data, the robot knows all objects within its reach and their position as well as the goal it is advised to reach.

The fusion algorithm used is hierarchical and works as follows:

1. Auditive and visual data are fused by matching the word number (derived from the speech sensor data) with one of the object identifiers (derived from the camera data) by means of a table. We overcome the binding problem by not dealing with sensor data themselves but by fusing classification results. The algorithm generates one of the following hypothesis:

   - A negative match result leads to the hypothesis "object not found". This requires no additional fusion of visual and proximity data and causes the robot to repeat the search.
   - A match of one of the object identifiers with the word number results in the hypothesis "object found"
   - The hypothesis "wall" or "stairs" is derived if one of those obstacle has been classified regardless the spoken command.

2. In the next fusion step the hypothesis generated by the visual sensor is verified by the data acquired from the proximity sensor. If the class derived from the distance function $z (\alpha, \beta)$ equals the hypothesis it is regarded as true. Otherwise the hypothesis is rejected.

This hierarchical approach results in a high specifity and a low sensitivity because in case of conflicting visual and proximity results they are rejected. We overcome this problem by repeating the search in this case. The robot moves to a different position before starting the renewed search as described below.

Currently we apply the fusion approach to differentiate 3 kinds of objects, a water bottle and bottles of 2 different kinds of soft drinks, as well as 2 different kinds of obstacles (wall and stairs).

Depending on the outcome of the sensor fusion the robot develops different execution plans and controls the robot motors accordingly:

- If the demanded object has been identified, the robot approaches it and grabs it in order to bring it to the user. During the movement towards the object its position relatively to the robot is permanently tracked.
- If no or the wrong object has been spotted or in case of conflicting results, the robot repeats the search by turning the camera head and the proximity sensors and by moving in order to change the position.
- If an obstacle has been detected the robot develops an approach to overcome it, i.e. it climbs stairs or avoids colliding with walls.

The robot grabs the objects by pressing its arms from left and right at them. It stops the arm movements if a feedback signal indicates a resistance.

6 Application Example

One typical example of the robot's performance is to search for objects and bring it to the user (Fig. 4).If the user says "Water Bottle", the robot understands its task and searches for the bottle. After detection, it grabs the bottle and brings it to the user. Even stairs can be climbed by a coordinated arm and leg movement and a stabilization of the robot with a tilt sensor.

In a scenario of 3 different bottles (water and soft drink bottles), a wall and a stair, the right bottle has not been found in 2 out of 20 cases. In 6 cases the robot had to repeat the search at least once due to a mismatch or conflicting data during the fusion process. In 1 case stairs have been wrongly classified as a wall. The number of search repetitions was limited in all 20 cases to 10.

Another application example are soccer robots which must search for the ball and kick them to the goal or another robot of their team. In order to coordinate these actions we develop a communication protocol via Bluetooth technology.

As for rescue robots, we focus on the scenario that an injured person (in this case a doll) lies on a stretcher. Two robots evacuate the injured person by jointly carrying the stretcher into a safe area. This task can be solved efficiently if they communicate with each other in order to synchronize their movements and to exchange information about the direction to go as well as to warn each other about obstacles. The robot on the top end operates as a master. When it grabbs the stretcher the robot on the back end does the same. The same is true for the synchronous movement. This ensures that the position of the stretcher is always almost horizontally and the injured person does not fall down.

Listen for a goal   Search

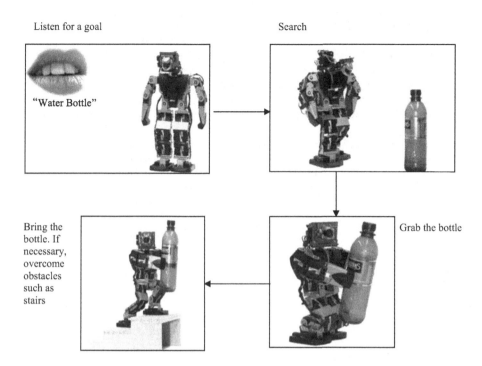

"Water Bottle"

Bring the
bottle. If
necessary,
overcome
obstacles
such as
stairs

Grab the bottle

Fig. 4. Goal Understanding and Achievement

7 Summary

A robot has been developed which understands spoken instructions, derives a goal from it and can act accordingly. If the user advises the robot to bring a specific object, the robot uses its smart camera and other sensors to search for the object and brings it to the user. As future work additional applications such as rescue robots are being developed.

Acknowledgments

The research was funded by the Fachhochschule Frankfurt a.M. and the Gesellschaft für technische Weiterbildung e.V.

References

[1] Gonzalez, R.C., Woods, R.E.: Digital Image Processing. Prentice Hall, Englewood Cliffs (2008)
[2] Haddaoui, A.E., Hamidi, R.: Intelligente Sensorik zur Steuerung eines humanoiden Roboters, Diplomarbeit, Fachhochschule Frankfurt a.M (2008)

[3] Hirai, K., Hirose, M., Haikawa, Y., Takenaka, T.: The Development of Honda Humanoid Robot. In: IEEE Int. Conf. Robot. Autom., pp. 1321–1326 (1998)

[4] Ivascu, E.-R.: Roboteransteuerung mit einem 32-Bit Mikrocontroller, Diplomarbeit, Polytechnische Universität Bukarest (2007)

[5] Jin, T.-S., Lee, B.-K., Lee, J.M.: AGV Navigation Using a Space and Time Sensor Fusion of an Active Camera. International Journal of Navigation and Port Research 27(3) (2003)

[6] Krieger, O.: Entwicklung einer intelligenten Kamera zur Objekterkennung, Diplomarbeit, Fachhochschule Frankfurt a.M (2007)

[7] Nauth, P.: Embedded Intelligent Systems. Oldenbourg Verlag (2005)

[8] Siciliano, B., Khatib, O.: Handbook of Robotics. Springer, Heidelberg (2008)

[9] Stubbs, K., Wettergreen, D.: Anatomy and Common Ground in Human-Robot Interaction: A Field Study. IEEE Intelligent Systems (March 2007)

Sequential Authentication Concept to Improve WLAN Handover Performance

Andreas Roos[1,2,3], Arne Keller[2], Andreas Th. Schwarzbacher[3], and Sabine Wieland[1]

[1] Institute of Telecommunication-Informatics, University of Applied Sciences,
Gustav-Freytag-Straße 43-45, 04277 Leipzig, Germany
{roos,wieland}@hftl.de
[2] Deutsche Telekom AG Laboratories,
Deutsche-Telekom-Allee 7, 64295 Darmstadt, Germany
[3] School of Electronic and Communications Engineering, Dublin Institute of Technology,
143-149 Rathmines Road, Dublin 6, Ireland
andreas.schwarzbacher@dit.ie

Abstract. Service provisioning in customer satisfying quality is an important issue for current and future network operators. Real-time services suffer from network performance influences, e.g. delay, jitter and packet-loss. This paper evaluates the handover performance in WLAN access networks with regard to different WLAN security mechanisms, such as WPA2 PSK and WPA2 EAP-TLS. Performance investigations show that WPA2 EAP-TLS influences the handover performance and thus the network performance in a significant manner. A major impact is the authentication process introduced by the IEEE 802.1X EAP-TLS. The proposed sequential authentication concept based on WPA2 PSK and WPA2 EAP-TLS decreases the influence of authentication time in a handover process. The validation of the sequential authentication concept in a real network environment has shown that a reduction of 97.5 % of data communication interruption can be archived compared to the traditional WPA2 EAP-TLS behaviour. This is beneficial for real-time services.

Keywords: AAA, WLAN security, handover, IEEE 802.1X, VoIP quality.

1 Introduction

The motivation of this work is to enhance network performance to provide carrier grade services via Wireless Local Area Networks (WLANs) for mobile users. The focus is on the Voice over IP (VoIP) service. The number of supported calls via an access network is important for network operators but also the quality of the calls. Bad voice quality of VoIP will not satisfy customers' expectancy of a voice service. This means, the Quality of Experience (QoE) with regard to traditional telephony will not be achieved by a VoIP service. As a result, the acceptance of VoIP services on customers decreases. For this reason a network operator aims for VoIP quality that is comparable with traditional telephony.

The VoIP quality itself mainly depends on the parameters delay, jitter and packet-loss of VoIP packets. A general relation of a delay chain in a speech communication

D. Tavangarian et al. (Eds.): IMC 2009, CCIS 53, pp. 295–306, 2009.

path and the influence of data loss is described in [1]. In the case of wireless networks, such as WLAN, delay, jitter or packet-loss occurs due to the fact of a shared medium that is influenced by factors interference, propagation and shadowing. An additional factor that influences network performance is the aspect of customer mobility in a WLAN that comes along with handover processes between user equipment (UE) and access points (APs). The handover process comprises sending of probe messages, to scan for new APs, authentication and re-association messages that leads to data transmission delay and packet-loss, as investigated in [2]. The authors of [3] examine detailed the influence of the handover process components, such as probe delay, authentication delay and re-association delay, concluding that the probe delay is the significant part of the handover delay with up to several hundreds of milliseconds. However, the reduction of the probe delay is possible by means of handover triggers controlled by e.g. location based information. Consequently, the scanning process can be avoided but the authentication and re-association delay still remains. Further, [3] observes only the two authentication types *open system* and *shared key* specified in IEEE 802.11 standard. Investigations in [4] show, that the open system authentication impacts the handover time in a lowly dimension of 1 ms. However, there are more complex authentication mechanisms, e.g. IEEE 802.1X [5] using Extensible Authentication Protocol (EAP) – Transport Layer Security (TLS) [6], that require the authentication and authorisation data exchange with external authentication, authorisation and accounting (AAA) servers. The authors of [7] describe that integration of security mechanisms within network architectures comes along with time and resource consumption, which poses a problem if delay critical applications, such as VoIP, should be provided in user satisfying quality. Beside the authentication and authorisation time in a single handover process the frequency a handover process occurs while customers' mobility influences the parameters delay, jitter and packet-loss as well. Resent investigations in [8] show that voice communication interruptions greater than 40 ms in conjunction with interruption intervals less than 11,7 s leads to voice quality that is not sufficient to provide carrier grade voice quality. Investigations in [8] are based on the specification of ITU-T G P.862 [9] the perceptual evaluation of speech quality (PESQ) value. This circumstance asks for network access control mechanisms providing reduced data connectivity interruptions in handover processes of secured WLANs.

This paper investigates the handover process in WLAN. Particularly the impact of wireless interface configuration tools, such as iwconfig and wpa_supplicant on handover time performance. Furthermore, the influence of different authentication and encryption methods are investigated with focus on the authentication time. Finally, a sequential authentication concept based on WPA2 Pre-Shared Key (PSK) and WPA2 EAP-TLS is presented that is able to overcome the drawback of data connectivity interruption due to the authentication and authorisation process of a traditional IEEE 802.1X EAP-TLS authentication.

The remainder of the paper is organised as follows. Section 2 gives a brief overview of related work while Section 3 investigates the handover time behaviour depending on the used security mechanism and the used wireless card configuration tool. The sequential authentication concept to reduce authentication time in a handover process is described in Section 4. Section 5 validates the sequential authentication concept. Finally, Section 6 concludes the paper.

2 Related Work

Several approaches have been suggested to enhance the handover performance in secured WLAN. A brief overview is given as follows. In [10] a pre-registration mechanism for Inter Access Point Protocol (IAPP) to reduce the handoff latency has been proposed. For that purpose six new IAPP packets are designed with the drawback of arising more handshakes in the network. IEEE 802.11r [11] describes a fast Basic Service Set (BSS) transition to reduce the communication interruption time. However, this approach describes a new protocol that comes along with additional handshakes among the involved entities of the handover process. IEEE 802.11i [12] describes a pre-authentication method with a key caching solution that carries out the authentication process between UE and the new AP while the UE is connected to the old AP. This behaviour can lead to impairments on applicability of the mechanism in inter-provider scenarios due to the required link layer connectivity.

3 Handover Time Behaviour Dependent on Security Mechanisms

The integration of security mechanisms in wireless communication comes along with data overhead and increased data transmission delay [13]. Furthermore, security mechanisms influence VoIP quality as described in [14] derived from PESQ investigation of voice communication. In this section the influence of network security mechanisms on the WLAN handover time behaviour in a real environment is investigated. Derived from the results the influence of handover time on voice quality can be concluded.

3.1 Handover Measurement Setup

The handover measurement setup, presented in Fig. 1, consists of two APs to connect the user equipment to the network. The Communication Server (CS) represents the communication partner of the UE to carry out VoIP or ping communication. Furthermore, there is a local AAA (LAAA) server and an external AAA (EAAA) server to setup up different authentication and authorisation scenarios. The LAAA is used to carry out UE authentication and authorisation within the local network, while the EAAA is used to carry out UE authentication and authorisation within a remote network. Both locations of AAA servers are important in the measurement setup to investigate the influence of different AAA entity locations on the authentication time behaviour. A hub interconnects APs and servers in the measurement setup.

The following security mechanisms have been investigated: WEP, WPA2 PSK and WPA2 EAP-TLS. The used configuration tools to configure the wireless card are iwconfig for WEP encryption and wpa_supplicant for WEP, WPA2 PSK and WPA2 EAP-TLS encryption and authentication. Both tools are used to investigate the influence of different software implementations on the wireless card configuration time. Even if WEP encryption should not longer be used to setup a secure WLAN connection the measurement series with WEP encryption provides an important reference value of WLAN card configuration time in the case of a handover process for further evaluations and conclusions.

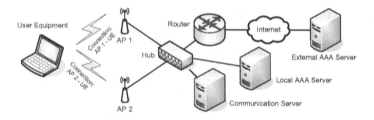

Fig. 1. Handover measurement setup

The handover measurement is controlled by a script on the UE. Before a handover is initiated the script starts a traffic trace by means of TCPDUMP that captures all network communications send and received by the UE. After that, the script starts a ping series. The ping is carried out every 10 ms for the duration of 1 sec. Ping intervals less than 10 ms led to no more detailed results. Each series of handover measurement has been carried out 100 times. The handover interval itself is configured in the script as well. The script controls the handover by means of re-configuration of the UE wireless interface to connect to the AP 1 and AP 2 respectively. At this the Basic Service Set Identifier (BSSID), the wireless channel, the key as well as the Extended Service Set Identifier (ESSID) is configured. Furthermore, the background scanning functionality of the wireless interface is disabled. Only a single connection between UE and APs is established, this means no connection to AP 1 and AP 2 are established at the same time.

3.2   Investigation of Handover Time Behaviour

In the following the so called communication interruption time is the synonym for handover time. The handover time consists of two parameters the configuration time and the authentication time, as presented in Fig. 2. The time needed to re-establish the Internet Protocol (IP) connectivity after a handover is called the configuration time of the wireless card while the time needed to carry out UE authentication is called authentication time.

The first handover measurement focuses the WEP encryption investigating the influence of the wireless card configuration tools iwconfig and wpa_supplicant on handover performance. A detailed investigation of communication interruption can be carried out by means of the network analyser WIRESHARK [15]. The results depending on the tools iwconfig and wpa_supplicant are presented in Table 1. The interruption time is determined by the time delta between last received ping reply before the handover has taken place and the first successfully answered ping request after the handover has taken place. Table 1 shows minimum (min), average (avg) and maximum (max) communication interruption times using WEP encryption. It can be seen that the usage of different wireless configuration tools influences the handover time behaviour in a distinctly manner. Comparing the maximum interruption time the wpa_supplicant requires up to 222 ms longer re-establishing the IP data connectivity before a communication between UE and CS is possible. This behaviour is founded in the different implementations and functionalities of the tools. Iwconfig interacts via the application programming interface wireless extension with the driver to configure the wireless parameters only while

Table 1. Interruption time using tool iwconfig and wpa_supplicant – WEP encryption

	iwconfig	wpa_supplicant
Min	45 ms	254 ms
Avg	90 ms	300 ms
max	130 ms	352 ms

wpa_supplicant is a daemon program that runs in the background and controls the whole wireless connection. During the controlling process a lot of state machines have to be passed leading to computation time and thus to the additional interruption time.

WEP and WPA2 PSK comprise no authentication process that requires the interaction with an authentication server. This means the occurred handover time consist of the configuration time only. The next measurement investigates the handover time behaviour when using WPA2 with EAP-TLS. WPA2 with EAP-TLS defines IEEE 802.1X to carry out authentication. This means the handover time will consist of the configuration time and the authentication time. Two authentication scenarios have been investigated in this context. The first scenario focuses the RADIUS authentication server within the local network and the second scenario focuses the RADIUS authentication server within an external network.

In most mobility scenarios a customer aims to cover a distance and moves from location A to location B. In other words, the UE handovers from location A while moving into the direction of location B each time to new APs. This means, the UE has not been connected to the same AP before. This movement characteristic is important for the handover time investigation and has to be considered in the measurement setup. In short the IEEE 802.1X EAP-TLS mechanism derives key material to encrypt the communication. The derivation of the key material comes along with handshakes between UE and authentication server. The runtimes of these handshakes are a major factor that influences the all over handover time. In the case of re-connection to an AP that knows the UE's valid key due to a previous authentication process no new key derivation is needed. This means no new authentication process is initiated by the AP and no handshakes between UE and authentication server occurs. For this reason it is important to prepare the measurement setup that a full authentication process with key derivation is carried out for each handover process. This behaviour has been emulated by rebooting the APs. This means after the handover from the old AP to the new AP the old AP has been rebooted. Due to this fact all previous derived encryption keys in the old AP are deleted. The next handover of the UE to this rebooted AP requires a full authentication process with key derivation. Thus the handover time influencing mobility scenario has been emulated.

Fig. 2 summarises all carried out handover measurement results relating to the investigated encryption and authentication mechanisms respectively. The dark (blue) marked part of the bar presents the configuration time needed to configure the wireless card depending on the used configuration tool iwconfig or wpa_supplicant. The bright (orange) marked part of the bar presents the authentication time required to carry out UE authentication, authorisation and key derivation to get network access.

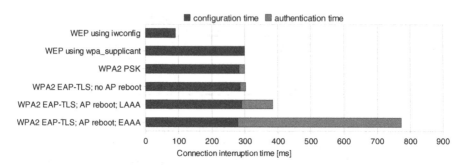

Fig. 2. Handover time behaviour measurement results

The most connection interruption time intensive authentication and authorisation mechanism is WPA2 using EAP-TLS in conjunction with an EAAA server, as shown in Fig. 2. The average time of authentication, authorisation and key derivation is 494 ms. This time is caused by the runtime of required handshakes between AP and remote located EAAA server. A clear shorter authentication time arises in the case of WPA2 using EAP-TLS and LAAA server. This behaviour is due to the fact that the runtime between AP and LAAA server is much shorter compared to the EAAA server. The short authentication time when using WPA2 PSK is due to the 4-way handshake needed to exchange the encryption keys between UE and AP. Furthermore, WPA2 PSK needs no interaction between AP and AAA Server to exchange authentication information. The average authentication time is 18 ms. The authentication time when using WPA2 EAP-TLS, but no AP reboot, is comparable with the authentication time of WPA2 PSK, as shown in Fig. 2. This behaviour is based on the fact that the AP stores information and keys of previous connected UEs. Handovers the UE back to the old AP, the old AP comprises information about the previous connection of UE and carries out a 4-way handshake only between UE and AP to provide re-keying instead of a full authentication process.

3.3 Conclusion of Handover Measurement

This subsection interprets the results of handover time measurement by keeping the results of PESQ [9] simulations of [8] in mind. The PESQ method simulates the human speech quality rating by comparing an original speech signal with a transmitted speech signal. The conclusion of [8] is that communication interruptions greater than 40 ms in conjunction with interruption intervals less than 11.7 s are leading to PESQ values that are less than 4. PESQ is an indicator to describe the quality of a voice communication. Investigated voice communications with determined PESQ values greater than 4 fulfil the requirements on a carrier grade voice service. The knowledge of [8] with regard to the investigated handover time using WPA2 EAP-TLS leads to the assumption that voice quality in mobility scenarios can be improved by shortened authentication times providing a faster handover process. Improvement of the configuration time can be achieved by fitted configuration tool implementations for fast handovers. However, this aspect is out of focus in the further investigation because the focus is on authentication time improvement.

4 Sequential Authentication Concept

IEEE 802.1X describes three components supplicant, authenticator and AAA server. The supplicant is located in the UE, the authenticator in the AP and the AAA server can be realised by a RADIUS server. This section provides a brief description of IEEE 802.1X drawback with regard to fast authentication. Furthermore, the sequential authentication concept is presented.

4.1 Drawback of IEEE 802.1X Authentication Time Behaviour

The authentication method of IEEE 802.1X with EAP-TLS comprises four sequences to carry out UE authentication and to establish a secure encrypted wireless link. The first sequence *EAP Initiation* exchanges UE identity information and negotiates the authentication method, in this case TLS. The second sequence *TLS Handshake* exchanges client (supplicant) and server (AAA server) certificates, coincidence values and encoded hash values. Furthermore, the premaster key is derived and mutually verified by the supplicant and the AAA server. This leads to the Pairwise Master Key (PMK) needed for the 4-way handshake. In the third sequence *EAP Termination* the successful TLS authentication will be confirmed additionally and the AAA server provides the PMK to the authenticator. Finally, in sequence four the *PMK 4-Way Handshake* is carried out. Based on coincidence values of authenticator and supplicant as well as the PMK the Pairwise Transient Key (PTK) is derived by the supplicant and the authenticator. Further, the Group Transient Key (GTK) is derived.

No. ·	Time	Time Delta	Source	Destination	Protocol	Info
7	0.313	0.313	Cisco-Li_a9:1c:ff	3com_37:f7:32	EAP	Request, Identity [RFC3748]
8	0.313	0.000	3com_37:f7:32	Cisco-Li_a9:1c:ff	EAP	Response, Identity [RFC3748
10	0.323	0.009	Cisco-Li_a9:1c:ff	3com_37:f7:32	EAP	Request, EAP-TLS [RFC2716]
11	0.324	0.000	3com_37:f7:32	Cisco-Li_a9:1c:ff	TLSv1	Client Hello
13	0.335	0.011	Cisco-Li_a9:1c:ff	3com_37:f7:32	TLSv1	Server Hello, Certificate,
14	0.348	0.012	3com_37:f7:32	Cisco-Li_a9:1c:ff	TLSv1	Certificate, Client Key Exc
18	0.384	0.035	Cisco-Li_a9:1c:ff	3com_37:f7:32	TLSv1	Change Cipher Spec, Encrypt
19	0.385	0.000	3com_37:f7:32	Cisco-Li_a9:1c:ff	EAP	Response, EAP-TLS [RFC2716]
20	0.394	0.009	Cisco-Li_a9:1c:ff	3com_37:f7:32	EAP	Success
21	0.395	0.000	Cisco-Li_a9:1c:ff	3com_37:f7:32	EAPOL	key
22	0.400	0.005	3com_37:f7:32	Cisco-Li_a9:1c:ff	EAPOL	key
24	0.404	0.003	Cisco-Li_a9:1c:ff	3com_37:f7:32	EAPOL	key
25	0.404	0.000	3com_37:f7:32	Cisco-Li_a9:1c:ff	EAPOL	key

Fig. 3. EAP-TLS communication; local AAA server

Sequences 1 to 3 require the communication between authenticator and AAA server. In the case of remote located AAA server interconnected via the Internet the runtime between authenticator and AAA server increases. This is the reason for the high authentication time shown in Fig. 2.

A transparent overview about the authentication communication and the ping communication is depicted separately in Fig. 3 and Fig. 4. Fig. 3 shows the authentication communication due to IEEE 802.1X using EAP-TLS among UE, AP and LAAA server respectively, while Fig. 4 presents the ping communication among UE and CS. The dark (red) marked frame number six in Fig. 4 shows the last successfully sent ping packet before the handover process is started. In Fig. 3 the dark (red) marked frame number seven presents the first successfully transmitted packet after the carried out handover. The time delta between frame number six, in Fig. 4, and frame number 7, in Fig. 3, is 313 ms. This time delta of 313 ms corresponds to the wireless card configuration time needed to establish IP connectivity. But in opposition to the WEP handover process there is no communication to the network possible after the wireless card configuration. This is shown in Fig. 4 when taken frame number nine, 12, 15, 16, 17 and 23 into account. Ping requests are sent to the network but no replies are received.

No. ◦	Time	Time Delta	Source	Destination	Protocol	Info
5	0.008	0.008	192.168.1.110	192.168.1.200	ICMP	Echo (ping) request
6	0.018	0.000	192.168.1.200	192.168.1.110	ICMP	Echo (ping) reply
9	*REF*	*REF*	192.168.1.110	192.168.1.200	ICMP	Echo (ping) request
12	0.016	0.016	192.168.1.110	192.168.1.200	ICMP	Echo (ping) request
15	0.032	0.016	192.168.1.110	192.168.1.200	ICMP	Echo (ping) request
16	0.048	0.015	192.168.1.110	192.168.1.200	ICMP	Echo (ping) request
17	0.063	0.015	192.168.1.110	192.168.1.200	ICMP	Echo (ping) request
23	0.082	0.018	192.168.1.110	192.168.1.200	ICMP	Echo (ping) request
26	0.096	0.013	192.168.1.110	192.168.1.200	ICMP	Echo (ping) request
27	0.096	0.000	192.168.1.200	192.168.1.110	ICMP	Echo (ping) reply

Fig. 4. Ping communication; local AAA server

This depends on the IEEE 802.1X mechanism that only allows interaction of authentication messages between UE and AP, as seen in Fig. 3. But full network access is granted after successful UE authentication. The bright (green) marked frame number 26 in Fig. 4 shows the first successfully transmitted ping request packet to the CS after full granted network access by the authenticator. The time delta between frame number nine and frame number 26 is 96 ms and corresponds to the required authentication time of IEEE 802.1X EAP-TLS using a LAAA server.

4.2 Sequential Authentication

The goal of the proposed sequential authentication approach is to provide status quo of most secure WLAN encryption based on standardised network access control mechanisms, such as WPA2 PSK and WAP2 EAP-TLS. This means no additional protocol interactions are integrated in the sequential authentication concept. The concept includes no mechanisms that improve handover performance, such as pre-authentication of IEEE 802.11i or IEEE 802.11r. The reason for this purpose is to avoid additional network load generated by exchanged information among the involved entities. Furthermore, the applicability in inter-provider handover scenarios should not be at risk due to the required link layer connectivity of e.g. IEEE 802.11i pre-authentication. Due to the known operation behaviour of WPA2 PSK and WPA2 EAP-TLS the implementation of the authentication concept in a testbed was focused to demonstrate the proper operation instead of evaluations based on simulations.

To overcome the drawback of long authentication times arising due to the communication between authenticator and remote AAA server, the behaviour of a secure WPA2 PSK authentication followed by a WPA2 EAP-TLS authentication is combined. The combination brings the benefit of both methods together and avoids the time of blocked network access in traditional IEEE 802.1X authentication phase. At first, the benefit of WPA2 PSK authentication is used to carry out secure but with focus on authentication time short authentication. At second, the WPA2 EAP-TLS authentication provides currently the most secure authentication method to carry out mutual authentication among supplicant and AAA server. Due to the reduced authentication time a handover process can be enhanced. This means real-time service quality can be increased because of the reduced handover time.

Fig. 5 presents the flow diagram of the sequential authentication concept. Compared to the traditional IEEE 802.1X method the sequential authentication concept comprises 5 sequences to carry out UE authentication instead of 4 sequences. The first sequence is the PSK 4-Way Handshake to authenticate UE against authenticator and to derive the wireless encryption key for further secure communication. The following sequences, such as EAP Initiation, TLS Handshake, EAP Termination and PMK 4-Way Handshake are equal to the traditional IEEE 802.1X authentication using EAP-TLS. In general no redesign of the standardised mechanisms WPA2 PSK and EAP-TLS is needed for the novel concept.

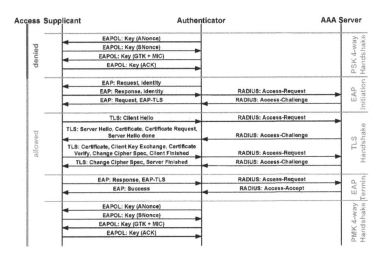

Fig. 5. Flow diagram of sequential authentication concept

The dark (red) and bright (green) marked line called access, in Fig. 5, shows that network access will already be granted after successful WPA2 PSK authentication - *PSK 4-Way Handshake*. As a result, data communication, such as VoIP traffic, can be provided while IEEE 802.1X using EAP-TLS authentication is processed.

The sequential authentication concept is realised by means of a temporary port parallel to the controlled and uncontrolled port of IEEE 802.1X. The temporary port is established after successful carried out WPA2 PSK authentication. This means based on the PSK the wireless link encryption key for further communication is derived and installed on supplicant and authenticator side. During the lifetime of the temporary port the UE has access to the network. As a result, data communication, such as VoIP traffic, can be provided while IEEE 802.1X with EAP-TLS authentication is processed. Thus, the reduction of network access interruption is achieved. The lifetime of the temporary port is configurable implemented and can be configured within the configuration file of the authenticator. With beginning of the temporary port lifetime the WPA2 EAP-TLS process is initialised and carried out. In the case of a successful EAP-TLS authentication the PMK is derived and installed for further data encryption on the wireless link. This means, the previous derived wireless link encryption key of WPA2 PSK will not longer be used. In the case of unsuccessful authentication the temporary port will be closed and the UE disconnected from the AP. Furthermore, the MAC address of the UE is blocked for a configurable time within the authenticator to avoid Denial of Service (DoS) attacks of malicious UEs. Base of authenticator implementation is *hostapd* in version 0.6.4 and supplicant implementation is *wpa_supplicant* in version 0.6.6.

5 Validation of Sequential Authentication Concept

The validation is based on 100 measurements using a LAAA server for authentication purpose. Fig. 6 presents exemplarily the authentication communication among UE and authenticator as well as the ping communication among UE and CS. The bright (yellow) marked rows represent the packets from the RADIUS server forwarded by the authenticator to the UE. Frame number seven presents the first transmitted packet after the handover. Frame number seven, eight, nine and ten represents the PSK 4-Way Handshake of the WPA2 PSK authentication followed by the start of WPA2 EAP-TLS authentication in frame eleven. With regard to aimed the goal of reduced communication interruption time and fast network access after a handover, the benefit of the sequential authentication concept can be seen in frame number 15 and 16. The first ping request after the handover and WPA2 PSK authentication is send in frame number 15 and the ping reply is provided in frame number 16. This means, network access is granted while the second authentication phase with WPA2 EAP-TLS is still

No. ▴	Time	Time Delta	Source	Destination	Protocol	Info
5	0.018	0.008	192.168.1.100	192.168.1.200	ICMP	Echo (ping) request
6	0.018	0.000	192.168.1.200	192.168.1.100	ICMP	Echo (ping) reply
7	*REF*	*REF*	3com_37:f7:b0	3com_37:f7:af	EAPOL	Key
8	0.005	0.005	3com_37:f7:af	3com_37:f7:b0	EAPOL	Key
9	0.006	0.000	3com_37:f7:b0	3com_37:f7:af	EAPOL	Key
10	0.007	0.001	3com_37:f7:af	3com_37:f7:b0	EAPOL	Key
11	0.008	0.000	3com_37:f7:b0	3com_37:f7:af	EAP	Request, Identity [RFC3748]
12	0.008	0.000	3com_37:f7:af	3com_37:f7:b0	EAP	Response, Identity [RFC3748
13	0.010	0.002	3com_37:f7:b0	3com_37:f7:af	EAP	Request, EAP-TLS [RFC2716]
14	0.011	0.000	3com_37:f7:af	3com_37:f7:b0	TLSv1	Client Hello
15	0.012	0.000	192.168.1.100	192.168.1.200	ICMP	Echo (ping) request
16	0.013	0.000	192.168.1.200	192.168.1.100	ICMP	Echo (ping) reply
17	0.020	0.007	3com_37:f7:b0	3com_37:f7:af	TLSv1	Server Hello, Certificate,
18	0.024	0.003	3com_37:f7:af	3com_37:f7:b0	EAP	Response, EAP-TLS [RFC2716]
19	0.025	0.000	192.168.1.100	192.168.1.200	ICMP	Echo (ping) request
20	0.025	0.000	192.168.1.200	192.168.1.100	ICMP	Echo (ping) reply
21	0.029	0.003	3com_37:f7:b0	3com_37:f7:af	TLSv1	Server Hello, Certificate,
22	0.029	0.000	3com_37:f7:af	3com_37:f7:b0	EAP	Response, EAP-TLS [RFC2716]
23	0.034	0.004	192.168.1.100	192.168.1.200	ICMP	Echo (ping) request
24	0.034	0.000	192.168.1.200	192.168.1.100	ICMP	Echo (ping) reply
25	0.035	0.000	3com_37:f7:b0	3com_37:f7:af	TLSv1	Server Hello, Certificate,
26	0.048	0.013	192.168.1.100	192.168.1.200	ICMP	Echo (ping) request
27	0.048	0.000	192.168.1.200	192.168.1.100	ICMP	Echo (ping) reply
28	0.055	0.006	3com_37:f7:af	3com_37:f7:b0	TLSv1	Certificate, Client Key Exc
29	0.057	0.001	192.168.1.100	192.168.1.200	ICMP	Echo (ping) request
30	0.057	0.000	192.168.1.200	192.168.1.100	ICMP	Echo (ping) reply
31	0.059	0.001	3com_37:f7:b0	3com_37:f7:af	EAP	Request, EAP-TLS [RFC2716]
32	0.060	0.000	3com_37:f7:af	3com_37:f7:b0	TLSv1	Certificate, Client Key Exc
33	0.069	0.009	192.168.1.100	192.168.1.200	ICMP	Echo (ping) request
34	0.070	0.000	192.168.1.200	192.168.1.100	ICMP	Echo (ping) reply
35	0.081	0.011	192.168.1.100	192.168.1.200	ICMP	Echo (ping) request
36	0.082	0.000	192.168.1.200	192.168.1.100	ICMP	Echo (ping) reply
37	0.089	0.007	3com_37:f7:b0	3com_37:f7:af	TLSv1	Change Cipher Spec, Encrypt
38	0.091	0.002	3com_37:f7:af	3com_37:f7:b0	EAP	Response, EAP-TLS [RFC2716]
39	0.092	0.000	192.168.1.100	192.168.1.200	ICMP	Echo (ping) request
40	0.092	0.000	192.168.1.200	192.168.1.100	ICMP	Echo (ping) reply
41	0.097	0.004	3com_37:f7:b0	3com_37:f7:af	EAP	Success
42	0.097	0.000	3com_37:f7:b0	3com_37:f7:af	EAPOL	Key
43	0.097	0.000	3com_37:f7:af	3com_37:f7:b0	EAP	Response, EAP-TLS [RFC2716]
44	0.103	0.005	3com_37:f7:af	3com_37:f7:b0	EAPOL	Key
45	0.103	0.000	3com_37:f7:b0	3com_37:f7:af	EAPOL	Key
46	0.105	0.002	3com_37:f7:af	3com_37:f7:b0	EAPOL	Key
47	0.106	0.000	192.168.1.100	192.168.1.200	ICMP	Echo (ping) request
48	0.107	0.001	192.168.1.200	192.168.1.100	ICMP	Echo (ping) reply

Fig. 6. EAP and ping communication in sequential authentication concept

in progress. But network access is granted after 12 ms calculated from the time delta between frame number seven and 15. The IEEE 802.1X authentication ends with frame number 41 followed by the PMK 4-way handshake. In frame number 46 the successful WPA2 EAP-TLS authentication is presented. Summarised, Fig. 6 presents the proper operation of the sequential authentication concept.

The configuration time of the wireless card still exists and takes 293 ms. However, the impact of WPA2 EAP-TLS authentication time on the handover performance has been avoided. The sequential authentication method enables real-time service continuity after 12 ms of interruption. Due to the reduced interruption time the concept is able to contribute to service quality improvement in UE mobility scenarios. This means freezing effects or artefacts in IPTV sessions can be reduced or avoided and enhanced voice quality in VoIP communication can be achieved.

Furthermore, the characteristic of the sequential authentication concept avoids the location influence of the remote located AAA servers on the handover performance. Due to the second authentication phase that performs WPA2 EAP-TLS in parallel to the already granted network access after the first WPA2 PSK authentication phase the required EAP-TLS negotiations does not affect the communication interruption time any longer. Network access is still granted after successful first authentication phase and a service can be provided. Thus, the authentication time of 494 ms using EAP-TLS in the traditional behaviour does not influence the handover time any longer.

6 Conclusion

This paper has investigated the handover performance in WLAN. The evaluation of different wireless card configuration tools, such as iwconfig and wpa_supplicant shows, that the usage of wpa_supplicant takes up to 338 ms for wireless card configuration to enable IP connectivity to the network. Further investigation shows that encryption and authentication mechanism does not influence the configuration time of a wireless card. Moreover, the investigation of security mechanism WPA2 EAP-TLS presents authentication times with up to 494 ms needed to carry out negotiation handshakes with external authentication servers. Thus the overall handover time consisting of configuration time and authentication time is more than 750 ms. From the reduction of authentication time point of view the proposed and validated sequential authentication concept, combining WPA2 PSK and WPA2 EAP-TLS, has the capability to decrease communication interruption time of a handover process. An interruption time of 12 ms has been archived instead of 494 ms., i.e. a reduction of 97.5 % of interruption time in comparison to traditional WPA2 EAP-TLS authentication. This reduces the impairment on maintained real-time communications significantly and leads to reduced freezing effect, artefacts or interruptions in multimedia sessions, such as IPTV or VoIP. From today's point of view the sequential authentication concept provides a high level on network access control and communication security. The transmitted data are encrypted all over the handover process even in the first authentication phase due to the WPA2 PSK process. The novel concept needs no redesign of the mechanisms WPA2 PSK and WPA2 EAP-TLS only a reimplementation in supplicant and authenticator is needed. Thus the sequential authentication method is easy deployable in existing network architectures.

References

1. Schel, M.: Konvergenz der Zugangsnetze. In: WissenHeute (October 2007)
2. Vatn, J.-O.: An experimental study of IEEE 802.11b handover performance and its effect on voice traffic, Telecommunication Systems Laboratory, Department of Microelectronics and Information Technology (IMIT), KTH, Royal Institute of Technology, Stockholm, Sweden (July 2003)
3. Mishra, A., Shin, M., Arbaugh, W.: An Empirical Analysis of the IEEE 802.11 MAC Layer Handoff Process, http://citeseer.ist.psu.edu/567990.html
4. Velayos, H., Karlsson, G.: Techniques to Reduce IEEE 802.11b MAC Layer Handover Time, Telecommunication Systems Laboratory, Department of Microelectronics and Information Technology (IMIT), KTH, Royal Institute of Technology, Stockholm, Sweden (April 2003)
5. IEEE Standard 802.1X, IEEE Standard for Local and metropolitan area networks – Port-Based Network Access Control, Stand (2001)
6. Aboba, B., Simon, D.: RFC 2716 - PPP EAP TLS Authentication Protocol (October 1999)
7. Martinovic, I., Zdarsky, F.A., Bachorek, A., Schmitt, J.B.: Measurement and Analysis of Handover Latencies in IEEE 802.11i Secured Networks. In: Proceedings of European Wireless 2007, Paris, France (April 2007)
8. Roos, A., Wieland, S., Schwarzbacher, A.Th.: Investigation of security mechanisms and mobility influence on VoIP Quality – Towards VoIP Quality Improvements. In: Proceeding of Science Days 2008 – HfTL, Leipzig, Germany (November 2008)
9. ITU-T Recommendation: P 862 - Perceptual evaluation of speech quality (PESQ): An objective method for end-to-end speech quality assessment of narrow-band telephone networks and speech codec (2001)
10. Huang, P., Tseng, Y.-C., Tsai, K.-C.: A Fast Handoff Mechanism for IEEE 802.11 and IAPP Networks. In: Proceedings of Vehicular Technology Conference 2006-Spring (2006)
11. IEEE Standard 802.11r-2008, Amendment 2: Fast Basic Service Set (BSS) (July 15, 2008)
12. IEEE 802.11i/D10.0. Security Enhancements, Amendment 6 to IEEE Standard for Information Technology. IEEE Standard (April 2004)
13. Liang, W., Wang, W.: A Quantitative Study of Authentication and QoS in Wireless IP Networks. In: Proceedings of INFOCOM 2005 (2005)
14. Passito, A., Mota, E., Aguiar, R., Biris, I., Mota, E.: Evaluating Voice Speech Quality in 802.11b Networks with VPN/IPSec. In: IEEE ICON. Kuala Lumpur – Malaysia (2005)
15. Network analyser, WIRESHARK, http://www.wireshark.org/

Simulation and Analysis of Ad Hoc Privacy Control in Smart Environments

Christian Bünnig*

University of Rostock
Department of Computer Science
Research Group for Information and Communication Services
christian.buennig@uni-rostock.de

Abstract. Services in smart environments usually require personal information to customize their behavior for the specific needs of a user. Traditionally users express privacy preferences in precompiled policies to control which information is disclosed to services within smart environments. A limitation of policies is that they are hard to create and maintain when the potentially communicated information or the context that influences a disclosure decision are highly diverse and hard to predict. Managing privacy ad hoc, in the moment when a service requests personal information, circumvents those problems. A drawback of ad hoc privacy control is the increased privacy related user interaction during service usage. This can be balanced by an assistance that handles personal information dynamically based on context information influencing a disclosure decisions. In this paper we describe a simulation environment to evaluate a context based, data mining driven disclosure assistance and present related results.

1 Introduction

In most cases privacy in ubiquitous computing environments is considered as a problem of protecting personal information to make it only visible to certain entities or from being misused by malicious entities. While this is an important aspect of privacy on the data level it neglects that privacy is much more than hiding personal information. Often people *want* to show certain information to other entities, e.g., to utilize personalized services, to receive information from other persons in return or to represent oneself to the public in a specific manner. In that sense privacy is a dynamic process that regulates the boundaries between private and public space [1,2]. Supporting this dynamic aspect of privacy within smart environments is the broad scope of our research. The special focus of this paper are simulations used to develop and evaluate data mining technologies for assisting users in ad hoc disclosure decisions when services request personal information

---

* Christian Bünnig is funded by the German Research Foundation (DFG), Graduate School 1424 (Multimodal Smart Appliance Ensembles for Mobile Applications - MuSAMA).

D. Tavangarian et al. (Eds.): IMC 2009, CCIS 53, pp. 307–318, 2009.

from users. In general there are two kinds of privacy related implications that influence a user's disclosure decision. The first is a technical one, e.g., a possible recording and post processing of the communicated information by the environment's infrastructure. The second relates to interpersonal implications because other persons within the environment directly or indirectly perceive information communicated with the environment. Consider preferences that alter the environments' physical setup or data to be shown on a public display as examples. In this work we focus on interpersonal implications and assume a non-malicious infrastructure which handles private data as publicly announced.

1.1 Related Work

Previous work mostly focused on precompiled privacy rule sets respectively policies or role concepts to express and enforce user privacy preferences.

An example for a policy based approach is Langheinrich's *pawS* [3], a privacy awareness system that extends the platform for privacy prefrences (P3P) and the P3P preference exchange language (APPEL) [4] for ubiquitous systems. Services within a smart environment announce their data handling policy expressed in P3P via service related privacy proxies. In return, users express privacy preferences using APPEL and personal privacy proxies. These proxies then negotiate the flow of personal information between a user and services within the environment. It is advantageous that this approach makes use of already existent concepts. On the other side, while there are user friendly tools for specifying privacy preferences and interacting with service-side policies in the realm of web activities [5], there is a lack of such tools for the domain of ubiquitous systems. Further *pawS* deals with privacy issues concerning the used infrastructure – our work focuses on interpersonal privacy implications.

In the domain of location privacy, Myles et al. [6] suggest a rule based system to decide disclosure of location information (also partly using P3P/APPEL). Location information is shared by a *location server* which contacts user specific *validators* when someone requests a user's location. Among other methods, these validators decide the location disclosure based on a set of rules defined by its users. The authors suggest that location provider offer appropriate rule set templates. Additionally "wizards" help users to comfortably set up rules that differ from the templates. This approach limits its use for managing location. It could be extended for other types of personal information but that would add complexity to the rule sets users have to specify in their validators. Actually Prabaker et al. [7] have shown that users already have difficulties to set up disclosure rules for location as the only type of information to manage.

Next to rules, there exist concepts which utilize virtual roles, identities [8,9,10] or faces [11] for managing disclosure of personal information in smart environments. The basic idea is to abstract a specific set of personal information to a role, e.g., "anonymous", "private", "job" or "public". Roles are supposed to provide an easy to grasp way of managing personal information. However, role concepts always conflict between simple but too general and subtle but too complex. Lederer highlights this problem of generality in a subsequent work [12].

Rule and role based approaches to control communication of personal information try to release users from repeatedly deciding information disclosure ad hoc. On the other side such preconfigured privacy contradicts to the way users normally practise privacy. Rules require users to specify their privacy preferences in advance in an abstract manner. This fails when upcoming situations and related disclosure decisions are not completely known or highly diverse. Roles, as a concept for managing the possible sets of information to disclose, get too complex if a user's privacy preferences extend a clear scheme like "private", "job" or "public" and require a more fine-grained selection of information.

The main message of this review is that existent work on user side control of personal information disclosure in smart environments focuses on a priori configured privacy preferences, which conflicts with the dynamic and intuitive aspects of privacy. There are cases when the decision which information to communicate within a smart environment can only be decided ad hoc, in the moment of disclosure: when the number of possible situations is very high, when there are situations which cannot be predicted or when there are many, subtly differing variances in the personal information to disclose.

1.2   Assisted Ad Hoc Privacy Control

The review of related work motivates to shift privacy control on service interaction in smart environments from a priori to ad hoc mechanisms. The closer disclosure decisions are linked to corresponding requests, the easier it is for users to identify potential privacy implications. Additionally, users do not need a priori knowledge about potential requests to come and related information to disclose. Finally a close link between request and control ensures users do not need to decide disclosures for requests which actually never happen.

A problem of ad hoc privacy control is the potentially high user interaction rate during service interaction. Ad hoc disclosure decisions cannot be regarded as an improvement for privacy control if the overall privacy related interaction significantly increases compared to those required for creating and maintaining predefined disclosure rules. To reduce user interactions in ad hoc privacy control, an assistance is needed which automates or suggests disclosure decisions. Our approach for an assistance is to partially automate ad hoc privacy control by learning user specific disclosure decision models (DDM) out of previous decisions. A DDM is supposed to describe a user's concept of which information to disclose to a specific service in a specific context. Of course there will never be a final DDM - privacy preferences may change and new services may request information. Thus a DDM needs to be updated respectively rebuilt regularly. Whether a DDM decides autonomously or only makes suggestions depends on the confidence of DDM decisions. Here users can set personal confidence thresholds to adjust the trust into DDM decisions.

In previous papers we discussed several learning algorithms concerning the suitability of output representations as human readable privacy preferences [13] as well as possibilities how to interact with DDMs depending on their output representation [14]. This paper focuses on evaluations of performance of different data mining algorithms for building DDMs.

Evaluations of DDM learning algorithms require a set of user disclosure decisions together with corresponding context information. There exists some monitoring data of users in real world ubicomp settings (e.g., the *RealityMining* project [15]) but those are mainly about user activity and location, not about privacy management. Capturing this data is a costly process, especially when a wide range of scenarios are to be considered. Another issue is that existing infrastructure limits the scenarios which may be used to to capture privacy related service interaction. Hence, we decided to develop and evaluate DDMs using simulations and to verify simulation based results in selected real environments and scenarios afterwards.

1.3   Overview

The next section describes the simulation setup, i.e., how service interaction, related context and disclosure decisions have been modelled. Section 3 deals with learning techniques for DDM building and presents comparative evaluation results, based on data generated by simulations. Finally we summarize this paper and highlight interesting challenges for future work in Section 4.

2   Simulation

The purpose of the simulations is to generate data which can be used to evaluate different data mining algorithms which predict disclosures based on context information. Advantages of simulations are that context as well as disclosure behavior of users can be modified freely. Thus, simulations are well suited to estimate for which kind of context patterns and disclosure behavior a data mining driven disclosure assistance may work. Simulating privacy interaction with services in smart environments requires to model a sequence of service interactions. A service interaction is described by a service request event and resulting disclosure decisions. Section 2.1 describes how service request events have been modelled, Section 2.2 is about modelling disclosure behavior.

2.1   Request Events

A service request event is described by a set of context information, a service request and persons participating at the event and responding to service requests. The simplest way to model events is to manually specify each single event. However, this a laborious work, not very flexible and always produces identical simulation output. In contrast, setting up a generative model with partly randomized parameters makes it possible to produce varying interaction data sets from repeated simulations using a single model. In principle there are no further requirements on modelling request events. Indeed it is advisable to do simulations with significantly differing generative models to evaluate DDMs learning algorithms with respect to different patterns of event sequences. Following the model is described which has been used to generate events for the simulations whose results are presented below, in Section 3. For better understanding at first the driving scenario shall be described.

Scenario. A typical use case for smart environments is the support of collaborative work. Consider the following scenario as an illustrative example. A room is equipped with a *collaboration board* – a desk or display with a touch screen surface used as a shared work space. Depending on a specific application this board may display and arrange various pieces of information, contributed by the persons working at the board. A team working on a film project meets at this board to discuss current results and upcoming tasks. Depending on the current state of the project, the persons present at the meeting and each person's task in the project, each team member wants to provide specific information to the meeting by disclosing them to the collaboration board service. Alice contributes some drafts for a poster, Bob has a story board ready and Clark has some suggestions concerning the crew casting. Dent, the organizer of the team, guides the meeting and controls and arranges the currently displayed information on the board. Additionally Dent requests to access the calendar of meeting participants to schedule upcoming events. All team members are working as freelancers – they may work at this board in other projects, in other roles, and with other team members too. Special characteristics of this scenario are that there is no distinct hierarchy among the persons and no fixed relationship between the persons and the room. Looking only at a person and a room there is no inherent structure that could be used for predefined rule based disclosure models. This emphasizes the in situ characteristic of information disclosure in such a meeting.

Based on this setting a model has been created which generates service request events for different groups which regularly conduct meetings while using the collaboration board service to share meeting related information items on the board. The groups defined are a promotion group, a casting group and a coffee break group. Each group has been assigned weighted dates at which a meeting at the board may occur, weighted rooms in which a meeting may take place, a list of persons together with participation probabilities and a list of devices together with presence probabilities. Thereby, a request event is described by a list of context attached with independent probabilities whether the context is on hand. Fig. 1 shows an excerpt of the model, describing instances of request events for one of the groups.

Limitations. The model used here is not capable of describing dependencies of variable context information, for instance, that certain devices are more likely to be present at an event if Doris is present too. To some extend it is still possible to describe such dependencies by splitting request event descriptions as seen in Fig. 1 into several descriptions so that each expresses a specific dependency. However, this blows up the model description and is not suitable for more complex dependencies between context information. In this case a Bayesian network is better suited to describe request events.

```
"REQUEST" :   "collaboration−board"
"DOW" :       (["mon"],  [0.5]),
"HOD" :       ([11,  15],  [0.8,  0.2])
"ROOM" :      (["ConfRoomBig" ,  "Cafeteria"],  [0.7,  0.3])
"PERSONS" :   [("Arthur",  0.81),  ("Ben",  0.75),  ("Claire",  0.4),
               ("Doris",  0.3),  ("Isaac",  0.5),  ("June",  0.5)]
"DEVICES" :   [("ProDev1",  0.8),  ("ProDev2",  0.7)]
"TOPIC" :     "promotion−group−meeting"
```

Fig. 1. Excerpt of the service request event model which describes a subset of events generated by the complete model. *REQUEST* names the service request to handle by persons at the event. Context items *DOW*, *HOD* and *ROOM* specify the time at and place where the event may occur. *PERSONS* and *DEVICES* specify probabilities of persons participating and devices present at the event. *TOPIC* is a special high level context token used for disclosure modelling, but finally is not part of the context information used for learning disclosure behavior (see Section 2.2).

2.2   Disclosure Behavior

According to Lederer et al. [16] the most important factor determining disclosures are information recipients, followed by the situation in which information gets requested. However, the cited work uses a simple linear disclosure model ranging from *show nothing* to *show all*. In ubicomp settings disclosures tend to be more sophisticated [12] in that they do not only range from nothing to all but additionally are scattered over different types or groups of information items. In that case the situation has a significant influence on a disclosure decision. In this regard disclosure behavior is modelled by information recipients and the request situation. Note that *request situation* does not mean a set of arbitrary context information composing a situation but a single high level context token (e.g., "coffee-break-at-work" or "meeting-on-project-x") which semantically summarizes circumstances relevant for privacy (besides the information recipients). The high level context token describing a situation on the privacy level is used to decouple the modelling of disclosure decisions from other context information which describes an event and which is used as input for the data mining process that builds a DDM. This is illustrated in Fig. 2. Examples for low level context are location, time and nearby devices. High level context is described by the mentioned context token and information recipients. Fig. 3 shows an

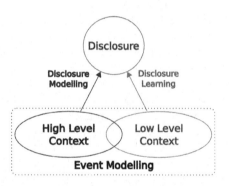

Fig. 2. An event is described by high and low level context. High level context is used to *model* disclosure decisions, low level context is used to *learn* disclosure decisions. Both types may overlap if, for instance, nearby persons (low level) are also information recipients (high level).

```
if situation == "meeting-on-project-x":
    if "Isaac" in recipients or "June" in recipients:
        disclose "final-version"
    elif "Doris" or "Claire" in recipients:
        disclose "draft"
    elif recipients < ("Arthur", "Ben"):
        disclose "all-working-materials"
    else:
        disclose "nothing"
elif situation == "meeting-on-project-y":
    ...
```

Fig. 3. Excerpt of a modelled disclosure behavior. In-order rules decide disclosures based on information recipients and request situation

exemplary excerpt of a modelled disclosure behavior for a specific person and service request. The model is basically a set of rules evaluated in-order until a matching rule has been found.

For each request event instance generated by the event model, the disclosure model is utilized to decide the disclosure for each person participating at the request event. Consequently a simulation produces a sequence of request events together with context information and disclosure decisions which can be used as input for supervised learning algorithms. Context items are used as features and decisions are used as labels to classify.

3 Analysis

The service interaction events produced by a simulation have been analyzed using RapidMiner/Yale [17], a data mining software which supports a wide range of algorithms, including those of the WEKA toolkit [18]. Table 1 lists the learning algorithms used to build DDMs. Initially some more algorithms have been evaluated, like boosting, linear, logistic and polynomial regression and neural networks. They finally have been discarded due to significantly low performance or long training time.

DDMs have been learned using the output of simulations which generated about 80 service interaction events. Best practice for validating learning algorithms are cross validations. However, this is not applicable here as in reality

Table 1. Learning algorithms used to build DDMs

Learner	Details on Algorithm
Naive Bayes	SimpleEstimator from WEKA [18]
Rule Learner	RIPPER [19]
Decision Tree	C4.5 [20]
k-Nearest Neighbour	k=5, weighted votes, features normalized and weighted
SVM	LibSVM [21], RBF kernel, features normalized

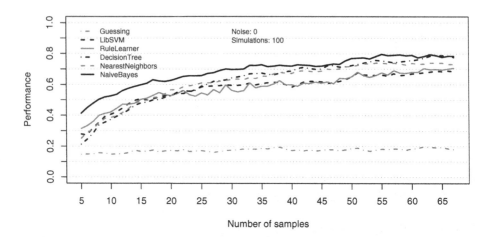

Fig. 4. Averaged fraction of correct disclosures of selected learning algorithms depending on the number of available training samples (used 15 regular attributes)

training samples to learn from grow over time and order is important. For that reason the algorithms have been evaluated in dependence of the number of available training samples. That is initially the first 5 samples have been used for DDM learning. Subsequent the sample size has been increased by 1 until the maximum number of training samples has been reached. In each evaluation step, the 10 service interaction events following those used for training have been used as test samples. This way algorithms can be qualified with regard to overall performance as well as required training samples. For each learning algorithm this evaluation has been done with the output of 100 simulations.

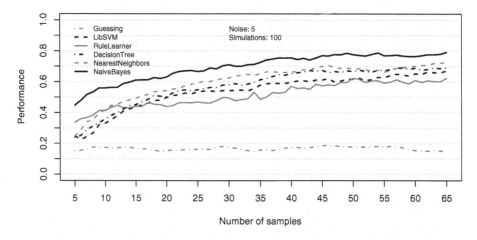

Fig. 5. Averaged fraction of correct disclosures of selected learning algorithms depending on the number of available training samples (added 5 noise attributes)

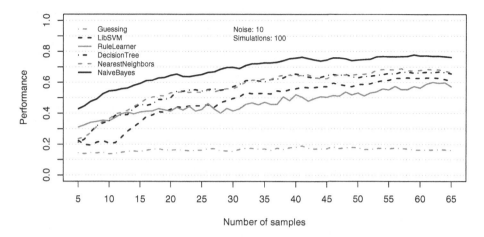

Fig. 6. Averaged fraction of correct disclosures of selected learning algorithms depending on the number of available training samples (added 10 noise attributes)

Additionally the same process has been repeated with added noise context. Figures 4 - 6 show the results of the evaluations for one person respectively it's modelled disclosure behavior. For comparison reasons additionally to the learners mentioned above the performance of a simple guessing is shown – it always predicts the disclosure which occurred most in previous situations.

Best results could be reached with the naive Bayes classifier, especially when there are few past service interactions to learn from and if additional noise data has been added. However, in future work these results need to get compared to evaluations made with data generated by simulations which use another model to generate service request events. Fig. 7 additionally shows the results of the naive Bayes classifier together with the 95% confidence intervals.

Whether the reached performance is sufficient for everyday use mainly depends on the sensitivity of the data to disclose. Here it would be useful if users rate manually disclosed information by sensitivity or assign a minimum

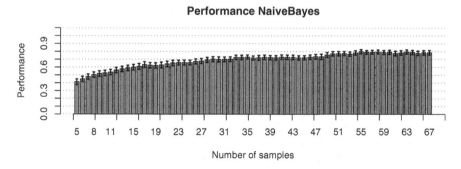

Fig. 7. Performance of the naive Bayes classifier with 0.95 confidence interval

confidence a DDM must have before disclosing a certain information. If the confidence assigned to an information by the user is higher than the confidence a DDM has when suggesting to disclose this information, the user can be queried for a final decision. For very sensitive information which should never get disclosed automatically, users could assign a minimum confidence > 1.

Finally, looking on the application level, a DDM driven ad hoc privacy control assistance should be integrated into a top level control scheme which enables users to set default behavior to either (a) deny all requests, (b) automatically reply all requests using a DDM or (c) query the user for manual disclosure. As mentioned before, the last two options can be merged by setting minimum confidence values required for automatic disclosure.

4   Conclusion and Outlook

In this work we described a concept for simulations to generate service interaction events in smart environments which can be used to apply data mining algorithms to evaluate disclosure assistance mechanisms for ad hoc privacy control. The results have shown that automatic disclosure decisions are correct in the majority of the cases with increasing performance. On the other side performance is not good enough to decide disclosure completely automatically. The autonomy of a DDM should be adjusted by users depending on the sensitivity of information to be handled by a DDM.

The main focus of this work was interpersonal privacy implications which cannot be generalized across users. In contrast, for privacy implications concerning the used infrastructure (handling of personal data by the service provider) similar preferences across users are more common and it is easier to predefine disclosure rules as the relevant factors are more static and generally known in advance (e.g., data retention and transfer policy). To follow an ad hoc approach anyway, disclosure decisions of other users could be used as suggestions, using concepts of trust networks. However, when using past disclosure decisions to suggest or predict new disclosures, it is important to differ between decisions based on interpersonal and technical privacy implications.

The results encourage to intensify research on ad hoc privacy control in smart environments. Concrete issues to tackle in future work are deploying further scenarios respectively service request event models to the simulation engine and to generalize concrete models as used here to event and context patterns. Concerning automatic disclosure decisions based on confidence it is further interesting to analyze data with respect to correlations between confidence and correctness of classifications.

References

1. Altman, I.: The Environment and Social Behavior: Privacy, Personal Space, Territory, and Crowding. Cole Publishing Company, Monterey (1975)
2. Palen, L., Dourish, P.: Unpacking "privacy" for a networked world. In: CHI 2003: Proc. of the SIGCHI Conference on Human Factors in Computing Systems, pp. 129–136. ACM, New York (2003)

3. Langheinrich, M.: A privacy awareness system for ubiquitous computing environments. In: Borriello, G., Holmquist, L.E. (eds.) UbiComp 2002. LNCS, vol. 2498, pp. 315–320. Springer, Heidelberg (2002)
4. W3C: The platform for privacy preferences 1.0 (P3P1.0) specification (April 2002), http://www.w3.org/TR/P3P/ (accessed December 12, 2008)
5. Cranor, L.F., Guduru, P., Arjula, M.: User interfaces for privacy agents. ACM Trans. Comput.-Hum. Interact. 13(2), 135–178 (2006)
6. Myles, G., Friday, A., Davies, N.: Preserving privacy in environments with location-based applications. IEEE Pervasive Computing 2(1), 56–64 (2003)
7. Prabaker, M., Rao, J., Fette, I., Kelley, P., Cranor, L., Hong, J., Sadeh, N.: Understanding and capturing people's privacy policies in a people finder application. In: UBICOMP 2007: Workshop on UBICOMP Privacy (September 2007)
8. Clauß, S., Pfitzmann, A., Hansen, M.: Privacy-enhancing identity management. The IPTS Report 67, 8–16 (2002), http://ipts.jrc.ec.europa.eu/home/report/english/articles/vol67/IPT2E676.htm (accessed January 26, 2009)
9. Jendricke, U., Kreutzer, M., Zugenmaier, A.: Pervasive privacy with identity management. Technical Report 178, Institut für Informatik, Universität Freiburg (October 2002)
10. Maibaum, N., Sedov, I., Cap, C.H.: A citizen digital assistant for e-government. In: Traunmüller, R., Lenk, K. (eds.) EGOV 2002. LNCS, vol. 2456, pp. 284–287. Springer, Heidelberg (2002)
11. Lederer, S., Mankoff, J., Dey, A.K., Beckmann, C.P.: Managing personal information disclosure in ubiquitous computing environments. Technical Report UCB/CSD-03-1257, EECS Department, University of California, Berkeley (July 2003)
12. Lederer, S., Hong, J.I., Dey, A.K., Landay, J.A.: Personal privacy through understanding and action: Five pitfalls for designers. Personal Ubiquitous Computing 8(6), 440–454 (2004)
13. Bünnig, C.: Learning context based disclosure of private information. In: The Internet of Things & Services - 1st Intl. Research Workshop, Valbonne, France (September 2008)
14. Bünnig, C.: Smart privacy management in ubiquitous computing environments. In: Smith, M.J., Salvendy, G. (eds.) Human Interface, Part II, HCII 2009. LNCS, vol. 5618. Springer, Heidelberg (2009)
15. Eagle, N., Pentland, A.: Reality mining - machine perception and learning of complex social systems (2009), http://reality.media.mit.edu/ (accessed June 12, 2009)
16. Lederer, S., Mankoff, J., Dey, A.K.: Who wants to know what when? privacy preference determinants in ubiquitous computing. In: CHI 2003: Extended Abstracts on Human Factors in Computing Systems, pp. 724–725. ACM, New York (2003)
17. Mierswa, I., Wurst, M., Klinkenberg, R., Scholz, M., Euler, T.: Yale: Rapid prototyping for complex data mining tasks. In: Proc. of the 12th ACM SIGKDD Intl. Conf. on Knowledge Discovery and Data Mining (KDD 2006), pp. 935–940. ACM, New York (2006)
18. Witten, I.H., Frank, E.: Data Mining: Practical machine learning tools and techniques, 2nd edn. Morgan Kaufmann, San Francisco (2005)
19. Cohen, W.W.: Fast effective rule induction. In: ICML, pp. 115–123 (1995)

20. Quinlan, J.R.: C4.5: Programs for Machine Learning. Morgan Kaufmann Publishers, San Francisco (1993)
21. Chang, C.C., Lin, C.J.: LIBSVM: a library for support vector machines (2001), http://www.csie.ntu.edu.tw/~cjlin/papers/libsvm.pdf (accessed June 12, 2009)

Passive Tracking of Transceiver-Free Users with RFID

Dominik Lieckfeldt, Jiaxi You, and Dirk Timmermann

University of Rostock
firstname.lastname@uni-rostock.de
http://www.imd.uni-rostock.de

Abstract. Providing location information while people move through a indoor environment is fundamental to smart environments. While many works address this problem, which is often referred to as tracking, the complex radio propagation and the need smart and unobtrusive localization system still represent challenges to current approaches.

We investigate through simulations the applicability of tracking a user with a passive RFID-System. The distinction to former approaches is that we do not constrain the user to wear any electronic devices to help localization. Our approach rather focuses on measuring the variations of signal strength which are caused by a human. For this purpose, we have spotted passive RFID to be very useful since the tags can be placed almost on any surface to measure the spatial distribution of the variations.

1 Introduction

The location of users and devices in smart environment has long been spotted as fundamental contextual information and, therefore, algorithms like intention recognition and task planning build on robust and accurate location information.

However, localization, the process of acquiring and tracking the location of users and devices using wireless communication, has to deal with several issues. Many existing approaches use the Time-of-Flight (ToF), Angle-of-Arrival (AoA) or received signal strength (RSS) to infer distances or directions to the target. However, the complex radio propagation in indoor environments represents a challenge for these methods since the aforementioned metrics are typically severely affected by multi path and interference of radio waves. For this reason, commercial localization systems use several metrics and fuse them to improve localization accuracy.

Observing that some of the negative effects on radio propagation are caused by the target to be tracked itself, an approach to track back these changes in order to localize a user has been reported to be feasible [1]. The distinction to previous approaches is that the user does not need to wear any communication devices and the resolution of the system can be adjusted by adding inexpensive passive tags.

The objective of the current paper is to investigate the applicability of this approach to tracking of the user with a particle filter. Special attention is paid to

D. Tavangarian et al. (Eds.): IMC 2009, CCIS 53, pp. 319–329, 2009.

Table 1. Overview of related work

	Passive Tags	Measurement	Transceiverless Target	Link Type
User/Object Localization				
Landmarc [2]	No	RSS	No	monostatic
SpotOn [3]	No	RSS	No	monostatic
Ferret [4]	Yes	Connectivity	No	bistatic
Robot Self-Localization				
Schneegans [5]	Yes	Connectivity	No	bistatic
Hhnel [6]	Yes	Connectivity/LR	No	bistatic
WSN Localization using RF-Propagation Effects				
Zhang et al. [7,8]	-	RSS	Yes	monostatic
Patwari et al. [9]	-	RSS	Yes	monostatic
curr. approach	Yes	RSS	Yes	bistatic

the sampling rate of the system which is a limiting parameter of our test bed and a function of number of passive RFID-Tags. Specifically, we aim at determining the minimum sampling rate of the system for which tracking still works with acceptable accuracy.

The rest of the paper is organized as follows. Section 2 reviews related works. Sections 3 and 4 reviews the theoretical models, their applicability to the current approach and introduces the particle filter framework. In Section 5, we present the set-up and results of simulations and draw conclusions on the applicability of a particle filter for tracking.

2   Related Work

Although the Global Positioning System (GPS) has been accepted as a reliable localization system for outdoor environments, its capabilities are very limited indoors since the satellite signals are typically strongly attenuated by walls and ceiling. Furthermore, in indoor environments a feasible localization system has to distinguish locations inside rooms and, therefore, an accuracy in the meter domain is expected.

The existing approaches to indoor localization can be classified in several ways: By the type of measurement, for example optical, ultrasound, infrared, pressure, RSS. Another distinction can be made concerning the system architecture, for example, whether the target can communicate over bidirectional or unidirectional links with the localization system. In some cases, the target does not need to carry a dedicated device to be located which makes these approaches especially interesting for ubiquitous environments.

Related to the distinction between uni- and bidirectional links is the distinction between monostatic and bistatic systems. In contrast to bistatic systems which use separate antennas for transmitting and receiving, monostatic systems have collocated transmitting and receiving antennas. Being either mono- or bistatic has strong impact on RSS-based localization with passive RFID because the mapping of RSS to distance is different. In addition, connectivity in bistatic systems depends on two physically different links as will be explained in greater detail later.

In contrast to our approach, Ni et al. utilize an active RFID-system for localizing a mobile target that has RFID tags attached [2]. The stationary deployed RFID-readers compare the measured power level of reference tags to improve localization performance.

Another well-known localization system using RFID is *SpotOn*. SpotOn researchers have designed and built custom hardware that serves as tags for localization. A 3D-localization algorithm uses the RSS readings between tags to determine their locations.

Ferret considers localization of nomadic objects and utilizes the directionality of RFID-readers [4]. The idea is to exploit different poses of the reader to narrow the object location down. This approach also utilizes a bistatic passive RFID-system.

The applicability of RFID to aid robot self-localization has been investigated in [6,5]. However, the connectivity information rather than the more informative RSS is used for localization.

Only few work have considered exploiting the change of RSS due to user presence for localization. Patwari et al. utilize the change of RSS to localize a person indoors [9]. The authors use a sensor network to measure the RSS and map its changes with a weighted linear least-squares error approach to estimated locations. Furthermore, Zhang et al. developed a system of ceiling mounted sensors that continuously measure the RSS between the sensor nodes. The absolute change of RSS is used to localize passing users. The authors recently proposed an extension of their original algorithm which allows for localization of multiple targets provided these are not too close [8].

Both approaches are related to ours since the impact of user presence on RSS is exploited. However, we point out the following significant differences: Our approach uses a passive bistatic RFID system which is advantageous for localization in ubiquitous environments. Such systems greatly differ in the way RSS are measured since they rely on backscattered signals. Furthermore, the resolution of our system depends on the number of inexpensive, passive RFID-Tags rather than full-fledged battery-powered transceivers.

3   Impact of Human Presence on RSSI

This section reviews findings obtained from an experimental testbed and focuses on the impact of user presence on RSS. A detailed investigation of these effects can be found in [1]. If not stated otherwise, we denote a pure sinusoid oscillation by signal.

3.1   Modeling of Human-Induced RF-Shadowing

We consider a bistatic, passive RFID-System consisting of a receiving and transmitting antenna and a RFID-Tag as depicted in Figures 1. These passive systems

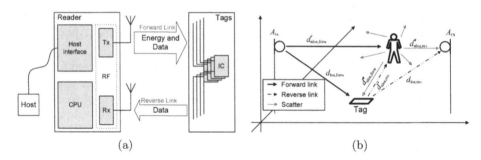

Fig. 1. a) Architecture of passive, bistatic RFID-Systems. b) Principle of radio scattering caused by human presence.

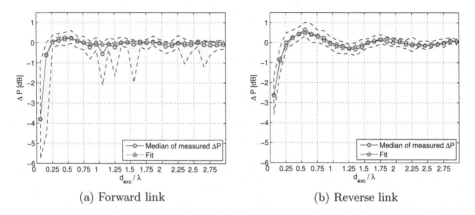

(a) Forward link   (b) Reverse link

Fig. 2. Human influence on RFID communication and relation between RSS variations and excess path delay

differ from active ones as the small tags are powered by impinging radio energy and thus do not need a battery. In the following, we seek to find a mathematical model for the RSS at the receiving antenna given a specific user location. Due to the characteristics of radio propagation, it is feasible to first describe the user location as the set of coordinates having the same excess path delay. Later, we will show how the excess path delays of several links can be combined for actual localization.

In Figure 1b, a user is situated in the deployment area and acts as scatterer to the ongoing wireless communications. As a result, radio signals reach the receiving antenna over several paths of different length and, therefore, show an *excess path delay*:

$$d_{\mathrm{exc}} = d'_{\mathrm{nlos}} + d''_{\mathrm{nlos}} - d_{\mathrm{los}} \tag{1}$$

The figure shows that for bistatic RFID systems we need to consider both forward and reverse links as the measured RSS depends on both. Furthermore, we are only able to observe a function of the actual RSS which is typically referred to as Received Signal Strength Indicator (RSSI). In the following, we assume that the RSSI is proportional to RSS that we only need to consider the change of RSSI to characterize the change of the true RSS.

To facilitate further considerations, we define the following quantities in dB

s_{init} is the initial RSSI measured without user presence in the deployment area.

s_{obst} is the RSSI measured with user presence at a specific location in the deployment area.

Δs denotes the difference or variation of RSSI $\Delta s = s_{\text{obst}} - s_{\text{init}}$.

To characterize the change of RSSI compared with the initial RSSI, we need to consider the relative excess path delay d_{exc} of the direct line-of-sight (LOS) and the scattered non-line-of-sight (NLOS) path. The ratio between excess path delay and signal wave length determines whether two interfering signals' amplitudes add or subtract. It is noted that lines of equal excess path delay form ellipsoids with A_{tx} and A_{tx} as focii. For example the region $d_{\text{exc}}/\lambda \leq 0.25$ is called the *First Fresnel Zone*. Obstacles in the First Fresnel Zone typically result in attenuations of RSS [10].

Table 2. Parameters of fitting the measurements

Parameter	Forward link	Reverse link
A	0.025	0.14
B	−1.32	−0.79
$\tilde{\lambda}$	0.37	0.43
Φ_{refl}	3.20	3.25

In a one excess path scenario, it can be shown that s_{obst} has the following form [1] with the parameter values in Table 2:

$$\Delta s(d_{\text{exc}}) \approx A d_{\text{exc}}^B \cos\left(\frac{2\pi}{\tilde{\lambda}} d_{\text{exc}} + \phi_{\text{refl}}\right) \qquad (2)$$

It is noted that in general there will be more than one scatterer and consequently more than one excess path. However, since we focus in this paper on system parameters, we constrain the investigations to the single-target case.

Figure 3 depicts simulated variation of RSSI. It is shown that there is ambiguity when we try to determine the location of the user given a specific Δs since lines of equal excess path delays form ellipsoids. In addition, Δs can not be attributed to either forward or backward link. To mitigate ambiguity, we need to consider several links between tags and antennas. This has the additional advantage of further narrowing down the possible location of the user the more tags are used. At this point it becomes clear that the inexpensiveness and small scale of passive RFID-Tags make such systems especially appropriate.

Following this approach, classical estimators like the method of least squared errors or the maximum likelihood method have been applied to the problem [11].

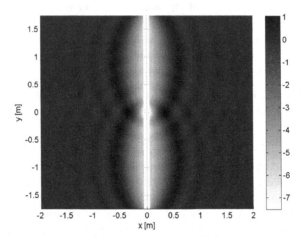

Fig. 3. Simulated s_{obst} for different user locations. Dark areas indicate no influence or amplification and white areas indicate attenuations. Receiving and transmitting antenna and the tag are situated at $(0, -1.75)$, $(0, 1.75)$ and $(0, 0)$ respectively.

4   Tracking Transceiver-Free Users

This section considers tracking a moving user and introduces the framework which will be used for tracking.

Concerning the localization problem, we desire to estimate the state sequence $\{\theta_k, k \in \mathbb{N}\}$ of the user which consists of its location and possible other parameters describing its movement. Here we assume a time discrete representation where k denotes the current time slot. Due to physics, the location of an object can not change abruptly but typically can be modeled by a set of state transition equations

$$\theta_k = \mathbf{f}_k(\theta_{k-1}, \mathbf{v}_{k-1}) \tag{3}$$

where $\mathbf{f}_k$ is a possibly nonlinear function, $\mathbf{v}$ is the an i.i.d. process noise and $\mathbb{N}$ are the natural numbers. The objective of tracking is to estimate the sequence $\{\theta_k, k \in \mathbb{N}\}$ given noisy measurements $\mathbf{z}_k$

$$\mathbf{z}_k = \mathbf{h}_k(\theta_{k-1}, \mathbf{n}_{k-1}) \tag{4}$$

Classical estimation methods regard the parameters to be estimated as deterministic yet unknown variables. In contrast thereof, Bayesian estimators assume that the parameters are random and, hence, can be described by probability distributions [12].

In this work, we consider the application of the Extended Kalman Filter (EKF) and the Particle Filter to the tracking problem. Since both algorithms have been extensively studied in the literature [13,14,15], we omit the mathematical details here.

5   Simulation

We conducted computer simulations to investigate the following:

- Relation between tracking error and number of RFID-Tags
- Compare tracking error of Particle Filter and Extended Kalman Filter.

We consider an indoor deployment of $N_{ant} = 4$ antennas and N_{tag} passive RFID-Tags. The tags are deployed in a regular, quadratic grid on the floor. The antennas are located at the four corners of the deployment area in a height of 1.8 meters. A target is assumed to move through the deployment area while the RFID system measures the vector of RSS of all tags in discrete time steps with sampling period T.

5.1   Simulation Set-Up

A schematic of the computer simulations is shown in Figure 4. The movement of the target is described by the process model. We assume 2D coordinates and the associated velocities, i.e. the state $\theta = [x, y, v_x, v_y]^{\mathrm{T}}$ and the state transition function are given by:

$$\theta_k = \begin{bmatrix} 1 & 0 & T & 0 \\ 0 & 1 & 0 & T \\ 0 & 0 & 1 & 0 \\ 0 & 0 & 0 & 1 \end{bmatrix} \theta_{k-1} + \mathbf{v}_{k-1} \tag{5}$$

Where $(\cdot)^{\mathrm{T}}$ denotes the transpose. To facilitate simulation, we predefined a S-shaped trajectory and calculated the evolution of the state accordingly.

The observation model describes the relation between the vector of measured RSS $\mathbf{z}$ and the state. We define the matrix of antenna sequence (AS) $\mathbf{S}_{ant} \in \mathbb{N}^{N_{as} \times 2}$. The first and second element of the i-th row of $\mathbf{S}_{ant}$ denote the i-th transmitting and receiving antenna, respectively. Theoretically, there are $\binom{N_{ant}}{2}$ possible antenna pairs. However, we choose for the simulation $N_{as} = 2$

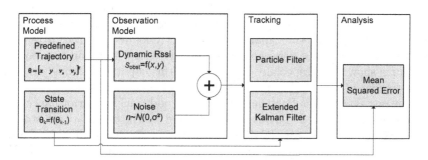

Fig. 4. Data flow of computer simulations

antenna pairs to limit the complexity of calculations. Consequently, the vector of observations is given by

$$\mathbf{z} = \left[\Delta s^{(1,1)}, \ldots, \Delta s^{(N_{\text{tags}},1)}, \Delta s^{(1,2)}, \ldots, \Delta s^{(N_{\text{tags}},N_{\text{as}})} \right]^{\text{T}} + \mathbf{n} \qquad (6)$$

We assume a lognormal fading model and add iid Gaussian noise with distribution $N(0,1)$ to the RSS given in dezibels. It is noted that each measured RSS, i.e. each element of $\mathbf{z}$, corresponds to the link between sending and transmitting antenna and tag. Consequently, the measurement vector has a size of $\mathbf{z}_k \in \mathbb{R}^{N_{\text{as}} N_{\text{tag}} \times 1}$.

We point out that this observation model assumes knowledge of the static RSS s_{init} associated with the absence of the target. Recognizing that it is possible to measure s_{init} during run-time, e.g. during nights when their is no activity, we regard this assumption as tractable.

Equation (1) and (2) are used to calculate the obstacle-dependent RSS which is a function of the current target position. For the calculation of the excess path length d_{exc} we need several quantities (see eq. (1) and Figure 1b). However, since the complexity of the human body prohibits an analytical calculation, we apply a simplified model and regard it as a cylinder of radius 0.1 m and height 1.9 m. This way, the path length of each NLOS line segment in Figure 1b can be determined using simple ray tracing.

To facilitate a simple implementation of the computer simulations we further assume that all tags are in range of every antenna.

5.2   Simulation Results

In order to analyze tracking performance, we calculate the Mean Square Error (MSE) of each estimated position $(\tilde{x}, \tilde{y})$ for each point of the simulated trajectory.

$$MSE = E\left[(x - \tilde{x})^2 + (y - \tilde{y})^2 \right] \qquad (7)$$

$$RMSE = \sqrt{E\left[(x - \tilde{x})^2 + (y - \tilde{y})^2 \right]} \qquad (8)$$

Figures 5 show the tracking error. Estimated positions are depicted by red crosses and the black ellipses and triangles denote the $1 - \sigma$-area of position errors and the average estimated positions. It is shown that the accuracy of tracking using the approach presented strongly depends on the number of tags. To further elaborate on this point, the capability to correctly follow the true trajectory is indicated by the distance between average estimated position and true position. The figures show that, especially for the EKF, this capability strongly depends on the number of tags deployed.

In contrast thereof, the Particle Filter shows good tracking performance for all tag numbers investigated. This is also supported by the cumulative histograms of Root Mean Square Error (RMSE) in Figure 6. It is shown that the tracking error of EKF slowly approaches that of the Particle Filter. In particular, the EKF achieves only for 36 tags feasible position estimates while the accuracy of the Particle Filter only marginally improves when the number of tags is increased.

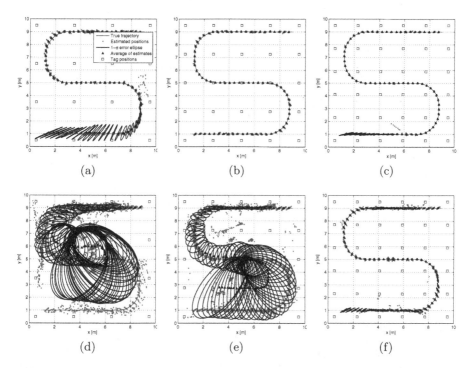

Fig. 5. MSE tracking error of a)-c) Particle Filter and d)-f) Extended Kalman Filter. The four antennas are situated at the corners at (0,0), (0,10), (10,10) and (10,0).

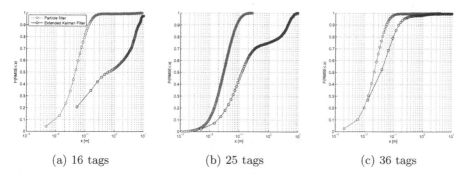

(a) 16 tags   (b) 25 tags   (c) 36 tags

Fig. 6. Cumulative histogram of RMSE tracking error

6   Conclusions

We have investigated the applicability of both Particle Filter and Extended Kalman Filter to tracking a user by merely measuring the changing received signal strength with passive RFID. The simulations indicate that the tracking error strongly depends on the number of passive tags.

In contrast to the Particle Filter which showed good tracking accuracy for all tag numbers, the Extended Kalman Filter proved to be very susceptible to the tag number and its estimates were only feasible when using 36 tags.

Future work will consider relaxing the assumption of a-priori known static RSS to make the approach applicable to changing environments. Although the observation model has been calculated using real measurements, we will investigate the tracking performance using our test-bed.

Acknowledgment

This work was partially financed by the German Research Foundation (DFG) within the graduate school **M**ulti modal **S**mart **A**ppliance ensembles for **M**obile **A**pplications (MuSAMA, GRK 1424).

References

1. Lieckfeldt, D., You, J., Timmermann, D.: Characterizing the influence of human presence on bistatic passive rfid-system. In: 5th IEEE International Conference on Wireless and Mobile Computing, Networking and Communications (2009)
2. Ni, L.M., Liu, Y., Lau, Y.C., Patil, A.P.: Landmarc: Indoor location sensing using active rfid. Wireless Networks 10(6), 701+ (2004)
3. Hightower, J., Want, R., Borriello, G.: SpotON: An indoor 3d location sensing technology based on RF signal strength. In: UW CSE 00-02-02. University of Washington, Department of Computer Science and Engineering, Seattle, WA (February 2000)
4. Liu, X., Corner, M.D., Shenoy, P.D.: Ferret: Rfid localization for pervasive multimedia. In: Dourish, P., Friday, A. (eds.) UbiComp 2006. LNCS, vol. 4206, pp. 422–440. Springer, Heidelberg (2006)
5. Schneegans, S., Vorst, P., Zell, A.: Using RFID snapshots for mobile robot self-localization. In: Proceedings of the 3rd European Conference on Mobile Robots (ECMR 2007), Freiburg, Germany, September 19-21, pp. 241–246 (2007)
6. Haenggi, M.: On distances in uniformly random networks. IEEE Transactions on Information Theory 51(10), 3584–3586 (2005)
7. Zhang, D., Jian, M., Chen, Q., Ni, L.: An rf-based system for tracking transceiver-free objects. In: 5th Annual IEEE International Conference on Pervasive Computing and Communications, PerCom 2007, White Plains, NY, pp. 135–144 (2006)
8. Zhang, D., Ni, L.M.: Dynamic clustering for tracking multiple transceiver-free objects. IEEE International Conference on Pervasive Computing and Communications 0, 1–8 (2009)
9. Patwari, N., Agrawal, P.: Effects of correlated shadowing: Connectivity, localization, and rf tomography. In: International Conference on Information Processing in Sensor Networks, IPSN 2008, April 2008, pp. 82–93 (2008)
10. Lee, W.: Mobile communications engineering. McGraw-Hill Professional, New York (1982)
11. Lieckfeldt, D., You, J., Timmermann, D.: Exploiting rf-scatter: Human localization with bistatic passive uhf rfid-systems. In: 5th IEEE Wireless and Mobile Computing, Networking and Communications (2009)

12. Kay, S.M.: Fundamentals of Statistical Signal Processing, Volume I: Estimation Theory. Prentice Hall PTR, Englewood Cliffs (1993)
13. Arulampalam, M., Maskell, S., Gordon, N., Clapp, T.: A tutorial on particle filters for online nonlinear/non-gaussian bayesian tracking. IEEE Transactions on Signal Processing 50(2), 174–188 (2002)
14. Doucet, A., Johansen, A.: A Tutorial on Particle Filtering and Smoothing: Fifteen years later. In: The Oxford Handbook of Nonlinear Filtering. Oxford University Press, Oxford (to appear, 2009)
15. Ljung, L.: Asymptotic behavior of the extended kalman filter as a parameter estimator for linear systems. IEEE Transactions on Automatic Control 24(1), 36–50 (1979)

A New Generation Digital Video Assist System with Intelligent Multi-Camera Control and Support for Creative Work on the Film Set

Christian Märtin[1], Bernhard Prell[2], and Andreas Kesper[2]

[1] Augsburg University of Applied Sciences, Faculty of Computer Science
Postbox 11 06 05, 86031 Augsburg, Germany
Christian.Maertin@hs-augsburg.de
[2] Vantage Film GmbH, Digital Division
Fuggerstrasse 7, 86150 Augsburg, Germany
{BernhardPrell,AndreasKesper}@vantagefilm.com

1 Computer-Supported Film Set

Digital video-assist systems store the video signal received from the integrated video system (IVS) embedded in the view-finder of conventional electronic film cameras (e.g from ARRI, Panavision) or digital film cameras (e.g. from ARRI, Red, DALSA, Panavision, Sony). They allow for easy playback of takes and better administration of the recorded takes, long before the developed celluloid film or the high-definition digital raws become available for post-production.

The term computer-supported film set (CSFS) was introduced in [1] to describe a new category of high-end systems for on-set support that combine classic video assist features with simultaneous support of multiple attached cameras, intelligent software functionality for on-set effects simulation (slow-motion, time-lapse, ramping, filtering, mix-and-overlay of takes, blue-, green-screen effects, editing), shooting day organization, rehearsal assistance for actors, and hard- and software-support for active camera control and communication between on-set devices. The development process used for all generations of Vantage Film´s touchsreen-based PSU® (pre-screen unit) systems followed a contextual design approach [2] combining contextual inquiry of film experts with extensive iterative hard- and software prototyping and a six months trial period, before the final products were released.

2 Vantage Film PSU-3® Digital Video Assist System

To arrive at the rich software functionality of the current PSU® systems and to allow for unprecedented user experience on the set, major HCI challenges had to be met. In contrast to their contenders the PSU® systems stand out by their overall UI look and feel, complexity reduction by UI layering, UI upward compatibility between all generations, dynamic configuration of camera-to-attached-screen-mappings, and transparent system behavior in mixed human-operated/automatic shooting situations [3].

The CSFS based on the new Vantage Film PSU-3® digital video assist system discussed in this paper surpasses its predecessors with high-speed/high-quality graphics

D. Tavangarian et al. (Eds.): IMC 2009, CCIS 53, pp. 331–332, 2009.
© Springer-Verlag Berlin Heidelberg 2009

functionality, new image processing features, simultaneous support of up to four attached film cameras, HD recording support, asynchronous input-channel-to-output-screen-mapping, multiple sound recordings, advanced shooting control for automatic recordings, post-production support, visualization of varying target screen formats, advanced camera status checking, and novel networking features.

The PSU-3® runs under Linux and uses the dual-core Intel T9400 45 nm processor and SSD technology. The broader and more sophisticated software and user interface functionality requires extensive embedded FPGA and USB controller support. Compared to its direct predecessor, the PSU-2Plus®, power consumption was reduced by a factor of two (now between 92 and 112W). Weight and form factors could also be massively reduced. Figure 1 shows the PSU-3®-based distributed CSFS environment.

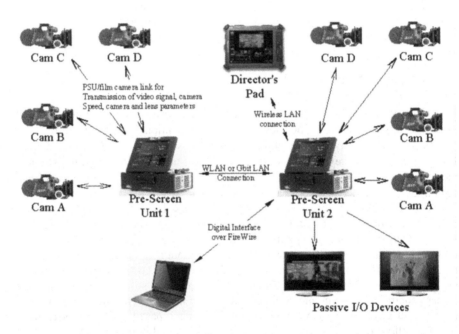

Fig. 1. Distributed CSFS environment around the PSU-3® digital video assist system

References

1. Märtin, C., Prell, B.: Contextual Design of a Computer-Suppported Film Set: A Case Study. In: Jorge, J.A., Jardim Nunes, N., Falcão e Cunha, J. (eds.) DSV-IS 2003. LNCS, vol. 2844, pp. 392–405. Springer, Heidelberg (2003)
2. Beyer, H., Holtzblatt, K.: Contextual Design. Interactions, 32–42 (January/Febuary 1999)
3. Märtin, C., Prell, B., Schwarz, A.: Managing User Interface Complexity and Usability in Computer-Supported Film Sets. In: Proc. of HCI International, Las Vegas, Nevada USA, July 22-27, vol. 3. Lawrence Erlbaum, Mahwah (2005)

RfM: A Radio Flashing Tool for Microcontrollers

Stefan Goldmann and Ralf Salomon

University of Rostock, 18051 Rostock, Germany
{stefan.goldmann,ralf.salomon}@uni-rostock.de

1 Introduction and Problem Description

During its lifetime, an embedded system's software is subject to recurrent changes, such as bug fixes, upgrades or even complete replacements. Traditionally, programming the system with a new application, i.e., *flashing*, requires a cable-connection between a PC and the system's microcontroller. In effect, the cable connects the PC to the controller's program (flash) memory, via a dedicated hardware flasher located on the chip.

While this procedure is acceptable in many scenarios, it might be impossible in others. For example, in the domain of automated factories, detaching a controller from a 10-meters height ceiling is but convenient. For those cases, flashing over an existing radio communication capability would provide a very convenient solution. However, when flashing the controller over its radio interface, the hardware flasher cannot be used to establish a connection between the radio interface and the program memory. Instead, the received data must flow from the radio interface through the actual controller into the flash. This approach imposes the problem, that, during flashing, the software flasher eventually overwrites its own machine code. This, in turn, aborts the flashing process prematurely and leaves the controller in a useless state. For the remainder of this paper, this phenomenon is referred to as the self-overwriting problem.

Therefore, the next section proposes a new software radio flasher, called RfM (Radio flashing tool for Microcontrollers), which circumvents this problem by utilizing a two pass approach in conjunction with a three-parted program memory layout. In the first pass, the application is received into a temporary storage, and in the second pass the application is transfered to its final location. This approach ensures a valid program memory state at any time, and it allows to correctly cope with the consequences of the missing support for stack operations, which can be found in many microcontrollers. The next section also reports on the experiences the authors have made with their RfM implementation during the last months, and concludes this paper with a brief discussion.

2 Solution and Results

Any software flashing tool must meet the following requirements: 1) Avoiding the self-overwriting problem by placing the flashing software at a fixed location.

D. Tavangarian et al. (Eds.): IMC 2009, CCIS 53, pp. 333–335, 2009.

2) Continuing execution of the old application in case of a radio breakdown.
3) Ensuring correct parameter passing between the user application and the flashing software.

RfM fulfills these requirements by utilizing a three-parted program memory layout: a) a little less than half the program memory for the user application and one part of the flashing software; b) a chunk of the same size as temporary storage; c) the remaining minor part for the other part of the flashing software. With this layout, RfM employs a two pass flashing approach: In the first pass, the new application is received from the radio interface into the temporary storage. The code responsible for this task is located in the user application area and is therefore exchangeable. In the second pass, the new application is transfered from the temporary storage to its final location, i.e., the user application area. The code for this task is located in the third, minor part. This code is fixed and therefore not replaceable.

Obviously, the RfM approach avoids the self-overwriting problem, as the actual application overwriting, i.e., the second pass, is performed by the code located in the minor program memory part, which remains untouched at all times. Furthermore, RfM can return to the old application in case of a premature radio breakdown, as the overwriting does not happen before the new application has been *completely* received. Finally, passing parameters correctly between the user application and the flashing software is ensured due to the division of the actual flashing software into two parts: The only part that requires parameters from the user application is actually embedded into the user application. It originates from the same compilation pass as the user application and is exchanged with it in conjunction. Therefore, it does not play a role, whether the controller provides a stack-based, register-based, or absolute-address-based parameter passing model. The price for these positive properties is that only about half of the program memory can be used for the user application.

The authors have implemented RfM within their office, where they have built up a small office automation instance [3], which utilizes the CC1010 [2] microcontroller. In contrast to some other controllers, such as the ARM series [1], this controller is poor with respect to memory sizes, speed, and instruction set capabilities. Especially, it does not support the stack-based parameter passing model. For these reasons, RfM should easily be portable to other architectures.

Up to the point of writing, RfM performed well within the test scenario for several months. Especially, RfM has proven its robustness against failing radio connections due to the temporary storage concept. In the future, RfM could be enhanced, such that during the second flashing pass, the old application is not overwritten, but merely swapped with the new one. With appropriate modifications to RfM's reboot behavior, RfM could switch back to the old application, if the new one crashes right away.

References

1. Furber, S.: ARM System-on-Chip Architecture. Addison Wesley, New York (2000)
2. Texas Instruments. Cc1010 data sheet (2004),
   http://www-mtl.mit.edu/Courses/6.111/labkit/datasheets/CC1010.pdf
3. Salomon, R., Goldmann, S.: Age-p: A platform for open evolution. In: Rudolph, G.,
   Jansen, T., Lucas, S., Poloni, C., Beume, N. (eds.) PPSN 2008. LNCS, vol. 5199,
   pp. 1111–1119. Springer, Heidelberg (2008)

Adequate Assistance for Elderly People in Homely Rehab

Alexander Mertens[1], Philipp Przybysz[1], Bernhard Kausch[1], Daniel Dünnebacke[2], and Christopher Schlick[1]

[1] Chair and Institute of Industrial Engineering and Ergonomics of RWTH Aachen University
{A.Mertens,P.Przybysz,B.Kausch,C.Schlick}@iaw.rwth-aachen.de
[2] Research Institute for Operations Management (FIR) at RWTH Aachen University
Daniel.Duennebacke@fir.rwth-aachen.de

Abstract. This paper presents an approach for arranging, allocating and interchanging the gain in knowledge and experience during projects of the eHealth sectors and related domains. The know-how is transcribed into design-patterns, whose concept has proven its effectiveness in versatile areas. A framework for specifying the pattern-structure that meets the specific requirements of this area is defined.

Keywords: design patterns, pattern language, telehealth, eHealth, AAL.

1 Motivation and Objectives

In times of demographic change, the development of systems with adequate assistance especially for elderly people becomes more and more important. But for all that the specific restrictions and requirements of the elderly target group are often not respected to a sufficient degree [1]. Solutions to problems of the eHealth sector have to be ´reinvented´ although they were already solved in related domains [2]. To improve this dilemma, the purpose of the pattern approach presented in this paper is:

- Design of a semiformal model of a pattern language for assistance of elderly people with technical systems in their domestic environment
- Creating of a domain specific vocabulary to support the internal communication
- Providing a framework in which novice can acquire domain specific proficiency, designers can express their ideas and experts can share their knowledge/experience

2 Pattern Language for eHealth-Domain

To ensure a common understanding, consistent creation of new patterns, as well as supporting people in finding auxiliary patterns for their eHealth-scenarios, a framework with ten *sections* is specified. Each pattern has a short *NAME* that communicates the central idea briefly, can be used as reference, and builds a vocabulary. The usage of medical terms should be avoided to ensure a common understanding. The *RANKING* (max. three asterisks) reflects the pattern author´s belief in how valid the

D. Tavangarian et al. (Eds.): IMC 2009, CCIS 53, pp. 337–338, 2009.

specific pattern can be applied for designing adequate assistance and whether it is the only one solution or one among many. The *CONTEXT* classifies in which phase of the medical process (check-up, emergency, hospital stay, rehabilitation, aftercare, etc.) the pattern is valid and therefore respects the particular demands of the patient/medical staff. The definition of a *TARGET GROUP* is momentous for this domain as it enables the reader to decide if the design pattern is adequate for his scenario. There should be at least a rudimental differentiation between: patient ↔ medical staff ↔ technical equipment A more precise definition or a combination if more groups interact can enhance the comprehensibility. *USAGE SITE* defines the local place were the scenario takes place. The different surrounding conditions e.g. among domestic environment, surgery and intensive care narrow the possible application because of factors such as sterility, data protection and radiation. Next section is the *PROBLEM* description. Here the definition of the conflicting interests and opposing forces in regard to medical needs, physical limits/restrictions, cognitive psychology, social and economical issues, and individual preferences of the patients as well as the professionals is stated. Quintessence of each pattern is the *SOLUTION* section. It gives constructive recommendations that have proven to balance the conflicting forces in typical eHealth scenarios. To be significant, all involved (medical) equipment, technical auxiliary material, running period, activity sampling and the integration in clinical practice that were field tested have to be mentioned. An *ILLUSTRATION* in the form of a photograph, a sequence/operating diagram, or a technical draft helps to get an idea of how the implementation might look. In some patterns there might be *LIMITATIONS* because of spillover effects or contraindications in the context of several diseases that forbid an application in that case. On the other hand the application of the pattern might only make sense for special ailments (e.g. dementia, ametropia, and adynamia) and is therefore limited to these scenarios. The *REFERENCES* organize the isolated patterns to a pattern language by linking to additional patterns that are part of following process steps in the medical treatment or specific aspects that are inherent to the solution.

3 Conclusion

The application of this framework within a project on telemedical services for elderly persons showed its effectiveness. The results in research were transformed and restructured into a tentative pattern language that was used as lingua franca for discussing and communicating the system design to all the involved. The pattern specific vocabulary and solutions are reused and amended in continuative works.

References

1. Sommerlatte, T.: Technikgestaltung aus Sicht des Nutzers. In: Digitale Visionen, Springer, Heidelberg (2008)
2. Borchers, J.: A pattern approach to interaction design. Wiley, Chichester (2001)

Self-adaptation for Deployment Decision Making

Rico Kusber, Nermin Brgulja, and Klaus David

University of Kassel, Chair for Communication Technology (ComTec), Wilhelmshöher
Allee 73, 34121 Kassel, Germany
{rico.kusber,nermin.brgulja}@comtec.eecs.uni-kassel.de
klaus.david@comtec.eecs.uni-kassel.de

Abstract. In this paper we present an intelligent assistant for deploying services
and obtaining content in distributed computing network. We focus on how self-
adaptation is achieved and illustrate the capabilities and limits of self-adaptation
within our approach with the help of provider reputation values.

Keywords: Deployment decision making, autonomic computing, assistance.

1 Introduction and Groundwork

Considering an environment of multiple networked computing systems that enable
access to a multitude of services and content, service and content consumers may
need assistance when making deployment decisions. In this paper we present an intelligent assistant for deploying services and obtaining content while taking into account
users' preferences and needs. We focus on giving an overview of the potential and the
limits of self-adaptation within our Deployment Decision Making (DDM) system.

The rest of this section summarizes related work and main principles of DDM.
Section 2 explains how self-adaptation is achieved by exemplarily describing provider
reputation values. Section 3 concludes with an outlook on further work.

Putting autonomicity to computing systems and networks helps to handle their
rapidly increasing complexity [1]. In our approach, we apply principles and ideas of
autonomic computing to the field of deployment decision making. The process of
deploying services has been researched extensively (cf. e.g. [2]). Several approaches
exist for dedicated requirements. What we could not find, is a facility to autonomi-
cally decide which out of many deployment alternatives should be selected to suit a
user's preferences. Moreover, we miss a possibility to handle unreliable information
in a user independent way. This paper builds upon [3] and contributes by presenting a
concept of self-adaptation to handle unreliable information in DDM processes.

2 Self-adaptation in DDM

DDM addresses the question which alternative, out of many, to deploy a service or to
obtain content maximally suits the needs of a DDM system user. Here, a user can be
human or a computing system. Deploying a service or obtaining content means to

D. Tavangarian et al. (Eds.): IMC 2009, CCIS 53, pp. 339–340, 2009.

either copy or move it from a source to a target device or to access it remotely. Detailed information about DDM can be found in [3].

To assess multiple deployment alternatives, DDM uses three kinds of parameters: Service parameters describe conditions under which a service or content can be accessed; Decision parameters represent properties that are relevant for a user of DDM; Adaptable parameters embody experiences a DDM system learned from former DDM processes. The DDM algorithm achieves self-adaptation by modifying adaptable parameters based on service parameter values measured during deployment.

In a networked domain with multiple interacting entities, service describing information, i.e., service parameters can be unreliable for different reasons. It can be incomplete or missing at all. It can be wrong because of unforeseen effects. And it can be manipulated purposely. A DDM system can, to a certain extent, handle unreliable information with the help of self-adaptation based on experiences. To illustrate this capability, we developed the adaptable parameter *ProviderReputation*. This parameter creates a map of all service or content providers a DDM system interacted with, and associates a reputation value accordingly. During service deployment or content retrieval, the service parameter values of the selected alternative are measured (if possible) and compared to the corresponding values that have been denoted by the concerned provider. If each pair of denoted and measured values is similar, the provider reputation increases. It decreases otherwise. Experimental evaluations have shown that a cheating provider that denotes manipulated service parameter values will most likely not win a DDM process after only few bad experiences have been collected.

3 Conclusion and Further Work

In this paper we presented an overview of a deployment decision making system that adapts itself by learning from experiences. By means of the adaptable parameter ProviderReputation we illustrated how this can help to handle unreliable information.

Next, we will investigate further adaptable parameters like deployment success rates and unreliability trends. Evaluations we performed so far will be further elaborated and used to determine potential and limits of self-adaptation in a DDM system.

References

1. Huebscher, M.C., McCann, J.A.: A Survey of Autonomic Computing – Degrees, Models, and Applications. ACM Comput. Surv. 40(3), 1–28 (2008)
2. Hillenbrand, M., Müller, P., Mihajloski, K.: A Software Deployment Service for Autonomous Computing Environments. In: Proceedings of the International Conference on Intelligent Agents, Web Technology and Internet Commerce, Gold Coast (2004)
3. Kusber, R., Haseloff, S., David, K.: An Approach to Autonomic Deployment Decision Making. In: Hummel, K.A., Sterbenz, J.P.G. (eds.) IWSOS 2008. LNCS, vol. 5343, pp. 121–132. Springer, Heidelberg (2008)

Towards Building User-Centric Privacy-Respecting Collaborative Applications

Mohamed Bourimi[1], Thomas Barth[1], Bernd Ueberschär[2],
and Dogan Kesdogan[1]

[1] Information Systems Institute, University of Siegen, Germany
[2] Leibniz Institute of Marine Sciences at the University of Kiel, Germany
{bourimi,barth}@fb5.uni-siegen.de

1 Problem Statement: Requirements for Collaborative Systems

The Internet is accepted as the de facto information support system in most areas of our professional and leisure life. Nowadays, a shift from single-user-centered usage to support multi-user needs can be observed either in professional life (e.g. when participating in collaborative business processes) and in leisure life activities (e.g. when participating in non-profit communities). The needed environment is provided through collaborative systems and social software (e.g. wikis, blogs, etc.). These environments provide e.g. shared workspaces, where collaborative processes and activities like document sharing, group formation, coordination and communication activities, etc. can take place. For this, collaborative settings need some degree of user's information disclosure (e.g. partial or full identity revelation). Depending on the actual context and a users sensitivity to a (partial) loss of privacy in a given context a users trust in a system handling privacy is crucial for its acceptance and overall success. Many end-user expectations are covered by functional requirements (FRs), most end-user preferences (e.g. usability, response time) and concerns (e.g. privacy, security) are non-functional requirements (NFRs). Considering current approaches, non-functional requirements in general and being of special relevance in this context privacy requirements are not considered adequately in the development process and will become one key issue in future software development processes. In this short paper, we present four requirements derived from a case study in collaborative system design and implementation (CURE, s. [1] for details). A framework for adequate (i.e. earlier) consideration of NFR (e.g. privacy) is outlined.

2 Problem Analysis, Derived Requirements, and a Proposal for a Development Framework Satisfying these Requirements

Nowadays, many factors like globalization, market pressure, time-to-market, and need for compliance, implies an increased business complexity. Many end-users' increasing need for collaboration to fulfill their complex and knowledge-intensive tasks along the business processes results in increasingly complex IT

D. Tavangarian et al. (Eds.): IMC 2009, CCIS 53, pp. 341–342, 2009.

infrastructures comprising a plethora of applications, processes, platforms, etc. and the resulting interdependencies. Thus, efficient methods for requirement and software engineering are crucial in order to assure adequate systems and reduce development costs while fulfilling end-users' requirements in the presence of frequent changes. From the long-running project CURE [2], the following four requirements for development processes as well as implementation technology were derived considered as characteristic for collaborative systems subject to frequent changes: Systematically addressing NFRs (e.g. end-users' privacy concerns) early in the development process considering trade-offs with (N)FRs (HLR1:ANALYSIS); Addressing emerging changes in the business processes which can be efficiently tailored according to the steps or phases of the different existing development processes, practices and approaches (HLR2: AGILITY); Considering explicitly human factors (especially of end-users, developers) in the method answering HLR1 and HLR2 (HLR3:HUMAN_FACTOR); Supporting the method at the architectural and implementation level to assure meeting HLR1-HLR3 at minimal cost (HLR4:SYSTEM_ARCHITECTURE).

To satisfy HLR1-HLR4, the proposed framework consists of an iterative and agile method based on SCRUM ([3], HLR1-3) as a process for empirical control of software development, and its support through a generic software architecture (HLR4). Since HLR1-4 are located at a rather generic, high level of abstraction, answering those requirements either purely technical (e.g. by a software architecture) or purely organizational (e.g. by a process model) would be insufficient. Our method suggests the following informal steps (roles like the Scrum master are omitted due to space limits): (1) Involvement of all stakeholders and introducing the Scrum master role (HLR 1, 3); (2) Identification of use cases of the intended business process(es) (defining the set of FRs) (HLR 2, 3); (3) Alignment of all NFRs which have to be considered prioritizing them according to the use cases (HLR 1, 3); (4) Selection of responsible persons and experts for each use case as well as NFR (HLR 1, 2, 3); (5) Circulating a single, consistent document containing the use cases, their specification, and models (considering aligned FRs/NFRs simultaneously) (HLR 1, 2, 3). The inherently distributed nature of collaborative systems implies the use of Service- and Process-oriented concepts in the generic architecture. Widely accepted benefits of these concepts comprise design-time as well as run- and change time efficiency due to re-use, flexibility/agility, and loose coupling.

References

1. Haake, J.M., Schümmer, T., Haake, A., Bourimi, M., Landgraf, B.: Supporting flexible collaborative distance learning in the cure platform. Vol. 1. IEEE Computer Society Press, Los Alamitos (2004)
2. Bourimi, M., Kuehnel, F., Haake, J., Abou-Tair, D.I., Kesdogan, D.: Tailoring collaboration according privacy needs in real-identity collaborative systems. In: Fonseca, B. (ed.) CRIWG 2009. LNCS, vol. 5784, pp. 110–125. Springer, Heidelberg (2009)
3. Schwaber, K.: Scrum overview (2009),
   http://codebetter.com/blogs/darrell.norton/pages/50339.aspx

Author Index